Contents

New Headway Upper-Intermediate – the NEW edition

PHOTOCOPIABLE MATERIALS AND EXTRA IDEAS

Introduction

New Headway Upper-Intermediate – the new edition

Why a new edition of *New Headway Upper-Intermediate*?

The second edition of the Upper-Intermediate book appeared in 1998, so we felt that the Student's Book needed some refreshing.

The basic methodology remains steadfastly the same:
- both accuracy and fluency-based activities
- a blend of traditional and more recently developed communicative approaches
- in-depth treatment of grammar
- systematic lexical syllabus
- attention to all four language skills (listening, speaking, reading, and writing)
- authentic material and tasks throughout

The grammatical syllabus will also be familiar:
- work on the tense system
- perfect versus non-perfect verb forms
- simple versus continuous aspects
- narrative and future verb forms
- expressing quantity
- relative pronouns, participles and adverbial clauses, conjunctions, and determiners

There is work on new areas:
- modal auxiliary verbs are dealt with over two units, the first on all meanings, and the second on modal verbs in the past
- verbs related to modals, such as *able to*, *obliged to*, *manage to*, *supposed to* are covered

However, the main area of change is in the material. Nearly all texts, for presentation, listening, reading, and writing, are new. There are new speaking activities, and new focuses in the writing syllabus. Unit topics have largely been replaced too. If a topic has remained the same or similar, parallel texts have been found. This will hopefully ensure that teachers who have enjoyed using *Headway* at this level can continue using the book.

The upper-intermediate level

The upper-intermediate level is an interesting one for both students and teachers. From the students' point of view, they have successfully achieved a certain amount. They have been introduced to a significant selection of the English language, grammatically, lexically, functionally and situationally, and possess sufficient language proficiency to be able to express themselves in a variety of social contexts. They can interact with authentic material as long as it is not of too specialized a nature, and can begin to feel 'at home' with English. It is certainly possible to engage them in conversation on all sorts of subjects without the interaction being too laboured.

From the teachers' point of view, it requires a shift of attitude to deal with the upper-intermediate student. One cannot begin a presentation with the expectation of zero knowledge. On the contrary, a certain amount of understanding is to be expected, and this has to be acknowledged and exploited. Teachers might encounter a degree of frustration from their students – *We do already Present Perfect many times before – why we do again?* This (not invented) comment summarizes the upper-intermediate level. The students have covered a lot in their four or five years of English, but very little comes out of their mouths or pens that doesn't containing howling mistakes of some kind – tense, word order, wrong word, pronunciation, spelling, or whatever. So teachers need to give credit where it is due for what students have achieved, and be prepared to sort out areas of perennial difficulty – like the Present Perfect, for instance!

With all the instruction that students have received, they can have some challenging questions for the teacher. These questions might be very confused, very big (*I don't understand prepositions*), very interesting (*Why does English have so many words?*) or impossible to answer (*How can I learn to speak to people?*). You, the teacher, need to be prepared to field these questions in a succinct and insightful manner, without getting totally sidetracked from the main aims of your lesson. We strongly suggest that you research areas to be taught by reading the Grammar Reference at the back of the Student's Book, and by consulting a grammar book such as *Practical English Usage* by Michael Swan. The Teacher's Book notes contain further language analysis and a warning of possible problems that students might have with each language area.

the THIRD edition

New Headway

Upper-Intermediate
Teacher's Book

Liz and John Soars

Mike Sayer

Peter May

OXFORD

UNIVERSITY PRESS

OXFORD
UNIVERSITY PRESS

Great Clarendon Street, Oxford OX2 6DP

Oxford University Press is a department of the University of Oxford.
It furthers the University's objective of excellence in research, scholarship,
and education by publishing worldwide in

Oxford New York

Auckland Cape Town Dar es Salaam Hong Kong Karachi
Kuala Lumpur Madrid Melbourne Mexico City Nairobi
New Delhi Shanghai Taipei Toronto

With offices in

Argentina Austria Brazil Chile Czech Republic France Greece
Guatemala Hungary Italy Japan Poland Portugal Singapore
South Korea Switzerland Thailand Turkey Ukraine Vietnam

OXFORD and OXFORD ENGLISH are registered trade marks of
Oxford University Press in the UK and in certain other countries

© Oxford University Press 2005

ACKNOWLEDGEMENTS

Photocopiable pages designed by: Keith Shaw

The authors and publisher are grateful to those who have given permission to reproduce the following extracts and adaptations of copyright material: p97 *I'll Be There For You* Words and Music by Michael Skloff, Marta Kauffman, David Crane, Phil Solem, Allee Willis and Danny Wilde © 1995 Til Dawn Music, CA, USA. Warner/Chappell North America, London, W6 8BS. Reproduced by permission of International Music Publications Ltd. All Rights Reserved. p143 *Don't Leave Home* Words and Music by Dido Armstrong and Rollo Armstrong © Copyright 2003 Warner/Chappell Music Ltd (75%) BMG Music Publishing Limited (25%). Used by permission of International Music Publications Limited and Music Sales Limited. All rights reserved. International Copyright Secured. p145 *I Never Loved You Anyway* Words and Music by Andrea Corr, Caroline Corr, Sharon Corr, Jim Corr & Carole Bayer Sager © Copyright 1997 Universal-Songs Of PolyGram International Incorporated/Beacon Communications Music Company/All About Me Music/Warner-Tamerlane Publishing Corporation, USA. Universal Music Publishing Limited (66.67%)/Warner/Chappell Music Limited (33.33%).All Rights Reserved. International Copyright Secured. p159 *Fast Car* Words and Music by Tracy Chapman © 1988 EMI April Music Inc/Purple Rabbit Music, USA, reproduced by permission of EMI Songs Ltd, London WC2H 0EA. p162 *One Of These Things First* Lyrics by Nick Drake. Taken from the album *'Bryter Layter'* (Island Records 1970). Reproduced by permission.

Photography by: Punchstock pp143 (couple/Photodisc), 159 (blurred road/Comstock Images)

Illustrations by: John Batten p160

The organization of the units

The organization of the units remains very much the same.

- A *Test your grammar* unit opener, to launch the target language, and to allow students to show what they know. This is intended to be done quickly.
- A text, either reading or listening or both, to show the target language in context.
- Exploratory work in the *Language Focus*, with a reference to the Grammar Reference at the back.
- A *Practice* section, with a wide variety of activities using all skills, but with an emphasis on speaking and listening. Some exercises encourage deeper analysis of the language, such as *Discussing grammar*; many exercises are personalized, with students working in pairs to swap information about themselves.
- There follows a reading, a listening, and a speaking activity (though not in any particular order). They follow the *Headway* tradition of being authentic, taken from a wide variety of sources, and with a range of comprehension tasks, language exercises, and extension speaking activities with the *What do you think?* questions. There is also a reference to the Writing section at the back of the book. This is cued at an appropriate point in each unit, but can be used at the teacher's discretion.
- There is a strong emphasis on vocabulary. Some of the lexical focuses are the same, some are different. As in the previous book, we do work on *Hot words*, that is, very common words which combine with nouns, phrases, and particles to produce new meanings, for example, *do damage, That'll do fine, do away with the monarchy*.
- What was called the *Postscript* section in the previous book has now been called *Everyday English*, to bring it into line with other levels of *Headway*. It consists of the usual mix of social English, survival language, using the phone, understanding signs, etc. For the other main aim of this section, see below.

Spoken English

In the previous edition, we did quite a lot of work on the grammar of spoken English, trying to highlight areas that are more characteristic of the spoken rather than the written language. These sections appeared in the *Postscript* section, and covered topics such as exclamations, showing interest and surprise, being polite, exaggeration and understatement. All these exercises and more are in the *Everyday English* section of the new edition.

However, there is a new feature in this edition. The above exercises are presented and practised, as the language items are intended for active use by students. In the section called *Spoken English*, aspects of the language are pointed out because they are common features of English as it is used today. Whilst none of them would be inappropriate if used by the students, the aim is rather to draw attention to them rather than teach them for active production.

They include the following.

- informal language (missing words out; words like *stuff* and *hanging out*)
- being imprecise (*sort of; and things*)
- fillers (*I mean*)
- the word *thing* (*How are things? The thing is ...*)
- the word *like*, which litters the conversation of many young people these days
- giving news and responding to news (*Did you hear about ...? You're kidding!*)
- the use of the non-defining relative clause with *which*, to add a comment (*He gave me some flowers, which was kind*)
- expressions with modal verbs (*You might as well, I couldn't help it*)

Music of English

In the *Everyday English* sections we have often included a *Music of English* feature. These highlight the intonation and stress patterns of the key everyday expressions that are being presented. As students are keen to learn these high frequency expressions, it is well worth making sure that they know exactly how to use them, with the correct intonation and stress.

Teacher's Book, Workbook, Teacher's Resource Book, and online material

The Teacher's Book contains photocopiable materials with extra idea and songs, as well as Stop and Check revision tests, Progress Tests, and Wordlists.

The Workbook contains comprehensive practice of the grammar points covered in the Student's Book, and vocabulary exercises which revise items from the Student's Book, as well as providing extension of vocabulary areas. It also provides further listening and pronunciation exercises for self-study.

The Teacher's Resource Book provides photocopiable games and activities to supplement the main course material.

There is also a teacher's website with additional material for teachers at www.oup.com/elt/teacher/headway, and a student's site with interactive practice exercises at www.oup.com/elt/headway.

Finally ...

We hope that the new edition of *New Headway Upper-Intermediate* helps you and your students, and we hope you have fun in the process of teaching and learning English.

Note

Before you start the book, you may like to use the photocopiable worksheet on p142 of this book, *Getting to know your Student Book!* This serves as an introduction to the titles, topics, and sections of the Student's Book.

Introduction to the unit

The theme of this unit is living and working away from home. The main reading texts are two accounts of people living abroad. They describe the pros and cons of their new lives. The main listening text is a series of 'vox pops' in which people talk briefly about what they miss about home when they go abroad.

Note

Before you start the book, you may like to use the photocopiable worksheet on p142 of this book, *Getting to know your Student Book!* This serves as an introduction to the titles, topics, and sections of the Student's Book.

Language aims

The tense system   The aim is to revise the main tenses at the start of the course. The emphasis is on *recognition* of form and meaning.

Simple vs continuous   Basically, the verb action can be seen as a complete whole (simple tenses) or as an activity with duration (continuous tenses). Think about whether your students make this distinction in L1.

Simple vs perfect   The major confusion here is between the Past Simple (for an action completed at a specific time in the past) and the Present Perfect (for an action which happened or started before now but has a connection with the present). The key thing about the Present Perfect in English is that it expresses a past action in terms of its relation to the present. This is not always true in other languages.

Vocabulary   The vocabulary section looks at compound nouns, particularly those made from the words, *house* and *home*, e.g. *house-proud, homesick*.

Everyday English   This section introduces common social expressions, and introduces and provides lots of practice of the way intonation, stress and rhythm combine to produce the 'music' of English.

Notes on the unit

TEST YOUR GRAMMAR (SB p6)

This *Test your grammar* section aims to test the students' ability to use the main tense forms in English. It also aims to get students talking to each other, and finding out about each other, from the very beginning of the course.

1   Ask students to work individually to match the time expressions and the sentences. Go round monitoring to see how well students understand the way the tenses work. Let students check in pairs before going over the answers in class.

> **EXTRA IDEA**
> Before doing the matching task, check that students can recognize the uses of the tenses by asking the following questions:
> *Which sentences refer to the past?* (1, 3, 4, 6)
> *Which sentences refer to the future?* (7, 8, 10)
> *Which sentence talks about something that is always true?* (2)
> *Which sentences connect past and present?* (5, 9)

Answers

1 My parents met in Paris in the *1970s/ages ago/during a snowstorm*.
2 They *never/frequently/sometimes* travel abroad.
3 They were working in Canada *when I was born/in the 1970s/for ages/recently/for a year*.
4 I was born in Montreal *in the 1970s/ages ago/during a snowstorm*.
5 My grandparents have *never/recently* lived in Ireland./My grandparents have lived in Ireland *for ages/recently/for a year/since I was a child*.
6 I *never/frequently/recently/later/sometimes* wrote to my grandmother./I wrote to my grandmother *in the 1970s*/frequently/for ages*/ages ago/the other day/recently/during a snowstorm/later*.
7 I'm *never* going to work in the US *in a fortnight's time/for a year/later*.
8 My brother's *frequently* flying to Argentina on business./My brother's flying to Argentina on business *tonight/in a fortnight's time/later*.
9 He's recently been learning Spanish./He's been learning Spanish *for ages/recently/for a year/since I was a child*.
10 I'll *never* see you *tonight/in a fortnight's time/later/frequently/sometimes*.

* These are grammatically correct, but 'borderline' in terms of being 'natural'.

Note

Students may be surprised that the following sentence is possible:
They were working in Canada for ages/for a year.
Point out that we choose to use the Past Continuous rather than the Past Simple here because we are emphasising that the activity was 'temporary'.

2 Allow students three or four minutes to prepare things to say, then put them in pairs or threes to talk about themselves. In the feedback, ask a few students to summarize what their partners told them.

You could monitor students as they speak, and note down any errors made. At the end of the activity, write a few of the errors on the board, and ask the class to correct them.

WRITING HOME (SB p6)

Tense revision and informal language

This section practises forming and using questions in a variety of tenses. It also looks at the use of informal language and abbreviations in personal letters and emails.

1 You could lead-in by asking one or two questions about the boy in the picture: *Where is he? What is he doing? How does he feel?*

Ask students to read the letter, and answer the simple gist questions.

Answers

Who is writing? Max, a boy
Who to? His parents
Where is he? Grove Hill Summer Camp
What is he complaining about? Feeling bored and homesick, and not having enough money or a cell phone*
How old do you think the writer is? Probably between 10 and 14

> **CULTURAL NOTE**
> Summer camp is a common experience for young teens in the United States. They spend a few weeks of their summer holiday camping and doing outdoor activities, away from their parents, under the guidance of group leaders.
> * *Cell phone* is the common word in the USA, South Africa, Australia and New Zealand. But in the UK, it is usually called a *mobile (phone)*.

2 Ask students to complete the questions and then ask and answer them with a partner. Go round monitoring, prompting the students to correct any mistakes they make.

3 **T 1.1** [CD 1: Track 2]
Students listen and check their answers.

Answers and tapescript

1 'How long has Max been at summer camp?'
  'Just **two days**.'
2 'Is he **having** a good time?'
  'No, not really. He**'s feeling** very homesick.'
3 'Is this his first time at summer camp?'
  'No, it**'s not**. He**'s been** once before. Last year he **went** to Pine Trees.'
4 '**Did** he like it at Pine Trees?'
  'Oh, yes he **did**, very much.'
5 'Why was that?'
  'Because **they did things like archery and mountain biking**.'
6 'What**'s** he doing tomorrow?'
  'He**'s making** pancakes.'
7 'Why **does he want** his cell phone?'
  'Because **all the other kids have theirs**.'

4 Ask one or two questions about the photo to set the scene, then ask students to read the email and answer the questions.

Answers

What is it about? Travelling in New Zealand and missing Rob, Sophie's boyfriend.

What do you learn about Sophie's likes and dislikes? She likes small, cool places and wildlife. She likes getting news from Rob. She doesn't like heat and doesn't know much about cars.
Who is Rob? Sophie's boyfriend.
Who do you think Catherine is? Her friend and travelling companion.

Ask students in pairs to form the questions and find the answers in the text. Allow students to ask and answer the questions with a partner. Alternatively, ask students to ask and answer the questions across the class.

5 **T 1.2** [CD 1: Track 3]
Students listen and check their answers.

Answers and tapescript
1 How long has Sophie been in New Zealand?
   Nearly a week.
2 How long was she in Australia?
   Three weeks.
3 Who is she travelling with?
   Catherine.
4 Why does she like New Zealand?
   Because it's smaller and cooler than Australia.
5 Why did she like Kangaroo Island?
   Because of the wildlife. She saw some platypus there.
6 What's their car like?
   It's OK – the lights work and it has a big glove box – but it sometimes makes strange noises.
7 Which wildlife has she seen already?
   She's seen dolphins, whales, and enormous albatrosses.
8 Where are they going next?
   They're heading up the west coast.
9 Why is she sending Rob photos?
   So that he won't forget what she looks like.

LANGUAGE FOCUS

The *Language Focus* section in each unit aims to get students to think analytically about language. Students are asked to look at clear examples of how language works, then say why they think language is used in that way.

Rather than teaching from the front of the class, let students work in pairs or threes to deduce rules and explain them to each other. This frees you as a teacher to walk round the classroom, monitor understanding and answer questions. It also allows students to take responsibility for their learning, and to peer teach.

Don't forget to look at the *Language aims* section on TB p6, which looks at problems students may have. You should also read the Grammar Reference on SB pp140–141.

LANGUAGE INPUT

1 Ask students to look back at the two sets of questions and answers, and identify the tenses. Go round monitoring, and then have a brief class feedback.

Answers
Max's letter
1 Present Perfect Simple to talk about something that started in the past and continued to now
2 Present Continuous to talk about a temporary situation
3 Present Simple to express a state/Present Perfect to talk about an experience with indefinite time/Past Simple to talk about a finished action
4 Past Simple (the auxiliary verb *did* in questions and short answers) to talk about something previously referred to as definite past
5 Past Simple
6 Present Continuous to talk about a future arrangement
7 Present Simple to express a state
Sophie's email
1 Present Perfect Simple to talk about something that started in the past and continued to now
2 Past Simple to talk about a finished action
3 Present Continuous to talk about a temporary activity
4 Present Simple to express a state
5 Past Simple to talk about a past state and a past action
6 Present Simple to express a state
7 Present Perfect to talk about present results of past actions
8 Present Continuous to talk about future arrangements
9 Present Continuous to talk about something that is happening now./Future Simple

2 Read through the examples as a class.

3 Ask students in pairs to find colloquial words and express them less colloquially, then to find examples where words are missing and say which words they are.

Answers
1 Here *stuff* means activities, and *hanging in there* means not giving up, even though it is difficult.
   Examples in Sophie's email:
   missing you like crazy = missing you very much
   Like it lots = like it very much
   Oz = Australia
   loads of wildlife = lots of wildlife
   classy sounding = the name sounds fashionable and high quality (here used ironically)
   going OK = working alright
   nice and slowly = at a relaxed pace
2 The missing words are subject pronouns and auxiliary verbs. For example:

(I've) Got to go to sleep now.
(I'm) Still having a great time but (I'm) missing you...
(I've) Been in New Zealand...

Refer students to Grammar Reference 1 on SB pp140–141.

PRACTICE (SB p8)

Identifying the tenses

1 Ask students in pairs to complete the tense charts.

Answers

ACTIVE	Simple	Continuous
Present	he works	we are working
Past	she worked	I was working
Future	they will work	you will be working
Present Perfect	we have worked	she has been working
Past Perfect	I had worked	you had been working
Future Perfect	they will have worked	he will have been working

PASSIVE	Simple	Continuous
Present	it is made	they are being made
Past	it was made	it was being made
Future	they will be made	
Present Perfect	they have been made	
Past Perfect	it had been made	
Future Perfect	they will have been made	

2 The aim here is to get students to recognize the form and meaning of different tenses in spoken discourse.

Ask students to look at the example carefully. Ask them if they can think of any other contexts in which this might be said.

T 1.3 [CD 1: Track 4]

Ask students to listen to the lines of conversation and discuss what the context might be. Pause the recording after each line and ask for suggestions from the class.

T 1.3 Ask students to listen a second time. This time, ask students to identify the tenses, and say which lines have contractions.

Answers and tapescript

1 Possible context: Shop assistant and customer, in a clothes shop perhaps.
Present Continuous passive and active. *(I'm) just looking*.

2 Possible context: Friends gossiping, at work?/in school? Talking about a friend's new boyfriend.
Present Perfect and Present Perfect Continuous. *I've* (I have) *heard* and *she's* (she has) *been seeing*.

3 Possible context: Two friends or colleagues talking. One informs the other that she will pass on some good news.
Future Continuous and Future Simple. *I'll* (I will) *be seeing* and *I'll tell*.

4 Possible context: Friend telling a story about another friend, or perhaps someone in the news. *He* may be a criminal or drunken driver. *They* is probably the police.
Past Continuous and Past Simple.

5 Possible context: Somebody telling or recalling the story of when she met somebody from her past. *Her* could be an ex-neighbour's daughter, but could also be a relative that the speaker had become estranged from.
Past Perfect and Past Simple of *to be*. *Hadn't* (had not) *seen* and *she'd* (she had) *changed*.

6 Possible context: A person describing someone they know. It could be a school mate, colleague or even boss.
Future Simple/Present Simple of *to be*/Present Simple passive. *He's* (He is) and *isn't* (is not) *believed*.

7 Possible context: Somebody saying they are waiting to be told whether they have got a job or a place at college.
Present Perfect passive/Present Perfect/Future Simple passive. *Haven't* (have not) *seen*, *I've* (I have) *got* and *I'll* (I will) *be told*.

8 Possible context: Somebody enquiring about what has happened to a letter or parcel. Probably talking to somebody from a company.
Present Simple question form/Past Simple passive

T 1.3

1 A Are you being served sir?
   B Oh, er, just looking thank you.
2 I've heard that she's been seeing a lot of Patrick recently.
3 I'll be seeing Bill this afternoon – I'll tell him the good news then.
4 Apparently, he was overtaking on a bend at 70 mph when they stopped him.
5 I hadn't seen her since she was a little girl, and she'd changed beyond all recognition.
6 Nobody will listen to him. He's the kind of guy who isn't believed by anyone.
7 I haven't been told yet if I've got it. I'll be told in writing sometime next week.
8 Do you have any idea which address it was sent to?

Discussing grammar

Discussing grammar is a regular feature of New Headway Upper-Intermediate. It aims to get students to analyse and explain language. It enables you, as a teacher, to respond to and explain confusions that students may have. If you have a monolingual class, and speak the students' L1, you may wish to translate and contrast sentences to show how English may work differently from the students' own language.

3   Ask students in pairs to compare the meaning in the pairs of sentences. Go round monitoring, and find out how well your students understand how these tenses work. Answer queries, but don't spend too long explaining grammar at this stage.

Conduct a class feedback. To avoid a lengthy and frustrating discussion about grammar, think about controlling the feedback carefully. Rather than asking individual students to explain grammar, (which can be time-consuming and inaccurate), use check questions yourself. Check questions are a time efficient way of making sure students understand. For example, for number 1, ask,
Which sentence means that Klaus was born and brought up in Berlin?
Which sentence means that Klaus is at this moment on a train from Berlin, and will be here in an hour or two?

Answers

1   Klaus **comes** from Berlin.
    (Present Simple: to talk about a fact that is always true. Klaus was born in Berlin or usually lives there.)
    Klaus **is coming** from Berlin.
    (Present Continuous: to talk about something that is happening now/in progress – Klaus is on his way (on the plane or train) from Berlin. Or to talk about a future arrangement – Klaus is planning to come from Berlin. English abbreviates 'is going to come' to 'is coming', so this sentence could be expressing an intention.)

2   You**'re** very kind. Thank you.
    (Present Simple: a fact that is always true. Here, the verb *to be* is a state verb – *kind* is a state, a characteristic.)
    You**'re being** very kind. What do you want?
    (Present Continuous: a temporary activity that is happening now. In this sentence, the verb *to be* is active – somebody is temporarily behaving in a 'kind' way. The implication is that being kind is not their usual state, and that they are deliberately behaving in a kind way, perhaps because they want something from the other person.)
    Check question: *Which sentence is describing a temporary activity, and which a permanent state?*

3   What **were** you **doing** when the accident happened?
    (Past Continuous: to ask about the activity that was in progress in the past when the accident happened.)
    What **did** you **do** when the accident happened?
    (Past Simple: to ask about the next action that happened as a result of the accident.)

What **did** you **do** when the accident happened?
(Past Simple: to ask about the next action that happened as a result of the accident.)
Check questions: *Which sentence asks about something that started before the accident, and was in progress during it? Which sentence asks about what happened next – as a result?*

4   I**'ve lived** in Singapore for five years.
    (Present Perfect: to talk about the unfinished past – an action that began in the past and still continues.)
    I **lived** in Singapore for five years.
    (Past Simple: to talk about a finished action in the past.)
    Check question: *In which sentence does the speaker still live in Singapore now?*

5   When we arrived, he **tidied** the flat.
    (Past Simple: to say what happened next, or as a consequence of the first action *arrived*.)
    When we arrived, he**'d tidied** the flat.
    (Past Perfect: to say what happened before the first action *arrived*.)
    Check question: *Which event happened before they arrived, and which happened after?*

6   We**'ll have** dinner at 8.00, shall we?
    (Future Simple: to express a spontaneous intention. Here, functionally, it is a suggestion.)
    Don't call at 8.00. We**'ll be having** dinner.
    (Future Continuous: to talk about a temporary action that will be in progress at a time in the future.)
    Check question: *In which sentence does dinner start at 8, and in which one does it start before 8?*

7   How much **are** you **paying** to have the house painted?
    (Present Continuous active: a temporary activity or situation that is true now, but not necessarily happening right at this moment. Here, 'you' is the house owner.)
    How much **are** you **being paid** to paint the house?
    (Present Continuous passive: a temporary activity or situation that is true now, but not necessarily happening now. Here, 'you' is the painter.)
    Check question: *In which sentence is 'you' the painter, and in which the house owner?*

8   How **do** you **do**?
    (Present Simple: used as a greeting after you have been formally introduced to a stranger.)
    How **are** you **doing**?
    (Present Continuous: used informally to ask how a friend is, and how life is going.)
    Check question: *Which sentence is a formal greeting to a stranger, and which an informal greeting to a friend?*

Talking about you

4   Ask students to work individually to complete the sentences with their own ideas. Give students one or two of your own examples, to get them started.
    When they are ready, ask students to compare their answers with a partner.

Answers
Students' own ideas

T 1.4 [CD 1: Track 5]

Play the recording. Ask students to listen to the conversations. Pause the recording after each conversation, so that the students can tell you what responses they heard.

At the end of the activity, elicit and write up some of the typical 'responding' phrases the students heard. For example:

Absolutely!	*I know.*
Really?	*Just Mondays, eh?*
Well, don't ask me.	*Who on earth told you that?*

T 1.4

1 A At weekends I often don't bother getting up 'til lunchtime.
   B Absolutely! Why bother if you don't have to?
2 A My parents have never had a cross word in all their married lives.
   B Really? Mine are at it all the time.
3 A I don't think I'll ever master this DVD player.
   B Well, don't ask me. I can't even find the on/off button.
4 A I was saying to a friend just the other day that I hadn't seen you for ages.
   B I know. How long has it been?
5 A I hate Mondays because nothing ever goes right on a Monday.
   B Just Mondays, eh? Aren't you the lucky one!
6 A I'd just arrived home last night when I realized I'd left my briefcase on the bus.
   B Well, you won't see that again.
7 A I was just getting ready to go out this morning when my grandmother rang for a chat. It's so frustrating!
   B I know, and you feel really bad if you say it's not a good time.
8 A I've been told that our teacher wears purple pyjamas in bed!
   B Who on earth told you that?!
9 A In my very first English lesson I was taught to introduce myself and say 'hello'.
   B I was taught to say 'the cat runs after the mouse' and stuff like that – useful, uh?!
10 A The reason I'm learning English is because it's spoken all over the world.
    B True. But isn't Chinese spoken by more people?

5 Ask students to work with their partner again, and practise responding naturally to the sentences their partner wrote for exercise 4.

Ask students in pairs to decide which words are missing in the lines from conversations. Then ask students to take it in turns to read the lines aloud to a partner and make suitable responses.

To get students started, model the first dialogue. For example:
Heard about Jane and John splitting up?
No. Really? I don't believe it!

Answers
1 (Have you) Heard about Jane and John splitting up?
2 (Are you) Leaving already? What's wrong?
3 (Have you) Failed again? How many times is that?
4 (I'm) Sorry I'm late. (Have you) Been waiting long?
5 (Are you) Doing anything interesting this weekend?
6 (I) Like the car! When did you get it?
7 (Good) Bye Jo! (I'll) See you later.
8 (I'm) Just coming! Hang on!*
9 (Do you) Want a lift? Hop in.*
10 (Have you) Seen Jim lately?

* *Hang on* and *Hop in* are imperatives, so there are no words missing.

T 1.5 [CD 1: Track 6]

Play the recording. Ask students to listen and compare the recorded conversations with their own.

T 1.5

1 A Heard about Jane and John splitting up?
   B No, really? I always thought they got on really well.
   A Apparently not. John's been seeing his ex-girlfriend.
2 A Leaving already? What's wrong?
   B I just have a headache, that's all.
3 A Failed again? How many times is that?
   B OK, OK. There's no need to rub it in! They say the *best* drivers fail three times.
4 A Sorry I'm late. Been waiting long?
   B No, I've just arrived myself. Got caught in traffic.
5 A Doing anything interesting this weekend?
   B Yeah, if you call housework interesting. I've just *got* to tidy my flat this weekend.
6 A Like the car! When did you get it?
   B We've had it a while actually. Second-hand, you know.
7 A Bye Jo! See you later.
   B Yeah. I'll be round about eight!
8 A Just coming! Hang on!
   B Get a move on or we'll go without you!
9 A Want a lift? Hop in.
   B Great. Can you drop me in the centre?
10 A Seen Jim lately?
    B No, I haven't. I wonder what he's up to at the moment.

A long-distance phone call

6 Ask students to read through the lines of the phone conversation, and answer the gist questions. Let the students discuss their answers in pairs before feedback. In the feedback, encourage lots of speculation, but don't give the correct answers.

> **VOCABULARY NOTE**
> *jet-lagged* = feeling tired because you have moved from one time zone to another
> *huge* = very big
> *litter* = rubbish in the streets
> *tiny* = very small
> *You're kidding* = You're joking

Answers
Students' own ideas.
Answers from the tapescript: Kirsty is in Tokyo, Japan. She is there because she has a job with a big company. Her father is in London.

Ask students to work with a partner to complete Kirsty's father's lines in the conversation.

T 1.6 [CD 1: Track 7]

Play the recording. Students listen and compare their answers.

Ask students which tenses were commonly used in the conversation. You could refer the students to the tapescript on SB p124 so that students can check their answers and research the tenses used.

Answers and tapescript
Commonly used tenses
Present Simple, e.g. *And the trains come so regularly ...*
Present Continuous, e.g. *How's it all going?*
Past Simple, e.g. *I lay awake all night ...*
Present Perfect Simple, e.g. *Have you seen much of the city yet?*
Present Perfect Continuous, e.g. *I've been trying to find out ...*
Future Continuous, e.g. *Will you be moving somewhere else?*

T 1.6

K Dad! It's me, Kirsty.
D Kirsty! How are you? How's it all going?
K I'm fine, but still a bit jet-lagged.
D I can imagine. What exactly is the time difference over there?
K It's nine hours ahead. I just can't get used to it. Last night I lay awake all night, and then today I nearly fell asleep at work in the middle of a meeting.
D You poor thing. And what's work like?
K It's early days but I think it's going to be really good. It's a big company but everybody's being so kind and helpful. I've been trying to find out how everything works.
D And what about Tokyo? What's it like? Have you seen much of the city yet?

K I've seen a bit. It just seems such a big, busy city. I don't see how I'll ever find my way round it.
D I know. Big cities can seem really strange and frightening at first. Is it anything like London?
K No, it's nothing like London. It's like nowhere else I've ever been – masses of huge buildings, underground shopping centres, lots of taxis and people – so many people – but it's *so* clean. No litter on the streets or anything.
D And where are you living? What kind of accommodation have you got?
K Well, for the time being I've been given a tiny apartment, but it's in a great part of town.
D What do you mean 'for the time being'? Will you be moving somewhere else?
K That's right. I won't be living here for long. I'll be offered a bigger place as soon as one becomes available, which is good 'cos this one really is tiny, but at least it's near to where I'm working.
D How do you get to work then? Do you walk?
K Walk! You're kidding! It's not *that* close. It's a short subway ride away. And the trains come so regularly – it's a really easy journey, which is good 'cos I start work very early in the morning.
D It all sounds really interesting but are you enjoying yourself?
K Again it's too early to say. I think I really will be enjoying it all soon. I'm sure it's going to be a great experience. It's just that I miss everyone at home so much.
D Oh, we miss you too, very much. Make sure you email us regularly – it's the best way to keep in touch.
K I will. And you email me back with all your news. I just love getting news from home. Give everyone my love. Bye.
D Bye sweetheart. It's been great talking to you.

Writing Unit 1
Applying for a job – A CV and a covering letter   SB p110

ADDITIONAL MATERIAL

Workbook Unit 1
Exercises 1–3 The tense system
Exercise 4 Passives
Exercises 5–6 Auxiliary verbs
Exercise 7 *have* and *have got*

READING AND SPEAKING (SB p10)

A home from home

1 Divide your students into groups of three or four to make a list of reasons why people go to live abroad. In the feedback, ask each group to give you one or two reasons. You could build up a list on the board.

Personalize the activity by asking if any student knows a friend or relative who has gone to live abroad. Ask them to tell the class why they left home and where they went to.

2 Ask students to work in pairs or small groups to decide which lines they think are about Chile (**C**) and which are about Korea (**K**). Do the first as an example to get the students started. In the feedback, ask students what clues helped them decide, but don't confirm their answers.

3 Divide the students into two groups. An easy way to do this is to put students into pairs, and tell each pair what their letter is: **AA BB AA BB**, etc. Ask each pair to read the relevant text, and check their answers to the prediction work in exercise 2:

Students A read about Ian Walker-Smith in Chile on p10.
Students B read about Thomas Creed in Korea on p12.

Tell the students to check their answers to exercise 2 with their partner before feedback.

Answers
1 C 2 K 3 C 4 K 5 C 6 K 7 K 8 C

> **NOTE**
> *expat* is an abbreviation of *expatriate*, which means someone who lives in a foreign country.

4 Ask students to read their texts more carefully to answer the questions about Ian or Thomas. Encourage students to work with and check with their partner.

5 Pair each student with somebody who read the other text. This will depend on your class size and layout, but an easy way to do this is to get one student in each pair to turn to work with, or change places with, a student from a pair who read the alternative text: **AB AB AB**, etc.

Ask the students to compare their answers, and answer the follow-up questions. Have a brief class feedback, but don't spend too long going through answers – the students should by now have a good understanding of the texts.

Answers
Ian
1 He went to Antofagasto, Chile, because he had 'itchy feet' (he wanted to travel), and he wanted to escape an ex-girlfriend.
2 Four years.
3 He works at Paranal Observatory as part of the I.T. (Information Technology) team, making sure the computers run 24/7.
4 He has a girlfriend, Andrea, who is probably Chilean.
5 It is a mining town, and not very attractive. There is a pleasant walkway along the front and the beach has been improved.
6 Yes. He lost his baggage when he first arrived. He had little Spanish when he arrived, and still cannot communicate on a 'deeper level'. He has a long drive to work, and misses his girlfriend when he is away working shifts.
7 Paranal, where he works, is up a mountain in the desert.
8 No. He doesn't feel he belongs in Chile, and misses the culture and greenery of Britain.
9 He likes Andrea, his girlfriend, and the amazing sky. He doesn't like travelling to work, or working away from Andrea on shifts.
10 He misses the culture and greenery of Britain.

Thomas
1 He went to Seoul, Korea. His father is an officer in the US Army, and his 'tour of duty' took him to Korea.
2 Six years.
3 He is a school student.
4 His father is an officer in the US Army. His brother is in the US Army, too. His mother is a scientist.
5 Seoul is 'cool'. It's bigger than Boston, crowded and busy.
6 Yes. At first, he felt lonely because he couldn't understand what people said. He was scared when he started school.
7 He felt lonely when he first arrived because he couldn't understand anything, and people didn't smile at strangers.
8 Yes. He speaks Korean fluently, and has friends.
9 He likes soccer, the city, 'PC rooms', Korean books and stories, and the people. He dislikes learning Chinese characters.
10 He misses American comics, with superheroes like Spiderman, and he wishes people liked basketball.

Who do you think is happier about the move? Thomas.
Which new home would you prefer? Students' own opinions.

Language work

Ask students to study the texts again and answer the questions about the expressions, then explain the meanings to a partner who read the other text.

Ask the students to work together to express the lines marked with an asterisk (*) in more formal English.

Answers

Ian in Chile

1 Driving two hours to Paranal takes a toll on Ian and on his relationship with Andrea. 'It takes a real toll' means it is a difficult and tiring task. (A *toll* is the price you have to pay for travelling on some roads.)

2 Computers operate for 24 hours a day, 7 days a week.

3 He gets 'puffed' when he first arrives and when he exercises in Paranal because it is 2,600 miles above sea level. 'I easily get puffed' means 'I get out of breath very quickly'.

4 He got 'itchy feet' because he was bored with his job and wanted to escape an ex-girlfriend. 'Itchy feet' means 'a desire to travel'.

5 His own culture still fits him like winter gloves. In other words, no matter how long he stays away, he feels comfortable in England as soon as he gets home.

Thomas in Korea

1 He is a big fan. 'I'm really into...' means 'I'm a big fan of.../I'm very interested in...'

2 Soccer (football) is a big deal because Korea co-hosted the 2002 World Cup. 'A big deal' means 'very important/of great interest.'

3 Thomas' father doesn't get soccer because, as an American and a basketball fan, it isn't part of his sporting culture. 'He doesn't get it' means 'he doesn't understand it.'

4 His father is a big shot because he is an officer in the US Army. 'A big shot' is someone with an important position.

5 He's beating up Spiderman. 'Beat up' means hit repeatedly.

What do you think?

The aim here is to get students talking. It gives them an opportunity to talk about personal experiences and express opinions about the topic of the lesson. Unless you have a very small class, it is best done in small groups, which gives more students the opportunity to speak, and frees up the teacher to monitor, prompt, and note errors.

Divide students into groups of four, five, or six, then give them two or three minutes to read through the questions. Nominate one person in each group to be the discussion leader. It is their job to ask the questions, make sure everybody gets a chance to speak, and to decide when to move on from one question to the next.

Monitor the groups equally, and prompt. You may wish to monitor for errors – walk from group to group, and note any interesting errors made by the students. After the feedback on the discussion, write these errors (anonymously) on the board and discuss them as a class.

> **SUGGESTION**
> After students have worked on listing advantages and disadvantages of living abroad, ask them to 'act out' the points in pairs. One gives a reason not to live abroad, and the other replies with the relevant advantage.

For example:
The language barrier is a problem if you don't speak the language.
Yes, but (on the other hand) it gives you a great opportunity to learn a new language.

Possible disadvantages

The language barrier – maybe you don't speak the language.
You don't have any friends in the new country.
You miss your family.
The culture and customs are strange.
You miss simple things, e.g. food.
There are bureaucratic problems like visas, work permits, insurance and pension schemes.
You will always feel like a foreigner – you don't belong.

Possible advantages

But this is an opportunity to learn a new language.
You can make new friends.
Your family can visit – and it's easy to keep in touch nowadays.
Learning about a new culture is fascinating.
You get to enjoy the simple things about a new country.
The new country may be less bureaucratic than yours!
You find out how different people live and behave.

VOCABULARY AND PRONUNCIATION (SB p13)

House and home

The aim of this section is to introduce compound nouns and adjectives. It also practises stress and intonation.

> **Compound nouns and adjectives**
>
> 1 Look at the examples as a class. Ask the questions.
>
> > **Answers**
> > Nouns: lifestyle, life expectancy, life insurance
> > Adjectives: lifelong, life-size
>
> The nouns can be written as one word or two words.
>
> The adjectives can be written as one word or one hyphenated word.
>
> Point out that students should use a dictionary to check how compound nouns and adjectives are written (and that even native speakers often need to do this).
>
> 2 Read the compounds aloud. Or ask students to read them aloud. Point out the stress.
>
> > **Answers**
> > •   •   •   •   •
> > *lifestyle lifelong life-size life expectancy life insurance*
>
> 3 Ask students to research the texts on pp10–12, and find compounds. Let the students check what they have found with a partner before feedback.

Answers

Ian	Thomas
mining town	eleven-year-old
25-year-old	floor mats
two-hour	soccer fan
ex-girlfriend	leg cramps
12-strong	best friend
tourist destination	elementary school
ground station	baseball cards
home town	spicy foods
desktop	big shot
municipal beach	superheroes
sea level	PC rooms
seafront	basketball
	Internet
	slam dunk
	cross-legged
	soccer player

1   Ask students in pairs to make compounds and answer the questions. Encourage them to use learner dictionaries to check their answers.

Answers
Home: homework*, home-made, homesick, home town*, homecoming, homeless, home-grown, home page*
House: housewife*, house-proud, house plant, housebound, house-warming, housework
* Words marked with * are nouns. The rest are adjectives.

2   **T 1.7** [CD 1: Track 8] Play the recording. Ask students to listen to the conversations, and, after each conversation, discuss the questions.

Answers
1   Two neighbours – one is asking the other to water their house plants while they are away.
    Compounds: *house plants, house-proud*.
2   Mother is telling her daughter (Julie) that her sister (Anna) is returning home from the USA. Compounds: *homecoming, housewife, home-made, home-grown*.
3   Someone is inviting a friend to a house-warming party. Compounds: *house-warming, housework*.
4   Teenagers asks friend if he/she is going to Carly's party. Compound: *housebound*.

T 1.7

1   A   I'm going away on business for two weeks. Do you think you could possibly water my house plants for me?
    B   No problem. I'd be glad to. I'll keep an eye on your whole flat if you like.
    A   That would be great.
    B   Don't worry, I know how house-proud you are. I'll make sure everything stays clean and tidy.
    A   I'll do the same for you any time, you know.
    B   Thanks.
2   A   Julie, have you heard? Anna's just been made managing director of the UK branch of her firm, so she's coming back from the States!
    B   Oh, that's great news. Let's give her a spectacular homecoming party when she gets back. Hmmm. She's certainly the career girl of the family.
    A   Doing really well, isn't she?
    B   I know and I'm happy for her. Me? I'm just a housewife. Four kids, home-made cakes, and home-grown vegetables!
    A   And how are my wonderful grandchildren?
3   A   We're having a house-warming party on the 12th. Can you come?
    B   Yes, you bet. We'd love to! But I didn't know you'd moved.
    A   Yeah, two weeks ago. It's much bigger than the old one. Huge kitchen and three big bedrooms.
    B   Sounds great.
    A   Yeah. Mind you, there's much more housework to do!
    B   That's a drag!
4   A   Hey, you going to Carly's on Saturday?
    B   I dunno.
    A   It's a free house. It'll be great.
    B   Cool. Where are her parents then?
    A   Carly says they're visiting her grandma – she's sick and housebound, so they have to go and help.
    B   OK. Count me in. I'll be there.

3   Ask students in pairs to complete the lines from the conversations with compound words.

Answers
1   I'm going away for two weeks. Do you think you could possibly water my **house plants** for me?
2   Don't worry, I know how **house-proud** you are. I'll make sure everything stays clean and tidy.
3   Let's give her a spectacular **homecoming** party when she gets back from New York.
4   Me? I'm just a **housewife**. Four kids, **home-made** cakes and **home-grown** vegetables!
5   We're having a **house-warming** party on the 12th. Can you come? I'll give you our new address.
6   Mind you, with it being much bigger, there's much more **housework** to do!
7   Her grandmother's sick and **housebound**, so they have to go and help.

4 **T 1.8** [CD 1: Track 9] Ask students in pairs to practise saying the lines in exercise 3 with correct stress and intonation. Go round monitoring, and help with pronunciation problems.

Ask students to listen to the recording and check their pronunciation.

Ask students to practise the conversations with a partner, using the lines in exercise 3 as prompts.

5 Divide the class into groups of four. Ask the groups to make compounds by combining words from one of the boxes in **A** with as many words as possible from **B**. Give half of the groups the first box in **A** to work with, and the other half the second box in **A**. Give the students a time limit of, say, five minutes. Allow students to use a learner dictionary to help.

Find out which group got most compounds, then check the answers.

Ask students to share their words with a different group and explain the meanings. Go round monitoring and helping.

> **Answers**
> bookcase, book shelf, computer software, computer program, airline, airmail, junk food, food processor, food poisoning, word processor, tea bag, teapot, sleeping pill, sleeping bag, fire bell, fire escape, fire alarm, headline, headway(!), headlight, head office, headrest

Song [After T 1.13] [CD 1: Track 15]
Don't leave home, TB p143

LISTENING AND SPEAKING (SB p14)

Things I miss from home

This is a series of six short 'vox pops', with six people talking very naturally about the same topic: what they miss when they go away from home. The tasks involve note-taking for general comprehension, and looking at pronoun reference in a text.

1 Lead in and set the scene by asking students the questions in a brief class discussion.

2 Ask students to write down one thing they missed on a small piece of paper. Collect the pieces of paper, and save them until the end of the lesson.

3 **T 1.9** [CD 1: Track 10] Play the recording. Students listen and take notes to complete the table. Play the recording more than once, and pause between speakers, if necessary. When they have completed the table, let students compare their answers in groups.

> **Answers**
>
> | | WHAT THEY MISS | OTHER INFORMATION |
> |---|---|---|
> | Andrew | Listening to the radio | He takes a small short wave radio with him so that he can listen to an English language station. |
> | Helen | Hair straighteners | She takes them away with her. |
> | Gabriele | Her two cats | She takes a photo of them with her. |
> | Paul | His bed, particularly a comfortable pillow | He takes ear plugs with him. |
> | Sylvia | Her children, a good cup of tea, and a particular TV news programme and presenter | She takes a bag of snacks with her in case she is hungry while she is travelling. |
> | Chris | A lazy Sunday morning: newspaper, croissant, pot of coffee | |

T 1.9 See SB tapescripts p125

4 **T 1.9** Ask students in pairs to decide who is speaking, and what is being referred to in the extracts. Play the recording again so that they can check their answers.

You may wish to check the following vocabulary:
can't bear = can't stand/hate
reassuring = comforting
waving = moving from side to side
twiddling the knob = moving the knob (dial) on the radio backwards and forwards to try and get good radio reception

> **Answers**
> 1 Gabriele. *Them* refers to her cats.
> 2 Helen. *Them* refers to her hair straighteners.
> 3 Sylvia. *It* refers to the watching of the TV programme and presenter.
> 4 Andrew. *The aerial* and *the knob* are the parts of the radio you move to try and tune into a radio station.
> 5 Paul. *They* refer to ear plugs.
> 6 Chris. *The day* is Sunday.

5 End the class with the things that were written down in exercise 1. A good way of doing this is to hand out the slips of paper at random around the class. Ask a student to read out what is on the piece of paper. The rest of the class has to guess who wrote it. That person can then explain why they wrote it if they want to. Decide whose is the funniest and/or the most interesting.

ADDITIONAL MATERIAL

Workbook Unit 1

Exercises 8–9 Vocabulary

Exercise 10 Phrasal verbs

Exercise 11 Pronunciation – Vowel sounds and sentence stress

Exercise 12 Listening – A good mate

EVERYDAY ENGLISH (SB p15)

Social expressions and the music of English

The aim of this section is to introduce and practise a set of common, colloquial social expressions. It also looks at the way intonation, stress and rhythm combine to create the 'music' of the language. Students are encouraged to listen to the 'music' of English, and are given guided practice in trying to imitate it.

1 Ask students to read through the sentences carefully. Ask them to note or underline expressions that they don't understand. Check the students understand the vocabulary:

Let me see = Let me think about it

I don't think I'll bother with = I'm not interested in having/doing…

I was just passing = I was walking past/I was in the area

drop in = visit for a short time

That's a drag = that's annoying

can't make it = is not able to go (to a party, etc.)

don't feel up to = not in the right mood for (perhaps ill/tired, etc.)

How come… = Why?/For what reason?

swing it = manage to achieve it (perhaps by persuading someone to change their mind)

That's as maybe = that may be true but it is not the point

Ask students in pairs to match lines in **A** with lines in **B**.

Answers

1 b   2 d   3 e (g is possible, but is necessary for 6),
4 a   5 c   6 g   7 h   8 f

T 1.10 [CD 1: Track 11] Students listen and check their answers. Ask students to decide what they think the situation is before practising each conversation. For example:

Great to see you. Come on in.
I was just passing…

(Situation: a neighbour visiting/an old friend who is passing on his/her way to somewhere)

By deciding what the situation is, the students should be better able to use good stress and intonation.

T 1.10

1 A Great to see you. Come on in.
  B I was just passing and thought I'd drop in.
2 A Excuse me, don't I know you from somewhere?
  B No, I don't think so.
3 A What d'you mean you're not coming?
  B Well, I just don't feel up to going out tonight.
4 A I think I'll have the chocolate mousse. What about you?
  B Let me see. No, actually, I don't think I'll bother with dessert.
5 A My flatmate can't make it to your party.
  B Really! That's a drag. I was hoping to meet her.
6 A How come you're not having a holiday this year?
  B We just can't afford it.
7 A You'll make yourself ill if you carry on working at that pace.
  B That's as maybe but I have to get this finished by Friday.
8 A I've got you the last two tickets for the show.
  B Fantastic! I knew you'd swing it for us.

MUSIC OF ENGLISH

T 1.11 [CD 1: Track 12] Read through the information on the 'Music of English' in the box and play the examples. You can get students to repeat them.

2 **T 1.12** [CD 1: Track 13] Here, the students listen to a dialogue which they are going to read out loud for intensive practice of stress, intonation and rhythm. The aim, therefore, is to get them to listen for meaning, but, more importantly, to concentrate on the 'music' of the way the people speak.

Ask students to look at the gist questions, then close their eyes and listen to the conversation.

Answers

Who are the people? Two passengers on a train.
Do they know each other? No.
Where are they? On a train.

3 Ask students to look at the conversation on SB p153, and work in pairs to read it aloud. Go round monitoring, and correct students who are not using an appropriate stress and intonation pattern. When students have finished, ask them to change roles. It's important to keep encouraging students to work at this text, so keep interrupting pairs to model good stress or intonation.

T 1.12 Play the recording again. Pause after each line for students to repeat. Encourage choral repetition, then ask one or two students to attempt the line by themselves.

Put the students in pairs again to practise. You could ask one or two pairs to act out parts of the dialogue for the class.

Unit 1 · No place like home   17

A Excuse me, is this yours?

B Let me see. Yes, it is. Thank you. I must have dropped it.

A Are you going far?

B Yeah, all the way to London. What about you?

A I'm getting off at Bristol.

B Oh, d'you live there?

A Actually, no. I work in Bristol but I live in Bath.

B Lucky you! I think Bath's a beautiful city!

A Yeah, you and thousands of others!

B What d'you mean?

A Well, you know, the tourists. There are just so many, all year round.

B Ah yes, that's a drag. You don't like tourists then?

A Well, I shouldn't really complain.

B How come? You can complain if you want.

A Not really – you see I'm a travel agent so I make a living from tourists.

4 Ask students to read the two gapped conversations quickly. Ask them what the situation is and who might be speaking.

Sample answers

1 Two strangers meet, and one thinks he recognizes the other.

2 A friend or neighbour is visiting a friend.

Ask students in pairs to try to complete the lines, and practise saying them as they go.

Ask two or three pairs to act out the conversations for the class at the end.

5 **T 1.13** [CD 1: Track 14] Play the recording. Students listen and compare their ideas and pronunciation.

Answers and tapescript

1 **A** Excuse me, don't I know you from somewhere?

   B Actually, I don't think so.

   A Weren't you at Gavin's party last week?

   B Not me. I don't know anyone called Gavin.

   A Well, someone who looked just like you was there.

   B Well, that's as maybe but it certainly wasn't me.

   A I am sorry!

2 **A** Tony! Hi! Great to see you.

   B Well, I was just passing and I thought I'd drop in and say 'hello'.

   A Come on in! Have a drink!

   B You're sure? You're not too busy?

   A Never too busy to talk to you.

   B Thanks Jo. It'd be really nice to have a chat.

   A Fantastic! Let me take your coat.

2

Present Perfect • Simple and continuous
Hot verbs – *make, do* • Exclamations

Been there, done that!

Introduction to the unit

Been there, done that, (got the T-shirt!) is the cry of bored young people. The idea is that nothing about the world is of any interest because they have already been everywhere, done everything, and bought the T-shirt to prove it! It was used as an advert for Pepsi Cola, in which of course the only thing new and interesting was a can of Pepsi!

The theme of this unit is world travel past and present, from historical explorers to modern-day tourism. The main reading text is an article about the effects of tourism on host countries. There are two listening texts. The first features three people who talk briefly about their dream holiday experiences. In the main listening text, Tashi Wheeler, daughter of the founders of the *Lonely Planet* travel guides, is interviewed about her childhood on the move.

Note In the introduction to this listening, students are asked about their earliest memories of childhood holidays and, if possible, to bring in photographs. It's a good idea to ask students to start looking for these photographs well in advance of the lesson. If enough students bring in photographs on the day, it will make the lesson feel personalized in a very direct way.

Language aims

Present Perfect The aim is to revise and practise the Present Perfect Simple and Continuous tenses.

Present Perfect Simple It is difficult for students, even at upper-intermediate level, to be consistently correct in their use of the Present Perfect. This is because although many other European languages have a tense that is *formed* in the same way, (the auxiliary verb *have* + past participle), its uses in English are different.

Present Perfect Continuous The Present Perfect Continuous is similarly difficult. Moreover, it presents difficulty as to when it should be chosen instead of the Present Perfect Simple. Basically, the Present Perfect Continuous should be chosen in the following situations:

1 To suggest a temporary situation when talking about unfinished past.
   I've lived here for ten years.
   I've been living here for ten days.

2 To emphasize activity rather than completed action when talking about present result.
   I've painted the ceiling. (It's finished.)
   I've been painting the ceiling. (I'm tired.)

Vocabulary The vocabulary section looks at the hot verbs, *make* and *do*, and how they are used in expressions and with particles to form phrasal verbs.

Everyday English This section introduces and practises exclamations.

Notes on the unit

TEST YOUR GRAMMAR (SB p16)

The first part of the *Test your grammar* section aims to test the students' understanding of the difference between the use of the Past Simple (to talk about a finished past action), and the Present Perfect (to talk about unfinished past or a past action with a present result). The 'strangeness' in these sentences arises from misapplying these uses.

The second part tests the students' understanding of simple aspect (which describes states and complete actions) and continuous aspect (which focuses on the duration of an activity).

These exercises should be done quickly. Don't get involved in lengthy grammar explanations at this stage.

1 Ask students in pairs to discuss and correct the sentences. Go round monitoring to see how well students understand the way the tenses work.

Answers

1 Using the Present Perfect here suggests that this is recent news and that Columbus is still alive. The Past Simple should be used.
Columbus discovered America in 1492.

2 Although the use of the Past Simple is correct here, the sentence sounds incomplete without a time reference.
Man first walked on the moon in 1969.

3 It sounds as if the speaker is dead, which is impossible. The Present Perfect is correct.
I've travelled/been travelling all my life. I've been everywhere.

4 The use of the Present Perfect sounds strange here because it suggests that this is a completed action. It's saying, *Now I know English.* Learning a language is not a process we 'complete'! It's better to use the Present Perfect Continuous here, which suggests that the action is ongoing.
I've been learning English.

5 The use of the Present Perfect Continuous for an action of short duration (*lose my passport*) suggests that this has been happening frequently, i.e. I've been losing my passport and finding it again many times recently. The Present Perfect Simple should be used for a single action with a consequence that is strongly present.
I've lost my passport.

2 Ask students in pairs to discuss and change the sentences where possible. Monitor to see how well students understand the uses of simple and continuous aspect.

Answers

1 *What do you do in New York?*
That is, permanently. In other words, what's your job?
What are you doing in New York?
That is, temporarily. In other words, at this moment or these days, and not necessarily related to work.

2 *I know you don't like my boyfriend.*
Know and *like* are 'state' verbs that cannot be used in the continuous form.

3 *I had a cup of tea at 8.00.*
Here, used to talk about a completed past action.
I was having a cup of tea at 8.00.
Here, used to talk about an action in progress at that moment in time.

4 *Someone's eaten my sandwich.*
Here, the action is complete with a result now: The sandwich is gone.
Someone's been eating my sandwich.
Here, the action is incomplete. The speaker is looking at a sandwich with a couple of big bites taken out of it!

5 *I'm hot because I've been running.*
Here, the emphasis is on a result of the activity, not on the fact that the action of running is completed.
I'm hot because I've run.
This sentence is highly unlikely. We use the Present Perfect Simple when we want to emphasize the completed action, e.g. *I've run a marathon.*

EXPLORERS AND TRAVELLERS (SB p16)

Present Perfect

This section looks at the differences between the Present Perfect and Past Simple, with a particular focus on the Present Perfect Simple and Present Perfect Continuous. The practice activities emphasize question-forming.

1 Ask students to look at the pictures, and discuss the questions as a class.

Sample answers
In the past, people went exploring to find new countries, open up new markets, make money, or spread their religion. Nowadays, young people travel to see interesting places, have new and interesting experiences, find things out about themselves, meet new people, learn new languages.
Point out that an *explorer* tries to find new places that nobody knows about. A *traveller* goes to already-discovered places for interest and adventure.

2 Ask students to read the paragraphs quickly.

> **VOCABULARY NOTE**
> *get the travel bug* = become very enthusiastic about travelling
> *travel extensively* = travel to many places

T 2.1 [CD 1: Track 16] Ask students to match the sentences with the correct person. Do the first two as a class to get the students started. Let the students check in pairs before listening to the recording. Play the recording so that students can check their answers. In the feedback, ask the students what other information they heard.

Answers and tapescript
1 MP   2 TW   3 TW   4 MP
5 MP   6 TW   7 MP   8 TW

T 2.1
(New information in **bold**)
Marco Polo 1254–1324
Marco Polo was the first person to travel the entire 8,000 kilometre length of the Silk Route, the main trade link between Cathay (China) and the West for over two thousand years.

He was born in Venice, the son of a merchant. **In 1271**, when he was 17, he set off for China. The journey took him four years. His route led him through Persia, Afghanistan, **and Mongolia. He travelled by boat, but mainly on horseback, and he frequently got lost.**

He was met by the emperor Kublai Khan. He was one of the first Europeans to visit the territory, and he travelled extensively. **He went over mountain ranges, down rivers, and across deserts.**

He stayed in China for seventeen years. When he left, he took back a fortune in gold and jewellery. **He arrived back home in 1295.**

He wrote a book called *The Travels of Marco Polo*, which gave Europeans their first information about China and the Far East.

Tommy Willis, backpacker in Asia

Tommy Willis is in Fiji. He's on a nine-month backpacking trip round south-east Asia. He flew into Bangkok five months ago. Since then, he's been to Vietnam, Hong Kong, South Korea, and Japan.

He's visited royal palaces and national parks in South Korea, and climbed to the summit of Mount Fuji in Japan.

He's been staying in cheap hostels, along with a lot of other young people.

'I've met a lot of really great people, but it hasn't all been easy,' said Tommy. 'I've had diarrhoea a few times, **and I've been pickpocketed once. I've also been mugged, which was really scary.'** Apart from that, his only worry is the insects. He's been stung all over his body.

He's been travelling mainly by public transport – **bus, train, and ferry, but when he's been able to afford it, he's also taken the occasional plane.**

He's looking forward to taking things easy for another week, then setting off again for Australia. 'Once you've got the travel bug, it becomes very hard to stay in the same place for too long,' he said.

3 **T 2.2** [CD 1: Track 17] Ask students in pairs to match lines in **A** with lines in **B**. Then ask the pairs to practise saying the sentences. Play the recording so that students can listen and check their answers. Play the recording a second time so that students can repeat and practise their pronunciation.

Answers and tapescript
He's been stung all over his body.
He's visited royal palaces.
He's been staying in cheap hostels.
I've been pickpocketed and mugged.
I've met a lot of really great people.
He's been to Vietnam and Japan.

LANGUAGE FOCUS

See TB p8 for suggestions on how to teach this section.

Don't forget to look at the *Language aims* section on TB p19, which looks at problems students may have. You should also read the Grammar Reference on SB pp140–142.

LANGUAGE INPUT

1 Ask the students which grammatical clue let them know which sentences went with which person.

Answers
The main tense used about Marco Polo is the Past Simple, because he is dead, so all the events of his life are set firmly in past time.

The main tenses used about Tommy Willis are the Present Perfect Simple and the Present Perfect Continuous. Not only is Tommy Willis still alive, he is also in the middle of his trip. He's been travelling for five months and he is still travelling, and in the course of his travels he's seen and done many things. The Past Simple is used once to talk about an activity set at a particular time – *He flew into Bangkok five months ago.*

2 Ask students in pairs to compare the tenses. Go round monitoring to help the students with queries.

Answers
1 *I've read that book. It's good.*
   The reading of the book is finished.
   I've been reading a great book. I'll lend it to you when I've finished.
   The reading of the book is not finished.
   I've been reading a lot about Orwell recently. I've just finished his biography.
   Here, the continuous emphasizes repeated activities over a period of time.
2 *She's been writing since she was 16.*
   Here, the continuous emphasizes repeated activities over a period of time.
   She's written three novels.
   The Present Perfect Simple emphasizes the completed actions: the total of three novels that have been completed in her life so far.
3 *He's played tennis since he was a kid.*
   He's been playing tennis since he was a kid.
   There is very little difference in meaning between these two sentences.

Refer students to Grammar Reference 1 & 2 on SB pp140–142.

Questions and answers

1 Ask students in pairs to ask and answer the questions. Remind the students that the Past Simple is used with Marco Polo (dead) and the Present Perfect with Tommy (living/still travelling).

Answers
1 MP: *Where did he go?* He travelled the Silk Route to China.
   TW: *Where has he been?* He's been to Vietnam, Hong Kong, South Korea, Japan, and now he's in Fiji.
2 TW: *How long has he been travelling?* He's been travelling for five months.
   MP: *How long did he travel?* He travelled for four years.
3 MP: *How did he travel?* He travelled by boat, but mainly on horseback.
   TW: *How has he been travelling?* He's been travelling by public transport – bus, train, and ferry.
4 TW: *Who has he met?* He has met some really great people.
   MP: *Who did he meet?* He met the Mongolian emperor Kublai Khan.
5 MP: *Did he have any problems?* He frequently got lost.
   TW: *Has he had any problems?* He's had diarrhoea a few times, he's been pickpocketed once, and he's also been mugged. He's been stung all over his body by insects.

2 **T 2.3** [CD 1: Track 18] Ask students in pairs to write questions. Play the recording so that students can check their answers.

Answers and tapescript
About Marco Polo
1 When and where was he born?
   In 1254 in Venice.
2 How long did it take to travel to China?
   Four years.
3 How long did he stay in China?
   For seventeen years.
4 What did he take back to Venice?
   Gold and jewellery.
5 What was his book called?
   The Travels of Marco Polo.
About Tommy Willis
6 How long has he been away from home?
   For five months.
7 Which places has he been to?
   Thailand, Vietnam, Hong Kong, South Korea, and Japan.
8 Where's he been staying?
   In cheap hostels.
9 How many times has he had diarrhoea?
   A few times.
10 Has he been pickpocketed?
   Yes, once.

Discussing grammar

This section aims to get students to show their understanding of the contrast between Past Simple, Present Perfect and Present Perfect Continuous by putting the verbs in the correct tense. This activity enables you, as a teacher, to respond to and explain confusions that students may have. If you have a monolingual class, and speak the students' L1, you may wish to translate and contrast sentences to show how English may work differently from the students' own language.

3 Ask students to put the verbs in the correct tense. Let the students discuss their answers with a partner before feedback.

You may wish to use check questions to check the students' understanding in feedback. Check questions are a time-efficient way of making sure students understand. For example, for number 1, ask: *In which sentence do we say when it happened in the past? Which sentence talks about a repeated activity which is not finished?*

For number 2 ask: *In which sentence are we interested in the experience, not the time when?*

For number 3 ask: *In which sentence are we talking about experiences up to now?*

For number 4 ask: *Which sentence talks about a temporary situation? Which one talks about a permanent situation?*

For number 5 ask: *Which sentence talks about a single past action with a result now? Which sentence talks about repeated past actions up to now?*

Answers
1 Charles Dickens **wrote** Oliver Twist in 1837. (finished past action)
   I **have written** two best-selling crime stories. (at an unspecified time in the past – the 'experience' not the time is important)
   She **has been writing** her autobiography for the past eighteen months. (unfinished past – activity that started in past and continued to now)
2 **Have** you ever **tried** Mexican food? (at an unspecified time in the past – the 'experience' not the time is important)
   Did you **try** *chiles rellenos* when you were in Mexico? (finished past action – asking about a specific event during a specified time)
3 How many times **have** you **been married**? (experiences up to now)
   How many times **was** Henry VIII **married**? (events in finished past)
4 I **'ve lived** in the same house since I was born. (unfinished past – began in past and continued to now – permanent)
   He **'s been living** with his brother for the past week. (unfinished past – began in past and continued to now – temporary: *He's lived with his brother for the past week* is possible, but using the Present Perfect Continuous here

sounds more natural because, from the context, the action seems temporary.)

5 Cindy's very pleased with herself. She's finally **given up** smoking. She's **been trying** to give up for years. (present result – recent past action with results now/repeated activity over a period of time)

Simple and continuous

LANGUAGE FOCUS

See TB p8 for suggestions on how to teach this section.

Don't forget to look at the *Language aims* section on TB p19, which looks at problems students may have. You should also read the Grammar Reference on SB pp140–141.

LANGUAGE INPUT

Read through the rules as a class. Ask students for examples of other state verbs.

State verbs
Verbs of the mind: *believe, think, assume, consider, understand, suppose, expect, agree, know, remember, forget*
Verbs of emotion: *like, love, detest, envy, hate, hope, prefer, wish, want*
Verbs of having and being: *belong, own, depend, contain, cost, seem, appear, need, have*
Verbs of the senses: *see, hear, taste, smell*

Refer the students to the Grammar reference on pp140–141.

4 Ask students to match the sentence halves. Do the first as an example. Let students check in pairs before feedback.

Answers
a1 *Peter comes from Switzerland.* (Present Simple – action is seen as a complete whole. Here, it is not so much an action, as a statement of fact about something that is always true.)
b2 *Peter is coming round at 8.00 tonight.* (Present Continuous – here, used to talk about a future arrangement)
c2 *I wrote a report this morning. I sent it off this afternoon.* (Past Simple – a completed past action with a definite time reference)
d1 *I was writing a report this morning. I'll finish it this afternoon.* (Past Continuous – an action that was in progress and is incomplete)
e1 *I heard her scream when she saw a mouse.* (hear (someone) do – the infinitive form is used when the action is seen as a single, whole event)
f2 *I heard the baby screaming all night long.* (hear (someone) doing – the –ing form is used when it is seen as a long action in progress, and only a part of it may have been heard)
g2 *What have you done with my dictionary? I can't find it.* (Present Perfect Simple – action seen as a complete whole, an action with a result now)

h1 *What have you been doing since I last saw you?* (Present Perfect Continuous – asking about continuous or repeated actions over a period of time, actions starting in the past and happening up to now)
i1 *I've had a headache all day.* (Present Perfect Simple – although this is a long event, *have* here is a state verb and cannot be used in the continuous form.)
j2 *I've been having second thoughts about the new job.* (Present Perfect Continuous – a series of repeated actions over a period of time up to now. The speaker thinks one thing, then changes their mind. Note that *I've had* is possible, but it means that the action of having second thoughts is seen as one completed event: *I've had second thoughts – I don't want the job.*)
k2 *I've known Anna for over ten years.* (Present Perfect Simple – a single, whole event that started in the past and continued to now. *Know* is a state verb.)
l1 *I've been getting to know my new neighbours.* (Present Perfect Continuous – here, seen as a series of repeated actions up to now. There is also the idea of an action in progress, which is not yet completed.)
m1 *I've cut my finger. It hurts.* (Present Perfect Simple – seen as a single, whole event.)
n2 *I've been cutting wood all morning.* (Present Perfect Continuous – seen as a series of repeated actions that started in the past and continued to now, or until very recently.)

Writing Unit 2
Informal Letters – Correcting mistakes SB p112

Exchanging information

These two information gap activities aim to give the students lots of speaking practice in pairs. The students must show a reasonable degree of accuracy and fluency in manipulating a variety of tenses.

Lead in by asking students about the *Lonely Planet* travel guides: *Have you ever used one? Where did you go? What sort of information do you find in a Lonely Planet guide? Do you have a similar sort of guide in your country?*

CULTURAL NOTE
As stated in the texts, there are now over 650 *Lonely Planet* travel guides, translated into 17 languages. The books are written for 'travellers' rather than tourists. They provide information on how to travel around foreign countries by yourself, where to find accommodation, particularly budget accommodation, and where to go to get a 'flavour' of the real country. The books also give information about the history, culture and language of the country visited. The books are very popular with backpackers and budget travellers from Britain, New Zealand and Australia.

5 Divide the students into pairs. Ask Student A in each pair to look at the information on p153. Ask Student B to look at the information on p154.

Read through the instructions with the whole class. Model the example with a student. Make it clear that students must **take it in turns** to ask questions to fill the gaps in the text. Give the students five minutes to read their texts and prepare questions. Go round monitoring, helping with vocabulary and question-forming. When the students are ready, pair As with Bs and ask them to interview each other to find the missing information. Go round monitoring, first checking briefly that all the pairs are doing the activity correctly.

Feedback with the whole class by asking the students some of the questions. For example: *How many people does it employ? Where does it have offices?*

Completed text and sample questions

Lonely Planet is one of the outstanding publishing successes of the past three decades. It employs more than **500** people, and has offices in **the USA, France, England**, with its headquarters in Melbourne, Australia.

Tony and Maureen Wheeler have been writing *Lonely Planet* guide books for **over thirty years**. They have written **more than 650** guides. They sell **around 5.5 million** copies a year in 118 countries. The books have been translated into **17** languages.

Tony lived **in many different countries** when he was young because **his father's job took him all over the world**. He studied **engineering** at Warwick University, then business studies at **the London Business School**.

Maureen was born in **Belfast**. She went to London at the age of 20 because **she wanted to see the world**. Three days later she met Tony **on a bench in Regent's Park**. In 1972 they travelled overland across Europe, through Asia, and on to Australia. The trip took **six months**. They wrote their first book, called *Across Asia on the cheap* on their kitchen table in Melbourne. They have lived in Melbourne on and off for over **thirty years**.

Together they have been to **more than 100** countries. Tony says that the most amazing place he has ever visited is **a remote hilltop city called Tsaparang, in Tibet**.

They are currently travelling in **India, researching a new edition of their guide to the country**.

He is thinking of selling **his shares in the company**. He said, '**I've had a wonderful time, it's been terrific, but it has now got too much like a business.**'

Student A's questions

How many people does it employ?
How long have Tony and Maureen been writing *Lonely Planet* guide books?
How many copies a year do they sell?

Where did Tony live when he was young?
What did he study at Warwick university?
Where was Maureen born?
Where did she meet Tony?
What was their first book called?
How many countries have they been to?
Where are they currently travelling?
What is he thinking of selling?

Student B's questions

Where does it have its offices?
How many guides have they written?
How many languages have the guides been translated into?
Why did Tony live in so many countries when he was young?
Where did he study business studies?
Why did Maureen go to London?
How long did the trip take?
How long have they lived in Melbourne?
What is the most amazing pace that Tony has ever visited?
What are they doing in India?
What reason did he give for selling the shares?

6 Divide the class into groups of four. Ask half the groups to prepare questions from the prompts. Ask the other groups to read the information about Tony Wheeler on p154. Tell them that they must imagine they are Tony, and be prepared to answer questions about his life. Go round monitoring, helping with vocabulary and question-forming.

When the students are ready, ask two people from each 'question-forming' group to exchange places with two people from each 'Tony Wheeler' group. Ask the interviewers to interview Tony Wheeler.

Monitor and note down any errors the students make with the grammatical forms practised in this unit. At the end of the activity, write any errors the students have made on the board, and ask students in the class to correct them.

ADDITIONAL MATERIAL

Workbook Unit 2

Exercise 1 Present Perfect Simple or Continuous?
Exercise 2 Present Perfect and Past Simple
Exercise 3 Simple or continuous verb forms?
Exercise 4 Present Perfect passive
Exercise 5 *have something done*

READING AND SPEAKING (SB p19)

Paradise Lost

1 Lead in by asking students to look at the photos and answer the questions.

2 Discuss the questions as a class or in small groups.

3 Ask students to work in pairs or small groups to answer
   the questions. Give them a few minutes to think of
   problems. Then ask some of the pairs to report their
   ideas to the class. You could build up a list of 'main
   problems with the tourist industry' on the board.

Reading

4 Ask students to predict the content of the article from
   the title and the quotes.

5 Ask students to read the article and answer the
   questions. Let students check in pairs before feedback.

6 Divide students into groups of three or four, then ask
   them to read the article again and answer the questions.
   The aim here is to get students to read a text in detail for
   specific information, to take notes, and to share and
   discuss their information.

What do you think?

The aim of these two exercises is to use the text as a
springboard for discussion. The students are expected to
discuss, personally respond to and ask questions about
material in the text.

1 Ask students to work in their groups to prepare things to
   say. Go round monitoring and helping with sentence
   construction. Let students give their reactions in their
   groups, then have a brief class feedback, asking each
   group to make a comment.

2 Ask students to work in their groups to prepare questions.
   Give them four or five minutes, and go round monitoring
   to help with question forming. When the students are
   ready, either ask each group to take it in turns to ask the
   other groups questions, or mix the students into new
   groups so that they can ask their questions in groups.

Vocabulary work

1 Ask students in pairs to find and guess the meaning of
   the highlighted words in context.

Low-end package tourists = Package tourists are people who pay for all-inclusive holidays, with food and accommodation pre-paid. *Low-end* means their holiday packages are cheap.
cooped up in the hotel compound = Chickens are 'cooped up' – kept in small cages. So, here, metaphorically, it means kept within the walls of the hotel without going out.
the victim of its own success = It has lost (money/beauty/way of life) because it has been successful.
might have second thoughts = If you have second thoughts, it means you think again and possibly change your mind.

2 Ask students in pairs to match words in **A** with words that they collocate with in **B**. Let students look back at the text to check their answers.

Answers
the boom in world travel (what Maurice Chandler is reporting on)
tourism's vital contribution to the economy (Majorcans don't deny this)
per capita income (Majorca has become one of the richest parts of Spain in terms of this)
a major business venture (the reason 250 Filipinos were evicted from their homes)
foreign destinations (to millions of tourists, these are exotic paradises)
consume as much water (a golf course can consume as much water as a town of 10,000 people)
a prime example (Italy is a prime example of the tourist industry's need to keep the crowds at bay)
the best hope for development (tourism still offers this for many poorer countries)

SPEAKING AND LISTENING (SB p22)

Dreams come true

The speaking activity is a personalized ordering task. It is followed by three short 'vox pop' listening texts, which practise the students' ability to listen for gist.

1 Lead in and set the scene by writing on the board, *Which place in the world would you most like to visit? What activity would you most like to do?* Elicit a few responses.

Read through the list as a class, and use the pictures on the page to check any difficult vocabulary. Then ask the students to list their top 5 individually. When they are ready, put the students in groups of four or five to discuss their lists. Encourage them to say why they have chosen the things on their list.

Have a brief class feedback, and find out which place or activity was most popular in the class.

ALTERNATIVE IDEA
Ask students in their groups to agree on a list of five. To do this they will have to negotiate as well as discuss. When they are ready, ask each group to read out their list, and build up a 'class' list on the board.

CULTURAL NOTE
The Northern Lights, or *aurora borealis*, is a natural light show that can be seen in the far north.
Machu Picchu is the ruins of an Inca city in Peru.
The Great Barrier Reef is a huge coral reef off the coast of Australia.

2, 3 Ask the students to read the poll results on SB p155, and discuss the questions in their groups. Have a brief class feedback, encouraging students to tell the class about any personal experiences, or those of people they know.

4 **T 2.4** [CD 1: Track 19] Play the recording. Ask students to listen and answer the questions. Let them compare their answers in pairs or groups before feedback.

Answers
1 Alan is talking about the Northern Lights. He describes them as *a shimmering curtain – purply red* – and says they make a *buzzing noise*. He describes his feeling of awe on seeing the lights, and how they made him feel small.
2 James is talking about Machu Picchu. He talks about walking there in time for the sunrise, and looking down on the ancient city, which is extraordinary, especially before the thousands of tourists arrive.
3 Willow is talking about flying in a hot air balloon. She talks about *flying like a bird*, how small people seem, and how amazingly silent it is.

T 2.4
Alan
They are ... one of the most eerie ... and -er strange experiences you can possibly have. The first time I saw them, they appeared as a kind of shimmering curtain, over the top of a ridge of mountains, and they went from a greeny colour to a kind of purply red colour. And they just stayed there. The second time I saw them, it was the most amazing sight because they were right above our heads, and they covered the whole of the sky. The other interesting thing is that -er not everybody hears it, but they sometimes make a sound, a kind of -er buzzing noise. It was a real sense of wonder and awe. I just kind of sat there with my mouth hanging open, just feeling kind of small.
James
You start at the bottom of the valley, and slowly make your way up the hill, -er about a seven-hour hike until you get to a camp. Then you get up very early the next morning, about four o'clock, in order to get there for the sunrise. You walk for an hour or so, and suddenly you reach this point where you're

looking down on this ancient city, just as the sun is breaking through the clouds. It's the most extraordinary sight. And you walk around in the total silence of a city that's more than five hundred years old. At that point it's invaded by thousands of tourists, and -er it's time to go.

Willow

We got up about five o'clock in the morning. We went to the site, and set off. Because you're floating with the wind, there is no breeze on you, and it really was like ... flying like a bird. You could look down on everyone, and they were all so small, like ants. It was just amazing, and so silent. And we landed about seven o'clock, and suddenly we were back with the rest of civilization. It was just the most beautiful experience.

VOCABULARY (SB p23)

Hot verbs – *make, do*

The aim of this section is to introduce and practise the easily confused verbs, *make* and *do*. It also looks at phrasal verbs with *make* and *do*. This is the first of a series of exercises in both the Student's book and Workbook on *Hot verbs*. These are verbs which are much used in English, both in expressions and phrasal verbs.

Start the lesson by writing some common *hot verbs* on the board: *take, put, have, make, do, go, come*. Give students three minutes to write down *any* words that go with these verbs. Then elicit ideas and write them on the board. This builds awareness of how common these verbs are.

1 Read through the examples from the text on p20 as a class.

2 Ask students in pairs to put the words in the correct box. Do the first as an example. Let students have a guess first, then go through the answers as a class, building up the table on the board.

Answers	
make	**do**
a good impression	business
arrangements	research
a decision	your best
a difference	a good job
a profit/a loss	a degree
a start/a move	sb a favour
sth clear	
an effort	
a suggestion	

ALTERNATIVE IDEA

If you have a class set of learners' dictionaries, you could do this as a dictionary task. Ask some pairs to look up *do* and other pairs to look up *make*. Then pair the pairs to check their answers, and complete the table.

There is a kind of 'rule' for *make* and *do*. We tend to use *make* with the idea of creation or construction, e.g. *make a cake*. We tend to use *do* with the idea of work, e.g. *do your homework, do the ironing*. However, there are lots of exceptions.

3 **T 2.5** [CD 1: Track 20] Ask students to complete the sentences, then listen and check.

Answers and tapescript

1 When you go for a job interview, it's important to *make a good impression*.
2 I think we're all getting tired. Can I *make a suggestion*? How about a break?
3 A lot of *research* has been *done* into the causes of cancer.
4 I think the director is basically *doing a good job*. He's reliable, he's honest, and he gets results.
5 I'd like to *make it clear* right now that I am totally opposed to this idea.
6 Right. I think we should *make a start* and get down to business.
7 I don't mind if we go now or later. It *makes no difference* to me.
8 Could you *do me a favour* and lend me some money till tomorrow?

4 Ask students to match the sentences and underline the expressions.

Answers

1 She's made the big time as an actress. She can command $20 million a movie.
2 We'll never make the airport in time. The traffic's too bad.
3 'What does she do for a living?' 'She's an accountant.'
4 'You'll all have to do more overtime and work weekends.' 'That does it! I'm going to look for another job!'
5 'How much do you want to borrow? $20?' 'Great. That'll do fine.'
6 'How much Spanish do you speak?' 'I can make myself understood.'
7 'I hear the boss said you'd done really well?' 'Yeah. It really made my day.'

EXTENSION ACTIVITY

Ask students in pairs to act out the mini-dialogues 3–7 above. Or ask them to write their own 'statement and response' dialogue, using at least one *make* or *do* expression. Ask pairs to act out their dialogue for the class.

Phrasal verbs

5 **T 2.6** [CD 1: Track 21] Ask students in pairs to complete the sentences. Then play the recording so that students can listen and check.

Answers and tapescript

1 I'm so thirsty. I *could do with* a cup of tea.
2 We've bought an old flat. We're going to *do it up* over the next few years.
3 I think we should *do away with* the monarchy. They're all useless. And expensive.
4 I could never *do without* my personal assistant. She organizes everything for me.

6 **T 2.7** [CD 1: Track 22] Ask students in pairs to complete the sentences. Then play the recording so that students can listen and check.

Answers and tapescript

1 Thieves broke into the castle and *made off with* jewellery and antique paintings.
2 Jake's parents buy him loads of toys. They're trying to *make up for* always being at work.
3 What do you *make of* the new boss? I quite like him.
4 You didn't believe his story, did you? He *made* the whole thing *up*.

LISTENING AND SPEAKING (SB p24)

Tashi Wheeler – girl on the move

The aim of the listening is to give students practice in listening intensively to a long interview. The tasks involve predicting and listening to confirm, note-taking, correcting a text, and answering questions.

The Spoken English section looks at 'fillers' – vague words such as *stuff* and *like*.

1 Lead in by asking students to tell the class about their earliest holiday memories. It is a good idea to start this activity by talking about your own earliest memory first.

   If students have brought in their own photos, you could do this as a mini-presentation. Ask students to describe their memories to the class, or in groups, while circulating the photos they have brought in. This can generate a great deal of amusement and interest.

2 Remind students what they learnt about Tony and Maureen Wheeler (SB p18), and point out that Tashi Wheeler is their daughter. Ask students in pairs to look at the photos of Tashi and discuss the questions. Have a class feedback, and discuss their answers to the questions.

Answers

Top picture from right to left:
Tashi is about 7 months old, in Singapore, riding in a baby-carrier.
Tashi is 4 years old, in Puno on Lake Titicaca, Peru, riding on a delivery bicycle with her brother (apparently her parents were too breathless from the altitude to carry them!)

Bottom pictures from right to left:
Tashi is 6 years old, in a sculpture park in Villahermosa, Mexico, dancing beside an Olmec head.
Tashi is 8 years old, in Voi, Kenya, waiting for a bus at the bus stand.
Tashi is 8 years old, in Kenya, lying in a mosquito-netted bed at a safari lodge.
Tashi is 13 years old, in Arizona, looking at American-Indian jewellery at a street-side market.

3 Ask students in pairs to think of as many questions to ask as they can.

4 **T 2.8** [CD 1: Track 23] Play the first part of the recording. Ask students to listen and make notes under the headings. Let students check in pairs before feedback. In the feedback, find out which of their questions they heard answers to, then build up answers on the board under the headings.

Answers

Transport: *airports and bus rides*
Being on safari: *got chased by an elephant, had lion cubs jumping around the safari bus, monkeys swinging off the rear-view mirrors ...*
Her mother: *Mum used to say that when I was two years old she just put me down and I just ran off. And she wouldn't see me and then someone would pick me up and bring me back.*
Trekking in Nepal: *getting up at like four in the morning and looking over all the mountains, and then just walking all day, talking to porters, and coming into villages, and all the kids running out and seeing you...*

T 2.8 See SB Tapescripts p126

5 **T 2.9** [CD 1: Track 24] Play the second part of the recording. Ask students to listen carefully, then correct the information in the text. Let students check in pairs before feedback. You may need to play the recording again so that students can check their corrections.

Answers

On holiday, the Wheeler family are *not* relaxed – Dad, Tony, is 'hectic'. They get up *early* and go to bed *late*. They *don't spend time on the beach – they visit lots of sights.* Tony Wheeler *doesn't have time to* read the paper. They go *to lots of different restaurants.* Tashi and her brother spend a lot of time watching movies. She *feels that* travel broadens the mind.

T 2.9 See SB Tapescripts p126

6 **T 2.10** Read through the questions as a class. Then play the third part of the recording. Ask students to listen carefully, but not to try to write answers. After playing the extract, put students in pairs to discuss and write answers to the questions. You may need to play the recording again so that students can check their corrections.

Answers

1 She wanted to stay at home.
2 She didn't really know how to get along with kids her age and her own culture and country.
3 Because when you are travelling for so long in countries where you can't talk to boys, or you can't look at people in a certain way, or you don't wear certain clothing, it is difficult to adjust to life at home.
4 The kids at school had things going on, like watching TV, and she was never up to date. But at the same time, she had seen things, and had a broader view of life.
5 She feels comfortable at her home in Melbourne, and in Asia. She doesn't feel uncomfortable anywhere.
6 Try to fit as much of it in as you can when you're younger.
7 Tony Willis says that he's 'got the travel bug.'

T 2.10 See SB Tapescripts p126

SPOKEN ENGLISH – Fillers

Read through the explanation and extract with students. Ask them if they can think of any other language that English speakers use as fillers.

Ask students in pairs to look at the tapescript and find more examples of imprecise language and fillers.

Answers
Other fillers used in the tapescript:
...erm	...I don't know	...kind of...
...and so on...	...all that stuff	...I guess

EVERYDAY ENGLISH (SB p25)

Exclamations

The aim of this section is to introduce and practise exclamations.

1 Read through the examples as a class. Ask students when we use exclamations.

Answer
To express strong emotions. For example, *shock, surprise, disgust, amazement, delight*.
See exercise 5 for the grammar rule.

2 Ask students in pairs to match the exclamations and the sentences.

Answers
B	C
Mmm!	It's absolutely delicious.
Wow!	That's unbelievable! How amazing!
Hey, Peter!	Come over here and sit with us.
Oh, really?	How interesting!

Ah!	What a shame!
Ouch!	That really hurt!
Yuk!	That's disgusting!
Uh?	That's nonsense! What a stupid thing to say!
Phew!	What a relief! Thank goodness for that!
Whoops!	Sorry about that! I dropped it!

3 **T 2.11** [CD 1: Track 26] Play the recording. Ask students to listen and write the correct number next to each exclamation. Play the recording again. Ask students to listen and reply, using the correct exclamation and line of conversation.

Answers and tapescript
1 Mmm! It's absolutely delicious.
3 Wow! That's unbelievable! How amazing!
7 Hey, Peter! Come over here and sit with us.
9 Oh, really? How interesting!
2 Ah! What a shame!
4 Ouch! That really hurt!
6 Yuk! That's disgusting!
8 Uh? That's nonsense! What a stupid thing to say!
10 Phew! What a relief! Thank goodness for that!
5 Whoops! Sorry about that! I dropped it!

T 2.11
1 How's your steak? Is it OK?
2 We were all going on holiday to Spain next week. We were really looking forward to it, but my father's been quite ill so we've had to cancel the holiday.
3 A Has Ann had the baby yet? It must be due any time now.
   B Oh, yes. haven't you heard? She didn't have one baby. She had three! Tom's the father of triplets!
4 Mind your head as you come through this door. It's very low.
5 Do be careful. That bowl's really heavy.
6 Did you know that they eat horse-meat in some countries? And snails. And pigs' feet.
7 Look! Isn't that Peter over there, sitting on his own?
8 Sarah told me that you hated me. She said that you never wanted to see me ever again!
9 I saw Julie yesterday.
10 Tomorrow's test has been cancelled.

4 Ask students in pairs to match the next line of each conversation.

T 2.12 [CD 1: Track 27] Play the recording so that students can listen and check. Put students in pairs to practise the conversations. Ask two or three pairs to act out conversations for the class.

Answers and tapescript
5 Don't worry. I'll get you a new one.
3 Triplets! That'll keep them busy!
2 You must be so disappointed!
1 Just the way I like it.
10 I hadn't done any revising for it at all.

<u>6</u> You wouldn't catch me eating that!

<u>4</u> I told you! Well, it isn't bleeding, but you'll have a nice bruise.

<u>7</u> Let's have a chat.

<u>8</u> You know it's not true.

<u>9</u> I haven't seen her for ages. How is she?

T 2.12

1 A How's your steak? Is it OK?
   B Mmm! It's absolutely delicious! Just the way I like it.

2 A We were all going on holiday to Spain next week. We were really looking forward to it, but my father's been quite ill so we had to cancel the holiday.
   B Ah! What a shame! You must be so disappointed!

3 A Has Ann had the baby yet? It must be due any time now.
   B Oh, yes. haven't you heard? She didn't have one baby. She had three! Tom's the father of triplets!
   A Wow! That's unbelievable! How amazing! Triplets! That'll keep them busy!

4 A Mind your head as you come through this door. It's very low.
   B Ouch! That really hurt!
   A I told you! Well, it isn't bleeding, but you'll have a nice bruise.

5 A Do be careful. That bowl's really heavy.
   B Whoops! Sorry about that! I dropped it! Don't worry. I'll get you a new one.

6 A Did you know that they eat horse-meat in some countries? And snails. And pigs' feet.
   B Yuk! That's disgusting! You wouldn't catch me eating that!

7 A Look! Isn't that Peter over there, sitting on his own?
   B Hey, Peter! Come over here and sit with us. Let's have a chat.

8 A Sarah told me that you hated me. She said that you never wanted to see me ever again!
   B Uh? That's nonsense! What a stupid thing to say! You know it's not true.

9 A I saw Julie yesterday.
   B Oh, really? How interesting! I haven't seen her for ages. How is she?

10 A Tomorrow's test has been cancelled!
   B Phew! What a relief! Thank goodness for that! I hadn't done any revising for it at all.

MUSIC OF ENGLISH

Read the information as a class.

T 2.13 [CD 1: Track 28] Play the recording. Ask students to listen and repeat.

Tapescript
What awful shoes!
What a fantastic view!
How amazing!

5 Ask students in pairs to complete the exclamations. Point out that we use *What* + plural or countable noun, *What a* + singular, countable noun, and *How* + adjective.

Answers

1 What a silly mistake!	6 What a mess!
2 What a brilliant idea!	7 How awful!
3 How utterly ridiculous!	8 How wonderful!
4 What dreadful weather!	9 What a relief!
5 What rubbish!	10 What a terrible thing to happen!

Positive reactions: 2, 8, 9
Negative reactions: 1, 3, 4, 5, 6, 7, 10

6 **T 2.14** [CD 1: Track 29] Play the recording. Ask students to listen and respond, using the exclamations in exercise 5. A good way to do this is to play and pause each extract, and get the class to suggest the correct exclamation. Then play the recording again, and nominate individuals to respond. Correct errors, particularly poor intonation.

Answers and tapescript (with suggested answers in **bold**)

1 I've just won $25,000 on the lottery!
   How wonderful!

2 Let's have a long coffee break!
   What a brilliant idea!

3 Maria, you wrote 'at Rome' instead of 'in Rome'.
   What a silly mistake!

4 We were stuck in a traffic jam for four hours!
   How awful!

5 Look at the state of the kitchen! It hasn't been cleaned for weeks!
   What a mess!

6 Rain, rain, rain.
   What dreadful weather!

7 The teacher told us to learn the dictionary for homework.
   How utterly ridiculous!

8 We hadn't heard from our daughter for a month, then she phoned last night.
   What a relief!

9 My sister says it's possible to learn French in three months!
   What rubbish!/How utterly ridiculous!

10 Yesterday I got a tax bill for $20,000.
   What a terrible thing to happen!

7 Ask students in pairs to write a dialogue. Monitor and help the students with ideas and language. When the students are ready, ask some of the pairs to act out their dialogues.

ADDITIONAL MATERIAL

Workbook Unit 2

Exercises 6-7 Vocabulary

Exercise 8 Prepositions

Exercise 9 Pronunciation – Word stress

Exercise 10 Listening – A camping nightmare

Narrative tenses • News and responses
Books and films • Showing interest and surprise

Introduction to the unit

This unit is all about telling stories, an obvious theme for a unit covering the major narrative tenses: the Past Simple, Past Continuous, Past Perfect Simple and Past Perfect Continuous.

The main reading text is an extract from the novel *The Blind Assassin* by Margaret Atwood. The main listening text is an interview in which a girl tells a story about how she and her friend found some ripped up banknotes, and pieced them together. The vocabulary section introduces language that students can use to ask about and describe books and films.

Language aims

Narrative tenses   The aim is to revise and practise the narrative tenses, Past Simple active and passive, Past Continuous, Past Perfect Simple active and passive, and Past Perfect Continuous.

Past Simple v Past Continuous   Students at this level will be very familiar with these tenses. However, if the students' first language does not use the Past Continuous as English does, it is difficult to know when to use it. Two common errors are the following:

1   **I got back home at three in the afternoon. The sun shone. The trees blew in the breeze, but…*
Here, the student chooses to use the Past Simple because they see the above events as finished past actions. In English, however, we choose the Past Continuous to describe longer 'background' events or situations: *I got back home at three in the afternoon. The sun was shining. The trees were blowing in the breeze, but …*

2   **I was working in a factory for fifteen years when I was a young man.*
Here the student chooses to use the Past Continuous because it is an action that goes on for a long time. However, in English, we use the Past Simple to describe actions that are 'permanent'. We would only use the Past Continuous here if the action was 'temporary', for example *I was working in a factory for a few weeks last summer.* (But even here the Past Simple would also be correct.)

In brief, the Past Continuous is used to express activities in progress that are interrupted, incomplete and/or temporary.

Past Simple v Past Perfect   Similarly, the Past Simple and the Past Perfect are not new for students at this level, but are difficult to use correctly. Generally the Past Perfect is overused by students when it is not called for. A common example is the following error:

*When I was young, I had lived in Jamaica.

Here, the student uses the Past Perfect because it is a 'distant' past. Many languages have a past historic tense to refer to the far past, and they confuse it with the English Past Perfect. *Had lived* is wrong here because it does not happen before *was young*.

In brief, we use the Past Perfect to tell stories in a different order. For example:
I had a shower and then got dressed.
I got dressed when I'd had a shower.

If we don't use the Past Perfect in the second example, then the order of events could be misunderstood, with bizarre results. Note that this is not the case when we use clear time sequencers such as *after* and *before*, as these make the sequence of events very clear. If we use these sequencers, then the use of the Past Perfect is optional.

I got dressed after I had a shower.
I got dressed after I'd had a shower.

Vocabulary   The vocabulary section introduces language used to talk about books and films.

Everyday English   This section introduces and practises ways of showing interest and surprise.

Notes on the unit

TEST YOUR GRAMMAR (SB p26)

The *Test your grammar* section aims to test the students' understanding of how Past Perfect forms are used to refer back to things that happened before. In order to do the exercise, students have to recognize the tense forms, and realize which ones are referring back to an earlier time.

This exercise should be done quickly. Don't get involved in lengthy grammar explanations at this stage.

Ask students to read the story, then work in pairs to put the events into chronological order. Go round monitoring to see how well students understand the way the tenses work.

Answers
1   Mr and Mrs Gilbreath... moved to the house...
2   a man... had been acting suspiciously...
3   Mr and Mrs Gilbreath ... had seen (the) man...
4   Bob and Janet Gilbreath had left their house...
5   a neighbour had heard a loud noise
     the back door had been smashed
     money and jewellery stolen
     ...their house had been burgled
6   A couple came home/they got home
7   Mr and Mrs Gilbreath told police...
8   ...were able to give a description
9   A neighbour said... (this may have happened before 7)
10   A man... was later arrested

Ask students which tenses they recognized in the story.

Answers
Past Simple: *came, got, said, moved, told, were*
Past Simple Passive: *was arrested*
Past Perfect Simple: *had left, had heard, had seen*
Past Perfect Simple passive: *had been burgled, had been smashed/stolen*
Past Perfect Continuous: *had been acting*

Narrative tenses

This section looks at the differences between the narrative tenses. The aim is to get students to a point where they are able to manipulate the tenses when writing their own stories, and when speaking. The spoken English activity asks students to manipulate the tenses when giving and responding to news.

1   Ask students in pairs or small groups to look at the headlines and pictures. Check the difficult vocabulary, then ask students to discuss what they think the whole story is. Have a brief feedback, asking a few students for their ideas, but don't reveal the actual stories yet.

DIFFICULT VOCABULARY
plunge = fall
plea = appeal
nerd = derogatory term for somebody who is a computer enthusiast
hacked into = illegally entered somebody else's computer system
*You could point out that these words are examples of typical tabloid (i.e. popular) newspaper usage.

2   Ask students in their pairs or groups to write some questions. Monitor and prompt.

3   **T 3.1** [CD 1: Track 30] Play the recording. Ask students to listen and see which of their questions are answered. Have a brief class feedback.

Tapescript
1   **A** Did you read that story about the guy who went over the Niagara Falls?
     B No. What happened to him? Did he die?
     A No, he survived, amazingly enough.
     B Really? But I suppose he was wearing some kind of protection.
     A That's the incredible thing. He was just wearing ordinary clothes. He just jumped in, fell down 180 feet, and somehow managed to avoid hitting the rocks.
     B That's amazing! What did he do it for?
     A Apparently he just did it for a dare. He'd been talking about doing it for ages. His friends had bet him he wouldn't do it.
     B What a crazy guy!
     A You're not kidding. The strange thing is, before he jumped, people around him said he'd been smiling.
     B Wow! How weird!
2   **A** There was this story the other day about ... this woman mountain climber ...
     B Uh huh. What about her?
     A Well, she was stuck on top of a mountain, and she only managed to escape by sending text messages.

B Gosh! Where did this happen?

A In the Swiss Alps, I think. She was climbing with a partner. They'd been climbing for three hours when they got trapped in a terrible storm.

B You're kidding!

A No. But they built a shelter or something, and they hid in that.

B Then what happened?

A She started sending text messages to friends in London, and one of them sent a text back saying that the mountain rescue teams in Switzerland had been contacted.

B Uh huh.

A They tried to find them, but the weather was too bad – storms and everything.

B Oh, no!

A Anyway, they were rescued the next night, and now they're safe and sound.

B Thank goodness for that!

3 **A** I was reading in the paper the other day about a schoolboy who hacked into the United States military computers.

B No! Really? How old was he? 17? 18?

A Actually he was only 14.

B How did he do it?

A Well, he'd developed his own software program, and he'd been using this to download films and music from the Internet.

B I don't get it. What's that got to do with the US military?

A Well, he'd figured that if he broke into these powerful military computers, he could use them to download stuff even faster, so he wasn't really trying to get to their secrets.

B Oh, I see. I bet they were worried, though.

A They were. They got in touch with Scotland Yard, and this boy was tracked down to his house in North London.

B And he's only 14! They should give him a job!

4 Ask students in pairs to write the questions. You could replay the recording to help the students, if necessary. Monitor, prompt and correct.

Sample questions
1 What was he wearing?
2 What did he do it for?/Why did he do it?
3 How long had she/they been climbing (when she/they got trapped)?
4 Where did she/they hide?
5 What had he developed?
6 Why did he break/hack into the United States military computers?

5 Ask students in pairs to match the lines.

T3.2 [CD 1: Track 31] Play the recording so that students can check their answers. Then point out the following phonological features:
The weak /ə/ in *was*, *were*, and *had*.
The weak pronunciation of *been* /bɪn/.
Ask students to repeat the sentences after the model on the recording, or after your model.

Answers and tapescript
He was wearing ordinary clothes.
He'd been talking about doing it for ages.
His friends had bet him he wouldn't do it.
She was climbing with a partner.
They were rescued the next night.

LANGUAGE FOCUS

See TB p8 for suggestions on how to teach this section.

Don't forget to look at the *Language aims* section on TB p31, which looks at problems students may have. You should also read the Grammar Reference on SB pp142–143.

LANGUAGE INPUT

1 Ask the students to complete the chart. Let them check in pairs before feedback.

Answers

Past Simple	Past Continuous
fell	was/were reading
Past Perfect	**Past Perfect Continuous**
had heard	had been hearing *acting*
Past Simple passive	**Past Perfect passive**
was/were arrested	had been burgled

Ask students to look at **T3.1** on p127, and find examples of the tenses. Discuss the questions as a class.

Answers
Past Simple: Did you read, went, happened, Did he die, survived, jumped, fell, managed, did he do, jumped, said, stuck, managed, did this happen, was, got trapped, built, hid, happened, started, sent, tried, broke, could
Past Simple passive: were rescued, were worried, was tracked
Past Continuous: was wearing, was reading, wasn't really trying
Past Perfect Simple: had bet, had developed, had figured
Past Perfect Simple passive: had been contacted
Past Perfect Continuous: had been talking, had been smiling, had been climbing, had been using

We use the Past Perfect in order to tell a story in a different order. It allows the speaker to refer back to a past event that happened earlier.

We use the continuous tenses to express activities in progress.

2 Ask students in pairs to compare the tenses. Go round monitoring to help the students with queries.

> **Answers**
> *John cooked a lovely meal. His guests had a good time. They left at midnight.*
> Here, the Past Simple is used to describe three events in the past that happened one after the other. The narrative begins early in the evening
>
> *Just after midnight, John was looking at the mess. His guests had just left. He'd cooked a lovely meal, and everyone had had a good time.*
> Here, the narrative begins just after midnight. The Past Continuous is used to describe an activity in progress at a time in the past. The Past Perfect is used to refer back to events that happened earlier.

Refer students to the Grammar Reference on SB pp142–143.

PRACTICE (SB p27)

Discussing grammar

1 Ask students in pairs to compare the use of tenses. Go round monitoring, and helping. Then have a class feedback.

> **Answers**
> 1 *I read*: Past Simple to describe a finished action in the past.
> *I was reading*: Past Continuous to describe an incomplete activity in the past, (the book is not finished).
> 2 *I made a cake*: This was the next event after Alice's arrival.
> *I was making a cake*: This was the activity in progress when Alice arrived. I started making the cake before her arrival.
> *I had made a cake*: The cake was already finished before she arrived.
> 3 *The film started*: It happened soon after our arrival at the cinema.
> *The film had started*: It started before we arrived. We missed the start of the film.
> 4 *He had stolen some money*: It was one event that resulted in him being sacked.
> *He had been stealing money for years*: It was a repeated activity that resulted in him being sacked.
> 5 *Was being repaired*: in the process of being repaired – not finished yet
> *Had been repaired*; repair finished before I got to the garage

Writing narratives

2 Ask students in pairs to rewrite the sentences.

> **Answers**
> 1 Peter was tired when he got home because he'd got up at dawn, and had been driving for ten hours.
> 2 When I went to get my car, it wasn't there because I'd parked it on a yellow line, and it had been towed away.
> 3 Mick was a homeless beggar, but he hadn't always been poor, as he'd had a successful business, which, unfortunately, went/had gone bust.
> 4 When Jane and Peter arrived home, they were broke because they'd been shopping all day, and had spent all their money on clothes.
> 5 Last week John moved to the house which he'd first seen in Scotland while he'd been driving on holiday.

The news

3 **T3.3** [CD 1: Track 32] Play the recording. Ask students to listen to the news story, and correct the mistakes.

> **Answers and tapescript**
> 1 Ten workers have *been rescued*.
> 2 They had been trapped *underground*.
> 3 They had been digging a *tunnel*.
> 4 *The roof of their tunnel collapsed*.
> 5 *Sixty* men managed to escape.
> 6 *Two* men were fatally injured.
> 7 The men were recovering *in hospital*.
> 8 The cause of the accident is *not* known – an investigation into the cause of the accident is due to start tomorrow.

> **T3.3**
> This is the six o'clock news.
> Ten workers have been rescued from an accident 400 feet beneath the streets of London. They had spent the past 36 hours trapped underground. They had been digging a tunnel for a new Underground line when the roof collapsed. Sixty men managed to escape immediately, but two were fatally injured. Last night the ten men were recovering in hospital. An investigation into the cause of the accident is due to start tomorrow.

4 **T3.4** [CD 1: Track 33] Play the recording. Ask students to listen to the news story, and write the questions.

> **Answers and tapescript**
> 1 How long had the children been missing?
> 2 When did they disappear?
> 3 What had police issued?
> 4 Where had the police been searching?
> 5 Who were they spotted by?
> 6 Where had they slept?
> 7 Had they realized the concern they had caused?

SPOKEN ENGLISH – News and responses

The aim here is to get students to give and respond to news, using certain expressions. It also gives further practice in using narrative tenses, particularly question forms.

Read through the introduction as a class. Ask students in pairs to write G, R, or A after each expression. Do the first as an example.

Answers

1 G 2 A 3 R 4 A 5 G 6 R 7 R 8 A 9 G 10 R

Divide the students into pairs. Ask Student A in each pair to read the news story on SB p155. Ask Student B to read the news story on SB p156. Give the students five minutes to read their texts and prepare to talk about them. Go round monitoring, helping with vocabulary and prompting students to use the 'giving news' expressions. When the students are ready, ask them to tell their partner about their story. They could show their partner the headline and photograph from the article, and refer to it for detailed information, but discourage extensive reading from the text. The idea is that students use this activity as an exercise in paraphrasing information. It is a good idea to model the activity with a strong student first so that the students are clear that they need to listen and respond as well as tell stories.

Ask two or three pairs to act out their story-telling for the class.

Writing Unit 3
Narrative Writing 1 – Using adverbs in narratives SB p113.

ADDITIONAL MATERIAL

Workbook Unit 3

Exercises 1-4 Narrative tenses

Exercise 5 Past passives

Exercise 6 Revision of active and passive

VOCABULARY AND SPEAKING (SB p29)

Books and films

The aim here is to introduce vocabulary around the topic of books and films, and to practise question-forming.

Depending on the length of your lesson, you could do this section as a 'stand alone' lesson, ending with exercise 4, which provides a personalized speaking practice of the new vocabulary. Or you could do this section as a lead-in to the main reading text on p30. Exercise 5 asks the students to use the new vocabulary to predict the content of the reading text.

1   Ask students in pairs to look at the answers and write the questions. Monitor and prompt.

Answers

1 Who wrote it?
2 What kind/sort of book is it?
3 What's it about?
4 Where and when is it set?
5 Who are the main characters?
6 Has it been made into a film?
7 What happens in the end?/How does it end?
8 What did you think of it?
9 Would you recommend it?

2   Ask students how they could adapt the questions to ask about films. Ask them what extra questions they would ask.

Possible answers

3, 4, 5, 7, 8, and 9 could also be asked about a film. The others could be adapted thus:

1 Who directed it?
2 What sort of film is it?
6 Was it (adapted from) / Is it based on a novel?

Extra questions

Who is the main star of the film?/Who stars in it?
Who wrote the screenplay/ the music?

3   **T3.5** [CD 1: Track 34] Play the recording. Ask students to listen and take notes under the headings.

Answers and tapescript

1   **Paul: the film**
    Title
    Witness
    Setting
    The Amish community
    Characters
    A detective/city cop, an Amish child/boy, the boy's Amish mother
    Plot
    A detective goes to an Amish community after an Amish boy witnesses a murder, in order to protect him. It's a passionate love story in which the detective falls in love with the boy's mother. It's a thriller about police corruption that ends with a tense climax.
    Personal opinion
    A favourite film... wonderful scenes... intense and passionate love story... unbearably tense...the build up towards the end is incredible. It really, really does have you on the edge of your seat.

2 Kate: the book

Title

The Secret History by Donna Tartt

Setting

Within a group of students. She doesn't say, but we can assume that it's set in a university.

Characters

A group of students

Plot

It's about a group of students and somebody's desire to belong to a group. The group murder somebody.

Personal opinion

It made quite an impression on me... very claustrophobic. You feel sort of trapped inside the group and trapped inside their situation. It's completely compelling to read. It's not a comfortable read... I lived and breathed this book ... I would recommend it to anybody who wants to read something that psychologically is really dramatic.

T3.5 See TB Tapescripts p127

4 Give students a few minutes to think of their favourite book or film, and to think of answers to the questions in exercise 1. Allow students to make notes and ask for vocabulary as they prepare. Then put students in pairs or small groups to interview each other about their books and films. Monitor and prompt. Note down any errors that students make with the questions, and feedback on the errors at the end by writing them on the board, and asking students to correct.

EXTRA ACTIVITY

Write the following novels and authors on the board.

Gulliver's Travels by Jonathan Swift
Pride and Prejudice by Jane Austen
The Maltese Falcon by Raymond Chandler
The Lord of the Flies by William Golding
Lord of the Rings by J R R Tolkien
The Great Gatsby by F Scott Fitzgerald
Captain Corelli's Mandolin by Louis de Bernières
Tess of the d'Urbervilles by Thomas Hardy

Ask students if they know of or have read any of the books. Photocopy, cut out, and hand out the eight descriptions of novels on p144 of the Teacher's Book (2 students can use one card if the number of students in the class makes it necessary). Students must circulate, tell each other the number of the novel on their card, and ask each other questions about it using questions 2, 3, 4, 5, and 7 from exercise 1 on p29 of the Student's Book. They could take brief notes on the answers to questions 2, 4, and 5. When the students have asked about all the novels, have a class feedback. Students must say which novel from the list on the board goes with which card number, and can then try and answer questions 1, 6, 8, and 9 from p29.

Answers

(1) *Lord of the Rings* by J R R Tolkien (released as 3 films between 2001-2003, starring Elijah Wood and Ian Mckellen)
(2) *Pride and Prejudice* by Jane Austen (released as a BBC film in 1995, starring Jennifer Ehle and Colin Firth. A new version is planned for 2006 release, starring Judi Dench and Keira Knightley)
(3) *The Maltese Falcon* by Raymond Chandler (film released in 1941, starring Humphrey Bogart)
(4) *The Lord of the Flies* by William Golding (film released in 1963, directed by Peter Brook)
(5) *Tess of the d'Urbervilles* by Thomas Hardy (film released in 1980, starring Nastassja Kinski)
(6) *Captain Corelli's Mandolin* by Louis de Bernières (film released in 2001, starring Nicolas Cage and Penélope Cruz)
(7) *The Great Gatsby* by F Scott Fitzgerald (film released in 1974, starring Robert Redford)
(8) *Gulliver's Travels* by Jonathan Swift (many animated and live action film versions, including 1996 release starring Ted Danson)

5 Ask students in pairs to look at the book cover, and discuss which questions in exercise 1 they can answer.

Answers

1 **Who wrote it?**
  Margaret Atwood.
2 **What kind/sort of book is it?**
  It's a novel that combines elements of gothic drama, romantic suspense, and science fiction fantasy.
3 **What is it about?**
  It's about the secrets of the rich and influential Chase family, particularly the lives of the two sisters. One of the sisters dies by driving her car off a bridge, and an inquest report describes it as accidental. Then we learn that the husband of the other sister has been found dead on his sailing boat. There is also a novel within the novel, a science fiction story made up by two unnamed lovers.
4 **Where and when is it set?**
  In Ontario (Canada) in 1945.
5 **Who are the main characters?**
  Iris Chase Griffen and her sister Laura.
6 **Has it been made into a film?**
  No (and the book cover doesn't tell us).
7 **What happens in the end?/How does it end?**
  We are told that Iris is now the only surviving descendant of the Chase family.
8 **What did you think of it?**
  The cover describes it as 'profoundly entertaining', a 'brilliant and enthralling book by a writer at the top of her form.'
9 **Would you recommend it?**
  The cover certainly recommends it, with reviews describing it as 'Grand storytelling on a grand scale ... Sheerly

enjoyable' and 'Absorbing....Expertly rendered....Virtuosic storytelling'. The fact that it won the Booker Prize is also a recommendation.

READING AND SPEAKING (SB p30)

The Blind Assassin

NOTE ABOUT THE AUTHOR AND THE NOVEL
Margaret Atwood is a Canadian author, who lives in Toronto. She has written more than thirty books of fiction, poetry and critical essays. *The Blind Assassin*, which was published in 2000, is her tenth novel. It has won many literary awards.

Note that the author uses standard Canadian usages of English, so some words are spelt like American English (*tires, curb* = *tyres* and *kerb* in British English), and others are spelt like British English (*licence, grey* = *license* and *gray* in American English). Similarly, some American words are used (*streetcar, bureau* = *tram* and *writing desk* in British English), and some British ones (*taxi* = *cab* in American English).

1 Ask students to read the first part of the story, then discuss the questions with a partner.

Answers
The two words that students would be most likely to need explaining are *charred smithereens* (see *Vocabulary Note* below).
The facts are presented *coldly and clinically*.

VOCABULARY NOTE
ravine = a deep, narrow valley
creek = small, narrow stream (US/Canadian English)
chunks = big, heavy pieces of something (e.g. chunks of bread)
charred = burnt
*smithereens = tiny pieces
*Normally this word is only used in the expressions, *smash/blow to smithereens*. For example, *I dropped the vase and it smashed to smithereens.*

2 Ask students to read the second part of the story and then work in pairs or small groups to answer the questions.

Answers
1 Laura is Iris' sister.
Richard is Iris' husband, (the licence belonged to Iris, and had Richard's surname on it)
Mrs Griffen is Iris.
It's not clear who Alex is – perhaps Laura's husband, lover, brother...

2 The tires may have caught on a streetcar track.
The brakes may have failed.
Two witnesses had seen Laura deliberately drive the car off the bridge – i.e. she committed suicide.
Iris says that it was an accident because her sister was never a good driver.
She doesn't really believe this.
3 Because she had killed herself for her own 'ruthless' reasons.

3 Ask students to read the third and final part of the story. Then ask them to work in pairs or small groups to answer the questions.

Answers
1 Because she wants to be dressed appropriately – there might be reporters.
2 She probably comes from a privileged background, (as a child she had a nanny, Reenie, and her mother was busy). She is probably well-off and married to an important man, (the respectful policeman; the possibility of reporters at the morgue, and the need to warn Richard). She also feels the need to behave and dress according to her social status.
3 Reenie was Iris and Laura's nanny, or perhaps the cook. Their mother was 'resting' or 'doing good deeds elsewhere' – in other words, she didn't spend much time with her children.
4 It may refer to Laura, who killed herself. Or to Iris, who, from the tone of the whole extract, finds it difficult to 'tell where it hurts'.

4 Ask students to discuss the questions in pairs or small groups, then have a brief class discussion.

Answers
Iris appears calm when she talks to the police.
She is nostalgic when talking about Reenie.
She is very angry when thinking about what Laura has done.
She is clear thinking when preparing to visit the morgue.
She is cold and factual when describing the accident.

Evidence that Laura didn't care about people's feelings:
She was completely ruthless / She was washing her hands of me
Evidence that she felt guilty about something:
She had her reasons / penitential colours / She had left the exercise books for Iris to find – perhaps with a secret.
Evidence that she had bad experiences in life:
She had her reasons / She was washing her hands of me. Of all of us / of bad faith. Of our father and his wreckage / her fatal triangular bargain
Evidence that she had suffered even as a child:
When they were children, Reenie would say: *Tell me where it hurts. Stop howling. Just calm down and show me where. But some people can't tell where it hurts. They can't calm down. They can't ever stop howling.*

Language work

1 Ask students to match the words to the descriptions, then check with a partner.

Answers	
charred	badly burnt
smithereens	very small pieces
plunged	fell suddenly downwards
swirling	turning and twisting
suspended	hung
chattering	knocking together (teeth)
deeds	things people do
scoop	lift quickly
howling	making a loud cry (in pain)

What do you think?

1, 2 The aim of these two exercises is to use the text as a springboard for discussion. The students are expected to discuss, personally respond to and ask questions about material in the text.

Ask students to work in small groups to discuss the questions. Monitor and prompt, then have a brief class discussion. Encourage students to expand on their opinions by referring to parts of the story.

Sample answers
1 Students' own ideas. The author has not told us why Laura has killed herself, who Alex is, what their father's wreckage was, what Laura's fatal triangular bargain was. She hasn't told us what is in the school exercise books, or why Laura left them for Iris.
2 Students' own ideas. The rest of the novel reveals that Laura's notebooks are a record of a secret relationship, that she suffered because she had an unhappy love life, and that Iris feels responsible for her sister's death.

LISTENING AND SPEAKING (SB p32)

The money jigsaw

The speaking activity encourages students to tell each other stories from prompts, using narrative tenses. It creates a prediction task for the listening. The *Spoken English* section looks at the use of the filler, *like*.

1 Lead in by asking the students what they think the story might be about from the headline and photographs.

Put the students in pairs to tell each other the story, using the prompts in the boxes. Ask Student A in each pair to prepare to tell the story using the prompts in the first box. Ask Student B to prepare to tell the rest of the story, using the prompts in the second box.

When the students are ready, ask them to tell each other the two halves of the story. Monitor and prompt for correct use of narrative tenses. It doesn't matter whether the students' stories are similar to the actual story, and they should be allowed to let their imagination run free. The idea is that the students use the vocabulary to speculate about a possible story, which will increase their interest in what the actual story is, and help them to understand it.

Sample story
Two schoolgirls were walking to school when they saw some ripped up bank notes. They were flying all over the place. Then they saw that the bank notes were coming from a bin. In the bin was a plastic bag jammed full of torn up notes. Then the girls had to go to school.
After school the girls were playing when the police arrived. They told them where the banknotes were, and the police took them away to the Bank of England. After a long time, the police gave them back the banknotes and they decided to stick them together.

2 **T3.6** [CD 1: Track 35] Play the recording. Ask the students to listen and say whether Rachel's story is similar to theirs.

3 Play the recording again. Ask students to listen and answer the questions. Let students compare their answers in pairs or groups before feedback.

Answers
1 It was flying all over the floor. They traced the notes to a bin.
2 Some are bigger than stamps – some smaller.
3 Yes.
4 No. It has taken ages.
5 They have to get the two serial numbers, and a bit from the middle of the note, then they put sticky tape on the back so that they stay all together, and then put them in a bag.
6 About a year.
7 £1200 so far – probably about £2000 when they have finished.

T3.6
I = Interviewer   R = Rachel

I Well and one of those girls, Rachel Aumann, is on the line now as we speak. Good morning to you, Rachel.
R Good morning.
I Erm ... extraordinary, this. You saw these bits of bank notes just blowing in the wind?
R Yeah, it was ... erm ... **like** really out of the ordinary. We were just walking to school and there's ripped up notes flying all over the floor. And then we traced it to **like** a bin, so that's where the ... the big bag was full of them.
I How big a bag?
R Erm ...

I Like a bin bag or something?

R No, actually, not that big ... erm ... it's about, I think it was like a Sainsbury's bag, like one of those.

I And it was just jammed full of torn-up banknotes, what fivers and tenners and that sort of thing?

R Yeah, just fives, tens, twenties.

I And how little were the pieces?

R Erm ... some were bigger than stamp sizes.

I That small though?

R Yeah, some were smaller.

I And so what did you do? You took them to the police or something?

R Erm we, we had to go to school so we went to school and then ... erm ... after school we were playing outside around ... erm ... **like** on the same road and ... erm ... when the police arrived we were, we went over then and started talking to them and telling them when we found it.

I And they took them away at that stage, did they?

R Yeah.

I And then what happened?

R Erm ... they kept them for **like** a long time 'cos there's a certain amount of months that they have to keep them before you, they can give them back.

I Right.

R And I think they went to the Royal Bank of England and to Scotland Yard and umm ... when ... erm ... they said yeah, it's real money ... erm ... they gave it back and we put it together.

I You say you put it together, but tiny bits of bank notes it must have taken you forever to do ... I mean, what a jigsaw puzzle!

R Yeah it's taken ages 'cos it's been about a year and we still haven't finished.

I So how many have you got left now then?

R Erm ... we have all the fives to do and just a few twenties but the tens are all finished.

I Extraordinary! Is it ... how much time do you spend doing this?

R Erm ... well when we first got it we did **like** half an hour, an hour a day but then as **like** time passed we just slowly like died down and didn't do as much.

I But I'm trying to picture you doing this. What do you do, do you stick bits of sellotape or something, or do you stick them onto a piece of paper or what?

R Well you have to get, you get the two serial numbers and ... erm ... then you have to get **like** a little bit from the middle of the note and so once you've got that, you just put sticky tape on the back of them so that they all stay together and put it in a bag

I Good heavens! And you're going to carry on doing it, eh?

R Yeah, hopefully.

I £1,200 so far?

R Erm ... yeah.

I And how much do you reckon you will be worth at the end of it all?

R Erm ... I think we if stick to it we could probably get about £2,000.

I Well, I think that you've earned every penny of it, Rachel. Thank you very much.

R Thank you.

What do you think?

The aim here is to get students talking and speculating about the listening.

Read through the theories as a class, then put students in small groups to think of other explanations. In the feedback, see how many good explanations the class can come up with.

SPOKEN ENGLISH – *Like*

Point out the use of *like* and read the explanation. This use of *like* has become habitual amongst younger native speakers. Ask students to find further examples in the tapescript on SB p127 (highlighted in bold in the TB tapescript). The interviewer's use of *like* (the fourth time he speaks) is not a filler, but a correct use of *like* as a preposition. The use of *like* in Rachel's response to his question is the same.

ADDITIONAL MATERIAL

Workbook Unit 3

Exercise 7 Vocabulary

Exercise 8 Phrasal verbs

Exercise 9 Pronunciation – Dipthongs

Exercise 10 Listening – What an amazing coincidence!

EVERYDAY ENGLISH (SB p33)

Showing interest and surprise

The aim of this section is to introduce and practise ways of showing interest and surprise.

1 **T3.7** [CD 1: Track 36] Ask students to listen to the dialogue and write in B's answers.

Answers and tapescript

B shows interest and surprise by using echo and reply questions. Echo questions repeat the surprising information in the statement with rising intonation. Reply questions consist of auxiliary verbs and pronouns with rising intonation. The auxiliary verb must agree with the tense of the verb in the preceding statement. This is the same as in question tags, but in reply questions the auxiliary verb does not change positive to negative, negative to positive.

T3.7

A Jade's got a new boyfriend.

B A new boyfriend? Good for her!

A Apparently, he lives in a castle.

B Does he? How amazing!

A Yes. She met him in Slovenia.

B In Slovenia? That's interesting.

A Unfortunately, he can't speak much English.

B Can't he? I thought everyone could these days!

2 Ask students to say which questions are echo questions, and which are reply. Then read through the *Music of English* box and ask students to listen to the models (**T3.8** [CD 1: Track 37]) and repeat them. Put students in pairs to practise the conversation. Make sure that they use enough rising intonation in the echo and reply questions.

Answers

Echo questions	Reply questions
A new boyfriend?	*Does he?*
In Slovenia?	*Can't he?*

3 Ask students to complete the conversations, then check with a partner.

T3.9 [CD 1: Track 38] Play the recording. Ask students to check their answers.

Ask students in pairs to practise the conversations. Monitor and prompt for good intonation. Ask four or five pairs to act out dialogues for the class.

Answers and tapescript

1 **A** Sam wants to apologize.
  B Does he?
  A Yes. He's broken your mother's Chinese vase.
  B My mother's Chinese vase? Oh, no!

2 **A** We had a terrible holiday.
  B Did you?
  A Yes. It rained all the time.
  B Did it?
  A Yes. And the food was disgusting!
  B Was it? What a drag!

3 **A** I'm broke.
  B Are you? How come?
  A Because I just had a phone bill for £500.
  B £500? Why so much?
  A Because I have a girlfriend in Korea.
  B Do you? How interesting!

4 **A** It took me three hours to get here.
  B Did it?
  A Yes. There was a traffic jam ten miles long.
  B Ten miles long? That's awful!
  A Now I've got a headache!
  B Have you? Poor darling. I'll get you something for it.

5 **A** I'm on a mountain, watching the sun set.
  B Are you?
  A Yes. And I've got something very important to ask you.
  B Have you? What is it? I can't wait!
  A You'd better sit down. I'd like to marry you.
  B Marry me? Wow!

4 Prepare five or six statements about yourself, using a variety of tenses. The sentences should contain information that will be new and surprising to the students, e.g. *I'm going to buy a new car next week. / My sister's just had a baby.* You could invent some surprising statements that are not true, e.g. *I've been married five times. / I'm never going to give you any homework ever again.* Or, if you wish to take it, this is an opportunity to let your students into some of your personal secrets! Give your surprising statements to the class, and encourage appropriate responses.

You could then ask students to make similar surprising statements (either true or invented) about themselves.

4

Introduction to the unit

The theme of this unit is telling lies. In trying to get at the truth of stories, students will have lots of practice in forming questions and negatives, which is the grammatical focus of the unit. The title refers to the oath taken by witnesses in a court of law. They promise to tell '…the truth, the whole truth, and nothing but the truth.'

The main reading texts are about three conspiracy theories, (concerning the deaths of Princess Diana and John F. Kennedy junior, and the 'faked' Apollo moon landings). The main listening text involves six people talking about their most memorable lies.

Language aims

Questions and negatives   The aim is to revise and practise the formation of questions and negatives involving all the main tenses and modals.

Questions

Question formation is always a problem for learners of English. There are several reasons for this.

- Students must remember to invert the subject and the verb, and use the correct auxiliary verb.
- The subject of the sentence must always follow the auxiliary verb, no matter how long it is.
  How many times has the European section of your company won an award?
  Students often want to say **How many times has won an award the European section?*
- Students don't differentiate between the two questions *What … like?* and *How … ?* and overuse the question with *How … ?*
  **How's your flat?* **How's your city?*
- Having learned that questions always require an auxiliary verb, students encounter subject questions.
  *Who **wants** an ice-cream? What **happened** at the party?*
- Students are reluctant to end a question with a preposition.
  *Who are you waiting **for**? Who did you give the letter **to**?*
- Students often make errors with indirect or reported questions, forgetting that there is no inversion and no *do/does/did* in these questions.
  I wonder where she is. **I wonder where is she.*
  I asked her what she does. **I asked her what does she do.*
- It is unlikely that your students use negative questions appropriately and accurately. They are difficult to form and to pronounce. They have two quite distinct uses. The first expresses the speaker's surprise about a negative situation.
  '**Haven't** you **got** a computer?' 'No, I haven't.'
  Can't you **swim**? I thought everyone could swim.

  The other use means, *Confirm what I think is true.* In this use, it refers to a positive situation.
  '**Weren't** we at school together?' 'Yes, we were.'

In some languages, especially far eastern languages, the answer to negative questions is the opposite of what an English speaker would say, i.e. 'Yes' instead of 'No'.

A Can't you swim?
B **Yes.* (You're right.) I can't swim.

They answer the truth value of the question and not the reality of the situation.

Negatives

Making sentences negative doesn't usually present such a problem for upper-intermediate students. This unit concentrates on how other parts of the sentence can be made negative, not just the main verb.

*I told you **not to do** it.* = negative infinitive
*There are **no** onions left.*
'Who likes grammar?' *'**Not** me.'*

There is also practice of transferred negation. In English we usually say *I don't think* + affirmative verb rather than *I think* + negative verb. Other verbs like this are *believe*, *suppose*, and *expect*.

*I **don't think** you're right.*
*I **don't suppose** you know the answer.*

Vocabulary   The vocabulary section looks at making opposites, using prefixes (*un-*, *in-*, *im-*, etc.) and antonyms.

Everyday English   This section practises being polite. It looks at stress and intonation in polite requests and offers.

Notes on the unit

TEST YOUR GRAMMAR (SB p34)

The *Test your grammar* section aims to test the students' understanding of how to form negatives and questions. It tests many of the problem areas outlined in the *Language aims* section above.

This exercise should be done quickly. Don't get involved in lengthy grammar explanations at this stage.

1   Ask students in pairs to make the sentences negative. Go round monitoring to see how well students understand how to form negatives.

Answers
1   I disagree/don't agree with you.
2   I don't think you're right./I think you're wrong.
3   I didn't tell her to go home. (= I didn't say this to her.)
    I told her not to go home. (= I spoke to her, and told her to stay.)
4   'Isn't John coming?' (= a negative question, which either expresses surprise about a negative situation, or asks for confirmation of a positive situation, depending on the context.)
    'Is John not coming?' (= this is less likely, and means the same as above. It is used to emphasize the fact that he is '*not* coming.')
    'I hope not.' (= I hope that this is not true. Note that 'I think so' has two negatives, 'I don't think so' and the more formal, 'I think not'. However, *'I don't hope so'* is not possible. This is dealt with in detail in unit 5.)

5   I didn't know everybody at the party.
    I didn't know anybody at the party. / I knew nobody at the party. (= these two sentences mean the same. Note that in English, we cannot use a double negative: *'I didn't know nobody*.)
6   I haven't done my homework yet.
    I still haven't done my homework.
    (The use of the adverbs, *already*, *yet*, and *still*, can be confusing. We use *already* with positive sentences to mean, *before now* or *before expected*. We use *yet* with negative sentences to talk about something that has not happened but is expected to happen in the future. We use *still* with both positive and negative sentences to talk about a situation that continues to happen (or not happen), even though you expect it to have happened before now. Note the position of the adverbs in the sentence.)
7   You mustn't get a visa. (= prohibition)
    You don't have to get a visa. (= no obligation)
    You can't get a visa. (= not allowed/impossible)
    (Note that the negative of a modal verb is often a completely different modal verb.)
8   My sister doesn't like hip-hop either. (= *either* is used in negative statements to refer to both of two people or things)
    My sister dislikes hip-hop, too. (= but *either* is not used when the prefix *dis-* is used to make the negative)

2   Ask students in pairs to write in the missing word in each question.

Answers
1   What *sort/kind/type* of music do you like? (*what* + noun)
2   How *often/regularly/frequently* do you wash your hair? (*how* + adverb)
3   Who do you look *like*? (*look like* = resemble physically)
4   How *long* does it take you to get to school? (*How long* = how much time)
5   What were you talking to the teacher *about*? (Question with a preposition at the end)
6   Do you know what the time *is*? (There is no inversion and no *do/does/did* in indirect questions)

Ask students to practise the questions in pairs. Monitor and correct any errors.

TELLING LIES (SB p34)

Questions and negatives

This section looks at a variety of question and negative forms. The practice activities pay particular attention to indirect questions, questions with prepositions, negative questions, and the informal use of *How come?*

Lead in by asking students about *lies*. Ask, *Do you ever tell lies? What's the biggest lie you have ever told?*

1 Ask students in pairs or small groups to look at the people and think of what lies they might tell. Have a brief class feedback, asking a few students for their ideas.

Possible answers
A teenage girl to her parents: She might tell them she is staying with a friend when she is going to a party or seeing a boyfriend./She might lie about doing homework or getting a bad mark in tests.
A car salesman: He might say a car is better/faster/more reliable/more of a bargain than it really is.
A student to the teacher: He/she might say that he/she has done homework/revised for a test when they haven't. He/she might lie about why he/she hasn't done homework.
A politician: He might exaggerate the achievements of his/her government/say the economy is better than it is.
A husband to his wife: He might say that he is working late or meeting clients when he isn't./He might tell her that he likes her new dress or hairstyle when he doesn't.

2 Ask students in their pairs or groups to look at the cartoons and discuss the questions.

Answers
a She is lying to her boyfriend. She is saying that she's not ready for marriage, whereas, in truth, she probably doesn't love him enough. She's telling a white lie because she doesn't want to hurt his feelings.
b The boy is lying to his mother. He has probably been in a fight, and is probably lying because he knows his mother will be angry if he has been fighting.
c She is lying to a friend. She doesn't want to offend or upset her friend by telling the truth.
d She is lying to her father because she knows he would not approve of her going clubbing or to a party.
e He's lying to his boss. He wants to get a day off work to play golf.
f A secretary talking to a client. She is lying because her boss does not want to be disturbed by that particular client.

3 **T4.1** [CD 1: Track 39] Play the recording. Ask students to listen and answer the questions. Have a brief class feedback.

Answers and tapescript
1 The truth is that she doesn't love him. She lied because she didn't want to hurt his feelings.
2 The truth is he's being chased (bullied) by a group of lads (boys). He lied because he doesn't want his parents to complain to the head teacher and make the situation worse.
3 The truth is that she thinks the dress looks awful. She lied because she doesn't know how to tell her the truth.
4 The truth is that she is going clubbing. She lied because she has an exam next week and her dad would 'kill' her if he knew she was clubbing.

5 The truth is that he is going to play golf. He lied because he didn't want to sit in an office all day – he wanted to play golf.
6 The truth is that she is available, but she lied because she feels rough (unwell) after a late night.

T4.1
1 Oh dear! It's not that I *dislike* him, I just don't *love* him. How can I tell him I don't want to marry him without hurting his feelings? Trouble is, I actually fancy his best friend!
2 There's this group of lads you see – they're always chasing me and I don't think it's for fun. But I can't tell my mum and dad – if they find out, they'll go to the head teacher and complain and that would make everything much worse.
3 How do you tell someone when they look awful? That dress doesn't suit her at all. But I don't know how to tell her. She obviously thinks she looks great in it.
4 Me and Emma are going clubbing, but I daren't tell my dad – he'd kill me. I've got an important exam next week and I haven't done a thing for it. I haven't a clue when I'll be back.
5 I know I'm not really ill. But it's a beautiful day and I don't want to sit in a stuffy office all day. I'm off to play golf. I never have days off usually.
6 I don't care who it is. I had a late night and I feel really rough this morning. Tell them I'm in an important meeting and I don't want be disturbed at the moment.

4 Ask students in pairs to match the questions to the speakers in a-f. You could replay the recording to help the students, if necessary.

Answers
1 c 2 f 3 e 4 b 5 d 6 a

LANGUAGE FOCUS

See TB p8 for suggestions on how to teach this section.

Don't forget to look at the *Language aims* section on TB p41, which looks at problems students may have. You should also read the Grammar Reference on SB p144.

LANGUAGE INPUT

1 Ask the students to find and read aloud examples of the different question and negative forms.

Answers
Questions with auxiliary verbs: *What did you make that face for? Doesn't it look good? Can I speak to...? Haven't I told you...? Where are you going? How long will you be?*
Questions without auxiliary verbs: *How come you're ill today? Who gave you that black eye?*
Two ways of asking *why*: *What did you make that face for? How come you're ill today?*

A question with a preposition at the end: *What did you make that face for?*

A question word + an adverb: *How long will you be?*

An indirect question: *I want to know if you'll marry me.*

Negative questions: *Doesn't it look good? Haven't I told you...?*

A future negative: *...you won't be late.*

Negatives with *think* **and** *hope*: *I hope you won't be late. I don't think you will.*

2 Ask students to complete the indirect questions. In the feedback, point out that there is no inversion or use of *do/does/did* with indirect speech.

Answers
I don't know **where he works**.
Have you any idea **what the answer is**?
I wonder **whether/if she bought the blue one**.

Refer students to the Grammar Reference on SB p144

PRACTICE (SB p35)

Quiztime!

1 Naturally, organizing groups here will depend on the size of your class. With a small class, say 10, divide the class into two groups of five to prepare. Direct the students to the two sets of question prompts, on p155 for Group A, and p156 for Group B. Give the students a few minutes to prepare. Monitor and make sure all students are contributing to the question forming. Then hold the quiz. Nominate different students from each group in turn to ask questions. Write up points scored for correct answers on the board, and find a winner. In the feedback, correct any poorly-formed questions that you heard.

With a large class, say 20, either divide the class into four groups, two Group As and two Group Bs, then hold the quiz open class, but nominate speakers from different groups to ask questions. Alternatively, divide the class into smaller groups of three or four to prepare questions, then match Group As with Group Bs, so that you have perhaps three separate quizzes going on in class. Monitor, help and note errors for feedback.

Answers
Group A
MUSIC
1 What sort of music did Louis Armstrong play?   *jazz*
2 How many strings does a violin have?   *four*
SPORTS
3 What medal is given to the person who comes third in the Olympic Games?   *a bronze medal*
4 In which country was golf first played?   *Scotland*

SCIENCE
5 Which is the nearest star to the earth?   *The sun*
6 Who developed the theory of relativity?   *Albert Einstein*
GEOGRAPHY
Which country is Wellington the capital of?   *New Zealand*
8 What does the 'Richter Scale' measure?   *earthquakes*
HISTORY
9 Which year was President John F. Kennedy assassinated in?   *1963*
10 How long was Nelson Mandela in prison for?   *twenty-eight* years

Group B
MUSIC
1 What kind of music does Eminem sing?   *rap*
2 Whose brothers formed the pop group 'The Jackson Five'?   *Michael Jackson's*
SPORTS
3 What is the longest running race in the Olympic Games called?   *The Marathon*
4 Where and when was baseball first played?   *the United States* in the *19th century*
SCIENCE
5 How many legs does a butterfly have?   *six*
6 Which theory did Charles Darwin develop?   *the theory of evolution*
GEOGRAPHY
7 Which state is the biggest state in the US?   *Alaska*
8 Which oceans are linked by the Panama Canal?   *The Atlantic and Pacific Oceans*
HISTORY
9 Which town and state was President John F. Kennedy assassinated in?   *Dallas, Texas*
10 In which year did the last Concorde fly to New York?   *2003*

2 Ask students to work in their groups to think of comments about the answers in the quiz, using the prompts. Have a brief class discussion.

EXTRA IDEA
Here is an idea for extra indirect question practice. Ask students to write direct questions, one for each type of question word. They then read them out to each other in pairs. Their partner has to quickly make each question into an indirect question. For example.

Where's the nearest chemist?
Could you tell me where the nearest chemist is?

What time will he be arriving?
I wonder what time he'll be arriving.

Asking for more information

3 Read through the introduction and examples as a class. Ask students to write short questions to answer the statements. Let them check with a partner before feedback.

Here is a way of extending the exercise: Put students into pairs. Ask one student to read out the statements at random. The other student must respond with a short question, (without looking at the answers).

4 Ask students in pairs to make the questions longer.
   T4.2 [CD 1: Track 40] Play the recording so that students can check their answers.

Negative questions

5 **T4.3** [CD 1: Track 41] Play the recording and ask students to compare the use of negative questions in the two groups.

Play the recording again and ask students to listen and repeat the negative questions, imitating the stress and intonation patterns.

6 Read the examples, and then ask students in pairs to think of possible answers to the other negative questions in exercise 5.

7 Ask students in pairs to ask and answer about the topics listed, using negative questions. Monitor and make sure that students are forming the negative questions correctly and using appropriate intonation.

   T4.4 [CD 1: Track 42] Play the recording and compare the examples with the students' answers. Play the recording again and get students to repeat the examples, using the same intonation and stress patterns.

Making negatives

8 Ask students in pairs to check the words in their dictionaries, then make negative sentences. Have a brief class feedback.

9 **T4.5** [CD 1: Track 43] (part 1) Play part one of the recording. Ask students which words in exercise 8 describe Norman. Then ask students in pairs to write negative sentences about Norman.

T4.5 **(part 1)**
My mate Norman's a funny guy. He's an insomniac, he's dyslexic, and he's an atheist. He's single, unemployed, and lives all alone in a tiny one-roomed flat without even a pet for company. Also he's vegetarian and teetotal. He's -er pretty anti-social, actually.

SPOKEN ENGLISH *How come?*

Read through the box as a class.

Answers
How come you're going to work today? expresses surprise. *How come?* can be used instead of *Why?* when the question expresses surprise at the apparent irrational nature of the situation (it is a shortened way of saying *How has this come to be?*).

10 Ask students to read through the sentence halves, and think how they might complete the sentences using *How come?*

T4.5 **(part 2)** Play the recording. Ask students to listen, then work in pairs to complete the sentences. Ask the students if they understand the joke at the end. (*Because he is dyslexic, Norman spells 'OK' as 'KO', and 'God' as 'dog' – so, being an atheist, he worries about the existence of 'dog'.*)

Answers and tapescript
He's single, so how come his wife answered the door?
He hasn't got any pets, so how come his dog started barking?
He's an atheist, so how come he had been late for church?
He's dyslexic, so how come one of his favourite pastimes is doing crosswords?
He's unemployed, so how come all his friends from his office had been at his party?
He's teetotal, so how come he had a bit of a hangover?
He's vegetarian, so how come he had a barbecue with steaks and burgers?
He's anti-social, so how come he had a wild party?

T4.5 **(part 2)**
I went round to see him last Sunday. As I walked up the drive, his dog started barking. His wife answered the door, and she called for Norman to come downstairs and join us in the living room. He was in a bad mood because he'd overslept that morning and he'd been late for church. He also had a bit of an hangover, which he told me was the result of a wild party that they'd had at his house the night before. All his friends from his office were there. They'd had a barbecue in the garden with steaks and burgers. One of his favourite pastimes is doing crosswords, and while he was talking to me, he was doing one of those big puzzles from the newspaper.
'So how are you, Norman?' I asked him.
'KO, mate, KO. How about you?'
Anyway, as I said, Norman's an insomniac, dyslexic, atheist. So the joke is that he lies awake all night wondering about the existence of dog. Get it?

Who is it?

11 This activity provides light-hearted, written, personalized practice of negative forms. Model the activity by writing five negative statements about yourself on the board. Give students 3 or 4 minutes to write some sentences on a piece of paper, (not in their exercise books). Encourage students to use a variety of tenses. Collect in the pieces of paper, and hand them out at random around the class. Nominate students to read out the sentences in front of them. Ask the class to guess who is being described.

ADDITIONAL MATERIAL

Workbook Unit 4
Exercises 1-4 Negatives
Exercises 5-9 Questions

LISTENING AND SPEAKING (SB p37)

My most memorable lie!

The aim here is to improve the students' ability to listen for gist and specific information, and to get students talking about their personal experiences.

A useful vocabulary lead-in is to write the following phrases on the board, and ask students to give you an example of each:
tell a lie, tell the truth, tell a white lie, tell a fib*, exaggerate, be economical with the truth
*a fib is a small, inconsequential lie.
to be economical with the truth is an expression that became famous after being used by a British politician. When asked if he'd lied in court, he said that he hadn't lied, but admitted being 'economical with the truth'.

1 Lead in by telling the students about an 'interesting lie' that you told as a child.

Put students in small groups of three or four. Give them a minute to think of an 'interesting lie'. Then give the groups a few minutes to tell each other about their lies.

In the feedback, ask each group to briefly tell the class about their 'best' lie.

2 **T4.6** [CD 1: Track 44] Play the recording. Ask students to listen and correct each statement.

> **Answers**
> 1 Andrew was *playing pool* when his father came home.
> 2 Paul *regularly* lied as a child (because he wanted to have something to say to the priest).
> 3 Carolyn didn't go to America for her *male* friend's wedding.
> 4 Kiki *never* told her grandmother the truth.
> 5 Sean *didn't learn* judo at school.
> 6 Kate *was* punished for lying. She was spanked (hit on the bottom).

3 Give the students a couple of minutes to read through the questions. Check that the students understand the vocabulary. Play the recording again. Ask students to listen and answer the questions.

> **Answers**
> 1 He denied all knowledge of the cigarettes (and in fact pool, and the basement, and everything else). He had pushed the cigarettes through a kind of grate underneath the window.
> 2 Lying to a (catholic) priest at confession. It is bizarre because he is lying in order to have a sin to confess – but of course, lying is a sin!
> 3 She told her friends that the bride's dress was lovely. It was a white lie because she lied in order not to be rude or hurt feelings. The dress did nothing for the bride's figure – it didn't make her figure look good.
> 4 She lost a necklace with her initial on it. She lost it at a party. She told her grandmother that it had been stolen.
> 5 To get details of judo classes. He lied about being good at judo in order to avoid a fight.
> 6 She put her pet cat in the dressing up box. Her excuse for forgetting all about the cat is that she was only four or five at the time.

> **T4.6** See SB Tapescripts p128

4 Ask students in their groups to match each word to one of the lies. The students will need to use dictionaries to check the words. Let students look at tapescript 4.6 on p128 of the Student's Book to check their answers.

> **Answers**
> confession (of sins to a priest) = 2
> frumpy (dress that is *unattractive and unfashionable*) = 3
> dressing up box (full of clothes for dressing up) = 6
> gold-filtered (cigarettes *with gold coloured filters*) = 1
> a robbery (at Kiki's house) = 4
> spanked (*hit on the bottom with the hand as punishment*) = 6
> stubs (the *burnt ends* of cigarettes) = 1
> necklace (the necklace which she lost) = 4
> the playground (at school) = 5

> a princess (in a dressing up game) = 6
> a grate (*a frame of metal bars* – here under a window) = 1
> a soldier (in a dressing up game) = 6
> sins (confess your sins – admit to the *bad things you have done*) = 2

What do you think?

The aim of this exercise is to use the listening as a springboard for discussion. The students are expected to discuss their opinions and list examples.

Discuss the first set of questions as a class. Then ask students to work alone to list good and bad occasions to lie. Then ask them to discuss their ideas in their groups. End the discussion by eliciting lists of good or bad occasions to lie on the board.

> **Sample answers and ideas**
> 3 is a white lie, and, arguably, 4. Otherwise, answers are students' own ideas.
> **Other occasions when it might be good to lie:** when someone asks your opinion about their ability to do something, or a possession or purchase.
> **Other occasions when it is not good to lie:** anything involving being dishonest in a way that puts the blame for something on other people.

READING AND SPEAKING (SB p38)

Diana and Elvis shot JFK!

This is a jigsaw reading activity. The aim is to develop the students' ability to read for specific information. The activity also teaches vocabulary in context, and involves a lot of spoken interaction.

1 Lead in by asking students to discuss what they know about the events in small groups. In the feedback, encourage any 'knowledgeable' students to inform the class. If the students know little or nothing about the events, you may need to tell them a bit about the events yourself.

> **BACKGROUND INFORMATION**
> President John Fitzgerald Kennedy was assassinated by a sniper (Lee Harvey Oswald) on November 22nd 1963 in Dallas, Texas. He was being driven through the streets of the city in an open-top car at the time.
>
> John Lennon, the former Beatle, was murdered on December 8th 1980 in New York. He was shot by a deranged fan, Mark Chapman, as he left his apartment building.
>
> Princess Diana, the Princess of Wales, was killed in a car crash in a tunnel in Paris on August 31st 1997. She had left the Ritz Hotel with her male companion, Dodi Fayed, and was being driven at high speed to escape the

pursuing media. Dodi, who was also killed in the crash, was the millionaire son of Mohammed al Fayed, the Egyptian-born owner of *Harrods* department store in London.

The Apollo space project was started by President Kennedy, with the aim of landing a man on the moon. The first Apollo moon landing took place on July 19th 1969. Astronauts, Neil Armstrong and Buzz Aldrin, walked on the moon. 'That's one small step for a man, one giant leap for mankind,' said Armstrong, as he stepped down onto the lunar surface. A number of further landings were made by the Apollo program throughout the 1970s.

2 Ask the questions open class, or ask students to discuss the questions in their groups.

Answers

Conspiracy theories are explanations of events by people who don't believe the official explanation. They believe that there was some secret conspiracy behind the official explanation. Conspiracy theories are usually circulated on the Internet nowadays.

There are many theories about the events in exercise 1, particularly about Kennedy.

Some people believe that:

JFK was murdered by the CIA or Republican Party, Russian or Cuban spies killed him, there was more than one marksman (not just Lee Harvey Oswald). Oswald was murdered by Jack Ruby to keep him from telling the truth.

Elvis is not dead, but faked his death to escape attention.

Princess Diana did not die in an accident – she was murdered in plots by the Royal family or British secret service.

The Apollo moon landings were staged in a Hollywood studio.

3 Ask students to read the introduction and answer the questions.

Answers

Events mentioned: The CIA shooting of President Kennedy, Elvis being alive and well and living on the moon.

People like these theories because they appeal to the imagination, and seek to make sense of horrifying, historic events.

A 'juicy' theory is a theory that is very interesting and enjoyable to speculate about.

4 This is a jigsaw activity. Divide the class into groups of three. Ask the students to decide which person in their group is going to read which text. Ask students to read and answer the questions.

When the students are ready, ask them to share their information with people in their group.

Answers
The death of Diana

1 The death of Princess Diana in a car crash on August 31st 1997.
2 Four theories are mentioned: an MI6 plot to protect the monarchy; a murder plot by florists to sell flowers; a hoax so that Diana and her boyfriend Dodi could live together on a tropical island; a plot by a member of the Royal family to kill Diana (by tampering with the car's brakes), so that Charles, the Prince of Wales could marry again.
3 Diana was fed up with intrusions into her private life.
   We never saw the body.
   Diana wrote to her butler predicting her own death in a car crash (according to the butler).
4 To protect the monarchy. To enable Diana and Dodi to live in peaceful isolation.
5 Florists, Dodi Fayed and the Fayed family; Paul Burrell (Diana's butler); the Royal family; the Prince of Wales (Prince Charles).

The Apollo moon landing

1 The Apollo moon landing in 1969 (and after).
2 Two: The landing was a hoax, filmed in a film studio; the landing happened, but the astronauts discovered evidence of an ancient civilization.
3 The flag is fluttering, and there is no breeze on the moon; the astronauts' photos don't show the night sky; the shadows are coming from more than one angle; one of the moon rocks is marked with a 'C'.
4 To prove America won the space race; the idea of finding civilization is too terrifying to reveal.
5 Neil Armstrong; Fox TV network; Apollo astronauts.

The death of John F Kennedy Junior

1 The death of JFK Junior in a plane crash on July 17th 1999.
2 Murdered by Clinton supporters because he planned to stand against Hillary Clinton; terrorists placed a bomb on the plane; Carolyn was chatting on her mobile and it interfered with the controls; an Irish curse on the family.
3 Leaked FBI documents record explosives within the plane's tail; the use of the mobile phone is recorded; proof of the curse is that other Kennedy family members have had accidents near water.
4 –
5 John Kennedy Junior (John John); JFK; Carolyn Kennedy; Clinton supporters; Hillary Clinton; the Kennedy clan; Joseph Kennedy Jr; Teddy Kennedy.

Vocabulary work

Ask students to find the words in their text, then explain them to the rest of their group.

Answers
Diana
1 breathtaking
2 thought up/fiendish
3 elaborate hoax
4 buy into
5 hatched/tampered

Moon landing
1 circulating
2 fluttering/breeze
3 stunning array
4 unanimously/even the beginnings of a case
5 seeking to conceal

JFK junior
1 bizarre/wildest
2 glued
3 ran into turbulence
4 spookily
5 patently ridiculous/pretty plausible

What do you think?

The aim of this exercise is to use the text as a springboard for discussion.

Ask students to work in small groups to discuss the questions. Monitor and prompt, then have a brief class feedback.

Possible answers
What is it about the Internet that breeds such theories?
The internet is anonymous; you can express things which would be libellous in other contexts, with less risk of prosecution; it's full of chat rooms where anybody (no matter how crazy) can express their view; people who spend a lot of time on the Internet are the sort who like gossip, conspiracy theories and strange ideas; it's a place for obsessives to write about their theories.

Writing Unit 4
Linking ideas – Conjunctions SB p114

VOCABULARY (SB p42)

Saying the opposite

This section looks at antonyms and negative prefixes.

Antonyms

1 Ask students to compare the sentences. Ask the questions and elicit the answers.

Answers
The antonyms used are *implausible* (formed with a negative prefix) and *ridiculous*.
In context, the use of *ridiculous* sounds better, as native speakers tend to avoid repeating the same word.

2 Do one as an example, then ask students in pairs to think of the correct prefixes.

Answers
unbelievable	dishonest	irresponsible
illegal	incredible	improbable

In feedback, check that the students are aware that, although *un-* is the most common prefix, English has a variety of them. *Dis-* is often used with verbs and nouns as well as adjectives, whereas the others are largely used with adjectives and adverbs. *Il-* is often used before adjectives beginning with *l*. *Im-* is often used before adjectives beginning with *p* or *m*. *Ir-* is often used with adjectives beginning with *r*. There are exceptions to these, however, e.g. *unpopular, unreliable*.

1 Ask students in pairs to label the parts of speech and then write antonyms. Go round monitoring and prompting. In the feedback, build up a list on the board.

Answers

Word	Antonyms
fake **adj**	genuine, real, authentic
like **vb**	**dis**like, hate, can't stand, can't bear, detest, loathe
tiny **adj**	big, large, huge, enormous, massive, immense
happiness **n**	**un**happiness, sadness, misery, sorrow, **dis**contentment
guilty **adj**	not guilty, innocent, blame**less**
safe **adj**	**un**safe, **in**secure, dangerous, risky, hazardous
admit **vb**	deny, contradict
sincere **adj**	**in**sincere, **dis**honest
success **n**	failure, **dis**aster, flop
mature **adj**	**im**mature, childish, young, youthful
encourage **vb**	**dis**courage, **dis**hearten, criticize, undermine
kind/generous **adj**	**un**kind/**un**generous, mean, stingy, tight, tight-fisted
appear **vb**	**dis**appear, vanish

2 Ask students to complete the conversations. Do the first as an example to show that the words need to be changed to the correct form. Let students check in pairs before feedback.

T4.7 [CD 1: Track 45] Play the recording. Students listen and check their answers.

3 Read out the conversations. Ask students what the effect of using the antonyms is.

Ask students in pairs to write similar conversations.

T4.8 [CD 1: Track 46] Play the recording. Ask students to compare their conversations with those on the recording. Ask a few pairs to read out their conversations for the class.

4 Ask students in pairs to write opposites.

5 Ask students in pairs to match words and meanings. Point out to students that *used* is unusual in that it can be used with all these prefixes. With most adjectives and past participles, only some of the prefixes can be used, e.g. *unpaid, overpaid, underpaid* but not *~~mispaid~~, ~~abpaid~~, ~~dispaid~~*.

Song **After T 4.12** [CD 1: Track 51]
I never loved you anyway TB p145

ADDITIONAL MATERIAL

Workbook Unit 4
Exercises 10-11 Vocabulary
Exercise 12 Verb + preposition
Exercise 13 Pronunciation – Intonation in question tags

EVERYDAY ENGLISH (SB p43)

Being polite

The aim of this section is to introduce and practise ways of being polite.

1 This light-hearted lead-in aims to find out how well and naturally students use polite expressions. Ask students to read through the situations, then elicit some 'white lies'.
Ask students in pairs to improvise roleplays for each situation. Go round monitoring, and note any good

examples of being polite. In the feedback, ask a few pairs to act out one of their roleplays for the class.

2 **T4.9** [CD 1: Track 47] Play the recording. Ask students to listen to each pair of lines and conversations and say which is more polite, and in what ways.

Ask students in pairs to look at the tapescripts on p129 of the Student's Book, and practise the conversations. Go round monitoring, reminding students to avoid flat intonation.

Answers and tapescript
1 Line 1 is more polite. The speaker says *I'm sorry to bother you*, meaning *Excuse me*, and uses a polite expression, *could you possibly*, and an energetic intonation pattern.
2 Line 2 is more polite. The speaker uses a polite expression, *Could you tell me*, and says *please*. Intonation rises at the end.
3 Conversation 1 is more polite. The speaker uses expressions like *how kind* and *You shouldn't have*. The intonation is high and positive.
4 Conversation 2 is more polite. The speaker apologizes, says *what a pity* and *Thanks anyway*, and expresses disappointment through the intonation pattern.
5 Conversation 1 is more polite. The speakers use polite expressions and a positive intonation pattern.
6 Conversation 2 is more polite. The speakers use polite expressions, *I wonder if I could possibly* and *Would you mind*, and a positive intonation pattern.

T4.9
1 I'm sorry to bother you, but could you possibly change a ten-pound note?
   Have you got change for a ten-pound note?
2 Where's the station?
   Could you tell me where the station is, please?
3 A This is a present for you.
   B For me! Oh, how kind! You shouldn't have, really. Thank you so much.

   C This is a present for you.
   D Thanks.
4 A Can you come to a party on Saturday?
   B No, I can't.

   C Can you come to a party on Saturday?
   D Oh, what a pity! I'm already going out, I'm afraid.
   C Oh well, never mind!
   D But thanks for the invitation anyway.
5 A Excuse me! Do you mind if I sit down here?
   B No, not at all.

   C Is anyone sitting here?

   D No.
6 A Can you give me a hand? I need to carry this box upstairs.
   B OK, if you like.
   C I wonder if I could possibly ask you a favour? Would you mind helping me with this box?
   D No, not at all.

3 Ask students in pairs to make the requests and offers more polite. Do the first one or two as examples, to get students started, but also to check the rules of form and use here. Ask students which of the expressions are used to make requests, and which make offers. Point out that some of the expressions are followed by *-ing*, some by the base infinitive.

Answers
Requests (followed by base infinitive)
Could you possibly/I wonder if you could/Do you think you could
give me a lift/help me find my glasses/lend me your dictionary/look after my dog while I'm on holiday/stop whistling?
Requests (followed by *-ing*)
Would you mind giving me a lift/helping me find my glasses/lending me your dictionary/looking after my dog while I'm on holiday?
Would you mind not whistling?
Note that *Would you mind stopping whistling?* is grammatically correct, but sounds clumsy.
Invitations
Would you like to come for a meal tomorrow evening?
Offers
Would you like me to help you with this exercise?
Students may also change requests to offers by changing *me* to *you*. For example, *Would you like me to give you a lift?/Would you like me to help you find your glasses?*
Requests (using an indirect question)
Do you happen to know where the toilet is?

MUSIC OF ENGLISH

T 4.10 [CD 1: Track 48] Read through the information in the box as a class. It is a good idea to write the example sentence on the board, with the intonation pattern as shown. Model the polite request, or play the recording as a model, and ask the class to repeat chorally then individually until most of the class are attempting a reasonable intonation pattern.

You could point out that native speakers often use polite requests aggressively, in a sarcastic way, e.g. *Do you think you could possibly take our order now?* (to a waiter in a restaurant, after waiting 20 minutes to order). In this case, the intonation used is flat.

4 Model one or two mini-dialogues with a reliable student. Then ask students in pairs to practise making and refusing requests. Go round monitoring, correcting any flat intonation. At the end, ask a few pairs to act out a dialogue for the class.

T4.11 [CD 1: Track 49] Play the recording so that students can compare their dialogues.

Tapescript

1 **A** Do you think you could give me a lift to the station?
   B I'm terribly sorry, I can't. I have to be at work by 8.30. I'll order you a taxi, though.
2 **A** Could you possibly help me find my glasses? I can't find them anywhere.
   B Sorry! I'm afraid I have to dash or I'll miss the bus. I'm hopeless at finding things anyway.
3 **A** Hi! Listen, would you like to come round for a meal tomorrow evening? I'm cooking Chinese.
   B Oh, I'd love to, but I'm afraid I'm already going out.
   A Oh, what a shame! Another time perhaps.
4 **A** Would you mind lending me your dictionary?
   B I would if I could but I'm afraid I forgot to bring it with me today. Sorry.
5 **A** Hi, it's Susan here. Could I ask you a big favour? I wonder if you could look after my dog next week? I'm going on holiday.
   B I'm terribly sorry, Susan, but I can't. I'd love to have Molly, you know I adore dogs, but I'm going away myself for a few days.
6 **A** Do you happen to know where the toilet is?
   B Sorry. I'm afraid I've no idea. Ask the guy serving drinks, he'll know.
7 **A** Would you like me to help you with this exercise? I think I know the answers.
   B That's really kind of you but I want to try and work it out for myself. Thanks anyway.
8 **A** Excuse me. Would you mind *not* whistling?
   B I'm sorry. I didn't realise I was.
   A That's OK.
   [*Amusingly, **B** then begins humming!*]

Roleplay

Lead in by asking students to look at the photo. Ask, *Where are they? Why are they there?* Tell students to imagine they have been invited for dinner at an English person's house. Ask, *What do you say when you arrive/during dinner/when you leave?* Elicit lots of ideas.

5 Read through the introduction as a class. Ask students to work in groups of four to complete the conversation on SB p156. Go round monitoring, helping and correcting.

T4.12 [CD 1: Track 50] Play the recording. Ask students to listen and compare their conversation.

After playing the recording, ask students to each choose a role, (*Anna, Ben, Kim* or *Henry*), then roleplay the dinner party, using the main stress shading on Anna, Ben, and Henry's lines to guide pronunciation. They could choose to act out their own version or the version on the recording.

Answers and tapescript (main stress underlined)
A = Anna B = Ben H = Henry K = Kim

B Kim! Hello! Great to see you. Come on in. Let me take your coat.
K Thanks very much. Oh, these are for you.
A What lovely flowers! How kind of you! Thank you so much. Now, I don't think you know Henry? Let me introduce you. Henry, this is Kim.
H Hello, Kim. Nice to meet you. I've heard a lot about you.
K Oh, I hope it was all good!
H Where exactly are you from, Kim?
K Well, I'm Canadian. I was born in Saskatoon but I've been working in the US for the last couple of years.
H That's interesting. And what are you doing in London?
K Work, I'm sorry to say. Actually, I'm on my way to Amsterdam for a conference, and I thought I'd stop over in London to see Anna and Ben. We used to work together in New York.
H And how do you find London, Kim? Is it like home, or is it very different?
K Well, it's very different from Saskatoon and New York! I know London quite well, actually , I always love it here.
B Now, Kim. What would you like to drink?
K Oh, could I have a beer? No, sorry, I'll have a glass of red wine, if that's OK.
B Right. I'll just get that for you.
K Thanks.
A Right, everybody. Dinner's ready. Come and sit down. Kim, can you sit next to Henry?
K Yes, of course.
B Has everyone got a drink? Cheers, everybody!
K Cheers! It's great to be here.
A Kim, help yourself. Would you like some Parmesan parsnips?
K Parmesan parsnips? I don't think I've ever had them. What are they?
A Well, they're parsnips coated in Parmesan cheese and roasted? Would you like to try some?
K Well, I'd love to but I'd better not – cheese doesn't always agree with me.
B Another glass of wine, perhaps?
K No, I'm all right, thanks very much. But d'you think I could have a glass of water?
B Yes, of course. Sparkling or still?
K Just tap water would be fine. That's great. Thanks a lot.
A Well, *bon appétit* everyone!

5

Future forms
Hot verbs *take* and *put*
Telephoning

An eye to the future

Introduction to the unit

The theme of this unit is how people see their future. It contextualizes the main future forms. The title is an idiomatic expression. If you do something with 'an eye to the future' then you have the future in mind when you do it. For example, *She started a savings account with an eye to the future. He made a few sketches with an eye to making a larger painting in the future.*

The main reading text is about how young people are concerned about the future – their own future and that of society. The main listening text is a jigsaw listening. Students listen to friends from university planning a reunion. It revises future forms.

Language aims

Future forms   The aim is to revise and practise the uses of the main future forms, *will*, *going to* and the Present Continuous. It also introduces and practises the Present Simple, the Future Continuous and the Future Perfect.

There are two main reasons why students have problems with this area. Firstly, English has more forms to refer to future time than many other languages; and secondly, the choice of future form depends on aspect (that is, how the speaker sees the event) and collocation, and not on time, nearness to present, or certainty.

POSSIBLE PROBLEMS

1 Students over-use *will*, seeing it as the standard future tense. English doesn't have a standard future tense. Students may not see that the pre-arranged nature of the verb action sometimes requires the Present Continuous or *going to*.
 **What time will you meet your friends?*
 **Will you go to the cinema tonight?*
 **We'll go on holiday to Greece.*

2 They resort to a constant use of the Present Simple/verb stem 'tense' to refer to all time.
 **I go to Paris this weekend.*
 **What do you do tonight?*
 This mistake is common instead of the spontaneous use of *will*.
 **I open the door for you.*
 **It's very nice. I buy it.*

3 The Present Continuous is very common to refer to arrangements between people. It *cannot* be used when human arrangement is not possible.
 **It's raining tomorrow.*

4 Students need to remember the relatively restricted usage of the Present Simple for the future, for timetables, schedules, etc.
 The match/term/film starts at…
 The train/plane/bus leaves at…

Vocabulary   The vocabulary section looks at expressions and phrasal verbs with the hot verbs *take* and *put*.

Everyday English   This section introduces and practises ways of beginning and ending a telephone conversation.

Notes on the unit

TEST YOUR GRAMMAR (SB p44)

The *Test your grammar* section aims to test the students' ability to recognize the form and use of the main future forms.

This exercise should be done quickly. Don't get involved in lengthy grammar explanations at this stage.

1 Ask students to match the forms to the uses. Let students check in pairs before feedback.

Answers
1 a prediction
2 a future fact based on a timetable
3 an intention
4 an arrangement between people
5 a suggestion
6 a spontaneous decision/offer

2 Ask students to name the forms.

Answers
1 *will* + infinitive (Future Simple)
2 Present Simple
3 *going to* + infinitive
4 Present Continuous
5 *shall* + infinitive (first person form of the Future Simple – *shall* is usually used in the question form to make offers and suggestions)
6 *will* + infinitive (Future Simple)

HOW DO YOU SEE YOUR FUTURE? (SB p44)

Future forms

This section contextualizes, contrasts and practises the main future forms. The practice activities focus on choosing the correct form to use from the context.

Lead in by asking students about their future plans. Ask, *What are you doing at the weekend? What are you planning to do after this course/in the summer holidays? What do you think you will be doing this time next year?* Test the students' ability to use future forms, but don't worry about correcting or explaining at this stage.

1 Ask students to look at the pictures. Ask a few questions to set the scene and predict content. Ask: *How old do you think they are? What do you think their future plans might be?*

   T5.1 [CD 2: Track 2] Play the recording. Ask students to listen and match numbers to names.

Answers and tapescript
1 Katrina   4 Elsie
2 Mickey   5 Janine
3 Tony   6 Gavin

T5.1 (Katrina)
1 I did my A levels a few months ago, and I've just got my results. Fortunately they're good, so I'm going to study psychology at Bristol University. The course lasts three years.
(Mickey)
2 It's Saturday tomorrow, so I'm going to see the football with my boy and some mates. Oxford United are playing Bristol Rovers. It'll be a great game. Kick-off is at 3 o'clock, so we'll have a beer or two before the match.
(Tony)
3 Marie's having a baby soon, so we're both very excited. The baby's due in five weeks. If it's a boy, we're going to call him Jamie. And if it's a girl, she'll be Hatty.
(Elsie)
4 What am I doing tomorrow, you say? Well, it's Thursday tomorrow, so I'll be doing what I always do on a Thursday. My daughter will come to see me, she'll be bringing the little 'uns, and we'll all have a cup of tea and a good old chat. And I'll bake a cake. A sponge cake with jam in it. They like that.
(Janine)
5 At the moment I'm packing, because tomorrow I'm going to France for a year. I'm going to study literature at the Sorbonne. My plane leaves at 10.30. My mum and dad are taking me to the airport. I have absolutely no idea how I'm going to carry all this lot.
(Gavin)
6 Well, I work in the City. In the next few years I'm going to be even more successful. I hope I'll be earning twice what I'm getting now. I've set myself this goal. Before I'm twenty-five, I'll have made a million.

2 Ask students in pairs to write answers to the questions. Encourage whole sentences.

   T5.2 [CD 2: Track 3] Play the recording. Pause before each answer and ask the students for their answers before you play it.

Answers and tapescript
1 She's going to study psychology.
   It lasts three years.
2 He's going to a football match.
   The match starts at 3.00.
3 Because they're going to have a baby.
4 Her daughter and grandchildren will be visiting.
   They'll have a cup of tea and a chat.
5 Because she's going to France for a year.
   Her mother and father are taking her.
6 He's going to be successful. He'll be earning a lot of money.
   He'll have made a million pounds before he's twenty-five.

3 Ask students in pairs to write the questions. Monitor and help.

T5.3 Play the recording, pausing for the students to give their questions before you play each one. Play the recording again, asking students to listen and repeat. Then ask students to work open class or in pairs, asking and answering the questions.

> **Answers and tapescript**
> 1 Which university is she going to?
> 2 Who's he going to the match with? Who's playing?
> 3 What are they going to call the baby?
> 4 What sort of cake is she going to bake?
> 5 What time does her plane leave?
> 6 How much will he be earning?

LANGUAGE FOCUS

See TB p8 for suggestions on how to teach this section.

Don't forget to look at the *Language aims* section on TB p53, which looks at problems students may have. You should also read the Grammar Reference on SB pp144–146.

LANGUAGE INPUT

1 Ask students to discuss the sentences in pairs.

> **Answers**
> *Marie's having a baby soon...* (refers to the future)
> *At the moment I'm packing...* (refers to the present – something happening now)
> *I work in the City.* (present – always true)
> *The plane leaves at 10.30.* (future fact – timetable)

2 Ask students to discuss the difference between the sentences.

> **Answers**
> *What do you do in the evenings?* (asking about regular habits)
> *What are you doing this evening?* (asking about future arrangement)
> *Get in the car. I'll give you a lift.* (spontaneous decision/offer)
> *I'm going to give Dave a lift to the airport tomorrow.* (intention made before speaking)
> *We'll have supper at 8.00.* (spontaneous intention)
> *We'll be having supper at 8.00.* (activity in progress at a time in the future – we will be in the middle of supper at 8)
> *I'll write the report tonight.* (spontaneous intention – the report writing will start and finish tonight)
> *I'll have written the report by tonight.* (action completed before a time in the future – the report writing will be complete before tonight)

Refer students to the Grammar Reference on SB pp144–146

PRACTICE (SB p46)

Discussing grammar

1 Ask students to work individually to choose the correct forms. Tell them not to worry if they aren't sure, and give a time limit of four or five minutes to make sure students don't spend too long worrying about the answer. When students are ready, put them into pairs or threes to discuss their answers.

At this stage, go round monitoring, helping with any pairs of sentences that cause problems. A good way of helping is to use check questions. If students are confused, ask some of the check questions below:
Is it a spontaneous intention or a planned intention?
Is it an arrangement between people or a future fact based on a timetable?
Is it an activity in progress at a time in the future?
Is it an action completed before a future time?

T5.4 [CD 2: Track 5] Play the recording so that students can check their answers.

> **Answers and tapescript**
> 1 I'm very excited. **I'm going to see** all my family this weekend. I don't know if I have time to come this evening. **I'll see**.
> 2 So you're off to the States for a year! What **are you going to do** there?
> I'm sure you will pass your exams, but what **will you do** if you don't?
> 3 **I'll come** with you if you like.
> **I'm coming** with you whether you like it or not.
> 4 Your school report is terrible. What **are you going to do** about it?
> What **are you doing** this evening?
> 5 I've had enough of her lazy attitude. **I'm going to give** her a good talking to.
> **I'm giving** a presentation at 3.00 this afternoon. I'm scared stiff.
> 6 John! Peter **is leaving** now. Come and say goodbye.
> The coach **leaves** at 9.00, so don't be late.
> 7 **I'll see** you outside the cinema at 8.00.
> **I'll be seeing** Peter this afternoon, so I'll tell him your news.
> 8 You'**ll have seen** enough of me by the end of this holiday. I'm going to make a success of my life. You'**ll see**.

2 Ask students to look at the photo. Ask questions to set the scene: *What can you see in the picture? What do pilots say on a flight?* You may wish to pre-teach the set of vocabulary below.

> *flight   pilot   take off/land   cruising speed*
> *cabin crew   flight attendant   duty-free goods   passport*
> *landing card   runway   plane   airport*
> *check-in   passport control   departure lounge*

Ask students to put the verbs in brackets in the correct tense. Let them check in pairs before feedback.

T5.5 [CD 2: Track 6] Play the recording and pause after each gapped item to check their answers.

Answers

1	'll be taking	9	will ... be giving out
2	have reached	10	have filled
3	'll be flying	11	will be collected
4	'll be	12	go
5	will be serving	13	will be landing
6	need	14	has come
7	will come	15	will fly
8	will be coming		

T5.5 See SB Tapescripts p130

3 Ask students in pairs to complete the sentences.

Answers

1 I can book the tickets. I**'ll be going** past the theatre on my way home.
2 I'll say goodbye now. You **'ll have gone** by the time I get back.
3 He**'ll go** mad when I tell him I've crashed his car.
4 'Tea?' 'It's OK. I**'ll make** it.'
5 Dave is so ambitious. I bet he **'ll have made** a fortune by the time he's thirty.
6 You'll know where the party is. We**'ll be making** so much noise!
7 I'll lend you this book next time I see you. I**'ll have read** it by then.
8 We're studying Shakespeare next term, so I**'ll be reading** his plays over the summer.
9 I've just got an email from Megan. I**'ll read** it to you.

Talking about you

4 Ask students to complete the sentences. Go round monitoring, making sure that students have selected the correct tense carefully.

When the students are ready, put them in pairs to interview each other about their holiday plans. Model the activity briefly with a reliable student first. In the feedback, ask a few students to summarize their partner's holiday plans.

Answers

1 Where are you going on holiday this year?/Where will you be going on holiday this year?
2 How are you getting there?/How will you get there?/How are you going to get there?
3 How long will you be away for? How long are you going to be away for?
4 Which hotel are you staying in?/Which hotel are you going to stay in?/ Which hotel will you be staying in?
5 What time does your flight arrive?/ What time will your flight arrive?/ What time is your flight going to arrive?/ What time will your flight be arriving?
6 What are you going to do while you're on holiday?/ What will you do while you're on holiday?

GRAMMAR NOTE

The choice of possible tenses above is sometimes bewildering for students – why are they all possible?! Remind students that it all depends on the point of view of the speaker. If the speaker is asking about fixed arrangements, he/she chooses the Present Continuous, (*Where are you going on holiday this year? How are you getting there?*). If the speaker sees it as a plan rather than an arrangement, *going to* is possible. Note that in the examples above, most speakers would choose to use Present Continuous or Present Simple instead of *going to* in 2, 3, 4 and 5 because English speakers tend to use the shorter form when both are possible. In 6, *What are you going to do while you're on holiday?* is preferred because it is clearly asking about intentions – it's not asking about fixed arrangements. In 1, *Where are you going to go on holiday this year?* is unlikely because English tends to avoid *going to go/come*. Will + infinitive is sometimes possible when it refers to a future fact. The Future Continuous is chosen to talk about 'something happening in the normal course of events' (which is why it is used so much by the pilot in exercise 2). So, *Which hotel will you be staying in?* might be chosen by the speaker to imply that there are limited options, and they are all hotels that people normally stay in.

I hope so/I don't think so

The aim here is to revise these common ways of responding to *yes/no* questions, and to provide further practice in using future forms.

Lead in by asking the questions in the dialogue around the class. Ask, *Do you think you'll ever be rich? Are you going out tonight? Do you think the climate will change dramatically in the next fifty years?*

5 **T5.6** [CD 2: Track 7] Play the recording. Ask students to listen and complete the conversations.

Answers and tapescript

1 'Do you think you'll ever be rich?'
   'I **hope** so.'
   'I **might** one day.'
   'It's possible, but I **doubt** it.'
   'I'm sure I **will**.'
   'I'm sure I **won't**.'
2 'Are you going out tonight?'
   'Yes, I am.'
   'I think **so**, but I'm not sure.'
   'I **might** be.'
3 'Do you think the world's climate will change dramatically in the next fifty years?'
   'I **don't think** so.'
   'I hope **not**.'
   'Who **knows**? Maybe.'

Point out the following sentences from the dialogues:
I think so.
I hope so.
I don't think so.
I hope not.
Point out that *~~I don't hope so/not~~* is wrong, and that *I think not* is very formal and rarely used.

6 Ask students in pairs to prepare and practise dialogues using the prompts. You could personalize some of these prompts to match your students' experiences and interests. Go round monitoring, making sure that the students are using *I hope so/I think so* correctly. Ask one or two pairs to act out dialogues for the class.

ADDITIONAL MATERIAL

Workbook Unit 5
Exercises 1-6 Future forms
Exercise 7 Conjunctions in time clauses

READING AND SPEAKING (SB p48)

Nobody listens to us

The aim here is to improve the students' ability to read for specific information, and to get students talking about their personal views and experiences.

Lead-in idea: write the following vocabulary on the board, check the meaning, then ask students to use the vocabulary in the discussion that follows in activity 1.

lazy selfish workshy conscientious idealistic boring hard-working responsible critical demanding

1 Ask students to discuss the questions in small groups. Have a brief class feedback.

> **Answers** Students' own ideas.

2 Ask students to work in small groups to discuss the order of importance. In the feedback, refer students to SB p157. Have a brief class discussion as to whether the students agree.

3 Set the scene for the reading by discussing the questions as a class.

> **Answers**
> The contrast and complaint is that although young people 'work ... vote ... (and) care ... nobody listens to them.'

4 Ask students to read through the article and answer the questions. Let students check their findings in pairs before having a class feedback.

> **Sample answers**
> Students' own ideas. However, the following would be typical findings.

> **Surprise findings:** Young people are conscientious, idealistic, care deeply about issues. They are concerned about the National Health Service, crime and schools. They like to save money and have career plans. They are concerned with political issues and feel a responsibility to vote.
> **Frustrations:** Nobody listens. They have no voice. Disillusioned with politics and political leaders. They shoulder (carry) heavy debts.
> **Leisure time:** buying clothes, purchasing and listening to CDs, eating out, drinking alcohol, travel, going to the cinema or theatre, reading books, sporting events, gigs and concerts (*gig* is an informal word for a rock concert).

5 Ask students to read the case studies on p50 and answer the questions. Let students check their findings in pairs before having a class feedback.

> **Answers**
> 1 Joe   3 Bob   5 Alex   7 Ellie
> 2 Kylie and Amber   4 Amber   6 Peter

6 Discuss the questions as a class.

> **Answers**
> Amber is worried about having to pay off her student loan.
> Ellie is worried about rising interest rates.
> Peter is worried about the lack of affordable housing.
> Bob intends to leave the country.
> Kylie intends to start her own business.
> Joe intends to 'work his backside off' (*backside* = bottom – a very informal expression, meaning *work very hard*) so that he can 'make it' (be successful).
> Alex intends to have several careers in his working life.

What do you think?

The aim of this exercise is to use the reading as a springboard for discussion. The students are expected to discuss their opinions and personal aspirations.

You could do this as a class or in small groups.

Language work

Ask students in pairs to complete the charts and mark the stress. Tell them to check their answers by finding the words in the article on SB p48.

> **Answers**
>
> | Adjective | Noun |
> | --- | --- |
> | 'popular | popu'larity |
> | a'ware | a'wareness |
> | disi'llusioned | **disi'llusionment** |
> | po'litical | **'politics/poli'ticians** |
> | 'criminal | **crime** |
> | **in'triguing** | 'intrigue |
> | **'alienated** | alie'nation |
> | re'sponsible | **responsi'bility** |

| 'different | 'difference |
| 'powerful | 'power |

SPOKEN ENGLISH – *thing*

Read through the explanation and questions with the class.

The thing is, … = a spoken expression used to introduce an answer, comment or explanation.

not my kind of thing = not something that I enjoy or have any interest in.

Check that students understand what the questions mean. Give students four or five minutes to think of answers to the questions, then put students in pairs to ask and answer the questions.

DEFINITIONS OF THE EXPRESSIONS WITH *THING*
How are things? = How are you?
What's the thing you like most? = What's the feature/characteristic you like most?
to do the right thing = to behave correctly
doing your own thing = doing something independently rather than following the group
your kind of thing = your taste/what you enjoy
to say the wrong thing = to say something that is inappropriate
to have a thing about = to have strong personal feelings about
to make a big thing of it = to make something more important than it is

VOCABULARY (SB p51)

Hot verbs – *take, put*

This section looks at expressions and phrasal verbs using *take* and *put*.

1 Ask students to look at the examples. Check that they know what they mean, (here, *put off* = postpone). Ask the students if they can think of any other expressions with *take* or *put*.

2 Do one as an example, then ask students in pairs to put the words in the correct box.

This works well as a dictionary activity. Ask one pair to look up *put* in their dictionary, and find the expressions. Ask another pair to look up *take*. When they are ready, put the pairs together to compare and check their answers.

Answers
TAKE	PUT
offence	a stop to sth
place	your arm round sb
(no) notice	sb in charge of

sb/sth for granted	a plan into practice
my advice	your work first
part	pressure on sb
a risk	
responsibility for something	
ages	

3 Ask students in pairs to complete the sentences.
T5.7 [CD 2: Track 8] Play the recording. Students listen and check their answers.

Answers and tapescript
1 The wedding **took place** in an old country church. It was lovely, but it was miles away. It **took ages** to get there.
2 My son's buying cigarettes, but I'll soon **put a stop** to that. I won't give him any more pocket money.
3 Please don't **take offence**, but I don't think your work has been up to your usual standard recently.
4 I told you that boy was no good for you. You should have **taken my advice** and had nothing to do with him.
5 The older you get, the more you have to learn to **take responsibility** for your own life.
6 My boss is **putting pressure** on me to resign, but I won't go.
7 I tried to get the teacher's attention but she **took no notice** of me at all.
8 Children never say 'Thank you' or 'How are you?' to their parents. They just **take** them **for granted**.

4 Ask students in pairs to match lines in **A** and **B**, and underline the expressions with *take* or *put*.

Answers
A	B
1 Take your time.	There's no need to hurry.
2 The party's on the 21st.	Put it in your diary.
3 Their relationship will never last.	Take my word for it. I know these things.
4 'I told her a joke about the French, and it turned out she *was* French.'	'Whoops! You really put your foot in it, didn't you?'
5 Take it easy.	Calm down. There's no need to panic.
6 Put yourself in my shoes.	What would *you* do?
7 You always take things too personally.	No one's out to get you.

Phrasal verbs

5, 6 Ask students in pairs to complete the sentences. Let them check answers with their dictionaries.
T5.8 **T5.9** [CD 2: Tracks 9 & 10] Play the recordings. Students listen and check their answers.

Answers and tapescripts

T5.8

1 The shop **takes on** a lot of extra staff every Christmas.
2 The lecture was too complicated, and the students couldn't **take** it all **in**.
3 My business really **took off** after I picked up six new clients.
4 You called me a liar, but I'm not. **Take** that **back** and say sorry!

T5.9

1 **Put** some music **on**. Whatever you want.
2 That article about factory farming has really **put** me **off** eating chicken.
3 Could you **put away** your clothes, please. Your room's a total mess.
4 **Put** your cigarette **out**. You can't smoke in here!

ADDITIONAL MATERIAL

Workbook Unit 5
Exercises 8-9 Vocabulary
Exercise 10 Phrasal verbs
Exercise 11 Pronunciation – Sounds and spelling

LISTENING AND SPEAKING (SB p52)

The reunion

This is a jigsaw listening activity. You will need two CD or cassette players and two recordings of this listening activity. Ideally, you need two rooms. The whole activity takes about 30 to 40 minutes. The aim is to listen for specific information and take notes, and to share information.

1 Ask students to look at the photo. Ask, *Where are they? What are they doing?* Read the introduction as a class.

You may wish to check the place names, as they are very culture specific and could confuse. *Claypath* and *Sadler Street* are streets in Durham city centre. The *Lotus Garden* and the *Kwai Lam* are restaurants. *The County* and *The Three Tuns* are pubs. Leeds and Sunderland are cities. The Midlands is the region of England around Birmingham.

Divide the students into two equal-sized groups, **A** and **B**. Take Group A to another room. They must listen to Alan phoning Sarah, (**T5.10** [CD 2: Track 11]). Group B must listen to Sarah phoning James (**T5.11** [CD 2: Track 12]). Make sure everybody can hear the recording easily. Nominate one reliable student to take control of playing and replaying. Give the students ten minutes to listen and complete the chart. Tell them they can play the recording as often as they like.

Answers
Group A's answers
Travelling from?
Alan: the Midlands; Sarah: Leeds; James: –
How?
Alan: by car; Sarah: By train; James: –

Leaving / what time?
Alan: about 3.00; Sarah: 17.05; James: –
Arriving / Durham?
Alan: between 5 and 6 o'clock; Sarah: about 6 o'clock (less than one hour after 17.05); James: –
Staying where?
Alan: The County; Sarah: The Three Tuns; James: –
Which restaurant?
Alan: The Lotus Garden; Sarah: The Lotus Garden; James: –
Where is it?
Alan: Claypath; Sarah: Claypath; James: –
Where / meet?
Alan: in the bar of the County; Sarah: in the bar of the County; James: –
What time?
Alan: at about 6.30; Sarah: at about 6.30; James: –
Group B's answers
Travelling from?
Alan: – ; Sarah: – ; James: Sunderland
How?
Alan: – ; Sarah: – ; James: by bus
Leaving / what time?
Alan: – ; Sarah: – ; James: soon after 6
Arriving / Durham?
Alan: earlier than James; Sarah: earlier than James; James: about 7
Staying where?
Alan: – ; Sarah: – ; James: with a friend
Which restaurant?
Alan: – ; Sarah: The Kwai Lam (The Lotus Garden has closed down); James: The Kwai Lam
Where is it?
Alan: – ; Sarah: on the corner of Sadler Street; James: on the corner of Sadler Street
Where / meet?
Alan: Sarah is meeting Alan in the County; Sarah: Sarah is meeting Alan in the County. She is meeting James in the Kwai Lam; James: James is meeting Sarah in the Kwai Lam.
What time?
Alan: – ; Sarah: meeting James between 7 and half past (7.30), meeting Alan before that; James: between 7 and 7.30

2 Give students time to check their answers with people in their group.

3 Give each student in each group a number. Tell number 1 in Group A to sit with number 1 in Group B, and so on. Once students are in pairs, ask them to exchange information to complete the chart.

4 Draw the activity to a close by asking the questions open class.

Answers
When Alan spoke to Sarah they didn't know that the Lotus Garden closed three years ago, so at the time of Sarah's conversation with James, Alan thinks he is going to the Lotus

Garden. However, the arrangements should be OK because James is going to ring Alan, and Sarah is going to meet Alan in the County before they go to the restaurant. So, everything should work out all right.

Sarah is meeting Alan in the County, and Alan and Sarah are meeting James in the Kwai Lam.

T5.10 See SB Tapescripts p130

T5.11 See SB Tapescripts p130

Writing Unit 5
Emailing friends SB p115

EVERYDAY ENGLISH (SB p53)

The aim of this section is to practise ways of beginning and ending telephone conversations. In order to do exercise 5, you will need to photocopy the list of expressions to use on the phone (TB p146), and the role cards (TB pp147–148).

Beginning a telephone conversation

Lead in by asking students about making phone calls in English. Ask, *Have you ever made a call in English? Who to? Why? What did you say? What did you find difficult about having a conversation on the phone?*

1 **T5.12** [CD 2: Track 13] Play the recording. Ask students to listen and say what is the difference between the beginning of these three calls.

Discuss the other questions as a class.

Answers and tapescript
1 It's a formal call – booking a hotel room.
2 It's an informal call – two friends chatting, making small talk.
3 It's a recorded message.
We make small talk when we are chatting to people we don't know very well – often at parties, or with colleagues at work, etc., because we know that serious, 'heavy' conversation topics would not be appropriate. Small talk means talking about nothing in particular, nothing serious. We make small talk about the weather, sport, what we've been doing recently, holidays, friends and family, what we're doing at work.
Recorded menus are often used by companies that are called regularly, such as cinema and theatre booking lines, customer enquiries for gas or electricity companies. They are used because they are an inexpensive way of dealing with lots of enquiries.
People find them frustrating because it can take a long time to get to the menu option that you want, and you sometimes miss it and have to start all over again. It's also frustrating dealing with a machine rather than a real person.

T5.12
1 A Hello. The Regent Hotel. Kathy speaking. How can I help you?
   B Hello. I was wondering if I could book a room ...
2 A Hello.
   B Hello, Pat. It's me, Dave.
   A Dave! Hi! How are things?
   B Not bad. Busy, busy, busy, but life's like that. How's everything with you?
   A Oh, you know, we've all got the flu, and Mike's away on business, so I've got to do the lot. School, shop, kids, cook, clean. It's great! What are you up to?
   B This and that ...
   A How's your mother, by the way?
   B She's a lot better, thanks. Really on the mend.
3 Welcome to National Phones. To help us deal with your call more efficiently, please select one of the following options. For customer services, press 1. To query a bill, press 2. To request a brochure, press 3.
   To return to the beginning of this menu, press the hash key. To speak to an operator, please hold.

2 Ask students in pairs to put the conversation in order.
   T5.13 [CD 2: Track 14] Play the recording. Students listen and check their answers.

Answers and tapescript
(The order reading down the boxes would be 1, 7, 6, 9, 2, 5, 3, 8, 4, 10)
A Hello. TVS Computers. Samantha speaking. How can I help you?
B Good morning. Could I speak to your customer services department, please?
A Certainly. Who's calling?
B This is Keith Jones.
A (pause) I'm afraid the line's busy at the moment. Will you hold?
B Yes, please.
A (pause) OK. It's ringing for you now.
B Thank you.
C (ring ring) Hello. Customer services.
B Hello. I was wondering if you could help me ...

Ending a telephone conversation

3 Ask students in pairs to put the conversation in order.
   T5.14 [CD 2: Track 15] Play the recording. Students listen and check their answers.

4   Ask students to discuss the questions briefly in pairs, then have a class feedback.

5   Divide students into pairs. Then hand out the list of expressions to use on the phone. You need to photocopy them (TB p146). Give students a few minutes to read through the expressions, and ask if they don't understand any.

POSSIBLE DIFFICULT VOCABULARY

We're surviving = we're doing OK.
What are you up to? = What are you doing these days?
I've got a lot on. = I'm busy.
Things are looking up. = They are getting better.
I mustn't complain. = Life is OK.
I must fly. = I must go. I'm busy.

Hand out the role cards. You need to photocopy them, (TB pp147–148). Give students a few minutes to read their role card, and decide whether they need to make small talk. Some situations are 'formal', for example, booking a taxi, so small talk is inappropriate. Others, such as phoning a hairdresser you know well, require small talk.

Give the pairs of students a few minutes to think about and discuss what they are going to talk about, but don't let them write the conversations at length. When the students are ready, ask them to sit back to back (to simulate a phone conversation without the clues of facial expressions and gestures), holding up a little finger and thumb to mime a telephone, and ask them to roleplay their telephone conversations. Go round monitoring, prompting and noting errors. In the feedback, write errors you heard on the board for the class to correct.

6

Expressions of quantity
'*export* and *ex*'*port*
Business expressions and numbers

Making it big

Introduction to the unit

The theme of this unit is success in business. The expression used in the title of the unit, *making it big*, means 'being very successful'.

The main grammatical focus of the unit is expressions of quantity, and these are contextualized in a reading text about the successful British TV chef, Jamie Oliver.

The main reading text is about two famous brands, *Starbucks* and *Apple Macintosh*. The main listening text is a series of radio advertisements. Students are also asked to talk about a newspaper or magazine advert they like and you should ask them to bring in an advert for this lesson, or bring in a selection of magazines yourself, with a good selection of adverts. The focus on business continues with a business maze and everyday work expressions in the *Everyday English* section.

Language aims

Expressions of quantity   The aim is to revise and practise expressions of quantity.

POSSIBLE PROBLEMS

1 **Singular or plural?**
Students get confused as to which expressions are seen as plural or singular. For example, English says, *All the people are…*, but *Everybody is…*. Watch out for the following errors:
*Everybody are happy.   *There is a few people here.
*Both people is…   *Do you have many money?

2 **Countable or uncountable?**
Perhaps the most confusing area is that of countability. This is harder than it looks. Words that are uncountable in English are countable in other languages. Students need to remember that *many* and *(a) few* are used with countable nouns, and *much* and *(a) little* are used with uncountable nouns. Watch out for the following errors:
*I'd like some advices/informations.   *He hasn't got many money.

3 **Positive or negative?**
A feature of English is that it uses different expressions of quantity in affirmative sentences and negative sentences or questions. For example, *I have some money*, but *I haven't got any money. There are a lot of people*, but *There aren't many people*. Watch out for the following errors:
*She's got much money.   *Frank talks much.
The difference between *a few/a little*, which have a positive, 'optimistic' meaning, and *few/little* which have a negative, 'pessimistic' meaning is also confusing. For example, *I have a little time to spare – let's discuss this now*, but *I have little time to spare – can we discuss this another time?*

4 **Using *of***
Most quantifiers can use *of* when it is followed by a determiner, (*the/my/those*, etc), but not otherwise. Some expressions generally use *of*, (*a lot of/a great deal of*). This leads to confusions, particularly when the students' L1 behaves differently. Watch out for the following errors:
*I haven't got enough of money.   *Several my friends like music.

Vocabulary   The vocabulary section looks at the way stress shifts from the first syllable in nouns to the second syllable in verbs and some adjectives, e.g. '*export* / *ex*'*port*.

Everyday English   This section introduces and practises fixed expressions in a work context. For example, *It's a deal/I'll read that back to you*. It also looks at the different ways of saying numbers.

Notes on the unit

TEST YOUR GRAMMAR (SB p54)

The *Test your grammar* section aims to test the students' ability to recognize which expressions of quantity are used with plural countable nouns and which are used with uncountable nouns.

This exercise should be done quickly. Don't get involved in lengthy grammar explanations at this stage.

1, 2 Ask students to underline the words that go with the expressions of quantity in each of the three groups. Let them check in pairs and discuss the question in 2 with their partner before feedback.

> **Answers**
> *This group **only** collocates with plural countable nouns:*
> **a few** cars/hold-ups
> **not many** crimes/criminals/accidents
> **several** times/letters/rooms
>
> *This group **only** collocates with uncountable nouns:*
> **very little** time/room/hope
> **not much** unemployment/work/experience
> **a bit of** luck/fun/help
>
> *This group collocates with **both** uncountable and plural countable nouns*
> **a lot of** enthusiasm/energy/people/ingredients
> **enough** chairs/food/herbs/cutlery
> **plenty of** fresh air/fluids/sleep/walks
> **hardly any** money/experience/clothes/friends

THE NAKED CHEF (SB p54)

Expressions of quantity

This section contextualizes and practises expressions of quantity. The practice activities focus on the major problem of countability, and on the differences in form, use and connotation of confusingly similar but differently-used expressions, such as *few/a few* or *all/every*.

Lead in by asking students about the picture. Ask, *How old is he? What is he doing? What do you think he does for a living? Why do you think he is famous?*

A useful vocabulary lead-in is to write on the board, and check, the following set of words: *chef, recipe, ingredients, herbs, catering, college.*

1 Ask students to read the article. Ask them why they think Jamie Oliver is called *the Naked Chef.*

> **Answers**
> Because he is *natural in front of the camera* and his recipes are *bare and simple*, without *complicated cooking techniques.*

2 Ask students in pairs to answer the questions.

> **Answers**
> 1 five   6 some time
> 2 several   7 three
> 3 around twenty   8 very little
> 4 a bit of pocket money   9 plenty
> 5 two years   10 he had no interest

3 **T6.1** [CD 2: Track 16] Play the recording. Tell students they will hear different ways of expressing amounts to the ones they have found in the text. Ask students to listen and write down the differences.

> **Answers and tapescript**
> 1 quite a few   6 a little
> 2 four   7 a few
> 3 a large number of   8 hardly any
> 4 a little   9 lots
> 5 a couple of   10 didn't have any

T6.1 (differences in bold)
Jamie Oliver
At only 28, Jamie Oliver is now an extremely successful and well known chef, with his own acclaimed restaurant in the centre of London. He has made **quite a few** TV series, written **four** books, and still does **a large number of** live shows a year. He doesn't have **many free days** any more. How did he make it big?
Well, his rise to fame and fortune came early and swiftly. By the age of eight he had already started cooking at his parents' pub. It was an easy way to earn **a little** pocket money! After **a couple of** years in catering college, and **a little time** spent in France, he started working in restaurants. He worked under **a few** famous chefs in London, before he was spotted by a TV producer at 21, and his life changed.
Even though he had **hardly any** experience, he had **a lot of** enthusiasm for cooking, and was very natural in front of the camera. His first TV programme featured him zipping around London on his scooter buying ingredients and cooking for his friends, all to a rock and roll soundtrack. The recipes were bare and simple – they didn't involve complicated cooking techniques and used **lots** of fresh ingredients and herbs. It attracted a completely new audience that previously **didn't have any** interest in food programmes. Jamie Oliver became an overnight success.
So what's his recipe for success? 'A little bit of luck, a little bit of passion, and a little bit of knowledge!' he says.

LANGUAGE FOCUS

See TB p8 for suggestions on how to teach this section.

Don't forget to look at the *Language aims* section on TB p62, which looks at problems students may have. You should also read the Grammar Reference on SB pp146–147.

1 Ask students to discuss the question in pairs.

> **Answers**
> We use **a few** with countable nouns, and **a little** with uncountable nouns.
> We use **not much** with uncountable nouns, and **not many** with countable nouns.

2 Ask students to complete the chart with answers from the reading and listening text, then compare the ways of expressing quantity with their partner.

> **Answers**
>
> | Reading text | Listening text |
> |---|---|
> | five TV series | quite a few TV series |
> | several books | four books |
> | around twenty live shows | a large number of live shows |
> | doesn't have much free time | doesn't have many free days |
> | two years | a couple of years |
> | three famous chefs | a few famous chefs |
> | very little experience | hardly any experience |
> | plenty of enthusiasm | a lot of enthusiasm |
> | plenty of fresh ingredients | lots of fresh ingredients |
> | had no interest | didn't have any interest |

Refer students to the Grammar Reference on SB pp146–147.

4 Ask students to close their books, and, in pairs, tell each other what they remember about Jamie. Have a brief class feedback. The aim here is to see how well the students remember and use the expressions of quantity.

PRACTICE (SB p55)

Countable or uncountable?

1 Do the first two as examples, then give students a couple of minutes to think about how they can form the questions. Remind them to use *How much...?* with uncountable nouns, and *How many...?* with plural countable nouns. Ask students in pairs to ask and answer questions.

T6.2 [CD 2: Track 17] Play the recording so that students can compare their answers.

> **Answers and tapescript**
> 1 'How much money have you got in your pocket?'
>   'About twenty euros.'
> 2 'How many cups of coffee do you drink a day?'
>   'It depends. I have milky coffee for breakfast, sometimes another mid-morning, then maybe one or two, black, after lunch and dinner.'
> 3 'How many times have you been on a plane?'

> 'About five or six.'
> 4 'How much time do you spend watching TV?'
>   'A couple of hours a night, just before I go to bed, I suppose.'
> 5 'How much sugar do you have in your coffee?
>   Just half a spoonful in white coffee, and none in black.'
> 6 'How many pairs of jeans do you have?'
>   'Three. A black pair, a blue pair, and an old pair I wear when I do dirty jobs like cleaning the car.'
> 7 'How many books do you read in one year?'
>   'I honestly don't know. Ten? Fifteen? I read most when I'm on holiday.'
> 8 'How much homework do you get a night?'
>   'Too much! About two hours, maybe? It depends.'
> 9 'How many English teachers have you had?'
>   'Er ... let me see ... about ten, I guess.'
> 10 'How many films do you watch a month?'
>   'One or two in the cinema, and one or two on television.'

2 Read through the examples as a class.

> **GRAMMAR NOTE**
> Point out that *chocolate* is uncountable when we are talking about chocolate in general. It is countable when we are talking about the individual *chocolates* in a chocolate box. *Business* in general is uncountable. It is countable when we are talking about individual *businesses* – a shop or a company.
> Ask students to complete the sentences. Let them check in pairs before feedback.

> **Answers**
> 1 I'd like a single room for the night.
>   Is there room for me to sit down?
> 2 You mustn't let children play with fire.
>   Can we light a fire? It's getting cold.
> 3 Scotland is a land of great beauty.
>   You should see my new car. It's a beauty.
> 4 There was a youth standing in front of me.
>   Youth is wasted on the young.

3 Ask students in pairs to match the words and put them in the correct column.

> **GRAMMAR NOTE**
> Be careful. This is harder than it looks. Words that are uncountable in English are countable in other languages.
> It is a good idea, in the feedback, to ask students which words are different in their language.

Ask students in pairs to choose a pair of words and write sentences to show their use (you could give each pair a different pair of words to make sure they are all covered). In the feedback, write up the suggested sentences on the board, and ask for comments and corrections from the rest of the class.

Expressing quantity

4 Ask students to rephrase the sentences using the prompts. Let students check in pairs before feedback.

5 Ask students to choose the correct alternative. Let students check in pairs before feedback.

EXTRA IDEA

'Quantity noughts and crosses' is a good way of testing expressions of quantity. Draw a noughts and crosses grid on the board, and write in six expressions of quantity in the squares.

Divide the class into two teams: Team X and Team O. Team X must choose a square and make a correct sentence with the expression of quantity in the square. If they are correct, write X in that square. Then it is Team O's turn. If Team X are wrong, Team O can win the square by producing a correct sentence. The winner is the first team to get three of their letters in a row.

Read the introduction as a class. Ask students if they can think of any other 'spoken' ways of expressing quantity.

T6.3 [CD 2: Track 18] Play the recording. Ask students to listen and fill the gaps.

Answers and tapescript

masses of time	piles of washing
bags of money	tons of things
heaps of food	millions of people

T6.3

1 There's no need to rush. We've got masses of time.
2 She's got bags of money. I think she inherited it.
3 We've got heaps of food for the party. Don't buy any more.
4 When my daughter comes back from university, she always brings piles of washing.
5 I can't see you today. I've got tons of things to do.
6 There were millions of people at the sales. I couldn't be bothered to fight my way through them.

Give students two or three minutes to think of ways of answering the question, *What have your friends got a lot of?* Then put them in small groups to express their ideas.

A lifestyle survey

If you have a small class (up to about 12 students), do this as a class survey. Ask students to write the list of prompts in note form down the left side of a blank sheet of A4 paper. Ask them to stand up and walk round the class, asking their fellow students questions. For example, *Do you spend a lot of money on trainers?* Tell them to write each student's name, and put ticks and crosses to record their results. Tell them to interview at least six students. When they have finished, ask them to sit down with a partner and share their findings. Then ask the pairs to record their results using the expressions in the second box.

If you have a large class, divide the students into groups of six to eight. Ask them to interview each other to gather the information, then present their findings to the class.

Sample answers

All of us/Most of us like shopping.
Hardly anybody/Nobody spends a lot on trainers.
A few of us buy designer clothes.
Quite a lot of us go to coffee shops.
None of us go clubbing regularly.
Nearly everybody watches Friends.
Most of us like The Simpsons.
Quite a lot of us do a lot of exercise.

GRAMMAR NOTE

As you monitor, or in the feedback, watch out for errors involving the following rules of use:
Third person *s*: *Everybody watch …/None of us buys …
Using *of* and *the*: *All like shopping.

Writing Unit 6

Report writing – A consumer survey SB p116

ADDITIONAL MATERIAL

Workbook Unit 6
Exercises 1-5 Countable and uncountable nouns
Exercise 6 Compounds with *some, any, no, every*
Exercise 7 Expressing quantity

LISTENING AND SPEAKING (SB p57)

Advertisements

The aim here is to improve the students' ability to listen for gist and specific information. The radio advertisements are amusing, and many are for brands that your students will be familiar with.

The speaking activity is a group task in which students have to devise and present their own radio or television advert.

In exercise 2, students are asked to talk about a newspaper or magazine advert they like. You will need to tell students to bring in an advertisement for this lesson, or bring in a selection yourself.

1 Lead in by asking students about their favourite TV or radio advertisement. Encourage a light-hearted class discussion.

2 Ask students to present and talk about the newspaper or magazine advert they have brought to class. Ask, *What is it advertising? Why do you like it? How does it persuade people to buy the product?*

ALTERNATIVE IDEA

Bring in a pile of magazines which are full of adverts. Divide students into small groups and give them two or three magazines. Ask them to find an advert that appeals, then present it to the class.

3 **T6.4** [CD 2: Track 19] Play the recording. Ask students to listen and answer the questions. Let students check their answers in pairs before feedback.

Answers

a football match	3
a chocolate bar	5
soap powder	1
a new car	4
car insurance for women	2
a shop's opening hours	6

4 **T6.4** Play the recording again. Ask students in pairs to complete the chart.

> **Answers**
> 1 Soap powder; 'mummy' and her young daughter, Sarah; At home – kitchen/washroom
> 2 Swinton car insurance; Two men watching someone parking; Car park
> 3 Premier football; 'daddy' and his young daughter; Living room – dad is trying to watch football on TV
> 4 Ford escort; Father and daughter; At home – arguing
> 5 Kitkat; Sue and a boy calling her; Sue's answering machine
> 6 Ikea; Priest and couple getting married; In church
>
> **T6.4** See SB Tapescript p131

5 Ask students in pairs to say what the selling point of each advert is.

> **Answers**
> 1 New System Sudso Automatic's advanced formula can remove ground-in dirt even at low temperatures, and keep colours bright.
> 2 Since men are responsible for 81% of parking offences and 96% of dangerous driving offences, why should women have to pay the same for car insurance? Swinton provides policies with up to 20% reductions for women.
> 3 Manchester United – Bayern Munich is such a 'must see' game that nothing should disturb you from watching – not even your children.
> 4 All new Ford Escorts now come with one year's free insurance.
> 5 Kitkat's slogan is 'have a break', which is used here to mean 'have a break from life's stresses'.
> 6 IKEA is open till 10pm weeknights.

6 **T6.4** Ask students in pairs to answer the questions. You may need to play the recording a third time, playing and pausing, if students are not sure about some of the answers.

> **Answers**
> 1 It's pink, with fluffy yellow ducks./ New System Sudso Automatic's advanced formula can remove ground-in dirt even at low temperatures, and keep colours bright.
> 2 They think she's terrible at parking./They change their mind because they realize it is a 'bloke' (man), and then decide that the parking space was 'tight' and difficult.
> 3 She did (drew) a picture of her father, and she got two stars, and Miss Lewis (her teacher) said she was the best in class./Because he wants her to go away so that he can watch the football.
> 4 It comes with free insurance./She makes fun of him by mocking the way he says, 'When I was young...', by implying that he is over 80, and by having the last word.

> 5 To meet him for lunch, or a drink. / He keeps worrying he's said the wrong thing, and by trying to correct himself, he *does* say the wrong thing!
> 6 He tells the bride to 'just nod' and interrupts the groom, and 'summarizes' the marriage ceremony in broken sentences. / He is in hurry because he wants to get to IKEA before it closes.

Writing an advert

Divide students into groups of three or four. Ask them to choose a product or service to describe. Then give them five to ten minutes to write a script for their advertisement. Tell them to write a dialogue which gets their audience's attention, and a slogan or piece of information to sell the product or service at the end. You could write the following useful language on the board to help them.

> **USEFUL LANGUAGE**
> *Buy/Try/Get the new... It's...*
> *It comes with...*
> *It's available with...*
> *You won't find a better/faster/cheaper... than the new...*
> *It's all you could want from a...*

When the students are ready, ask them to present their advertisement for the class. If you have time and equipment, you could record the advertisements. Video the students as they make their presentations, or send each group out of the room in turn, with a cassette recorder, and ask them to record their advertisement. Play the recordings in class.

READING AND SPEAKING (SB p58)

Two famous brands

This is a jigsaw reading activity. The aim is to improve the students' ability to read for specific information, and to exchange information.

1 Lead in by asking students to look at the pictures and discuss the questions.

2 Divide the students into two groups. Ask Group A to read about *Starbucks* on p58, and Group B to read about *Apple Macintosh* on p59. Ask them to answer the questions and compare their answers with people in their group.

> **HOW TO DO A JIGSAW READING**
> The way you organize your class to do the jigsaw reading will depend on the size and layout of the class. You could simply ask all the students on the left to be Group A, and all those on the right to be Group B. Once they have read their text, and shared their information with students in their group, they will

need to find a partner from the other group. To avoid chaos, give each person in each group a number, then ask students to find and sit down with the student from the other group with the same number. Alternatively, divide the class into A pairs, then B pairs, A pairs, then B pairs. Students read and compare with their partner, then simply turn round to compare their texts.

Answers
Group A: Starbucks
1 Seattle in 1971.
2 Baldwin, Siegel and Bowker.
3 A character in the novel *Moby Dick*.
4 Determination to provide best quality coffee.
5 Yes.
6 Its blend of commercialism and comfy sofas.
7 Anti-globalization protesters feel that big corporations put independent companies out of business.
8 Skinny Latte, Almond Truffle Mocha, Raspberry Mocha Chip Frappuccino.
Group B: Apple Macintosh
1 Silicon Valley, California, in 1976.
2 Steven Jobs and Steven Wozniak.
3 Jobs' favourite fruit.
4 The first home computer to be user-friendly – introduced the public to point and click graphics.
5 No. Jobs argued bitterly with John Sculley, and was forced to resign after a power struggle. By 1996 Apple was in trouble due to the dominance of Windows software and the increasing number of PC clones.
6 The attention to design.
7 Their computers cost more than most PCs, and a more limited range of software is available.
8 The Apple Macintosh, the iMac, the iPod.

3 Ask students to share their information with a partner from the other group.

4 Ask students to write the questions that go with their article.

Answers
Starbucks
How many Starbucks stores are (being) opened every (single) day? *Three or four.*
How much is Starbucks worth? *$5 billion.*
How long did it take Schultz to open 150 new stores and buy the company? *Ten years.*
Why do small, independent companies go out of business? *Because they can't compete.*
Apple
Where did Apple begin?/Where was Apple founded? *In Silicon Valley.*

How did Jobs and Wozniak raise the capital to start Apple? *By selling some of their possessions.*
Why did Jobs resign? *Because he argued with his partner.*
When was the iMac launched? *In 1997.*

Vocabulary work

Ask students in pairs to find the adverbs and match them to meanings.

Answers

Starbucks	Apple Macintosh
a rapidly	a truly
b currently	b effectively
c originally	c bitterly
d passionately	d reluctantly
e initially	e gradually
f eventually	f vitally

What do you think?

The aim here is to use the text as a springboard for speaking.

1 Ask students in small groups to make a list of arguments against multi-nationals. In the feedback, ask students for their personal views.

Arguments against
They put small companies out of business.
They go into poorer countries and undermine local businesses.
They exploit cheap labour.
They have too much influence with governments.
They affect and change consumer habits in other cultures – thus undermining that culture.
They are not environmentally friendly.
It's a form of imperialism.

2 Find out about the students' own computer use.

VOCABULARY AND PRONUNCIATION (SB p60)

This section looks at the way stress shifts from the first syllable in nouns to the second syllable in verbs and some adjectives, ('*export*/ex'*port*). It looks at the way that some words have different meanings according to the stress.

export: /ˈekspɔːt/ **or** /ɪkˈspɔːt/?

1 **T6.5** [CD 2: Track 20] Play the recording. Ask students to listen and repeat the nouns and verbs. Ask students how the stress changes when the word is a noun, and when it is a verb.

T6.5 See SB Tapescripts p131

2 Model the activity with a reliable student. Then ask students in pairs to practise the words.

3 Ask students to complete the sentences. Ask them to work in pairs to read out the sentences to each other, paying attention to the correct stress.

T6.6 [CD 2: Track 21] Play the recording. Students listen and check their answers.

Answers and tapescript (stressed syllable underlined)

1 Scotland imports a lot of its food from other countries. Its exports include oil, beef, and whisky.
2 I'm very pleased with my English. I'm making a lot of progress.
3 Ministers are worried. There has been an increase in the number of unemployed.
4 But the number of crimes has decreased, so that's good news.
5 How dare you call me a liar and a cheat! What an insult!
6 There was a demonstration yesterday. People were protesting about blood sports.
7 He ran 100m in 9.75 seconds and broke the world record.
8 Don't touch the DVD player! I'm recording a film.
9 Britain produces about 50% of its own oil.

refuse: /'refju:z/ or /ri'fju:z/?

1 Ask students in pairs to check the meaning, part of speech, and pronunciation of the words in their dictionaries.

T6.7 [CD 2: Track 22] Play the recording. Ask students to listen and repeat.

Answers and tapescript

a 'refuse (n)	re'fuse (vb)
b 'present (n)	pre'sent (vb)
c 'minute (n)	min'ute (adj)
d 'desert (n)	de'sert (vb)
e 'content (n)	con'tent (adj)
f 'object (n)	ob'ject (vb)
g 'invalid (n)	in'valid (adj)
h 'contract (n)	con'tract (vb)

2 Model the activity with a reliable student. Then ask students in pairs to practise the words.

3 Ask students in pairs to ask and answer the questions using the words in exercise 1.

T6.8 [CD 2: Track 23] Ask the questions again, and play the recording after students give each answer. Students listen and check their answers.

Answers and tapescript

1 A refuse collector.
2 An unidentified flying object.
3 A desert in northern Africa.
4 Presents!
5 The contents pages.
6 con'tent, 'contract, in'valid, mi'nute, re'fuse

SPEAKING (SB p60)

A business maze

This is a maze, similar to the sort of activity often used in business training to develop team-building and decision-making skills. The aim is to create a lot of discussion and negotiation in class.

Preparation

Before class, you will need to photocopy and cut out the situation cards on TB pp149–157. You need one complete set of cards for each group of about four students. It's a good idea to stick the cards onto different-coloured stiff cardboard. That way, the cards will last longer, and you can easily put the sets of cards back together in different-coloured sets.

How to do the maze

Divide the students into groups of four. It is a good idea to mix strong and weak, quiet and noisy, students.

Read the introduction as a class. Then ask students in their groups to read the problem on the card and discuss the options. When the students have made their decision, hand out the relevant card. You will have to monitor each group equally, ready to hand out each card they request. Encourage students to take it in turns to read out each card to their group, and tell them to discuss their options fully before asking for the next card. Point out that the aim is not to get to the end quickly, but to make successful career decisions.

The maze itself should take about thirty minutes.

Inevitably, groups will finish at different times. Ask groups to consider their performance. Where did they go wrong? What should they have done?

What do you think?

Ask each group's spokesperson to summarize their group's decisions.

Have a brief class discussion about why these activities are used for management training.

Possible reasons

To help people who work in the same company to get to know each other and learn to work together.
To develop team building skills.
To find out who makes a good leader.
To develop problem-solving skills.

Business expressions and numbers

The aim of this section is to practise business expressions and numbers.

1 Ask students in pairs to match the expressions. Do the first as an example to get them started.

   T6.9 [CD 2: Track 24] Play the recording. Students listen and check their answers. In the feedback, you may need to explain the meaning of some of the more idiomatic language.

Answers and tapescript

1 A Mike! Long time no see! How are things?
   B Good, thanks, Jeff. Business is booming. What about yourself?
2 A I'm afraid something's come up, and I can't make our meeting on the 6th.
   B Never mind. Let's go for the following week. Is Wednesday the 13th good for you?
3 A What are your travel arrangements?
   B I'm getting flight BA 2762, at 18.45.
4 A Could you confirm the details in writing?
   B Sure. I'll email them to you as an attachment.
5 A They want a deposit of $21\frac{1}{2}$ percent, which is £7,500, and we … ge … t… the two thous …
   B Sorry, I didn't quite get that last bit. What was it again?
6 A I'll give you £5,250 for your car. That's my final offer.
   B Great! It's a deal. It's yours.
7 A I don't know their number offhand. Bear with me while I look it up.
   B No worries. I'll hold.
8 A OK. Here's their number. Are you ready? It's 0800 205080.
   B I'll read that back to you. Oh eight double oh, two oh five, oh eight oh.
9 A So what's your salary, Dave? 35K? 40K?
   B Hey! Mind your own business! You wouldn't tell anyone yours!
10 A Have you applied for that job?
   B There's no point. I'm not qualified for it. I wouldn't stand a chance.

VOCABULARY NOTE

Long time no see! = This is the first time I've seen you for a long time.
Business is booming. = Business is very successful.
something's come up = An unexpected problem or something urgent has just happened.
I can't make our meeting on the 6th. = I can't get to/keep the appointment for our meeting…
Never mind. = it doesn't matter/it's not important.

I didn't quite get that last bit. = I didn't understand the last thing you said (because it was unclear).
It's a deal. = It is agreed.
I don't know their number offhand. = I don't know the number without looking it up.
Bear with me while I look it up. = wait a moment while…
No worries. = It's not a problem (a common Australian expression).
Mind your own business! = This is my personal affair, not yours.
I wouldn't stand a chance. = There's no chance that I would be successful.

2 Ask students in pairs to practise the conversations, using the stress shading to help them get the rhythm of the sentences right.

3 Ask students to look at the conversations again and tell you how the numbers are said.

Answer

Oh eight hundred, twenty, fifty, eighty
Oh eight double oh, two oh five, oh eight oh.

4 Ask students in pairs to practise saying the numbers.
   T6.10 [CD 2: Track 25] Play the recording. Ask students to listen and repeat.

5 Ask students to work in pairs. Tell each student to write down five very different numbers. Then ask them to dictate their numbers to their partners. Ask them to read their numbers back. Find out who got them all right. You could ask students to think of numbers that have a personal meaning for them, and they can finish the activity by guessing what the numbers mean, e.g. *2008? Is that when you hope to go to university? 0778 329716? Is that your girlfriend's mobile number?*

EXTRA IDEA

Write down ten different types of numbers in a list on a sheet of paper. Photocopy the sheet of paper so that there are enough for each pair of students in your class. Then hand them out to Student A in each pair. Tell the students that Student A will read a list of words to Student B. Student B must write them down. It's a race. Who can read and write down the numbers the quickest? Say, *Go.* Check the numbers carefully before announcing the winners.

ADDITIONAL MATERIAL

Workbook Unit 6

Exercise 8 Vocabulary

Exercise 9 Prepositions

Exercise 10 Listening – A business problem

Exercise 11 Pronunciation – Shifting word stress

7

Modals and related verbs 1
Hot verb *get*
Exaggeration and understatement

Introduction to the unit

The theme of this unit is relationships between people. The main grammatical focus of the unit is modal auxiliary verbs.

The main reading texts are about families in which the grown-up children don't leave home. The listening text is an interview with an Indian lady, who had an arranged marriage.

Language aims

Modal verbs   The aim is to revise and practise modal auxiliary verbs, and the way they are used to express ability, advice, obligation, permission, probability, and (un)willingness. The unit also looks at related verb forms, such as *be bound to* and *be supposed to*, which are used to express similar concepts.

POSSIBLE PROBLEMS

Students often avoid using modals because their L1 expresses the same ideas using different structures, and because they feel unconfident about using modals which have subtle and varied uses. Watch out for students using the following sort of structure.

*Is it possible to leave early?

1 **Probability**

Basically, *may, might* and *could* express uncertainty, *will* and *must* express certainty, and *won't* and *can't* express negative certainty. An error to watch out for is the misuse of *can* here.

*I'm not sure, but it can be Sally.

2 **Advice and obligation**

Should and *ought to* express advice (mild obligation), whereas *must* and *have to* express strong obligation. The difference between *must* to express a personal obligation, (*I'm tired. I must go home*), and *have to* to express an obligation based on laws or rules, (*In the UK, you have to drive on the left*) is very subtle. You could interchange the verbs in the above examples. The possible confusion that misusing the negative forms can cause is worth focusing on, however. *Don't have to* is used to express no obligation, (*You can go if you want to. You don't have to stay.*). *Mustn't* expresses negative obligation, (*Don't move! You mustn't leave until the end.*).

3 **Permission and requests**

An area of confusion here is that we use different modals to ask for permission from those we use to make a request.

Permission: *May/Can/Could I...*

Requests: *Can/Could/Will/Would you...*

4 **Negatives and past forms**

One thing to be aware of is that modals, often illogically, have different negatives and past forms depending on their meanings. For example:

Must (obligation)		*Must* (probability)	
Positive	**Past**	**Positive**	**Past**
She must leave.	*She had to leave.*	*It must be late.*	*It must have been late.*
She has to leave.			
	Negative		**Negative**
	She mustn't leave.		*It can't be late.*

Vocabulary The vocabulary section looks at the hot verb *get*, which is commonly used in expressions and phrasal verbs.

Everyday English This section introduces and practises ways of expressing exaggeration and understatement. Many of the expressions introduced use modal verbs.

Notes on the unit

TEST YOUR GRAMMAR (SB p62)

The *Test your grammar* section aims to test the students' ability to recognize the form and meaning of modal verbs. It also asks students to practise their pronunciation of the verbs.

This exercise should be done quickly. Don't get involved in lengthy grammar explanations at this stage.

1 Ask students in pairs to read the sentences 1–10, and underline the modal verbs. Go round monitoring, checking that they are pronouncing the words correctly.

Then ask students in pairs to rewrite the sentences, using the correct expressions a–j. Do the first as an example.

NOTE ON REGISTER

Tell students that although the modals 1–10 have the same meaning as the expressions a–j, they often have different register. For example, *You are required to…*, *You're allowed to…*, and *You aren't permitted to …* are more formal than the modal use they correspond with. *You're bound to…* and *Is it OK if…* are less formal.

2 **T7.1** [CD 2: Track 26] Play the recording. Ask students to listen and compare their answers.

Answers and tapescript
1 g If I were you I wouldn't wear red. It doesn't suit you.
2 e Is it OK if I make a suggestion?
3 f You're allowed to smoke in the designated area only.
4 a I'll be able to take you to the airport, after all.
5 d You are required to obtain a visa to work in Australia.
6 i It's always a good idea to make an appointment.
7 c You're bound to pass. Don't worry.
8 j You aren't permitted to walk on the grass.
9 b I didn't manage to get through, the line was engaged.
10 h I refuse to discuss the matter any further.

3 Ask students to complete the lines a–j with their own ideas.

EXTRA IDEA

Ask students in pairs to write three-line dialogues, using expressions from 1–10 and a–j. Ask the pairs to act out their conversations for the class. For example:
May I make a suggestion?
Yes, of course, but I won't change my mind.

OK. *That's fine. But if I were you, I really wouldn't wear that hat!*

WE CAN WORK IT OUT (SB p62)

Modals and related verbs

This section contextualizes and practises modals and related verbs. The practice activities focus on meaning and use.

Lead in by asking students about the picture. Ask, *What can you see in the pictures? How do the people feel? What do you think they are saying?*

1 **T7.2** [CD 2: Track 27] Play the recording. Ask students to listen and read the conversations. Ask the questions. Ask students to find the modal verbs, then check with a partner. (The modals are in bold in the tapescripts below).

Answers and tapescript
1 Speakers: two male car drivers. One is trying to turn illegally into a road with a 'No entry' sign. The other is angry.
2 Speakers: two women are chatting. One is telling the other a secret – that she is going to get married for the second time.

T7.2
1 A What the … where d'you think you're going?
   B What d'you mean?
   A Well, you **can't** turn right here.
   B Who says I **can't**?
   A That sign does mate. 'No Entry'. **Can't** you read?
   B I **couldn't** see it, **could** I?
   A You **should** get your eyes tested, you **should**. You're not fit to be on the roads.
2 A You **won't** tell anyone, **will** you?
   B Of course I **won't**.
   A You really **mustn't** tell a soul.
   B Trust me. I **won't** say a word.
   A But I know you. I'm sure you**'ll** tell someone.
   B Look. I really **can** keep a secret, you know. Oh, but **can** I tell David?
   A That's fine. He's invited too, of course. It's just that Ben and I want a really quiet affair. It being second time around for both of us.

2 **T7.3** [CD 2: Track 28] Play the recording. Tell students they will listen to similar conversations, using expressions in place of modal verbs. In the feedback, build up a list of the expressions on the board. (The expressions are in bold in the tapescripts below).

Answers and tapescript

1. A What the ... where d'you think you're going?
   B What d'you mean?
   A Well, you're **not allowed** to turn right here.
   B Who says it's **not allowed**?
   A That sign does mate. 'No Entry', you **ought to be able to** read that.
   B It's **impossible** to see.
   A You'd **better** get your eyes tested, you **had**. You're not fit to be on the roads.

2. A **Promise not to** tell anyone!
   B I **promise**.
   A It's really **important not to** tell a soul.
   B Trust me. I **won't** say a word.
   A But I know you. You're **bound to** tell someone.
   B Look. I really **am able to** keep a secret, you know. Oh, but **is it OK if** I tell David?
   A That's fine. He's invited too of course. It's just that Ben and I want a really quiet affair. It being second time around for both of us.

3. Ask students in pairs to choose and learn a conversation by heart. Ask them to act it out for the class. Learning by heart is a useful and fun way of learning expressions.

LANGUAGE FOCUS

See TB p8 for suggestions on how to teach this section.

Don't forget to look at the *Language aims* section on TB p71, which looks at problems students may have. You should also read the Grammar Reference on SB pp147–149.

LANGUAGE INPUT

1. Ask students in pairs to match the sentences in **A** with the meanings in **B**.

Answers

A		B
1	He can ski.	ability
2	Can I go to the party?	permission
3	You must stop at the crossroads.	obligation
4	You must see the film.	advice
5	He must be rich.	probability
6	I'll help you.	willingness
7	I won't help you.	unwillingness
8	You should stop smoking.	advice
9	It will be a good party.	probability
10	It might rain.	probability

2. Ask students to match the related verbs to the meanings.

Answers

be able to* = ability
manage to* = ability
be allowed to = permission
be bound to = probability (certain)
be supposed to = advice/mild obligation
promise to = willingness
refuse to = unwillingness
have (got) to = obligation
be required to = obligation
be likely to = probability
had better = advice
Why don't you... = advice
*Note the difference between *be able to* and *manage to* for ability. We can use both to express an ability on a specific occasion: *The wall was very high but Sam **managed to/was able to** climb it*. But we can only use *be able to* to express general ability: *One day, I hope I'll **be able to** swim much faster*.

3. Ask students to change the sentences into the various forms – first the question, negative, and third person, and after checking those forms, the past and future.

Answers

I **can** speak Japanese.
Question: *Can you speak Japanese?*
Negative: *I can't (cannot) speak Japanese.*
Third person: *He/She can speak Japanese.*
Past: *I could speak Japanese.*
Future: *I'll be able to speak Japanese.*

I'm **able to** speak three languages.
Question: *Are you able to speak three languages?*
Negative: *I'm not able to speak three languages.*
Third person: *He/She is able to speak three languages.*
Past: *I was able to speak three languages.*
Future: *I'll be able to speak three languages.*

I **must** go.
Question: *Must you go?*
Negative: *I mustn't go.(not allowed)/I don't have to go. (no obligation)*
Third person: *He/She must go.*
Past: *I had to go.*
Future: *I'll have to go.*

I **have to** go.
Question: *Do you have to go?*
Negative: *I don't have to go. (no obligation)*
Third person: *He/She has to go.*
Past: *I had to go.*
Future: *I'll have to go.*

I've **got to** go.
Question: *Have you got to go?*
Negative: *I haven't got to go. (no obligation)*
Third person: *He/She has got to go.*
Past: *I had to go.*
Future: *I'll have to go.*

Note that *can* does not have a future form, so we use *be able to*, and *must* does not have a past or future form, so we use *have to*. *Have got to* is a 'spoken' form of *have to*, which is not generally used in past or future forms.

Refer students to the Grammar Reference on SB pp147–149.

PRACTICE (SB p 63)

Negotiating

1 Ask students to look at the picture, and predict the situation. Ask, *What do you think they are saying?* Then ask students to read the dialogue and tell their partner what it is about.

Answers
A woman is advising her friend to forgive her partner or husband for the sake of their children.

2 Ask students in pairs to replace the words in italics with modal verbs. Do the first as an example. Go round monitoring and prompting.

T7.4 [CD 2: Track 29] Play the recording so that students can compare their answers.

Answers and tapescript
A **I think you should** swallow **your** pride and forgive and forget.
B Never! I **will not**.
A You**'ll have to** in the end. You **can't** ignore each other forever.
B I **might** forgive him but I **can** never forget.
A **It must be** possible to talk it over, and work something out. You **must** for the sake of the children.
B Oh dear! I just don't know what to do for the best.

3 Repeat the procedure in **1** for this next conversation.

Answers
A schoolboy is explaining to a friend why he can't come to football practice.

Ask students in pairs to replace the words in italics with modal verbs.

T7.5 [CD 2: Track 30] Play the recording so that students can compare their answers.

Answers and tapescript
A I don't know if I **can** come this evening.
B But you **must**. You **said you would**.
A Yeah, but I **can't** go out on weekday evenings. My parents won't let me.
B **You could** tell them that you're coming over to my house to do homework.

A **I can't**. Somebody **will** see me and tell them.
B We**'ll have to** cancel the match then. Lots of kids **can't** come to practice in term time.

4 Ask students to practise the conversations in pairs. You could ask them to try to memorize a conversation.

Discussing grammar

5 Ask students in pairs to decide which verbs or phrases fill the gaps.

Answers
1 a won't (unwillingness)
 b ~~can't~~ (we cannot use *can't* + be able to – they both express ability)
 c might (probability)
 d may (probability)
2 a ~~could~~ (don't use *did* with a modal auxiliary)
 b manage to (ability)
 c ~~able to~~ (the form is *be able to*, so use the auxiliary *be* not *do* here)
 d have to (obligation)
3 a must (probability – logical deduction)
 b ~~can~~ (we cannot use *can* to express probability here)
 c ~~had better~~ (It is just about possible to construct a context to make this correct – but it is unusual. We don't really use an advice expression here)
 d are bound to (probability – certainty)
4 a ~~mustn't~~ (*mustn't* expresses prohibition – negative obligation – so it contradicts 'optional')
 b don't have to (no obligation)
 c don't need to (no necessity)
 d ~~aren't supposed to~~ (expresses a mild obligation or expectation which contradicts 'optional')
5 a will not (unwillingness)
 b should not (obligation)
 c ~~might not~~ (*might* expresses uncertainty and doubt so it contradicts 'absolutely')
 d refuse to (unwillingness)
6 a Are you able to (ability)
 b Can you (ability – or, possibly, a request here)
 c ~~May you~~ (*may* is not used for ability or with *you* for requests)
 d Could you (past ability, or a request – an odd request but possible!)
7 a ~~May you~~ (*may* is not used with *you* for requests)
 b Could you (request)
 c ~~Are you able to~~ (we use this form for ability – not requests)
 d Can you (request – not as polite as *Could you*)
8 a Could (permission)
 b May (permission)
 c ~~Will~~ (used to express willingness not permission)
 d ~~Would~~ (used to express willingness not permission)
9 a ~~can~~ (can't use modal auxiliary with another auxiliary to make a question)

b be able to (ability)

c be allowed to (permission)

d ~~may~~ (can't use modal auxiliary with another auxiliary to make a question)

10 a should (advice)

b don't have to (no obligation)

c ~~mustn't~~ (prohibition – this is grammatically possible but highly improbable advice!)

d could (suggestion)

11 a mustn't (prohibition – here, strong advice)

b shouldn't (advice)

c ~~don't have to~~ (no obligation – so contradicted by 'you'll make yourself ill')

d ~~can't~~ (don't use *can't* to express obligation or advice)

12 a 'd better (obligation)

b ought to (obligation)

c am likely to (probability)

d had to (obligation)

6 Ask students to rewrite the sentences. Let them check in pairs before feedback.

> **Answers**
>
> 1 It's (just) bound to rain at the weekend.
> 2 He managed to give up smoking after three attempts./He succeeded in giving up smoking after three attempts.
> 3 Are you able to tell which twin is which?
> 4 My parents say I'm not allowed to have a puppy./My parents say they won't let me have a puppy.
> 5 If I were you, I'd take it back and complain./You'd better take it back and complain.
> 6 I'm supposed to wear a suit for work, but I often don't.
> 7 You'd better not tell anyone about it./Promise not to tell anyone about it.
> 8 He refused to put out his cigarette.

Note some of the complex forms here, which may catch students out: *succeed in* + ing; *allow (sb) to do* but *let (sb) do*; *had better not do* and *promise not to do*.

Exciting news

Lead in by asking about the picture. Ask, *Where is the place in the photo? What do you think is the connection between the place and the girl?*

7 Ask students to read the one side of the telephone conversation and discuss the questions in pairs.

> **Answers**
>
> Miranda is excited because she has won a competition.
> She is going to stay at the Ritz Carlton which overlooks Central Park (in New York).
> David is probably her ex-boyfriend.
> Miranda and Rick are good friends. They might become boyfriend and girlfriend.

8 Ask students in pairs to write in Miranda's exact words. Encourage them to use modal verbs and expressions from the lesson. Then ask the pairs to practise the conversation. Ask one or two pairs to perform their conversations for the class.

9 **T7.6** [CD 2: Track 31] Play the recording. Ask students to listen and compare.

> **Tapescript**
> **Exciting News**
> **R** Hello?
> **M** Rick, Rick is that you? I've got to talk to you.
> **R** Miranda, hi! Why all the excitement?
> **M** Well, can you remember that competition I entered, just for a laugh, a few weeks ago?
> **R** Yes, I can. I remember you doing it in the coffee bar. It was the one in the *Daily Sun*, wasn't it? Didn't you have to name loads of capital cities?
> **M** Yeah, that's it. You've got it. Well, get this, I've *won*! I came first!
> **R** Never! I don't believe it! What's the prize?
> **M** A trip to New York.
> **R** You must be kidding! That's brilliant. For how long?
> **M** Just three days – but it's three days in the Ritz Carlton, of all places!
> **R** Well, you should be able to do quite a lot in three days. And the Ritz Carlton! I'm impressed! Doesn't that overlook Central Park?
> **M** Yes, it does.
> **R** I thought so. Not that I've been there, of course.
> **M** Well, you can now.
> **R** What do you mean? How would I ever be able to?
> **M** Well, it's a trip for two and I'd really love it if you would come with me. Will you?
> **R** You can't be serious? You know I'd love to! But why me? Surely you should be taking David?
> **M** Haven't you heard? David and I have split up.
> **R** Oh, I'm sorry! I didn't know. When did this happen?
> **M** Well, a couple of weeks ago. We haven't been getting on well for ages.
> **R** Well, what can I say? How could I possibly refuse an offer like that?
> **M** You'll come then?
> **R** I certainly will.

ADDITIONAL MATERIAL

Workbook Unit 7

Exercises 1-3 Revision of all modals

Exercise 4 Verbs related to modals

Exercise 5 Modal verbs of probability

Exercise 6 *need*

Getting married

The aim here is to improve the students' ability to listen in order to confirm their expectations, and for specific information. The *Spoken English* section also looks at declarative questions and questions ending with the question word.

If you have a multicultural class, you could lead in by asking students to tell the class what is typical or unusual about getting married in their country.

A useful vocabulary lead-in is to teach vocabulary around the topic of marriage. Write the following words on the board, and ask students to check their meaning:

a wedding ceremony an arranged marriage a honeymoon get engaged get married get divorced a chaperone an engagement party bride groom bridesmaid

1   Ask students to look at the photographs of the three weddings. Ask them to describe them.

> **Answers**
> The first photo is of a very traditional 'white' wedding in the UK, with the bride and groom, a bridesmaid, and family members. This is a very posed photo for the wedding album. The second photo is of a traditional Indian wedding, with the bride and groom in traditional wedding clothes. The groom also wears the gifts of money that are customarily given by wedding guests. The third photo shows a 'drive thru' wedding in Las Vegas. The bride and groom are actually wearing traditional formal wedding outfits, but are getting married without getting out of their car!

2   Ask students to discuss good and bad reasons to get married. One fun way of doing this is to divide students into two teams. One team must think of good reasons, and the other team bad reasons. Find out which team has most reasons.

> **SUGGESTED REASONS**
> This will depend on the age and culture of your class. However, here is a list a class might produce.
> *Good reasons*
> love; wanting to start a family; wanting to show commitment to another person; for religious reasons
> *Bad reasons*
> money; to get a visa/citizenship; tax avoidance; unwanted pregnancy; because your parents want you to; to get away from home; to have a good party

3   Look at the picture, and read the introduction as a class. Ask students in pairs to prepare some questions.

4   Read through the questions as a class.
    T7.7 [CD 2: Track 32] Play the recording. Ask students to listen and answer the questions. Tell them not to write while they listen. When the recording has

finished, let them write their answers and check with a partner. You will probably need to play the recording a second time.

> **Answers**
> 1   Students' own answers.
> 2   He asked friends and relatives.
> 3   Their education, their background, and their family's background.
> 4   The first man was very wealthy, well-dressed, and had good manners, but not a good education. The second man was not wealthy, badly-dressed, well-educated, and from a very good background.
> 5   He thought that education was more important than money.
> 6   He hoped her father would refuse him – he didn't want to get married.
> 7   There was a special day when they met each other's families. They phoned every day and met regularly with a chaperone.
> 8   She says, 'Oh yes, I do.' She thinks that the couple entering the marriage don't expect too much.

T7.7 See SB Tapescripts p132

SPOKEN ENGLISH – other question forms

1   Read through the examples and explanation as a class. Ask the questions.

> **Answers**
> What is unusual is that these declarative questions do not have an interrogative form – they are statements with rising intonation at the end.
> **More examples from the tapescript**
> And ... it's been a successful marriage?
> Your father made a good choice?
> And your sons want it?
> But you still believe that the system of arranged marriages is a good one?

Point out the danger for non-native speakers of using these declarative question forms inappropriately, usually because their L1 uses them as a standard question form. Native speakers hearing them might assume that the speaker is expressing surprise (and even disapproval!), e.g. *'You're married?' 'Yes…why shouldn't I be?!'*

2   Read the example and question as a class. Then ask students in pairs to make similar questions. In the feedback, ask students to read and respond across the class.

T7.8 [CD 2: Track 33] Play the recording. You can have fun by encouraging students to exaggerate the fall and rise in intonation on the question word as they repeat the questions on the recording.

What do you think?

Divide students into groups of three or four. Ask them to make a list of advantages and disadvantages of arranged marriages. Ask a spokesperson for each group to present their list to the class.

Advantages
Your partner is an appropriate match according to education, wealth and background
It is easier than finding your own partner
Your parents and family are happy with your choice
Arranged marriages are often successful
The couple enter the marriage not expecting too much

Disadvantages
You marry someone you don't know – you might not like them
It isn't a marriage for love
You take away the right to make an individual choice
It contravenes western ideas of individual liberty and women's rights
It is often difficult to get out of a loveless or unsuccessful marriage

Encourage a class discussion about whether arranged marriages are a good idea. Ask students what other ways people meet their marriage partners. You could personalize this by asking the students how their parents met.

ALTERNATIVE IDEA
Speaking roles
Speaking roles is an alternative way of doing this speaking activity. Divide students into groups of four to six. Photocopy and cut out the cards on p158 of the Teacher's Book. Hand out a different card to each student in the group. When they speak in groups, they must play the role on the card.
It is a good idea to laminate the cards, or stick them on cardboard, for later use. *Speaking roles* work well with group discussions and problem-solving activities.
This idea is based in part on *Six Thinking Hats*, which was originally developed by the psychologist, Edward de Bono.

Writing Unit 7
Arguing your case – For and against SB p118

Meet the *Kippers*

This is a jigsaw reading activity. The aim is to improve the students' ability to read for specific information, and to exchange information.

A useful vocabulary lead-in is to teach expressions used to describe relationships between people. Write the following phrases on the board, and ask students which ones describe a positive relationship. Ask students to tell you about a friend or family member using some of the phrases.

I get on well with…   *I have a lot in common with…*
…gets on my nerves.   *I keep in touch with…*
I've fallen out with…

1 Lead in by asking the questions. Then divide the students into two groups to make the lists. When they are ready, ask a spokesperson from each group to present their lists.

CULTURAL NOTE
In Britain young people generally leave home between 18 and 25, and it has long been considered a sign of immaturity to continue living at home after the age of 21. However, rising house prices and the rise of the *Kipper* culture, has meant that there has been a recent tendency for young people to stay at home longer. Because this is a change in traditional patterns of behaviour, it is a topical issue in Britain. Your students may find nothing strange in the idea of young people living at home in their late twenties and early thirties, but the fact that it is considered an issue in other cultures can still lead to thought-provoking discussion.

Group B: a list from the parents' point of view

For:
Want to be free of children so they can be independent
Don't want financial burden of children anymore
Don't want to be cleaning and tidying up after kids
Don't want noise of children and their friends
Don't want arguments
Want to rent out 'spare' room or make it an office
Eating into retirement or dream holiday savings

Against:
Will miss having the children around
Will worry that they are all right
Will cost more money to help them to buy or rent houses than it will to keep them at home
Want kids to do well – studying or working – and home provides a better environment than an uncomfortable flat
Worried about feeling lonely or old
Worried about losing touch

2   Ask students to read the introductory text, then discuss the questions briefly as a class.

Answers
1   They are young people who refuse to leave home.
2   Kippers is an acronym: 'Kids in Parents' Pockets Eroding Retirement Savings'.
3   It means gradually using up all the money you have saved to spend on your retirement. *Erode* means 'gradually wear away, e.g. the surface of rock by the weather or sea'. Here, it is used metaphorically.
4   Leave home. A metaphor from what young birds do when they are grown.

3   Divide the students into two groups. Ask Group A to read about *Vicki* and Group B to read about *Martin*. Ask them to answer the questions and compare their answers with people in their group. Then put students with a partner from the other group to share their information.

> **HOW TO DO A JIGSAW READING**
> See TB p67

Answers
Group A: Vicki
1   She lives with her dad. They get on very well.
2   Because she wouldn't be able to afford such a beautiful house. She has her father for company and money for a social life.
3   Only for three months when she went travelling in her early twenties.
4   **Advantages**: living in a beautiful house; father for company; money for a social life; father spoils her – meals out; doesn't pay rent
     Disadvantages: none really
5   Her friends say she is living in a bubble away from the real world.

Group B: Martin
1   His mum and dad, Kathy and Robert Gibbs. They get on really well – but his parents get on his nerves when they tell him what to do.
2   Because he's spoiled, and because he got into debt and doesn't have to pay rent. It's a lovely, cosy place.
3   Yes. He moved out for two years when he was 23.
4   **Advantages**: spoiled; no rent so spends his money on enjoying himself; lovely, cosy place to bring girls back to.
     Disadvantages: parents sometimes get on his nerves; gets called 'a mummy's boy.'
5   Girls say he's a 'mummy's boy.'

4   Ask students in groups or pairs to read both texts by parents of Kippers. Ask them to answer the questions and compare the parents' views.

Answers
1   Bill is happy because family is more important than money, and it helps him postpone getting old. Sandra is unhappy because her son is expensive to keep.
2   Sandra. 'I'm at my wits' end' means *I've had enough of a difficult situation but I don't know what to do to change it.*
3   Bill says he would forfeit (give up) foreign travel for the sake of his family. Sandra is angry that her dream cruise is now merely a dream because she has had to spend so much on her son.
4   Bill says money isn't everything. Sandra says that her son accumulated £4000 in debt, that he couldn't and wouldn't pay rent, but he's always got money to go out.

Vocabulary work

Ask students to complete the sentences and decide who they refer to, then discuss their answers with a partner or in groups before feedback.

Answers
1   rent (Vicki)
2   afford/off/debt (Martin)
3   strapped/cash/high (Vicki)
4   contributes/bill (Vicki)
5   charge/rent (Sandra)
6   accumulated (Alan)
7   off (Alan)
8   spend/salary (Martin)
9   money/everything (Bill)
strapped for cash (informal) = short of money
sponge off [his mother] (informal and negative) = constantly using his mother's things for free

What do you think?

The aim here is to use the text as a springboard for speaking.

Divide students into small groups to discuss the questions about the text. Make one member of each group the 'chairperson'. They have to ask the questions and make sure everybody in the group has a turn to express their view. At the end, the chairperson must summarize their group's discussion briefly for the class.

VOCABULARY AND SPEAKING (SB p68)

Hot verb *get*

This section looks at the hot verb *get*, a very common verb, often used in expressions and phrasal verbs.

1   Read through the introduction and examples as a class. Then ask students in pairs to match the examples with the expressions.

> **Answers**
> 1 have a good relationship
> 2 understand
> 3 annoy/irritate me
> 4 growing
> 5 become
> 6 contacting
> 7 buy
> 8 has

Talking about you

2   Ask students in pairs to ask and answer the questions. Alternatively, this would work well as a mingle. Ask students to walk round the class, interviewing as many people as they can in the time limit you set.

Then ask students in pairs to rewrite the sentences.

> **Answers**
> 1 Do you have a good relationship with your parents?
> 2 What do you have to do when you get home tonight?
> 3 How do you go/travel to school?
> 4 What time do you usually arrive at school?
> 5 How many TV channels can you receive?
> 6 When did you last become angry?
> 7 Do you have a pet/PC?
> 8 How often do you have your hair cut?
> 9 In what ways is your English improving?
> 10 What are two things that always annoy you?
> *Get* is generally more informal.

> **EXTENSION**
> Ask students to write their own personalized questions for the class. Tell them to work in pairs to write six questions, each using a different meaning of *get*. When they are ready, ask them to walk round the class and ask at least three people the questions they have prepared.

Phrasal verbs with *get*

3   Do the first as an example. Then ask students in pairs to complete the sentences.

> **Answers**
> 1 You always get **out** of... (avoid)
>   How did our secret get **out**? (become known)
>   I got a great book **out** of the library... (borrowed)
> 2 You're always getting **at** me? (criticizing)
>   What are you getting **at**? (trying to say)
>   I can't get **at** the sugar. (reach)
> 3 It took me ages to get **over** the operation. (recover from)
>   He couldn't get his point **over** to me at first. (communicate/express clearly)
>   I can't get **over** how much... (used for saying how endlessly surprised you are)
> 4 That boy is always getting **up** to something naughty! (doing)
>   We got **up** to page 56... (reached)
>   I had to get **up** at 5 a.m. (get out of bed)
> 5 I couldn't get **through** to Joe... (connect by phone)
>   We got **through** loads of money... (spent)
>   I failed, but Sue got **through** the exam... (passed)
> 6 She can always get **round** her father... (persuade/manipulate)
>   I'm sorry. I just haven't got **round** to replying... (found the time to)
>   I can't see how we can get **round** this problem. (deal with successfully, by avoiding)

> **EXTENSION**
> Ask students to close their books. Write the particles at random on the board. Divide the class into three or four groups, depending on the size of your class. Tell group 1 that they can win a point by producing a sentence, using *get* and one of particles. If it is correct, they win a point. Then move on to group 2. Go from group to group, asking them for a sentence. The sentence must be correct, and the verb and particle must have a different meaning from any used earlier. Keep going until the students can't produce any more sentences.

Exaggeration and understatement

The aim of this section is to practise ways of exaggerating or understating what you say.

1 Lead in by asking students the questions.

Answers
Students' own suggestions. However, Italians, Spanish, and Latin Americans are generally seen as passionate, spontaneous, and temperamental. English, Nordic nations, and Japanese are well-known for being more controlled and reserved.

2 Ask students in pairs to categorize the 'declarations'.

Answers
Exaggerated:
I adore you and can't live without you.
I'm absolutely crazy about you.
I worship the ground you walk on.
Understated:
I'm really rather fond of you.
We get on pretty well, don't you think?

3 Ask students in pairs to match lines in **A** with lines in **B**.

4 **T7.9** [CD 2: Track 34] Play the recording. Students listen and check their answers. Examples of exaggeration are in bold. Examples of understatement are in italics.

Answers and tapescript
1c **A** **I'm absolutely dying for** a drink.
   B Yes, my throat's *a bit dry*, I must say.
2i **A** His family *are pretty well off*, aren't they?
   B You can say that again! They**'re absolutely loaded**!
3h **A** You must have **hit the roof** when she told you she'd crashed your car.
   B Well, yes, I was *a bit upset*.
4d **A** I think Tony was *a bit rude* last night.
   B Too right! He **was totally out of order**!
5j **A** **I can't stand the sight of him**!
   B I must admit, *I'm not too keen on* him, either.
6b **A** He *isn't very bright*, is he?
   B You're not kidding. He's **as thick as two short planks**.
7e **A** I'm fed up with this weather! It**'s freezing**.
   B I suppose it *is a bit chilly*.
8a **A** Well, that was a **fantastic** holiday!
   B Yes, it was *a nice little break*, but all good things must come to an end.
9g **A** **I'm knackered**. Can we stop for a rest?
   B OK. I feel *a bit out of breath*, too.
10f **A** They're obviously **madly in love**.
   B Yeah, they do seem to *get on quite well*.

Read through the *Music of English* box with the class.
T 7.10 [CD 2: Track 35]Play the recording. Ask students to listen and repeat the example sentences.

Point out that this use of *a bit* for understatement is useful when complaining to native speakers, who find the directness of non-native speakers slightly shocking! If you complain to a native speaker, e.g. a teacher, and say '*This text is boring*', he/she will assume you are being rude, and feel hostile towards you. However, if you add *a bit* and say '*This text is a bit boring*', the native speaker will be open to answering the comment as friendly criticism ('*Yes, it is a bit boring, I agree, but it's got some really useful vocabulary in it, and it's good practice for the exam*'). Native speakers use this form of understated complaint to avoid hostility, and if students wish to have complaints dealt with sympathetically, they should do the same!

Ask students in pairs to practise the conversations, paying attention to their intonation.

5 Ask students in pairs to read the statements and give exaggerated replies. Do the first one or two with reliable students to get students started. Go round monitoring, insisting on good intonation patterns.

T7.11 [CD 2: Track 36] Play the recording. Ask students to listen and compare.

Tapescript
1 **A** Is that a new watch? I bet that cost a bit.
   B A bit!? It cost a fortune!
2 **A** It's a bit chilly in here, don't you think?
   B You can say that again! I'm absolutely freezing!
3 **A** These shoes are rather nice, aren't they?
   B They're *gorgeous*! I want them!
4 **A** Can we stop at the next service station? I could do with something to eat.
   B Me too. I'm starving! I didn't have breakfast this morning.
5 **A** I think those two like each other, don't you?
   B *Like*'s the wrong word. They're obviously crazy about each other.
6 **A** I bet you were a bit upset when your team lost.
   B Me? Upset? I only cried myself to sleep!

SONG **After T 7.11** [CD 2: Track 37]
Fast Car TB p159

ADDITIONAL MATERIAL

Workbook Unit 7
Exercise 7 Vocabulary
Exercise 8 Phrasal verbs
Exercise 9 Listening – Not getting on
Exercise 10–11 Pronunciation and Sentence stress – Consonant clusters

8 Relative clauses • Participles
Adverb collocations
The world around

Going to extremes

Introduction to the unit

The theme of this unit is extreme experiences and extreme places. The expression in the title of the unit, *going to extremes*, is generally used negatively to describe doing something much more than is reasonable.

The main grammatical focus of the unit is relative clauses and participles, and these are contextualized in a reading text about the 'extreme' lifestyle of film star John Travolta, who flies his own jets.

The main reading text is about Chukotka, a remote territory in Russia, which is the coldest place on earth. In the main listening text, two people describe their extreme experiences of heat and cold.

Language aims

Relative clauses   The aim is to revise and practise relative clauses and participles, two grammatical ways of forming complex sentences.

> **POSSIBLE PROBLEMS**
> **Defining and non-defining?**
> A defining relative clause is essential to the meaning of a sentence:
> *The people who live across the road are friendly.*
> If you remove the relative clause, leaving *The people are friendly*, then the meaning of the sentence is changed or unclear. (*Which people? All people?*)
> In contrast, a non-defining relative clause adds extra, non-essential information.
> *My next-door neighbour, who has a nice car, is friendly.*
> If you remove the relative clause, leaving *My next-door neighbour is friendly*, then the meaning of the sentence is still perfectly clear.
> Non-defining relative clauses are mainly a feature of written English. The clause is contained within commas, which affect pronunciation when the clause is spoken, because the speaker pauses before and after it.
> A common error is to define a noun which is already completely identified. For example:
> *~~My best friend who lives abroad is coming over next week.~~
> Students think the clause here is defining the friend, but it isn't (the word *best* has already told us which friend it is), it's just adding information, and should be *My best friend, who…* . Compare *the man who…* (needs defining) with *my brother, who…* (we already know who you're talking about).
> **Who or which?**
> English uses *who* for people, *which* for objects, but other languages use the same pronoun for both, changing the form depending on the gender of the noun. Watch out for errors such as *the people which…*
> Students often avoid omitting the pronoun when it defines the object of the clause, which results in unnatural (though not grammatically wrong) use. Watch out for *the place which I went to…* .
> Students get confused by the complexity of the sentence, inserting subject pronouns when the relative pronoun already expresses the subject.
> *~~The teacher who he helped me…~~

Participles Present and past participles can be used as adjectives (*a boring man/an exhausted athlete*). Present participles describe actions still happening. Past participles describe actions that have happened. They are both used as reduced relative clauses (*There was a man (who was) selling newspapers*), and in adverb clauses (*He woke up feeling ill*).

The subject of the main verb clause and the participle clause must be the same:
The house stood at the end of the road. It appeared large and friendly.
Standing at the end of the road, the house appeared large and friendly.

If the subject of the two clauses are different, then they must both be used with main verbs:
I looked through the window. The house appeared large and friendly.

If a participle clause were used here, then it would mean that *the house* was looking through the window!
~~Looking through the window, the house appeared large and friendly.~~

Vocabulary The vocabulary section looks at adverb collocations. It introduces extreme adjectives that collocate with *absolutely*, and it looks at the different meanings of *quite*.

Everyday English This section introduces and practises dialogues in shops and places providing other services.

Notes on the unit

TEST YOUR GRAMMAR (SB p70)

The *Test your grammar* section aims to test the students' ability to use relative pronouns, and to recognize past and present participles.

This exercise should be done quickly. Don't get involved in lengthy grammar explanations at this stage.

1 Ask students to complete the sentences with the correct relative pronoun. Let them check in pairs before feedback.

> **Answers**
> 1 The man **who** you met was my brother.
> 2 My older brother, **who** lives in London, is a teacher.
> 3 He suddenly decided to give up teaching, **which** came as a bit of a shock.
> 4 He says that **what** he wants to do is move to Australia.
> 5 His girlfriend, **whose** parents live in Melbourne, is delighted.
> 6 They don't know exactly **where** or **when** they are going.
> 7 Their flat, **which** they bought only last year, is up for sale.
> 8 The flat **which** I want to buy is in Acacia Avenue.

2 Ask students the question.

> **Answers**
> *That* can replace the relative pronoun in sentences 1 and 8. It can replace *who* or *which* in defining relative clauses. (Note that the pronoun can also be completely omitted in these sentences because they are object pronouns.)

> Note that *what* means *the thing that* and cannot be replaced by *that*. Students often make an error here, (for example, *~~Everything what she said was funny~~*), because in many languages *what* and *that* are the same word.

3 Ask students to underline the participles and replace them with relative pronouns.

> **Answers**
> 1 The woman <u>standing</u> next to him is his wife.
>   The woman who is standing...
> 2 Most houses <u>built</u> in the sixteenth century are listed buildings.
>   Most houses which were built...

PILOT SUPERSTAR (SB p70)

Relative clauses and participles

This section contextualizes and practises relative clauses and participles. The practice activities focus on recognizing when a relative clause is defining or non-defining, and on forming long, complex sentences using relative clauses and participles.

1 Lead in by asking students what they know about John Travolta. Ask students to read the text quickly and answer the gist questions.

> **Answers**
> We learn that Travolta lives in Jumbolair, Florida, where he keeps a row of aeroplanes. His house looks like an airport terminal. He also has a heliport, swimming pool, stables and runway. He is a family man. His passion is flying planes. He has a commercial pilot's licence.

> **BIOGRAPHICAL INFORMATION**
> John Travolta (1954 –)
> An actor and dancer, Travolta became famous in the films *Saturday Night Fever* (1977) and *Grease* (1978). His career was less successful in the 1980s, but he had great success in the 1990s, notably in *Pulp Fiction* (1994) and *Get Shorty* (1995). In the mid 1990s he was Hollywood's highest paid actor. He is married to actress Kelly Preston.

2 Ask students to read the text again and complete it with the clauses a-j. Let them check in pairs.

T8.1 [CD 2: Track 38] Play the recording. Students listen and check their answers.

> **Answers and tapescript**
> Welcome to JUMBOLAIR, Florida – the world's only housing estate (1d) **where the super-rich can commute** to work by jet plane from their own front doors. Jumbolair's most famous resident is Hollywood film star John Travolta, (2f) **whose $3.5 million mansion** is big enough to park a row of aeroplanes, (3e) **including a Gulfstream executive jet**, a two-seater jet fighter, and a four-engined Boeing 707, (4i) **previously owned by Frank Sinatra**. Travolta holds a commercial pilot's licence, (5h) **which means** he is qualified to fly passenger jets. He can land his planes and taxi them up to his front gates. His sumptuous Florida home, (6a) **which is built** in the style of an airport terminal building, is the ultimate boys' fantasy house made real. As well as the parking lots for the jets, there is a heliport, swimming pool and gym, stables for 75 horses, and of course a 1.4-mile runway. Family man Travolta, (7b) **who lives** with wife Kelly, daughter Ella Bleu, and aptly named son Jett, flies daily from his home when filming. (8g) **Walking out of his door** and into the cockpit, he is airborne in minutes. His neighbours, (9j) **most of whom share** his love of aviation, don't seem to mind the roar of his jets. They say that it's nice to meet a superstar (10c) **who isn't full of his own importance**. 'He's just a regular guy, very friendly', says one neighbour.

3 Ask students to discuss the questions in pairs. Then have a class feedback.

> **Answers**
> 1 Super-rich people who like flying planes.
> 2 More than three. (*including...* implies more than three)
> 3 Frank Sinatra.
> 4 It's a $3.5 million mansion, built in the style of an airport terminal building.
> 5 Because boys like the idea of flying a plane, and that's exactly what Travolta's house allows him to do.
> 6 His name is Jett. It is 'apt' (appropriate) because his father loves jet engines.
> 7 Because they share his love of aviation.
> 8 No. He's a regular, friendly family man. However, he does fly jet planes and live in a mansion, which is very Hollywood.

LANGUAGE FOCUS

See TB p8 for suggestions on how to teach this section.

Don't forget to look at the *Language aims* section on TB p81, which looks at problems students may have. You should also read the Grammar Reference on SB pp149–150.

Relative clauses

Read the explanation as a class.

1 Ask students in pairs to read the sentences aloud and underline the relative clauses.

> **Answers** (the speaker should pause at the commas)
> I met a man <u>who's a pilot</u>.
> My friend Adam, <u>who lives in London</u>, is a pilot.
> The house <u>which you walked past</u> is my aunt's.
> My aunt's house, <u>which I don't like</u>, is very modern.

2 Ask students to discuss in pairs. Then have a whole class feedback.

> **Answers**
> The (underlined) relative clauses in *I met a man <u>who's a pilot</u>* and *The house <u>which you walked past</u> is my aunt's* tell us exactly who or what is being talked about. They are defining relative clauses.
> *My friend Adam, <u>who lives in London</u>, is a pilot* and *My aunt's house, <u>which I don't like</u>, is very modern* give us an extra piece of information. They are non-defining relative clauses.
> We use commas in non-defining relative clauses. They go before and after the relative clause showing that it isn't an essential part of the sentence. The speaker pauses at the commas.

3 Discuss the question as a class.

> **Answers**
> The relative pronoun can be omitted from *The house which you walked past is my aunt's*. This is because the relative pronoun can be omitted from a defining relative clause when it replaces the object of the sentence. In speech, the sentence sounds more natural if the pronoun is omitted: *The house you walked past is my aunt's*.

Present and past participles

Ask students in pairs to underline the participles and discuss the questions.

> **Answers**
> Who is that <u>boring</u> man <u>standing</u> at the bar?
> The curtains and carpets <u>included</u> in the sale were old and <u>worn</u>.
> They own four houses, <u>including</u> a <u>ruined</u> castle in Scotland.
> <u>Having</u> lost all his money, he was a <u>broken</u> man.
> *boring, worn, ruined* and *broken* are adjectives
> *boring, standing, including* and *having* are present participles
> *included, worn, ruined* and *broken* are past participles

Refer students to the Grammar Reference on SB pp149–150.

Pronunciation and punctuation

1 Do the first two as examples, then ask students in pairs to read aloud and write in the punctuation. Go round monitoring and prompting.

T8.2 [CD 2: Track 39] Play the recording so that students can compare their answers. Ask students to listen and repeat.

Answers and tapescript
1 The area of London I like best is Soho.
2 My father, who's a doctor, plays the drums.
3 The book that I'm reading at the moment is fascinating.
4 Paul passed his driving test first time, which surprised everybody.
5 People who smoke risk getting all sorts of illnesses.
6 I met a man whose main aim in life was to visit every capital city in the world.
7 The Channel Tunnel, which opened in 1995, is a great way to get from England to France.
8 What I like best about work is the holidays.
9 A short bald man, seen running away from the scene of the crime, is being sought by the police.

Discussing grammar

2 Do the first two as a class. Then ask students in pairs to discuss and decide on the rest.

Answers
2, 3, 5, 7, 8 need more information.

3 Ask students in pairs to rewrite the sentences. Do the first as an example.

Answers
1 The apple tree in our garden, which my grandfather planted sixty years ago, needs to be cut down.
2 People who do regular exercise live longer.
3 She married a man she met on holiday in Turkey.
4 The Great Barrier Reef, which is situated off the north-east coast of Australia, is the largest coral reef in the world.
5 Did I show you the photographs we took in Barbados?
6 Let me introduce you to Petra James, who works in our Paris office.
7 I'm looking for a book which practises German grammar.
8 I was speaking to someone you know.

Depress -ed or *depress -ing*?

4 Ask students in pairs to match the adjectives and topics. Naturally, there are no definitive answers here – just likely ones.

Answers

A	B
1 exam results	disappointing/disappointed
2 a holiday	relaxing/relaxed
3 gossip	shocking/shocked
4 a journey	exhausting/exhausted
5 a job	challenging/challenged
6 a hard luck story	amusing/amused
7 a TV documentary	boring/bored
8 a social situation	embarrassing/embarrassed

GRAMMAR NOTE
Remind students of the grammar rule for using -*ing* and -*ed* adjectives. Basically we use -*ing* to describe the situation.
The weather is depressing.
We use -*ed* to describe how you feel about it.
It's raining! I'm depressed/I feel depressed.

T8.3 [CD 2: Track 40] Play the recording. Ask students to listen and describe the situation, using -*ing* and -*ed* adjectives.

Sample answers and tapescript
1 She is/feels disappointed./The exam results are disappointing.
2 She feels relaxed./The holiday was relaxing.
3 She is shocked./It's shocking that Doug and Maggie behaved in this way.
4 She feels exhausted./The journey was exhausting.
5 She feels challenged by having to deal with so many new things./The job is challenging.
6 She was amused by the funny story./The story was amusing.
7 She is bored because there is nothing on TV./The documentary looks boring.
8 She feels embarrassed./It's embarrassing that she thought the woman was pregnant.

T8.3
1 A How did you do in the maths test?
  B Oh! Don't ask! It's too awful.
  A Oh, dear. What did you get?
  B Twenty-two per cent. I came last and I thought I was going to do really well.
2 A How was your holiday?
  B Great, thanks. Just what we needed.
  A Did you do much?
  B Not a lot. We just sat by the pool, read books, and took it easy for two whole weeks. Absolute bliss.
3 A Have you heard about Dave and Maggie?
  B No. Tell me, tell me!
  A Well, last week they went to a party, had this huge row in front of all these people and … .
  B Did it get physical?

A Oh yeah! Maggie shoved Dave into a flowerpot, told him to get lost and went off with another bloke!

B What! I'm amazed! I just can't believe Maggie'd do such a thing. It doesn't sound like her at all.

4 **A** Come on in. You must be shattered!

B Oof, I am. I've been travelling for the past thirty hours and I haven't slept a wink.

A I know – I can never sleep on a plane, either. Just sit down, take it easy and I'll get you a drink.

5 **A** How's the new job going?

B Good, thanks, very good – but it's quite difficult. I'm having to deal with so many new things. Still, I'm enjoying it all.

A Mmm – I know what you mean.

B It's great to be doing something that's so satisfying, and meeting so many people from abroad.

A Absolutely.

6 **A** So, anyway, just to end the perfect evening, I had to walk back home because I'd lost the car keys and I didn't have any money for a taxi. I didn't get home until three in the morning.

B That's the funniest thing I've heard for ages. Poor you. Oh, sorry I'm laughing.

A Well, I'm glad you think it's so funny – I didn't think it funny at the time.

7 **A** There is just nothing good on TV tonight!

B What about that wildlife programme?

A D'you mean the one about the life of frogs?

B Yeah – does it look any good?

A You're kidding. It looks absolute rubbish.

8 **A** What's the matter with you?

B Oh my gosh – I've just put my foot right in it.

A What d'you mean?

B Well, I was talking to that lady over there and I asked her when her baby was due, and ... er ... she told me she wasn't pregnant.

A Oh, no! That's awful!

5 Ask students to complete the sentences with the correct participle. Let students check in pairs before feedback.

Answers

1 I hurt my leg **playing** football.
  Bridge is a card game **played** by four people.
2 It says *Made in Korea* on my camera.
  I have a job in a café **making** sandwiches.
3 I've spent the whole morning **writing** an essay.
  On the wall was some graffiti **written** in big letters.
4 Goods **bought** in the sales cannot be refunded.
  I've spent all my money **buying** Christmas presents.
5 The police caught the burglar **breaking** into a house.
  Careful! There's a lot of **broken** glass on the floor.

Making descriptions longer

The activities in this section should provide lots of speaking practice as well as practising participles.

6 Ask students in pairs to make a long sentence. Give them time to discuss and try out various alternatives before reading out their sentence for the class.

T8.4 [CD 2: Track 41] Play the recording. Students listen and check their answers.

Answers and tapescript

Lost in her thoughts, a beautiful, young woman was sitting in her country garden, watching a bee lazily going from rose to rose gathering honey.

7 Ask students in pairs to make longer sentences. Go round monitoring and helping. Give them time to discuss and try out various alternatives before reading out their sentences for the class.

ALTERNATIVE IDEA

An alternative idea is to give each pair of students in your class one of these sentences at the top of a sheet of paper. They must copy the sentence, adding an adjective, adverb or participle or relative clause. Then they pass it on to another pair who must add something to the previous pair's sentence before passing it to another pair.

T8.5 [CD 2: Track 42] Play the recording. Ask students to listen and compare their answers.

Answers and tapescript

1 Exhausted after a hard day's work, a balding, middle-aged man wearing a crumpled suit, and carrying a briefcase, walked slowly along the road that led from the station to his home, pausing only to look up at the night sky.
2 Peter, who's very wealthy, has a huge, sixteenth century farmhouse, surrounded by woods in the heart of the Devon countryside.
3 Ann Croft, the world famous actress, who married for the sixth time only last month, was seen having an intimate lunch in a London restaurant with a man who was definitely not her husband.
4 The two-week holiday in Mauritius, which we had looked forward to so much, was a complete and utter disaster from start to finish.
5 A ten-year-old boy, walking home from school, found an old, battered, leather wallet filled with £5,000 in £50 notes in the High Street.

8 Bring some magazines into class, and ask students to flick through and find an interesting picture to describe. Give them a minute or two to think of ways of describing the picture, using participles. Then ask them to describe the picture so that their partner can draw it.

EXTRA IDEA

Pictures of two scenes are provided on p160 of the Teacher's Book. Photocopy these pictures, and use them to practise the language of the lesson.

1 Hand out the pictures so that students in each pair have a different picture. Ask the students to take it in turns to describe the picture to their partner. Their partner must try to draw it.

2 Ask students to prepare a story based on their picture, using language from the lesson. For example, *A woman was sitting in a café, dressed in summer clothes, drinking coffee when…*You could ask students to work in pairs in class to think of a short story, then tell it to the class. Or you could ask students to write their story for homework.

ADDITIONAL MATERIAL

Workbook Unit 8

Exercises 1-5 Defining and non-defining relative clauses

Exercises 6-7 Participles

Exercise 8 Revision of relatives and participles

LISTENING AND SPEAKING (SB p73)

Extreme experiences

The aim here is to improve the students' ability to listen in order to confirm their expectations and for specific information. It also looks at how we add a comment with *which* as an afterthought.

1 Lead in by asking students to describe their coldest, hottest or wettest experiences to the class.

EXTENSION

A useful vocabulary area to focus on is 'hot' and 'cold'. Write the following words on the board, and ask students to tell you which ones are connected with 'hot' and which ones with 'cold'.

stuffy bitter frozen sweating boiling arctic
icy scorching freezing heat exhaustion below zero

Answers

hot

stuffy = when there isn't enough air in a room
sweating = producing drops of liquid on the skin because it's hot
boiling = extremely hot (as if the temperature was high enough to make water boil)

scorching = extremely hot (in the sun)
heat exhaustion = a medical condition resulting from being in the heat for too long
cold
bitter = when the air is biting cold
frozen = literally turned to ice, but used to mean 'very cold'
arctic = meaning that the weather is similar to that at the North Pole
icy = when water had turned to ice
freezing = similar to 'frozen'
below zero = used to describe freezing temperatures

2 Ask students in pairs to predict the experiences from the words in the box. You will need to check the words first, particularly *nostrils*, (the two holes in your nose that you breathe through) and *rehydration salts* (tablets or powder that you need to take when you've lost a lot of water in hot weather).

Ask a couple of pairs to briefly tell the class what they predict the two stories will be.

3 **T8.6** [CD 2: Track 43] Play the recording. Ask students to listen to Simone's story and answer the questions.

Answers

1 Cairo.
2 Between 40 and 45 degrees centigrade.
3 She decided to go dancing, danced for hours, and got dehydrated.
4 Taxi and motorbike.
5 The Pyramids – she wanted to see the sunrise.
6 The sun was just starting to come up.
7 A man in a village with a motorbike. He lent/hired out his motorbike to them.
8 She became dehydrated, lost energy, then, back home, felt strange. She had a headache. She felt confused, sick, nauseous. Her brain didn't work properly. She was suffering from heat exhaustion.
9 She learnt a lesson on how to behave in such high temperatures. She always carries rehydration salts now.

T8.6 See SB Tapescripts p133

4 Ask students in pairs to predict what the answers to the questions might be in Anna's story. Let students check in pairs before feedback.

5 **T8.7** [CD 2: Track 44] Play the recording. Ask students to listen to Anna's story and answer the questions in exercise 3. Let students check in pairs before feedback.

Answers

1 In a small town in central Russia.
2 −30° or colder.
3 She wanted to be independent so she told her friends she could find their house – no problem. She should have let her friends meet her at the tram stop.
4 Tram.
5 To see some friends.
6 Huge snow-covered white blocks, fifteen or sixteen floors high.
7 An old lady. She wasn't helpful.
8 Her feet and hands were beyond hurting – she couldn't feel them. It was difficult to breathe.
9 Her friends came to find her and took her home.

T8.7 See SB Tapescripts p134

Language work

6 Ask students in pairs to complete the sentences. Let them check their answers by looking at the tapescript on p134 of the Student's Book.

Answers

1 It was **extremely** hot and **stupidly** we decided to go dancing.
2 We were sweating **profusely**. (= very much)
3 The temperature rises **dramatically**.
4 My brain wasn't working **properly**. (= correctly)
5 It was **completely** anonymous this landscape.
6 They all looked **exactly** the same.
7 I was beginning to **really**, **seriously** panic.

SPOKEN ENGLISH – Adding a comment

Read through the explanation as a class.

1 Ask students in pairs to match the comments.

T8.8 [CD 2: Track 45] Play the recording. Students listen and check their answers. Then ask them to practise saying the comments. Remind students that there is a pause at the comma.

Answers and tapescript

1 We went dancing in temperatures of over 40°C, which was rather a stupid thing to do.
2 My friends were worried I'd get lost, which was understandable.
3 We visited the pyramids at sunrise, which was just amazing.
4 My nostrils actually froze, which is hard to believe.
5 This motorbike broke down in the desert, which was no laughing matter.
6 The old lady didn't understand a word I said, which is hardly surprising because my Russian's lousy.

2 Ask students to write their own sentences, ending with comments from **B**. Nominate various students to tell the class what they have written.

READING AND SPEAKING (SB p74)

Chukotka, the coldest place on earth

The aim is to improve the students' ability to read for specific information.

1 Lead in by asking students to look at the pictures and asking the question. Let students speculate. It doesn't matter if they don't know the correct answer.

Answers

Roman Abramovich, a Russian oil billionaire 'oligarch', is governor of the Russian province in the photos – Chukotka, and owner of Chelsea Football Club.

2 Ask students to read the facts and discuss them with a partner. Have a brief class discussion. However, the aim here is to predict the text, so don't explain why at this stage.

Answers

Surprising facts are that the capital is a boom town and that one of the world's richest men lives there. Students will probably predict that the two are connected, or suspect major mineral reserves such as oil or gold. The fact that there's no crime may be surprising – but then it is very cold.

3 Ask students to read the text quickly to find the information. Let them check in pairs, then share their information with the class.

Answers

1 *Where yesterday collides with today*
Refers to the fact that Chukotka lies right behind the International dateline – nowhere on earth is earlier than Chukotka.
From hospitals and cinemas to supermarkets
Refers to what Abramovich has done for Anadyr – he has built hospitals, cinemas, supermarkets.
−42°C and falling
Refers to the temperature in Chukotka – last winter the wind chill took the recorded temperature of −42°C down to −100°C.
From reindeer meat to French camembert
Refers to what Abramovich has done for the region. Before he came, people ate reindeer meat. Now, they have luxury products in the supermarket, like camembert.
Why doesn't anyone believe I find this place interesting?
Refers to people's suspicions of Abramovich's motives for his involvement in Chukotka.
2 *The people don't use fridges or freezers.* They hang their meat outside in plastic bags.
There's no crime. It's just 'too damn cold'.
It is a remote territory of Russia. It covers 284,000 square miles of frozen landscape, bordering the Bering Strait and straddling the Arctic Circle.

Its capital, Anadyr, is a boom town. (Abramovich) has spent $300 million and rebuilt the hospital, dental clinic, primary school, modernized the airport, opened a supermarket and cinema. The supermarket is full of luxury goods.

It's too cold to play football. Too cold for outdoor sports.

One of the world's richest men lives there. Abramovich has built a Canadian-style wooden house and visits monthly.

The only flowers are the plastic ones. There are no gardens or woodland. The plastic flowers are on restaurant tables.

4 Ask students to read the article again and answer the questions. Let them check in pairs before feedback.

Answers
1 It covers 284,000 square miles of frozen landscape, bordering the Bering Strait and straddling the Arctic Circle.
2 It's extremely cold. It's the coldest place on earth, with eight week Springs and Summers, and frozen seas. Last winter the wind chill took the recorded temperature of −42°C down to −100°C. Perhaps the weirdest fact is that the wind is so strong that people have to hold onto ropes in the streets to stop themselves being blown away!
3 The people don't use fridges or freezers. They hang their meat outside in plastic bags. They drink vodka. There's no crime – it's just 'too damn cold'. They have ropes in the streets so they don't blow away. Schools are closed in extreme weather. They can't play outdoor sports, and there's no café society.
4 Abramovich is governor of Chukotka and owner of Chelsea Football Club.
5 Abramovich has spent $300 million and rebuilt the hospital, dental clinic, primary school, modernized the airport, and opened a supermarket and cinema. He's also sent children on holiday. The supermarket is full of luxury goods, so people eat differently.
6 Why Abramovich chose them and spends time there.
7 Chelsea Football Club, his Boeing 767, and his homes all over the world in expensive places.
8 Because it is interesting and he wants to change things. People suspect he is interested in the oil, gas, and gold.

What do you think?

The aim here is to use the text as a springboard for speaking.

Divide students into small groups to discuss the questions about the text. Make one member of each group the 'chairperson'. They have to ask the questions and make sure everybody in the group has a turn to express their view. At the end, the chairperson must summarize their group's discussion briefly for the class.

VOCABULARY AND PRONUNCIATION (SB p76)

Adverb collocations

This section looks at extreme adjectives that collocate with *absolutely*, and at the different meanings of *quite*.

Extreme adjectives

1 Ask students in pairs to match words with similar meanings. Then ask them to match the adjectives with *very* or *absolutely*.

GRAMMAR NOTE
Remind students that *very* goes with gradable adjectives like *good*, *bad* and *beautiful*. *Absolutely* goes with extreme adjectives like *marvellous* and *fascinating*.

Answers

VERY	ABSOLUTELY
good	excellent/marvellous/ fabulous/wonderful
bad	awful
nice	fantastic
wet	soaking
clever	brilliant
excited	thrilled
surprised	amazed
valuable	priceless
small	tiny
silly	ridiculous
funny	hilarious
interesting	fascinating
pleased	delighted/thrilled
big	huge/enormous
beautiful	gorgeous

2 Ask students in pairs to complete the conversations. Then ask the students to practise them in pairs.

3 **T8.9** [CD 2: Track 46] Play the recording. Students listen and check their answers. Ask students to make up their own similar conversations in pairs. Ask them to act out their conversations for the class.

Answers and tapescript
1 A Did you get very wet in that shower?
  B Shower! It was a downpour. We're **absolutely soaking**!
2 A I bet you were quite excited when your team won.
  B Excited! We were **absolutely thrilled**!
3 A I thought she looked rather silly in that flowery hat, didn't you?
  B Silly! She looked **absolutely ridiculous**!
4 A Come on, nobody'll notice that tiny spot on your nose.
  B They will, I just know they will! It's **absolutely enormous**!

5 **A** I thought the last episode of *Friends* was **absolutely hilarious**.
  B Mmm. I wouldn't say that. It was quite funny but not hilarious.
6 **A** Len left early. He wasn't feeling well.
  B I'm not surprised. When I saw him this morning he looked **absolutely awful**!

Quite

4 **T8.10** [CD 2: Track 47] Play the recording. Ask students to listen and repeat the sentences. Then ask students to tell you which sentence is more positive in each pair.

> **Answers** 1b and 2b are more positive.

> **PRONUNCIATION NOTE**
> When *quite* is stressed it has a less positive meaning – it means 'not very'. The intonation rises on 'quite' and falls on the adjective. When it isn't stressed it has a more positive meaning – the stress is on the adjective, and it means that this adjective is true 'more than expected'. The intonation rises and falls on the adjective.

5 Ask students in pairs to decide which uses of *quite* have a positive meaning, and which less positive. Then ask them to practise reading the sentences aloud.

  T8.11 [CD 2: Track 48] Play the recording. Ask students to listen and compare their pronunciation, then repeat the sentences.

> **Answers and tapescript**
> 1 The film was quite <u>interesting</u>; you should go and see it.
> 2 The film was <u>quite</u> interesting, but I wouldn't really recommend it.
> 3 I'm quite <u>tired</u> after that last game. Shall we call it a day?
> 4 I'm <u>quite</u> tired, but I'm up for another game if you are.

A night at the Oscars

6 Ask students to read the speech, and say who is speaking.

> **Answer**
> An actor receiving an Oscar at the Academy Awards ceremony in Hollywood.

Ask students in pairs to make the speech more extreme and colourful by adding adjectives and adverbs. Go round monitoring and helping.

7 **T8.12** [CD 2: Track 49] Play the recording. Ask students to listen and compare their choices.

> **Answers and tapescript**
> I am absolutely amazed and delighted to receive this award. I'm truly grateful to all those wonderful people who voted for me. *Red Hot in the Snow* was an absolutely fantastic movie to act in, not only because of all the brilliant people involved in the making of it, but also because of the fabulous, thrilling and often extremely dangerous locations in Alaska. None of us could have predicted that it would be such a huge success. My special thanks go to Marius Aherne, my excellent director; Lulu Lovelace, my gorgeous co-star; Roger Sims, for writing a script that was both fascinating and hilarious, and last but not least to my marvellous wife, Glynis, for her priceless support. I absolutely adore you all.

> **EXTENSION**
> Ask students to write and present their own speeches. Tell them that they have been presented with an award for a book they have written, a scientific discovery they have made, or something they have invented. Ask students to present their speeches to the class.

ADDITIONAL MATERIAL

Workbook Unit 8
Exercises 9–10 Vocabulary
Exercise 11 Prepositions
Exercise 12 Pronunciation – Silent consonants

EVERYDAY ENGLISH (SB p77)

The world around

The aim of this section is to look at some of the signs outside shops and other places providing services. These signs might confuse students if they see them in Britain or on TV and in films. Students also listen to and practise conversations that might take place in these places.

1 Ask students in pairs to look at the signs and identify where they could do the things described. Have a brief class feedback.

> **Answers**
> *borrow money to buy a flat*
> Building Society (see Ex 2)
> *buy a hammer, a screwdriver, and some glue*
> DIY (Do-it-yourself) store (these are extremely popular in Britain, as most people own their own houses and spend a lot of time repairing and improving them).
> *go to get fit*
> Health Club
> *get rid of your newspapers and bottles*
> Recycling centre (see Ex 2)
> *get an inexpensive bed for the night*
> B & B (Bed and Breakfast)

get help with legal problems
   Citizen's Advice Bureau (see Ex 2)
have your body decorated
   Tattoo and Body piercing (specializing in tattoos (body painting) and making holes in the body for body jewellery to be put in)
replace some of the parts on your car
   Tyre and Exhaust Centre (similar to a garage, but specializing in quickly replacing tyres and exhausts)

2 **T8.13** [CD 2: Track 50] Ask students to listen to the five conversations and discuss in pairs where they think they are taking place. Then have a class feedback. Ask students which words helped them to identify the place.

Answers and tapescript
1 Vets (Veterinary Surgeon)
   A golden retriever is a type of dog. She's been brought to the vets because she's *gone off* (lost interest in) *her food* and *lies around all day long.*
2 Recycling Centre
   A place where you can take rubbish, but instead of it being buried or burnt, the materials in the rubbish are recycled. The woman is trying to get rid of some *old carpet*, a *washing machine that doesn't work*, and some *old cardboard*.
3 Building Society
   Although building societies were originally created to lend people money to buy houses, they now also operate as normal banks.
   The student is opening a *savings account*. One account has *24 hours a day access* and pays *3% interest*. Another requires *one week's notice for withdrawals* (taking money out), and both offer *overdraft facilities* (the ability to take out more money than is in the account).
4 Citizens Advice Bureau
   These are offices, run by a registered charity, which provide free information to help people with legal, money and other problems. Here the person has *fallen behind* (got into debt) with their rent.
5 Removal Services
   Will take all your furniture and belongings to your new home in a removal van.
   The woman is *moving to Edinburgh in a couple of months* and says she wants to '*move all my stuff from a house in the south-west of England up to Scotland*'.

T8.13

1
A Hello. Could I make an appointment for our golden retriever, Molly?
B Sure. What seems to be the problem?
A Well, she's gone off her food, which is most unusual for her, and she has no interest in going out for walks. She just lies around all day long.

2
A What have we got here?
B Some old carpet, a washing machine that doesn't work anymore, and a whole load of cardboard.
A Right, well the carpet can go in there, and all old electrical appliances go over there.

3
A Hello. I'd like to open a savings account, please.
B Are you a student?
A Yes, I am.
B Well, we have a couple of special accounts for students. One allows you 24 hours a day access, and pays 3% interest. Another requires one week's notice for withdrawals and pays 3.5% interest. For both accounts you need a minimum of one hundred pounds, but we can offer overdraft facilities ...

4
A Yes, please. How can I help you?
B Yeah, I've got a few money problems.
A Mmm huh.
B You see, I've fallen behind with my rent, about three months, and they're threatening to cut off the electricity.
A Because you haven't paid the bills?
B Yeah, right. And I keep getting all these credit card demands, and I just don't know what to do. I just can't cope any more ...

5
A Hello, can I help you?
B Yes, please. I'm trying to get some quotations to move all my stuff from a house in the south-west of England up to Scotland. Do you go as far as that?
A Oh, yes, madam. We will deliver anywhere in the world. Now whereabouts are you in the south-west?
B Not far from Bristol, and we're moving to Edinburgh in a couple of months time ...

3 Ask students in pairs to write their own dialogues for two or three of the other places shown in the signs. The dialogues should be quite short, like the examples in T 8.13, and use some of the key vocabulary that identifies the places. Ask students to read their dialogues out, and other students in the class to guess where they are taking place.

Writing Unit 8
Describing places – My favourite part of town SB p119

9

Expressing habit • *used to do/doing*
Homonyms/Homophones
Making your point

Forever friends

Introduction to the unit

The theme of this unit is remembering people. The main grammatical focus of the unit is ways of expressing habit, and these are contextualized in an email from a woman to an old school-friend that she hasn't seen for a long time.

The main reading text is about *Friends*, the popular American TV sitcom. In the main listening text, four people describe a teacher they will never forget.

Language aims

Expressing habit   The aim is to revise and practise ways of expressing present habit: the Present Simple, the Present Continuous with a frequency adverb, and *'ll/will* + infinitive. It also looks at *used to* and *would* to express past habit, and the confusion between *used to* + infinitive to describe a past state or habit, and *be/get used to* + *ing* to talk about situations that are or are becoming familiar.

Present habit   Students at this level should be comfortable with using the Present Simple to express present habits. Consequently the focus here is on how to use other forms to express habit. It is worth emphasizing, however, that the Present Simple is by far the most common form. The other forms are:

She's always asking me for money. (Present Continuous with *always* to express annoying habit)
He'll spend hours doing nothing. (unstressed *'ll* + infinitive to express typical behaviour)
*He **will** keep asking me for money.* (stressed *will* + infinitive to express irritation)

These uses are very context specific, so it is important to make sure students are clear about which situations they should use them in, and about how they feel when they use them. Stress and intonation are also important when using these forms, so it is important to practise this area.

Past habit

used to
Although the Past Simple can be used, English often prefers *used to* + infinitive to express past states and habits, particularly when emphasising the idea of 'no longer true'. Although *used to* is often taught at elementary level, students tend to avoid using it, so it is important to encourage them to start incorporating it into their spoken use.

Compare the following sentences.
Once, when I was young, I went to London. (*used to* + infinitive cannot be used because this is one finished past event)
When I was young, I went to the local barber's. (this is possible, but unclear – does it mean once or often? – we need to add a time adverbial to make it clear. For example, *I went to the local barber's every month.*)
When I was young, I used to go to the local barber's. (this is preferable because the meaning – *past habit that is no longer true* – is clear)

> **POSSIBLE PROBLEMS**
> 1 Students try to use *used to* in the present: *~~I use to get up early.~~* They should say: *I (usually) get up early.*
> 2 The pronunciation of *used to* /juːstə/ is difficult, and because the *d* is not pronounced, students miss it out when writing: *~~I use to live…~~*
> 3 Students often have problems with question and negative forms because the *d* is dropped: *~~Did you used to live…~~*

would

We use *would* as an alternative to repeating *used to* when talking about past habits.

As a child, I used to get up early, then I'd go downstairs…

However, *would* cannot be used to express past states.

~~I'd like eating chips when I was young.~~

We tend to prefer *would* when we want to be 'nostalgic' and when there are a number of past habits to mention.

Those days in Rome were wonderful. We'd get up with the sunrise, then we'd spend the day…

When *would* is stressed it expresses irritation.

*As a child, my younger brother **would** always spoil my games.*

used to + infinitive and be used to + ing

These two are confused because the forms are similar and both are to do with habit.

I used to get up early. (a past habit that is no longer true – *used* is a verb)

I'm used to getting up early. (something you are accustomed to – *used* is an adjective)

POSSIBLE PROBLEMS

1 Students are confused that *to* is a preposition in the form *be/get used to*, and is therefore followed by *-ing*.

2 Students overuse *be used to doing*, e.g. **In Italy we're used to eating pasta.* This form should only be used when we are talking about the difficulty of adapting to something unfamiliar, e.g. *I find it difficult to eat potatoes so often in England, because I'm used to eating pasta.* It's also used to stress that there *isn't* a problem with unfamiliarity, when people suggest that there might be, e.g. *Don't worry. I'm used to sleeping on the floor.* When there is no suggestion of anything being difficult or unfamiliar in the situation, the Present Simple should be used: *In Italy, we (usually) eat pasta.*

Vocabulary   The vocabulary section looks at homonyms and homophones.

Everyday English   This section introduces and practises ways of making your point in arguments and debates.

Notes on the unit

TEST YOUR GRAMMAR (SB p78)

The *Test your grammar* section aims to test the students' ability to recognize the forms of different ways of expressing present and past habit, and *be used to*.

This exercise should be done quickly. Don't get involved in lengthy grammar explanations at this stage.

1 Ask students in pairs to match the lines and underline the words that express habit.

Answers

1 A reliable friend <u>will</u> never <u>let</u> you down.
2 In the 1960s, hippies <u>used to wear</u> flowers in their hair.
3 I think my sister's in love. She<u>'ll spend</u> hours staring into space.
4 When I was a kid my dad <u>would read</u> me a story at bedtime.
5 My first girlfriend was Alice. We <u>used to go</u> to the cinema on a Friday, and then we<u>'d go</u> for a pizza afterwards.
6 Big-headed people are always talking about themselves.

2, 4 and 5 are past habit. The others are present habit.

---

2 Ask students to match the endings to the sentences

Answer

He used to work hard but now he's retired. (a past habit)
He's used to hard work because he's a builder. (something he's accustomed to)

FRIENDS REUNITED (SB p78)

Expressing habit – *used to do/doing*

This section contextualizes and practises ways of expressing habit. The practice activities focus on the importance of context in choosing and using these forms. Students have to describe people and describe relationships to show their ability to manipulate the forms.

Lead in by asking students to think of an old friend that they used to know but don't see anymore. As a class, or in pairs, ask questions. Ask, *Who was your friend? When did you last see him/her? What do you think he/she is doing now? Would you like to get in touch, and if so how?*

1 Read the introduction and ask the questions.

CULTURAL NOTE

Friendsreunited.co.uk has been phenomenally successful in the UK. It enables people to place information about themselves on their website, which old friends can access. That way you can find out what happened to people from your past, and even contact them by email and have a reunion.

---

2 Ask students to read the email and complete it. Let them check in pairs before feedback.

T9.1 [CD 3: Track 2] Play the recording. Students listen and check their answers.

Answers and tapescript

| 1 e | 2 c | 3 a | 4 k | 5 f | 6 b |
| 7 h | 8 g | 9 i | 10 l | 11 d | 12 j |

T9.1

Dear Sally

I'm sending this through Friends Reunited. Do you remember me? We (1e) **used to go** to Allendales School together. You were the first person I (2c) **got** to know when I started there. We (3a) **used to sit** next to each other in class, but then the teachers made us sit apart because we (4k) **were always giggling** so much.

I remember we (5f) **'d go** back to your house after school every day and listen to music for hours on end. We (6b) **'d get** all the Beatles records as soon as they came out. Once we ate all the food in your fridge and your mother (7h) **was** furious. Do you remember that time we nearly blew up the science lab? The teacher (8g) **went** crazy, but it wasn't our fault. We (9i) **used to call him** 'Mickey Mouse' because he had sticky-out ears.

I still see Penny, and she's still as mad as ever. We meet up every now and again, and we (10i) **'ll always end up** chatting about old times together. She (11d) **'s always talking** about a school reunion. So if you're interested, drop me a line.

Looking forward to hearing from you.

Your old schoolmate

Alison Makepeace

PS I'm not (12j) **used to calling** you Sally Davies! To me, you're still Sally Wilkinson!

3 Ask students to discuss the questions in pairs. Then have a class feedback.

Answers
1, 3, 4, 5, 6, 9, 10, and 11 describe actions that happened again and again. The point here is that the Past Simple, used in 2, 7 and 8, is used to describe events that happened once. 12 describes a situation that is not familiar.

4 Ask students to discuss the sentences in pairs. Then have a class feedback.

Answers
We used to go to school together… is more factual.
We'd go back to your house… is more nostalgic.
Basically, when talking about past habits, *used to* and *would* can both be used. However, we tend to use *would* to avoid repeating *used to*, and to make our stories or memories more nostalgic. Using *would* gives a real sense of a time that has been lost.

5 Ask students in pairs to match lines **A** and **B**.
T9.2 [CD 3: Track 3] Play the recording. Ask students to listen and check. Then ask students to listen and repeat the sentences after the recording, or after your model. The key areas to focus on here are the contracted form of *we'd* /wiːd/, the weak form of *were* /wə/, and the pronunciation of *used to*, in which the d is silent and *to* is pronounced with a weak schwa sound, /juːstə/.

Answers and tapescript
we used to go to school together
we used to sit next to each other
we were always giggling so much
we'd go back to your house
we used to call him 'Mickey Mouse'
I'm not used to calling you Sally Davies

LANGUAGE FOCUS

See TB p8 for suggestions on how to teach this section.

Don't forget to look at the *Language aims* section on TB p91, which looks at problems students may have. You should also read the Grammar Reference on SB pp150–151.

LANGUAGE INPUT

1 Ask students to tell you the names of the tenses used. Then ask them in pairs to match the sentences to the rules.

Answers
a Simple Present – expresses a simple fact about her
b Present Continuous with *always* – expresses my attitude to this habit of hers (I find it annoying)
c *will* or *'ll* + infinitive – expresses characteristic behaviour (this is typical of her)

2 Ask students in pairs to change the sentences.

Answers
a My sister worked in a bank./My sister used to work in a bank.
b She was always borrowing my clothes without asking me.
c She'd go out on a Friday night and wouldn't be back till morning.

3 Ask students to look at the sentences and work in pairs to discuss the questions. In the feedback, point out the form. In b *I used to live in Rome…*, *used* is a verb followed by the *to* infinitive. In the other sentences, *used* is an adjective followed by the preposition *to* + *ing*.

Answers
b *I used to live in Rome…* a past habit now finished.
a *…so I'm used to the noise.* a situation which is familiar and no longer strange.
c *I'm getting used to travelling…* a situation which is still strange, but becoming easier.

Refer students to the Grammar Reference on SB pp150–151.

What's she like?

1 Do the first as an example, then ask students in pairs to match the adjectives to the sentences. Go round monitoring and prompting.

In the feedback, check that the students fully understand the descriptive vocabulary, particularly the likely new words, *clumsy* and *stubborn*, and the common false friends, *sensible* and *sensitive*. You could also check the stress, and check some of the difficult words in the sentences.

> *bump into* = knock into
> *bloke* = man
> *pick a fight* = start a fight on purpose

> **Answers**
> 1 absent-minded   5 sensible
> 2 sensitive   6 stubborn
> 3 easy-going   7 mean
> 4 clumsy   8 argu'mentative

2 Ask students in pairs to write sentences. Encourage them to use expressions of present and past habit. Do the first as an example.

> **Sample answers**
> 1 He never does any housework./He's always leaving his things all over the house.
> 2 He never lets me go out with other people./He's always asking me where I've been./He'll ring me in the evening to find out where I am.
> 3 He always wears great clothes./He'll say something or do something that's so cool.
> 4 She's always criticising me./She's always telling me what to do.
> 5 She used to give me sweets and presents./She'd take me on picnics.
> 6 I used to take him for long walks. We'd walk for miles and miles./He used to follow me around.
> 7 You're always talking about yourself./You'll spend hours in front of the mirror.
> 8 She'll always try to find out what I'm doing./She's always asking me questions.

Discussing grammar

3 Ask students in pairs to match the lines.

> **Answers**
> 1 My friend Joe buys and sells cars. He earns loads of money.
> 2 He's always buying new things for himself – a DVD, a palm top. He's a real techno-geek. (a *geek* is someone who is obsessed with technical systems and equipment)
> 3 He'll buy a shirt and only wear it once. Don't you think that's wasteful of him?

4 When I was young, we used to have holidays by the sea-side. We'd go to the same place year after year.
5 My dad and I would build sandcastles and go swimming together. I remember those days with such fondness!
6 One year we went to East Africa. What an adventure that was!
7 John usually does the cooking but he isn't tonight. I am.
8 He used to do the cooking but then he stopped.
9 He's used to doing the cooking because he's been doing it for years.
10 He's getting used to doing the cooking but he still burns things. Maybe one day he'll get it.

Parents

4 **T9.3** [CD 3: Track 4] Play the recording. Ask students to listen to the four people talking, and answer the gist question.

> **Answers and tapescript**
> 1 It was/is a good relationship with her mother. Her father left when she was three.
> 2 It wasn't a good relationship with his father. He was very strict.
> 3 It isn't a good relationship – mother is always complaining. Dad is laid-back – doesn't mention relationship with him.
> 4 It was a good relationship – fond memories of family trips and treats.
>
> **T9.3**
> 1 I got on very well with my mother. She was my best friend, still is. We had to get on, really. Dad left when I was three. I used to tell her everything, well, nearly everything. And she'd talk to me very openly, too. Sometimes she'd say to me 'Don't go to school today. Stay with me'. And we'd go out shopping, or something like that. It's a wonder I had any education at all, the number of days I missed from school.
> 2 I don't remember much about my childhood. My wife's always asking me questions like erm 'When you were a boy, did you use to ...?', and I reply 'I don't know. I can't remember'. We didn't ... er ... really we didn't use to talk very much, we weren't very close, or if we were, we didn't show it. I remember I used to have my hair cut every Friday. My father was in the army, and he had a thing about short hair, so every week he'd take me to the hairdresser. I had the shortest hair in the school. I used to hate it. And him.
> 3 I'm not a very tidy person, but my mother's very house-proud, so she's always telling me to pick things up and put them away, and do this and do that. She'll go on for hours about 'Cleanliness is next to godliness' – that just makes me want to scream. My father isn't like that at all, he's much more laid-back. I think he's just learned to blank out my mother.

4 I have very fond memories of my childhood. To me it represented security. We used to do a lot together as a family. I remember walks, and picnics, and going for car rides on a Sunday afternoon. Every Friday when my Dad came home, he'd bring us each a treat, just something little. My mother used to say he was spoiling us, but why not? It didn't do us any harm.

5 **T9.3** Ask students in pairs to rewrite the sentences with actual words from the recording. Do the first as an example. You may need to play the recording again so that students can check their answers.

Answers
1 she'd talk to me very openly... we'd go out shopping
2 My wife's always asking me questions... we didn't use to talk very much... every week he'd take me to the hairdresser...
3 she's always telling me to pick things up... she'll go on for hours...
4 We used to do a lot together as a family... he'd bring us each a treat...

6 Give students three or four minutes to write a few sentences. Then ask them to read them out to their partner. Encourage them to use expressions of habit.

Answering questions

7 Ask students in pairs to answer the questions.
T9.4 [CD 3: Track 5] Play the recording. Students listen and check their answers.

Answers and tapescript
1 You don't like your new teacher, do you?
Not a lot, but **we're getting used to her**.
2 How can you get up at five o'clock in the morning?
No problem. **I'm used to it**.
3 How come you know Madrid so well?
I used to live there.
4 How are you finding your new job?
Difficult, but **I'm getting used to** it bit by bit.
5 Do you read comics?
I used to when I was young, but not any more.
6 You two argue so much. How can you live together?
After twenty years' marriage we**'re used to** each other.

ADDITIONAL MATERIAL

Workbook Unit 9
Exercises 1–5 Present and past habit

A teacher I'll never forget

The aim here is to improve the students' ability to listen for specific information. It also looks at compounds that collocate with and intensify the meaning of adjectives.

1 Ask students to look at the pictures and discuss the questions.

Answers
In the top picture the teacher is standing at the board with a pointer, and the students are sitting in rows of desks, all paying attention to the teacher at the front. In the second picture, the teacher is mingling with the students, giving them individual attention, while other students work together in pairs and groups. In the cartoon, the teacher is monitoring a student who is working on his own on a computer.
The pictures reflect the change in teaching styles over the years, from strict teacher-led lessons carried out from the front of the class only, to more relaxed pair and group work with the teacher working amongst the students. The cartoon looks humorously at a more recent and possible future trend, where students do much of the learning by themselves, using computer technology, and the teacher becomes more of a 'facilitator'.

2 **T9.5** [CD 3: Track 6] Play the recording. Ask students to listen, then tell their partner what good and bad characteristics they heard mentioned. It doesn't matter if they don't hear everything – just find out what they caught.

Answers
Good characteristics: sense of humour; good at controlling the class and making students pay attention; making the subject memorable; treating students fairly; keeping a distance
Bad characteristics: scaring students; teaching like a soldier; causing physical pain; trying to be like a teenager

3 Ask students in pairs to write answers to the questions. Play the recording again so that students can check and add to their answers.

Answers and tapescript
1 Because he had a terrific sense of humour, and had an ability to control the class in such a way that the students always paid attention when he wanted them to pay attention, but he could always get them to laugh at the same time. He'd stand on a desk and recite a poem, or he'd draw funny pictures on the blackboard, or tell jokes.
2 Because he taught out of fear – all the kids were scared of him. Students had to stand in a line outside his classroom, and when he was ready, he'd shout 'Get in, men!', and they'd all march into class. He'd pace up and down the

classroom, and he used to wear those kind of shoes that didn't make a noise. He picked students up by the hairs on the back of their neck.

3 She wore amazing clothes. She brought history to life – she made the characters from history memorable. Liz will never forget the fact that she brought history to life.

4 Because on one hand he's great – he'll joke with the students. But on the other hand, if a student misbehaves, he is head of discipline in the school, and he shouts and scares students.

5 1 Mr Sparks, which I think is a fantastic name for a teacher, anyway.

  2 Colin Tivvy. I'll never forget that name. It sends shivers down my spine just to hear it.

  3 Miss Potts ... another teacher who was called Miss Potts would probably have been called 'potty' ... she just never had a nickname.

  4 Mr Brown. We call him Brownie, but not to his face.

T9.5

Alan

I was very fortunate in high school to have erm ... one particularly good teacher for a subject called -er social studies, which incorporates history and erm .. geography. And I think the thing that made this teacher so good was that he not only had a terrific sense of humour but he also had an ability to control the class in such a way that we always paid attention when he wanted us to pay attention, but he could always get us to laugh at the same time. So he had a way of kind of being very fluid in his teaching style. And erm ... he'd do crazy things like ... -er you know, sometimes he'd stand on a desk and recite a poem, or he'd erm ... he'd draw funny pictures on the blackboard. But I never, never forget him. His name was Mr Sparks, which I think is a fantastic name for a teacher, anyway. And -er he'd stand at the front of the class ... he had this kind of -er ... he had a sort of, of a funny er ... short, pointy beard, and glasses and er ... this kind of greying, slicked back hair and erm ... he'd, he'd stand there and look at us with a, an imperious look on his face, and then tell a joke! He'd just make us all laugh!

John

I had a teacher at school who was just awful. He taught French and German, and his name was Colin Tivvy. I'll never forget that name. It sends shivers down my spine just to hear it. It wasn't that he was a bad teacher. In fact he used to get very good results. It was the way he got those results. He taught out of pure fear. All the kids were scared stiff of him, so you'd do his homework first and best, because the last thing you wanted was to make a mistake. If you made any mistake, in homework or in class, you had to write it out one hundred times that night. He'd been a soldier in the army, and he'd worked as an interrogator, and that was just how he taught. We had to stand in a line outside his classroom, and when he was ready, he'd shout 'Get in, men!', and we'd all march into class. As the lesson went through, he'd pace up and down the classroom, and er ... he used to wear those kind of shoes that didn't make a noise, you know? And the worst

feeling in the whole world was when you knew he was just behind you. You were waiting for a smack on the back of the head. But the worst was when he picked you up by the hairs on the back of your neck. That hurt.

Lizzie

The teacher I remember most from schooldays was ... erm ... a teacher called Miss Potts. She was a history teacher and I was about thirteen or fourteen years old. We were all very interested in fashion, and Miss Potts used to wear the most amazing things to come in to teach – so she was a very memorable teacher. Every day we'd be asking ourselves 'What's she gonna wear today?' She'd wear blue tights with red skirts and very red jumpers, and very bright red lipstick and she'd come teetering into the classroom on very high heels and we thought she looked wonderful. But the very best thing about Miss Potts was the way, in fact, she taught history – it's what makes her most memorable. She not only brought history to life, but she made it seem dead easy, she didn't just act it out for us, ... erm ... but the way she described the characters from history made us feel as if we knew them and, and sometimes instead of writing essays we would do cartoon strips ... erm ... of the, of the different tales from history and we loved it.

She was a brilliant, brilliant teacher. It's interesting 'cos I think another teacher who was called Miss Potts would probably have been called 'potty' or ... er ... given such a name as that, but there was something about her that we respected so much that ... er ... she just never had a nickname.

Kate

My favourite is called Mr Brown. We call him Brownie, but not to his face. We wouldn't dare. He's my PE teacher, and he's great. He'll joke and make fun of you, but never in a horrible, nasty way. And we like to pull his leg, too. He's bald, poor guy, totally bald, but when it's his birthday, we'll ask him if he wants a comb or a brush, or something like that. But there's a line we all know we can't cross. We have a lot of respect for him as a teacher, and he treats us totally fairly, but he also keeps his distance. He never tries to be one of us, oh no! If a teacher ever tries to be, you know, a teenager like us, same music, same clothes, same jokes, it just doesn't work. But there's another side to Brownie. He's also head of discipline in the school, so whenever a student you know ... misbehaves or cheeks a teacher, they get sent to Mr Brown and he scares the pants off them. And when he shouts, boy he is absolutely terrifying. No one, but no one, messes with Mr Brown.

What do you think?

The aim here is to use the listening as a springboard for personalised discussion.

Give students a few minutes to think of a favourite teacher, and prepare to speak about him or her (you could ask them to think of teachers from a previous, e.g. primary, school, if you prefer them not to talk about teachers in their current school). Divide the students into small groups to talk about their teachers. Monitor, prompting students to use expressions of past habit if they are avoiding them.

READING AND SPEAKING (SB p82)

Friends past

The aim is to improve the students' ability to read for specific information. There is also contextualized practice of ways of expressing habit.

1 Ask students to discuss the questions in pairs.

  1 Ask students to define the TV programmes, or show their understanding by giving you an example of each type of programme from TV in their country. Ask what their favourite TV programmes are and why.

Answers
a soap opera = a long-running TV series about the imaginary lives of a group of people – often shown every day or three or four times a week
a sitcom = a situation comedy, a weekly TV series in which a particular group of characters deal with an ongoing situation in a humorous way
a quiz show = involving a quiz, sometimes with prizes
a documentary = a programme that deals with real-life stories in an informative way
reality TV = a TV programme in which ordinary people are put in situations that make interesting viewing, (for example, *Big Brother*, in which a group of strangers are filmed living in a house together)
current affairs = a type of news programme that investigates a current political or social issue

Vocabulary extension
You may wish to pre-teach other 'TV' words that come up in the text. Ask students how these words relate to sitcoms:
long-running series show episode characters cast viewers ratings

> **EXTRA IDEA**
> Print out the evening sections of a TV guide from the Internet (www.guardian.co.uk/TV is a good example) or cut and paste them into a Word document, to create a handout covering 3, 4, or 5 channels. Hand it out to students in pairs, and ask the students to scan it quickly and find an example of each type of programme in the box in exercise 1.
> Alternatively, use the TV guide as a role-play activity. Divide the class into group of 3 or 4. Ask each student to decide which programmes they would like to watch in the evening, then tell the groups that they only have one TV, so they must negotiate to plan an evening's viewing together.

2 Ask students to tell you which American TV programmes they know and watch.

Sample answers
Some well-known recent American sitcoms: *Friends, Frasier, Will and Grace, Seinfeld*. Other popular programmes include *ER, The West Wing*, talk shows hosted by David Letterman and Jay Leno, and programmes that 'investigate' people's real-life problems, such as *Oprah* and *Jerry Springer*.

2 **T9.6** [CD 3: Track 7] Play the recording. Ask students to listen to the theme tune. Ask them if they can remember any lines.

Note that this song is fully exploited on p126 of the photocopiable section of New Headway Pre-Intermediate Teacher's Book.

Tapescript
So no-one told you life was gonna be this way
Your job's a joke, you're broke
Your love life's gone away
It's like you're always stuck in second gear
When it hasn't been your day, your week,
Your month or even your year

But I'll be there for you
When the rain starts to pour
I'll be there for you
You know I've been there before
I'll be there for you
'Cause you're there for me too

3 Ask students to look at the photos on the page. Find out how much your students know about *Friends*. Ask, *What are the names of the characters? Where is it set? Do you*

*know anything about the personalities of the characters?
Do you know the names of the stars and anything about
their lives and careers? Why was the programme successful?*

4   Ask students to read the first half of the article and
    answer the questions. Let them check their answers in
    pairs before feedback.

Answers
1 ... flat-mates, sharing the trials of their lives, loves and
   careers in a trendy New York apartment.
2 A decade (ten years).
3 Because we all wanted a life like theirs.
4 The cool New York flat with table football and easy chairs,
   and the social circle of beautiful, supportive friends.
5 The rise of coffee culture/the Rachel haircut/using *so*/the
   comfort the show provided after the September 11th bomb
   attack.
6 Because viewers sought a feel-good factor after the bomb
   attack.
7 *Language*: It popularized the common intensifier *so*, (as in,
   he's so cool)
   Hair: Rachel's haircut was copied by millions of women.
   Drinking habits: coffee culture and cappuccinos

5   Ask students to read the second half of the article and
    answer the questions. Let students check their answers in
    pairs before feedback.

Answers
1 Monica is Ross' sister.
   Ross is in love with Rachel. Chandler is in love with
   Monica.
   It is a mixture of envy and disdain (feeling that someone is
   not worthy of respect).
2 *Ross*: a bore, a geek – he's always whining, (relationship
   with Rachel keeps going wrong)
   Chandler: a comedian – he's constantly telling jokes and
   making everybody laugh
   Joey: a simple character – dense, loveable, charming, with
   total self-belief (he'll cheer himself up with food or
   women)
   Rachel: a prima donna – spoilt, terrible in a crisis (she will
   throw her arms up in despair)
   Phoebe: a hippy – wild, eccentric, (always communicating
   with the dead, chanting about auras, unique guitar playing)
   Monica: a neurotic – insecure, bossy, (always tidying up,
   needs to have her own way, wants to settle down)

6   **T9.7** [CD 3: Track 8] Play the recording. Ask students
    which character is being described.

Answers and tapescript
1 Phoebe   4 Chandler
2 Joey   5 Rachel
3 Monica   6 Ross

T9.7
1 I like her because she's so different from the others. She
   thinks differently, she behaves differently. She'll say the
   craziest of things in the most serious way.
2 I like him because he's so cute and so amazingly self-
   centred. He's so uncomplicated. What you see is what you
   get. So charmingly dumb and unsophisticated.
3 I can't stand her because she's so fussy and uptight. She has
   to have control over everything and everybody. And she
   screeches.
4 He really annoys me because he's so hopeless with women.
   But he's so funny. He uses his humour and sarcasm as a
   defence mechanism to get out of difficulty. How he ended
   up with Monica I'll never know.
5 She's my favourite because she's incredibly good-looking.
   She's a bit scatty, she's always losing things. She's a real
   daddy's girl. She was so popular at school.
6 He's my favourite because he's always falling in love with
   the wrong woman. He's the coolest of the non-cool crowd.
   He's so sensible, his parents think he can do no wrong, but
   he's always getting into trouble.

EXTRA IDEA
Ask students to prepare their own description of a
Friends character. Ask them to read out their
descriptions to other students. Who are they
describing?

Language work

Ask students in pairs to match the words.

Answers

A	B
the small screen	television
trials	difficulties
trendy	fashionable
encountered	met
grieving	feeling deep sadness
sought (past of *seek*)	looked for

What do you think?

The aim here is to use the text as a springboard for
speaking. Encourage students to keep using all the different
ways of expressing habit.
Divide students into small groups to discuss the questions.

Homonyms and homophones

This section looks at homonyms, (words with the same spelling but different meanings), and homophones, (words with the same pronunciation, but different spellings and meanings). English has plenty of examples of each.

1 Ask students to work alone to think about the meanings of the words.

2 **T9.8** [CD 3: Track 9] Play the recording. Ask students to continue working alone to listen and write down the words they hear.

3 Ask students in pairs to compare their answers. It is likely that the students will have thought of different meanings for the words in 1, and spelt the words in 2 in different ways. In the feedback, elicit different meanings and spellings, and introduce the concept of homonyms and homophones.

> **Answers** (to 1 and 2)
> 1 **Homonyms**
> *fine* = well (person) / bright and sunny (weather) / payment you must make for breaking the law
> *match* = small stick for lighting cigarettes / game between two players or teams / a person who is as good as you / a person suitable for you to marry / to be similar / to be equal
> *park* = open public area with grass / to move a vehicle into a place where you want to leave it
> *book* = something you read / reserve a table in a restaurant or seat in a cinema
> *cross* = go from one side to the other / a shape with an upright line and a line across it / angry
> *mean* = signify / intend / not willing to spend money / cruel / unkind
> 2 **Homophones**
> where / wear   break / brake
> nose / knows   through / threw
> mail / male   sent / scent

Homonyms

4 Read through the explanation and examples as a class. Then ask students in pairs to complete the sentences.

> **Answers**
> 1 cool   2 date   3 set   4 fit   5 bear

5 Ask students in pairs to think of two meanings for the words.

> **Answers**
> *wave* = move your hand to say hello (verb)/the sea coming into the land (noun)
> *suit* = formal matching jacket and trousers or skirt (noun)/go well with (verb)
> *fan* = (sports) supporter (noun)/machine or paper device used to keep you cool (noun)
> *miss* = unmarried woman (noun)/not hit (with a throw or shot) (verb)/feel sad because you are not with someone (verb)
> *type* = sort or kind (noun)/write with a keyboard (verb)
> *point* = indicate with your finger (verb)/idea or opinion in an argument (noun)/unit for counting the score in a game or sport (noun)
> *train* = vehicle on rails (noun)/practise to improve in a sport (verb)
> *tight* = not loose (adjective)/mean (adjective)
> *mind* = what you think with (noun)/be careful of (verb)/look after (verb)/feel unhappy about (verb)
> *fair* = light-coloured (adjective)/just (adjective)/pleasant (adjective)/an event where companies sell products (noun)/an event where people ride on fun rides (noun)

> **EXTRA IDEA**
> Ask students in pairs to choose two words from the list, then write two pairs of sentences showing different spellings or meanings of the word. Ask them to give their sentences to another pair with the homonyms or homophones missing. Can the other pair guess which words are missing?

Homophones

6 Read through the explanation and examples as a class. Then ask students in pairs to write the words.

> **Answers**
> 1 the **whole** world
>   a **hole** in the ground
> 2 a **piece** of cake
>   war and **peace**
> 3 a rose is a **flower**
>   **flour** to make bread
> 4 a yacht has **sails**
>   buy clothes in the **sales**
> 5 salespeople **sell** things
>   a prisoner lives in a **cell**

7 Ask students in pairs to think of homophones.

> **Answers**
> | board | court | wore | higher | pear |
> | plane | waste | seize | shore | allowed |

8 **T9.9** [CD 3: Track 10] Play the two jokes. Ask students to listen and read, and explain how the homonyms make the jokes.

Answers and tapescript
A How do you keep cool at a football match?
B I don't know.
A Sit next to a fan!
(*fan* = supporter/machine that blows air to keep you cool)

A Why did the teacher wear sunglasses?
B I don't know.
A Because her students were so bright.
(*bright* = intelligent/shining)

T9.10 [CD 3: Track 11] Play the rest of the jokes and see if the students can 'get' them. Ask them to practise telling the jokes to each other.

Answers and tapescript
Customer Waiter! I'm in a hurry. Will my pizza be long?
Waiter No, sir. It'll be round.
(*long* = long shape/long time)

Teacher You missed school yesterday, didn't you Johnny?
Johnny No, sir. Not a bit.
(*missed* = failed to attend/felt sad because of not having something)

What's the difference between a sailor and someone who goes shopping?
One goes to sail the seas, the other goes to see the sales!
(*sail the seas/see the sales* = homophones)

What's the difference between a jeweller and a jailer?
One sells watches and the other watches cells.
(*sells/cells* = homophones. *cell* = prison cell)

What sort of crisps can fly?
Plain crisps.
(*plain/plane* = homophones. *Plain* = ordinary – with no extra flavour)

Why was the doctor angry?
Because he had no patients!
(*patients/patience* = near homophones)

What did the sea say to the beach?
Nothing. It just waved.
(*wave* = water that comes onto shore from sea/movement of hand to say hello or goodbye)

What's black and white and red all over?
A newspaper.
(*red/read* = homophones)

What do you get when 5,000 strawberries try to go through a door at the same time?
Strawberry jam!
(*jam* = sweet food from fruit you put on toast/blocked movement – e.g. traffic jam)

EVERYDAY ENGLISH (SB p85)

Making your point

The aim of this section is to introduce and practise ways of making your point in arguments and debates.

Lead in by writing on the board, *Fast food is bad for you. We should pay more tax on it.* Ask students for their opinion.

1 **T9.11** [CD 3: Track 12] Play the recording. Ask students to listen and answer the questions.

Answers and tapescript
For: 3 Beth-Anne   *Against*: 1 Vicky   *Undecided*: 2 Al

T9.11
Vicky
If you ask me, this is a terrible idea. Firstly, it would be an infringement of individual freedom. Secondly, another way of saying fast food is convenience food, and that means it really suits the kind of lifestyle of people today. Another thing is that it would be a tax on people who are less well off. Personally, I don't eat in these places, but that's not the point. The point I'm trying to make is that people should be allowed to eat what they want.
Al
To tell you the truth, I haven't really thought about it. I suppose the problem is that we don't know what's in these burgers and pizzas. As far as I'm concerned, people can do what they want. I don't see what's wrong with that. Actually, I'm seeing a friend for lunch and we're going to have a burger. There's that new place just opened, you know, down by the square. It's supposed to be quite good. Anyway, as I was saying, I don't really feel strongly one way or the other.
Beth-Anne
If you want my opinion, I think this is a really good idea. There are far too many people who have a terrible diet, and they just go to the nearest hamburger joint and fill themselves up with rubbish. Basically, it's laziness. As I understand it, they just can't be bothered to buy fresh food and cook it. But the main point is that fast food, or junk food, is too cheap. If it was taxed, people would think twice before buying. What really worries me is that the next generation is going to have so many problems with kids being overweight.

2 Ask students in pairs to match the lines.

T9.12 Play the recording. Students listen and check their answers. Read through the *Music of English* box as a class. Play the recording again. Ask students to listen and repeat the lines, practising their stress patterns (underlined in the tapescript here).

Answers and tapescript
If you <u>ask</u> <u>me</u> ...
An<u>oth</u>er thing is that ...
That's <u>not</u> the <u>point</u>.
The <u>point</u> I'm <u>try</u>ing to <u>make</u> is that ...

> To <u>tell</u> you the <u>truth</u> ...
> I suppose the <u>problem</u> is that ...
> As <u>far</u> as <u>I'm</u> concerned ...
> Anyway, as I was <u>saying</u> ...
> If you <u>want</u> <u>my</u> opinion ...
> As I <u>understand</u> it ...
> But the <u>main</u> <u>point</u> is that ...
> What <u>really</u> worries <u>me</u> is that ...

3 Ask students to look at tapescript 9.11 on SB p135 and write the adverbs that end in –*ly*.

Answers
Firstly, Secondly, Personally, really, actually, strongly, basically

4 Ask students in pairs to match the lines. Ask students to practise saying the expressions in pairs or small groups, imagining they are in a debate, and trying to say things forcefully.

Answers
1 <u>First</u> of <u>all</u>, I'd like to <u>look</u> at the <u>general</u> <u>problem</u>.
2 As <u>well</u> as <u>this</u>, there are <u>problems</u> with the <u>cost</u>.
3 <u>Finally</u>, I'd like to <u>give</u> my conclusion.
4 <u>In</u> my <u>opinion</u>, fast <u>food</u> should be <u>totally</u> <u>banned</u>.
5 <u>Generally</u> <u>speaking</u>, as a <u>nation</u> we <u>don't</u> do <u>enough</u> <u>exercise</u>.
6 The <u>problem</u> <u>is</u>, how do you <u>educate</u> people to <u>have</u> a <u>better</u> <u>diet</u>?
7 As <u>far</u> as <u>I</u> know, <u>this</u> <u>problem</u> is <u>quite</u> <u>common</u>.
8 To <u>be</u> <u>exact</u>, there are <u>five</u> others like <u>this</u>.
9 To be <u>honest</u>, I <u>don't</u> know the <u>answer</u> to this <u>problem</u>.

5 As a class, choose a topic that everybody feels strongly about. If you know your class well, why not choose a different topic from those in the list? Then conduct a class debate.

HOW TO CONDUCT A CLASS DEBATE
Write on the board a 'motion' for the debate. For example, *Being a vegetarian is better than being a meat-eater. / Smoking in public places should be banned.*
Divide the class into groups of four or five. You could do this at random, then ask the students of each group to decide whether to support or oppose the motion. Or, you could ask students to form groups in the first place depending on whether they are supporters or opposers of the motion.
Ask the groups to write a list of arguments in favour of their view. Monitor and help. Then ask the groups to prepare to speak, ordering their arguments, and using some of the expressions from the lesson. Ask the students to decide who is going to speak from their group.

When the groups are ready, start the debate. Ask one group to argue in favour of the motion, then another group to oppose it. Make sure every group has a chance to present their ideas. When each group has formally presented their ideas, open the debate to the floor. Ask if any individuals have any further points to make. At the end, have a class vote to find out whether the majority supports or favours the motion. Ask: *Did anybody change their mind as a result of the debate?*

ALTERNATIVE IDEA
Speaking roles
Speaking roles is an alternative way of doing this speaking activity. Divide students into groups of four to six. Photocopy and cut out the cards on p158 of the Teacher's Book. Hand out a different card to each student in the group. When they speak in groups, they must play the role on the card.
It is a good idea to laminate the cards, or stick them on cardboard, for later use. *Speaking roles* work well with group discussions and problem-solving activities.
This idea is based in part on *Six Thinking Hats*, which was originally developed by the psychologist, Edward de Bono.

Writing Unit 9
Writing for talking – What I want to talk about is ... SB p120

ADDITIONAL MATERIAL

Workbook Unit 9
Exercises 6-7 Vocabulary
Exercise 8 Phrasal verbs
Exercise 9 Listening – A small disagreement
Exercise 10 Pronunciation – Weak and strong forms

10

Modal auxiliary verbs 2
Synonyms
Metaphors and idioms – the body

Risking life and limb

Introduction to the unit

The theme of this unit is taking risks. The expression that makes up the title of the unit, *risking life and limb*, means 'taking great risks – risking everything'. It is often used ironically, e.g. 'I've decided to risk life and limb and teach Belinda how to drive.'

The main grammatical focus is past modals, and these are contextualized in a discussion between two people speculating about why an ancient hunter risked his life climbing in the Alps.

The main reading text is about how the wild west of America was colonised by pioneers in the nineteenth century. The listening text is a humorous poem, about a child who takes unnecessary risks with a lion.

Language aims

Modal auxiliary verbs in the past   Unit 7 looked at the way that modal verbs have many meanings, (obligation, permission, willingness, etc.). In this unit, the aim is to revise and practise modal verbs that are used with the perfect infinitive (modal verb + *have* + past participle).

Past form

It is important to check and practise the complex form, (modal verb + *have* + past participle). Students will need to revise their past participles. They will also need to practise pronunciation here, notably the weak form of have /əv/.

Degrees of probability

The use of *may*, *might* and *could* to express possibility is straightforward. An area of difficulty, however, is the subtle difference between *they'll (won't) have arrived* (an assumption based on our knowledge of people and things) and *they must (can't) have arrived* (a logical conclusion).

should/need/could have…

The form *should(n't)* + *have* + past participle is used to express advice or criticism about a past event. *Need(n't)* + *have* + past participle says that a past action was not necessary. *Could* + *have* + past participle expresses past abilities or possibilities that didn't happen, and can also be used to criticize people for not doing things. Students often get confused between the uses here, using *mustn't* for *shouldn't*, for example. Students tend to avoid using these forms altogether. It is important to practise the uses carefully in context.

Vocabulary   The vocabulary section looks at synonyms in the context of a humorous poem.

Everyday English   This section also has a vocabulary focus. It looks at metaphors and idioms based on parts of the body, e.g. *a head for business* and *face the facts*.

Notes on the unit

TEST YOUR GRAMMAR (SB p86)

The *Test your grammar* section aims to test the students' ability to recognize when modal verbs are expressing probability, and when they have other meanings. There is also some introductory practice in forming past modals.

This exercise should be done quickly. Don't get involved in lengthy grammar explanations at this stage.

1　Ask students in pairs to tick the sentences that express degrees of probability.

Anwers
1　She must be very rich. ✓ (a logical deduction)
2　I must do my homework. ✗ (a personal obligation)
3　I can't sleep because of the noise. ✓ (an (in)ability)
4　They can't be in. There are no lights on. ✓ (a logical deduction)
5　I think that's Jane but I might be wrong. ✓ (a possibility)
6　You should see a doctor. ✗ (advice)
7　I could swim when I was five. ✗ (an ability)
8　Cheer up! Things could be worse. ✓ (possibility)
9　The train may be late due to bad weather. ✓ (possibility)
10　May I make a suggestion? ✗ (permission)

2　Ask students to put sentences 1 to 6 in the past.
T10.1 [CD 3: Track 15] Play the recording so that students can check their answers.

Answers and tapescript
1　She must have been very rich.
2　I had to do my homework.
3　I couldn't sleep because of the noise.
4　They can't have been in. There were no lights on.
5　I thought that was Jane but I might have been wrong.
6　You should have seen a doctor.

ÖTZI THE ICEMAN (SB p86)

Modal auxiliary verbs in the past

This section contextualizes and practises modal auxiliary verbs in the past. The practice activities focus on choosing the correct modal in context.

1　Lead in by asking students about the pictures. Encourage as much speculation as you can. Assess whether your students naturally use modals to speculate, or whether they tend to avoid them.

2　**T10.2** [CD 3: Track 16] Play the recording. Ask students to listen and match the speakers' answers to the questions in exercise 1.

Answers and tapescript
–　He could have been a hunter, or he could have been some kind of shepherd, you know, looking after his sheep up in the mountains.
–　I suppose he ...wore stuff like animal furs.
–　I guess they ate a lot of meat, and berries and fruit. They might even have grown crops, you know, like cereals to make bread.
–　I suppose he lived in a cave.
–　They reckon he fell asleep sheltering from a snowstorm, so he may have died from cold and starvation.
–　They think he was maybe forty to forty-five.

T10.2
A　You know that prehistoric man, the one they discovered in Italy years ago ...
B　You mean that guy in the Alps?
A　Yeah, that's the one. He's supposed to be about five thousand years old. They've done all sorts of tests on him, you know DNA tests and things, to find out about his life.
B　What was he? Some sort of hunter?
A　Well, they aren't sure. He could have been a hunter, or he could have been some kind of shepherd, you know, looking after his sheep up in the mountains. The mystery is 'What was he doing up there?' He might have just got lost for all we know.
B　It must have been cold up there. How did he keep warm?
A　I suppose he lived in a cave and wore stuff like animal furs. They reckon he fell asleep sheltering from a snowstorm, so he may have died from cold and – er starvation. He shouldn't have gone up so high without the right – erm ... you know, protective clothing.
B　I wonder what they did for food five thousand years ago. They hunted wild animals, didn't they, with – erm arrows and axes and things?
A　Yeah, I guess they ate a lot of meat, and, and berries and fruit. They might even have grown crops, you know, like cereals to make bread.
B　No, they can't have been that clever. I bet they didn't know how to do that. I'd have thought they just ate meat, you know, like – erm, like carnivores.
A　Who knows? Maybe these tests will tell us. I don't suppose they got around much. It would have been too difficult.
B　I'm sure. I wouldn't have thought they travelled much at all. I bet they stayed in the same area. How old was he when he died?
A　They think he was maybe forty to forty-five, which must have been quite old in those days.
B　I've bought the magazine *New Scientist*, so we can read all about the results.
A　Well, you needn't have bothered. I've downloaded them from the Internet. Let's have a look at them.

3　**T10.2** Ask students to write answers to the questions, using the modals in italics.

4　**T10.3** [CD 3: Track 17] Play the recording. Ask students to listen and check their answers to the questions in 3. Then ask students to practise the sentences in pairs, paying attention to contracted forms, (*can't*, *wouldn't*, etc.), and weak forms, (*have* /əv/). Alternatively, play the recording again and ask students to repeat, chorally and individually.

Answers and tapescript

1 *What was he?*
He could have been a hunter, or he could have been a shepherd.
2 *What was he doing in the mountains?*
He might have been looking after his sheep, or he might have got lost.
3 *Where did he live? What did he wear?*
He must have lived in a cave.
He must have worn animal furs.
4 *How did he die?*
He may have fallen asleep.
He may have died of cold and starvation.
5 *Was it a good idea to go so high?*
He shouldn't have gone so high on his own.
He should have worn protective clothing.
6 *What did he eat?*
He must have eaten a lot of meat and berries.
They might have grown crops like cereals to make bread.
They can't have grown crops.
I'd have thought they just ate meat.
7 *Did they travel much?*
I wouldn't have thought they travelled much at all.
They must have stayed in the same area.
8 *How old was he when he died?*
He could have been between forty and forty-five.
That must have been quite old in those days.

5 Ask students to look at the objects in the photographs. You could tell them what they are called, although this vocabulary is not necessary to do the activity.
an axe   dried grass   arrows   quiver   a dagger sheath   awl   a flint tool
Ask students to work in pairs or small groups to explain the objects. Model the activity by pointing to the axe and using some of the expressions given.

Sample answers
a **Axe**
That might have been for chopping firewood/killing animals.
He'll have used that to cut firewood.
b **Shoes and dried grass**
The shoes might have been made of leather.
I can't imagine what he could have used the dried grass for.
c **Arrows and quiver**
I suppose he used them to kill wild animals.
I'd have thought he killed wild animals using a bow and arrow.
d **Bearskin hat**
He'll have worn that when he was up in the mountains.
e **Flint knife/dagger and sheath**
I bet he used it to kill wild animals/defend himself/cut up his food.
That must have been for cutting up food.

f **Flint sharpening tool**
I reckon that's a tool for sharpening flint knives and arrowheads.
I bet he used that for sharpening knives and tools.
g **Awl**
He'll have used that for making holes in leather.
I wouldn't have thought that was a weapon.

6 Ask students to read the text on p157 of the Student's Book. Have a brief class discussion, asking whether the assumptions were correct.

Answers
Alan and Bill got the following wrong:
He was 46, not 40 to 45.
Although probably a herdsman or hunter, he was a warrior when he died.
Ötzi died from his battle wounds, not cold or starvation – he wasn't lost.

LANGUAGE FOCUS

See TB p8 for suggestions on how to teach this section.

Don't forget to look at the *Language aims* section on TB p102, which looks at problems students may have. You should also read the Grammar Reference on SB p151.

LANGUAGE INPUT

1 Ask students in pairs to write *certain* or *possible* next to the modals.

Answers	
They'll have	*certain* (an assumption based on our knowledge of people and things)
They must have	*certain* (a logical conclusion)
They might have	*possible*
They could have	*possible*
They may have	*possible*
They can't have	*certain* (negative certainty – a logical conclusion)
They won't have	*certain* (negative certainty – an assumption based on our knowledge of people and things)

2 Ask students in pairs to match the modals to the definitions.

Answers
You shouldn't have told a lie.
You did this but it was wrong.
You needn't have cooked. No one's hungry.
You did this but it wasn't necessary.
You idiot! You could have killed yourself!
This was possible but you didn't do it.

Refer students to the Grammar Reference on SB p151.

Discussing grammar

1 Ask students to underline the correct answer in the sentences. Let them check in pairs before feedback.

> **Answers**
> 1 Sorry I'm late. I *should have gone*/__had to go__ to the post office. (an obligation, *not* a regret)
> 2 I looked for Pearl but I __couldn't find__/*couldn't have found* her. (ability – the past of *can't* is *couldn't*)
> 3 I don't know where Paul is. He *had to go*/__must have gone__ home early. (logical deduction – he isn't here, so I deduce that he has gone home – note that the past of *must* is *had to* (obligation) or *must have + past participle* (probability)
> 4 I __had to work__/*must have worked* hard when I was at school. (an obligation – unlikely that this would be a deduction)
> 5 You *needn't have said*/__shouldn't have said__ anything to Pam about her birthday party. It was going to be a surprise. (a criticism about a past event, *not* expressing a lack of necessity)
> 6 You __needn't have bought__/*couldn't have bought* a new vacuum cleaner. I managed to fix the old one. (expressing that it was not necessary, *not* expressing an impossibility or something that you were unable to do)
> 7 You __should have asked__/*must have asked* me earlier. I *might have given*/__would have given__ you a lift. (expressing a criticism, *not* probability/an assumption, *not* a possibility)
> 8 You __can't have done__/*needn't have done* your homework already! You only started five minutes ago. (logically impossible, *not* unnecessary)
> 9 You __could have told__/*must have told* me the lesson had been cancelled! I *shouldn't have got*/__wouldn't have got__ up so early. (criticizing someone for not doing something, *not* a logical deduction/an assumption, *not* a regret)
> 10 You were lucky to get out of the car unharmed. You *would have been*/__could have been__ badly hurt. (a possibility that didn't happen)

2 Ask students to complete the sentences. Let students check in pairs before feedback.
T10.4 [CD 3: Track 18] Play the recording. Students listen and check their answers.

> **Answers and tapescript**
> 1 I *did* tell you about Joe's party. You **can't have been** listening.
> 2 Thanks so much for all your help. I **couldn't have** managed without you.
> 3 Flowers, for me! Oh, that's so kind, but really you **shouldn't have**.
> 4 Come on! We're only five minutes late. The film **won't have** started yet.
> 5 I don't believe that Kathy's going out with Mark. She**'d have** told me, I know she would.
> 6 We raced to get to the airport on time, but we **needn't have** worried. The flight was delayed.
> 7 We've got a letter here that isn't for us. The postman **must have** delivered it by mistake.
> 8 You **shouldn't have** gone swimming in such rough sea. You **could have** drowned!

Making assumptions

3 Ask students to look at the photograph and speculate on who the person is and what she is talking about.
T10.5 [CD 3: Track 19] Play the recording. Ask students to listen and answer the questions. In the feedback, encourage students to make assumptions, using modal verbs. You could give them the following prompts: *divorced, separated, kids, remarried, new girlfriend, upset, arrange.*

> **Sample answers**
> They must be divorced.
> They might be separated.
> They must have kids.
> He must have remarried.
> He might have a new girlfriend.
> She must have been very upset when he left.
> He must be ringing to arrange to see his kids.

4 Ask students in pairs to look at tapescript 10.5 on p136 of the Student's book. Ask them to write the other half of the conversation. Elicit one or two lines from the class to get the pairs started.

When the students have finished, ask them to compare their dialogues with other students. Ask one or two pairs to act out their dialogues for the class.

Alternatively, nominate a student, then play and pause the recording, asking the student to respond after each line.

> **Answers and tapescript** (with sample responses in italics)
> Hello.
> *Hello.*
> Oh, it's you.
> *Yes, it's me. How are you and the kids?*
> We're all right, no thanks to you. Why are you ringing?
> *Well, I'm ringing about next Saturday.*
> What do you mean, next Saturday? What about next Saturday?
> *It's my day for seeing the kids.*
> Already! Is it the second Saturday of the month so soon? Yes, I suppose it is. All right, then.
> *Great. I'll come over and pick them up.*
> Where are you thinking of taking them? The children always pester if they don't know, especially Daniel.

I was thinking of taking them to the zoo.

The zoo! Again! Can't you think of anything else? They hated it last time. Nicky did, anyway.

She said she had a great time.

That's not what she told me. Anyway, that's up to you. What time are you going to pick them up?

About two.

OK. I'll have them ready. By the way, when they come home after a day with you, they're always filthy. Can't Alison wash their clothes?

She's busy. She doesn't have the time.

Well, she has enough time to go shopping and have lunch with her friends, from what the kids have told me.

Well, that's hardly fair. She has a full-time job.

All right! I don't want to argue about it.

Tell the kids I love them.

I'll tell them you rang. Bye.

---

5 **T10.6** [CD 3: Track 20] Repeat the above procedure with the second dialogue. You could give students the following prompts: *holiday romance, visit, in love, disappointed.*

Sample answers
They must have had a holiday romance in Greece.
He may have told her to visit him.
She might still be in love with him.
She must be disappointed.

Ask students in pairs to look at tapescript 10.6 on p136 of the Student's book and write the other half of the conversation, as before.

Answers and tapescript (with sample responses in italics)
Hello.

Hello. Could I speak to Jeremy Brook, please?

This is Jeremy Brook speaking.

Hi Jeremy. This is Janice. Janice Frobisher.

Sorry – Janice who?

Janice Frobisher.

I'm sorry. I don't think I know anyone by that name.

We met on holiday.

On holiday? Did we? When was that?

In '99, in Skopelos, in Greece. Don't you remember?

In Greece! Of course! I remember! You're the American girl who was in the next room. That was years ago! How are you?

I'm fine. How are you?

I'm fine. What a surprise! What are you doing? Where are you?

Well, I'm travelling around Europe, and believe it or not I'm here in York.

Here? What are you doing here?

I was hoping to come over and stay with you for a few days.

Erm ... well ... I'd love to, but erm ... well, it's not very convenient, actually.

But you said that if I was ever in England I should come and stay at your place.

Yes, I know I said that, but that was a long time ago, and erm ... our flat isn't that big, and ...

Are you with someone else? Are you married?

Yes, I am. I got married last year.

Oh, I had no idea. I'm sorry I bothered you.

Well, I'm glad you understand. I'm sorry to let you down. I'd have liked to help, but er you see what I mean.

Yes, of course. Well, nice talking to you.

Well, maybe we could meet for a drink er ... you know, for old times' sake?

I don't think that would be a good idea, do you?

No, no, I suppose you're right. Well, it was nice to hear your voice again. Enjoy your trip round Europe.

OK. Well, all the best.

Thanks. Bye, Janice. Same to you.

SPOKEN ENGLISH – Expressions with modals

Ask students in pairs to match the expressions in **A** with the expressions in **B**.

T10.7 [CD 3: Track 21] Play the recording. Students listen and check their answers. Ask if they can identify the extra lines and work out what the contexts are. Then put students in pairs to practise the conversations.

Answers and tapescript
1b Extra line: *I'm bound to have failed.*
    Context: Two people talking about an exam they've just done
2d Extra line: *You never know, I might be just the person they're looking for.*
    Context: Deciding on whether to apply for a job.
3c Extra line: *I feel as fat as a pig now.*
    Context: Regretting eating too much ice-cream
4e Extra line: *It could get really nasty.*
    Context: Speaker is angry with someone and wants to say what they think – being advised against it
5a Extra line: *Everybody else does.*
    Context: Two friends talking – one of them is angry because they have said something about Jackie and Dave, not knowing they have split up
6g Extra line: *But I just can't get her out of my mind. I think it must be love./Oh no!*
    Context: friend advising friend to forget about his ex-girlfriend
7h Extra line: *Pedro was imitating the teacher, and he was so good, when the teacher walked in.*
    Context: Two students
8i Extra line: *It's common knowledge. Where have you been?*
    Context: friends gossiping
9j Extra line: *Maybe he does the same to every girl he meets.*
    Context: girlfriend telling friend about a date

10f Extra line: *It feels like this lesson's been going on for ages.*
Context: Two students in long, boring lesson

T10.7

1 **A** That exam was totally impossible!
B You can say that again! I couldn't answer a single question. I'm bound to have failed.

2 **A** You might as well apply for the job, even though you're too young.
B Yes, why not! After all, I've got nothing to lose. You never know, I might be just the person they're looking for.

3 I know I shouldn't have eaten a whole tub of ice-cream but I just couldn't help it. I feel as fat as a pig now.

4 **A** I'm going to tell her exactly what I think of her.
B I wouldn't do that if I were you. You've no idea how she'll react. It could get really nasty.

5 **A** You might have told me that Jackie and Dave had split up! I felt really stupid when I asked Jackie where they were going on holiday.
B Sorry! I thought you knew. Everybody else does.

6 **A** I think you should forget all about her and move on.
B Believe me, I would if I could. But I just can't get her out of my mind. I think it must be love.
A Oh no!

7 **A** You should have been here yesterday! You'd have died laughing!
B Why? What was so funny?
A Well, Pedro was imitating the teacher, and he was so good, and then the teacher walked in.

8 **A** Then I found out that Annie's been going out with ... guess who? Dave!
B Huh! I could have told *you* that. It's common knowledge. Where have you been?

9 I'd known this guy for five minutes when he asked me to marry him! I just couldn't believe it! Maybe he does the same to every girl he meets.

10 **A** I could do with a break.
B Me, too. I'm dying for a coffee. It feels like this lesson's been going on for ages.

Song **After T 10.10** [CD 3: Track 25]
One of these things first TB p162

Writing Unit 10
Formal and informal letters and emails – Do's and don'ts SB p121

ADDITIONAL MATERIAL

Workbook Unit 10
Exercise 1 Revision of modals
Exercises 2-6 Modal verbs of probability

It all went wrong!

6 Model this activity carefully. Write the following phrases from the Student's Book on the board:
Couldn't you have...? Why didn't you...?
You must have been terrified/shocked/upset!
Don't you think you should have...?
I'd have thought you could have...
Tell the students a brief story of a day when everything went wrong for you. For example, a journey involving a breakdown, or a dinner party when the electricity went off. Pause occasionally, point at the board, and encourage students to interrupt your story by asking questions or making statements using the expressions.

Ask students to think of a time in their life when everything went wrong. Then either ask them to tell the class, or divide the students into groups so that they can tell their stories that way. Tell both speakers and listeners to use the expressions from the lesson to make the story more interactive.

SPEAKING (SB p89)

The murder game

The aim of this task is to provide students with an opportunity for fluency practice, hopefully using past modals of deduction.

You will need to photocopy and cut up the cards on p161 of the Teacher's Book. There are fourteen cards. If you have less than fourteen students, then some students will get more than one card. If you have slightly more than fourteen students, some can share a card. If you have a large class, over twenty, then make two sets of cards, and have two groups.

HOW TO PLAY THE MURDER GAME

1, 2 Read the introduction as a class. Tell the students that you are not going to help or organize at all. However, if your class and room size allow, it is a good idea to get students sitting in a circle before they start the activity. Hand out the cards at random to the students.
Sit down somewhere in the room where you are not the focus of attention. Prepare to take notes on their performance, (i.e. How did they organize themselves? Was everyone involved? Did everyone listen?), and the linguistic performance of the class, (i.e. What errors did they make, particularly with the grammar of the unit?)
The students tend to be unsure about how to start, at first. Don't be tempted to help. Eventually, somebody will take the lead. They may decide to write up information on the board. They may decide to read out their cards to each other. In the authors' experience, the record for solving the murder is fifteen minutes; the average is about thirty-five.

---

3 When students have finished, ask them to discuss the questions in the Student's Book, which will help them assess their performance of the task. Then give your feedback from the notes you took while the activity was going on.

Answers
See the diagram below which shows the actual seating arrangement. Brown must have been the murderer because no-one else moved, so no-one else could have put poison in Jones' glass.
Games like these are used on management training courses because they test a group's ability to organize themselves and work co-operatively.

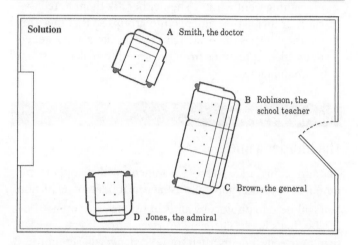

Solution
A Smith, the doctor
B Robinson, the school teacher
C Brown, the general
D Jones, the admiral

READING AND SPEAKING (SB p90)

How the West was won

The aim here is to improve the students' ability to read for specific information.

Here is a useful way of introducing the topic, predicting content, and pre-teaching key vocabulary:

Before asking students to open their books, write *How the West was won* in the middle of the board. Then write some or all of the words below at random all over the board. Ask, *How do these words relate to how the West was won, and how do they relate to each other?* Tell students to work in small groups to discuss the words. In the feedback, encourage groups to tell the class all they know about the Wild West.

native Americans settlers migration buffalo Sioux reservations Plains Indians covered wagons goldrush fur traders extinct Great Plains annihilation railroads

1 Ask students to tell you about their favourite cowboy films. Encourage a light-hearted class discussion.

2 Ask students to talk about the title and headings in pairs or small groups. Encourage lots of speculation in the feedback.

3 Ask students to read the first two sections and answer the questions. Let students check their answers in pairs before feedback.

Answers
1 To find new land to farm; to claim land promised to them by the government in Oregon and California; they believed it was part of God's plan to make America one continent and claim the land from the 'natives'.
2 Mountains, deserts, plains, blizzards, snowstorms, disease, dust storms, mud, plagues of insects.
  Many things could go wrong – if delayed, they faced fierce snowstorms in the mountains, and disease and self-inflicted gun deaths were common.
  They could have avoided shooting each other if they had been more experienced with guns.
3 1843: large-scale migration began
  14,000: number of settlers by 1848
  2,000 (miles): length of journey
  $4\frac{1}{2}$ (months): length of journey (time)
  15 (miles): distance covered in a day
  25: one in twenty-five migrants failed to reach their destination

4 Ask students to read the section about the Donner family, and complete the sentences. Let students check their answers in pairs before feedback.

Answers
1 They shouldn't have set out so late in the year.
2 They should have followed an established route.
3 They must have spent the winter in the mountains./They shouldn't have spent the winter in the mountains.
4 They should have taken enough food.
5 They must have been really starving to do what they did.

5 Ask students to read the rest of the article, and answer the questions. Let students check their answers in pairs before feedback.

Answers
1 Relations were generally friendly – trade was common and they inter-married. Attacks on wagons were rare, and the native Americans were amused by the new settlers. The Gold Rush caused the change – camps, roads and railroads were built on sacred hunting grounds.
2 They had a complex culture and social structure. They didn't believe that land should be owned by individuals, but should belong to all people. They believed that human beings were indivisible from the natural world. And they were hunters. They were bound to clash with the settlers who wanted to own and build on their sacred land.
3 They helped them by trading blankets, beads, mirrors and guns. They exploited them by developing their sacred hunting grounds, and hunting the buffalo to near extinction.
4 They lost the battle of Wounded Creek in 1890.
5 *White people*: pioneers, Americans, travellers, whites, new Americans, settlers, migrants, white Americans
Indians: native Americans, Plains Indians, primitive natives, Sioux, savages, hunters

What do you think?

The aim here is to use the reading text as a springboard for discussion.

Divide the class into small groups to discuss the questions. Nominate one person to be a chairperson. They must ask the questions, and make sure everybody in the group contributes. Nominate another student to be a secretary. They must make notes of what everybody says, then report what was said to the class.

Possible answers
• Settlers have taken the lands of natives in many countries. A common example is Australia, (many aborigines were corralled in reservations in the late nineteenth century; they died of disease; in Tasmania they were wiped out; today there are many land issues between aborigines and the government). In Canada, as in Australia, First Nation people were forced to give up their traditional way of life, and their children were taken from their families and forced to go to 'civilized' schools.
• *Arguments for developing remote parts of the world*: making the country rich; providing jobs; developing countries should be allowed to benefit from their natural wealth
Arguments against: destroying the environment/ozone layer; global warming; destroying our natural legacy; destroying traditional ways of life; the people who get rich are corrupt politicians and multi-nationals

Synonyms – the story of Jim and the lion

The aim is to introduce synonyms, and to get students to read and enjoy a humorous poem.

The poem includes lots of 'body parts', which leads neatly into the *Everyday English* section on 'body' metaphors. You may wish to pre-teach them: *jaws toes heels shins ankles calves knees*

There are a few words in the text that you may need to explain.
befell = happened to (archaic)
relate = tell
foible = strange, annoying behaviour that is relatively harmless
inauspicious = unlikely to be successful
keeper = zookeeper
bade (past of *bid*) = asked/commanded (archaic)
keep a-hold of = hold on to/hold hands with (archaic)

BACKGROUND INFORMATION
The illustrations are by Edward Gorey, and come from *Cautionary Tales for Children*, a book of humorous verses with a moral, first published in 1907. The author, Hilaire Belloc, (1870-1953), was a British essayist, historian, novelist and poet, of mixed French and English origin. He wrote travel books, biographies, and most famously, comic verse.
The humour in this poem arises from the hilariously detached air of the narrator. The author is mocking the detached way that parents viewed their children in this period.

1 Ask students to look at the title and pictures and discuss the questions in pairs or small groups, and guess the answers.
2 **T10.8** [CD 3: Track 22] Play the recording. Ask students to close their books and listen to the poem, then discuss the answers to the questions in 1 with their partner or group.

Answers
1 To the zoo
2 Naughty
3 Less than a yard (just under a metre) – before he was attacked by a lion
4 By gradual degrees, starting with his toes
5 The (zoo)keeper – it worked in that, on request, the lion dropped Jim – but Jim was already dead
6 They were very 'concerned' but not surprised, and his father used the opportunity to lecture the other children on good behaviour.

3 Ask students to work in pairs or groups to complete the lines in the first verse. Students may remember some of the words from the first listening, but should also be able to work out the answers by considering style, rhythm, and rhyme. Do the first word as an example. Point out that, although both *buddies* and *friends* are grammatically correct, only *friends* is possible because of style, (*buddies* sounds too informal and American), and rhythm, (*buddies* has two syllables, which, if inserted, makes the number of syllables in the line too great – each line always has eight syllables). Encourage students to say the lines out loud to get an idea of which word fits the rhythm.

4 **T10.8** Ask students to listen to the first verse and check their answers. Then ask them to complete the gaps in the rest of the poem, before playing the rest of the recording and checking their answers.

Answers and tapescript

Jim, who ran away from his nurse, and was eaten by a lion
There was a boy whose name was Jim;
His **friends** were very good to him.
They gave him tea, and cakes, and jam,
And slices of **delicious** ham,
And read him **stories** through and through,
And even took him to the zoo –
But there it was the **dreadful** fate
Befell him, I now **relate**.
You know – at least you ought to know,
For I have **often** told you so –
That children never are **allowed**
To leave their nurses in a crowd;
Now this was Jim's especial foible,
He ran away when he was able,
And on this **inauspicious** day
He slipped his hand and **ran** away!
He hadn't gone a yard when – bang!
With open jaws, a lion **sprang**,
And hungrily began to eat
The boy: **beginning** at his feet.
Now just **imagine** how it feels
When **first** your toes and then your heels,
And then by gradual degrees,
Your shins and ankles, calves and knees,
Are **slowly** eaten, bit by bit.
No wonder Jim **detested** it!
No wonder that he **shouted** 'Hi!'
The honest keeper heard his cry,
Though very **fat**, he almost ran
To help the little gentleman
'Ponto!' he cried, with **angry** frown
'Let go, sir! Down, sir! Put it down!'

....

The lion having reached his head
The **miserable** boy was dead!
When nurse **informed** his parents they
Were more **concerned** than I can say: –
His mother, as she dried her eyes,
Said, 'Well – it gives me no **surprise**,
He would not do as he was told!'
His father, who was **self-controlled**
Bade all the **children** round attend
To James' miserable **end**,
And always keep a-hold of nurse
For fear of finding something worse.

5 Discuss the questions as a class.

Answers
The moral, for children, is not to let go of your parent's or childminder's hand in dangerous places.
The tone is amusingly matter-of-fact and restrained, despite the horrific event it describes.
It is funny because you would expect parents to be upset, distraught, inconsolable. *Concerned* is not appropriate here, and suggests that the parents were very emotionally detached from their child.

What do you think?

The aim here is to use the poem as a springboard for speaking.
Ask students in small groups to discuss the questions. Ask a spokesperson from each group to summarize what was said.

EVERYDAY ENGLISH (SB p93)

Metaphors and idioms – the body

The aim of this section is to practise metaphors and idioms based on parts of the body.

1 Ask students in pairs to complete the gaps.

Answers
Your **head** is associated with intelligence.
Your **hands** are associated with manual skills.
Your **heart** is associated with emotions.

2 Ask students in pairs to decide which sentence uses a part of the body literally, and to rephrase the words used metaphorically.

3 Ask students in pairs to complete the sentences.

4 **T10.9** [CD 3: Track 23] Play the recording. Ask students to listen to the conversations. Ask a gist question, *What are they talking about?*

Put students in pairs. Ask them to think of ways of replacing some of the phrases with expressions from the lesson. Either play the recording again and pause after the relevant phrases (in italics in the tapescript above), and/or ask students to look at tapescript 10.9 on p136 of the Student's Book.

T10.10 [CD 3: Track 24] Play the recording so that students can check their answers.

5 Ask students in pairs to look up another part of the body, and find one or two idioms or metaphors which they think are useful. Ask students to tell the rest of the class what they have found. The following words are good ones to look up: *arm*, *ear*, *eye*, *finger*.

ADDITIONAL MATERIAL

Workbook Unit 10
Exercises 7-8 Vocabulary
Exercise 9 Prepositions
Exercise 10 Pronunciation – Rhymes and limericks

11

Hypothesizing • Expressions with *if*
Word pairs • Moans and groans

In your dreams

Introduction to the unit

The theme of this unit is regrets, wishes and dreams. The expression that makes up the title, *In your dreams*, can be read literally. However, it is also an expression used humorously to say, 'there is no chance of that happening'. The main language point is hypothesis, and is contextualized in dialogues in which people express wishes and regrets.

The main reading text is about things that people often wonder about, such as why we dream. In the listening text, someone describes a strange dream and students are asked to interpret this and other dreams.

Language aims

Hypothesis   The aim is to revise and practise ways of hypothesizing: using conditional sentences with *if*, and using other expressions like *wish*, *if only*, *supposing* and *should have done*.

Fact and non-fact   First conditional sentences are based on fact in real time. *If I see Paula* (the condition is possible), *I'll say hello* (the result is probable). Second and third conditionals, and *I wish* and *If only* are not based on fact. In fact, they say the opposite of reality.
If I saw Paula, I'd…
(the condition is hypothetical – I won't see Paula)
If I'd seen Paula, I would have…
(the condition is hypothetical – I didn't see Paula)
If only/I wish I'd seen Paula. (but, sadly, I didn't)

Actually, this concept is not as tricky as it looks. Most languages have a similar concept of hypothesis. Note that most European languages have a special subjunctive form to use with hypothesis, whereas English uses Simple Past and Past Perfect forms, (with the exception of *If/I wish I* **were**…).

POSSIBLE PROBLEMS
Problems with form
Students over-use *will* in the first conditional.
*If I will win the race, I will get a prize.
Because the past form is used in the second conditional and with *wish*, students think that the sentence refers to the past, not a hypothetical present or future.
*I wish I won the race last week.
The third conditional is a complex form, and it's difficult to remember all the parts! As *I had* and *I would* are both contracted to *I'd*, students sometimes get confused about which one should be used.
*I'd have told you if I would have known.
Problems with pronunciation
These forms involve a lot of contractions and weak forms. It is important to practise the pronunciation of *I'll/we'll* and *I'd/we'd*, and to practise the weak forms common with the third conditional *I'd have* /aɪdəv/, and other forms, e.g. *you should have* /ʃʌdəv/.

Uses of *wish*   *Wish* is used in a number of ways.
I wish I **were** *on holiday.* (wanting something to be different)
I wish I **had worked** *harder.* (regret about the past)
I wish you **would go** *away.* (irritation)

The major difficulty students have is knowing when they can use *would*. The answer is, when it expresses willingness, and not for wishes about yourself.

*I wish I would shut up.

I wish he would shut up. (I wish he was willing to...)

Vocabulary   The vocabulary section looks at word pairs, e.g. *now and then*, and *peace and quiet*.

Everyday English   This section practises ways of moaning and complaining.

Notes on the unit

TEST YOUR GRAMMAR (SB p94)

The *Test your grammar* section aims to test the students' ability to use the correct form after *wish*, showing whether they understand the 'one tense back' rule when hypothesizing.

This exercise should be done quickly. Don't get involved in lengthy grammar explanations at this stage.

1   Ask students to read Column **A** and say what Helen's problems are.

> **Answers**
> It's raining, she's bored, unhappy with her job, and she's depressed because she's split up with her boyfriend.

2   Ask students to join lines in **A** with wishes in **B**. Let them check in pairs.

> **T11.1**   [CD 3: Track 26] Play the recording so that students can check their answers.

> **Answers and tapescript**
> 1   It's raining again. I wish it wasn't.
> 2   I'm not going out tonight. I wish I was.
> 3   There's nothing good on TV. I wish there was.
> 4   I don't like my job. I wish I did.
> 5   My boyfriend and I split up last week. I wish we hadn't.
> 6   I know he won't call me. I wish he would.
> 7   I feel really depressed. I wish I didn't.
> 8   I can't talk to anyone about it. I wish I could.

3   Ask students to think of something they are not happy about. Then tell the class what they wish. For example, *I haven't done my homework. I wish I had.*

IF ONLY... (SB p94)

Hypothesizing about the past and present

This section contextualizes and practises ways of hypothesizing about the past and present. The practice activities focus on manipulating the form of these complex structures.

1   Lead in by asking students about the pictures. Encourage as much speculation as you can. Assess whether your students are able to express regrets and wishes accurately.

2   **T11.2**   [CD 3: Track 27] Play the recording. Ask students to listen and number the pictures in order. In the feedback, ask students if they can remember what people said.

> **Answers and tapescript**
> 1e   a student saying that she can't go out because she has to revise for an exam
> 2b   two mothers with kids, wishing they could go on holiday
> 3a   two teenagers wish they could buy a sports car
> 4d   father and grandfather talk about playing football
> 5c   car owner trying to persuade traffic warden not to give out a ticket

> **T11.2**
> 1   **A**   No, I can't possibly go out tonight. I shouldn't have gone out last night.
>   **B**   Come on – we had a great time. It was one helluva party!
>   **A**   I know it was.
>   **B**   So, when's your exam?
>   **A**   Tomorrow, 9 o'clock. If only I hadn't left all my revision 'til the last minute.
>   **B**   I wouldn't worry if I were you. You know you always do OK.
>   **A**   There's always a first time.
>   **B**   Good luck anyway.
> 2   **A**   If only we could just fly off to that island.
>   **B**   That would be fantastic. I'd sit on a beach and read all day.
>   **A**   I'd just sleep forever. I can't remember a full night's sleep.
>   **B**   Yeah. Sometimes I wish I'd never had kids. I mean, not really, but ...
>   **A**   I know what you mean. No – you can't have an ice cream. I said NO!
> 3   **A**   Oh boy! What would you give to drive one of those?!
>   **B**   Which one would you choose if you had the money?
>   **A**   That's one big 'if'! But ... mmm ... ... er ... if I won the lottery, I'd buy the Aston Martin.
>   **B**   I wouldn't – I'd go for the Ferrari.
>   **A**   In your dreams.
> 4   **A**   Brilliant shot Charlie! Well-done!
>   **B**   Don't you wish you still played football dad?
>   **A**   Me? No. I was never any good. But *you* could have been a brilliant player if you'd wanted.
>   **B**   Nah! I wasn't as good as Charlie. Aaah – oh nearly! YES!!
>   **A**   Yeah, he'll go far.
> 5   **A**   Look, I know I shouldn't have parked here but I was only gone two minutes.
>   **B**   I've already written the ticket.

A Surely you could cancel it if you wanted? It was literally one minute.

B One minute, two minutes. You can't park here, it's as simple as that.

A But I just had to dash into the chemist to collect a prescription for my sick grandmother. Supposing you cancelled it just this once?

B I don't care what you were doing. I can't cancel a ticket – it's more than my job's worth. You've got two weeks to pay.

3 **T11.2** Ask students to listen again and complete the lines, and say who is speaking. Let them check in pairs before feedback.

Answers
1 I shouldn't have gone out last night.
If only I hadn't left *all* my revision 'til the last minute.
I wouldn't worry if I were you.
(*two student friends are talking*)

2 If only we could just fly off to that island.
That would be fantastic.
I'd just sleep forever.
Sometimes I wish I'd never had kids.
(*two mums are talking*)

3 What would you give to drive one of those?!
Which would you choose if you had the money?
... if I won the lottery, I'd buy the Aston Martin.
I wouldn't – I'd go for the Ferrari.
(*two teenagers looking at sports cars*)

4 Don't you wish you still played football dad?
But *you* could have been a brilliant player if you'd wanted.
(*dad and son at football match*)

5 I shouldn't have parked here ...
Surely you could cancel it if you wanted?
Supposing you cancelled it just this once?
(*car owner talking to a traffic warden*)

4 Ask students to work in pairs, using the completed lines in 3 to improvise the conversations. Ask two or three pairs to act out a conversation for the class.

5 Ask students in pairs to look back at the lines in exercise 3, and discuss what the facts are behind the wishes and regrets. The aim of this exercise is to make sure students are very clear about the hypothetical 'non-fact' nature of these sentences – they are actually saying the opposite of reality. Note the tense change from non-fact to fact: *If only I **hadn't** left…/She **has** left…*

Answers
1 *I shouldn't have gone out last night.*
She *did* go out last night. She went to a party. (note the emphatic use of *did* here)
If only I hadn't left all my revision 'til the last minute.
She *has* left all her revision until the last minute.
I wouldn't worry if I were you.
She *isn't* her friend. Her friend *is* worried!

2 *If only we could just fly off to that island.*
But we *can't* just fly off to that island.
That would be fantastic. But it *won't* happen.
I'd just sleep forever.
Normally, I *can't* get any sleep because of the kids.
Sometimes I wish I'd never had kids.
But I *have* had kids.

3 *What would you give to drive one of those?!*
Not that you *can* give anything – it's impossible.
Which would you choose if you had the money?
You *don't* have the money.
If I won the lottery, I'd buy the Aston Martin.
There is very little chance of winning the lottery.
I wouldn't – I'd go for the Ferrari. I'm dreaming.

4 *Don't you wish you still played football dad?*
He *doesn't* play football any more.
But you could have been a brilliant player if you'd wanted.
He had the chance, but he didn't take it. He *wasn't* a brilliant player.

5 *I shouldn't have parked here.*
I *did* park here. I regret it.
Surely you could cancel it if you wanted?
You *can* cancel it but you don't want to.
Supposing you cancelled it just this once?
Here's a suggestion – cancel it.

LANGUAGE FOCUS

See TB p8 for suggestions on how to teach this section.

Don't forget to look at the *Language aims* section on TB p112, which looks at problems students may have. You should also read the Grammar Reference on SB pp151–152.

LANGUAGE INPUT

1 Ask students in pairs to decide what are the facts behind each hypothesis. In the feedback, make sure students are very clear about the hypothetical 'non-fact' nature of these sentences – they are actually saying the opposite of reality. Point out the tense change from non-fact to fact:

would $\longrightarrow$ won't
spoke $\longrightarrow$ don't speak
could $\longrightarrow$ can't
had helped $\longrightarrow$ didn't help

Answers
a I don't know the answer.
b I can't come.
c I didn't tell the truth.
d I do get nervous. I don't get better results.
e You didn't help us. We haven't finished.
f I didn't listen to your advice.
g I don't speak French well.
h You won't speak to him.

2 Ask students which sentences are about present time, and which are about past time.

Answers
a, b, d, g, h are about present time. Note that *b* and *h* could be referring to a future time, depending on the context. *c, e, f* are about past time. Note that hypothetical forms use a 'past' form to refer to the present, and a 'past perfect' form to refer to the past. The form, *should have done*, also refers to the past.

3 Ask students to tell you the full forms.

Answers
c *I'd* = I had
d *I'd* = I would
e *you'd* = you had, *we'd* = we would

4 Ask students in pairs to complete the sentences with the real facts.

Answers
It's time you **knew** the truth. The fact is that you **don't know** the truth.
I'd rather you **didn't smoke**. The fact is that you **do smoke**.
I'd rather they **hadn't come**. The fact is that they **did come/have come**.
Supposing you**'d fallen** and **hurt** yourself. Fortunately, you **didn't** (**fall** or **hurt** yourself).

Grammar note
In *I'd rather you didn't smoke*, *I'd rather…* is used as a polite way to tell someone to do something differently.

In *I'd rather they hadn't come*, the expression has a similar meaning to *I wish* – it expresses a regret or a wish that the situation had been different.

Refer students to the Grammar Reference on SB pp151–152.

PRACTICE (SB p95)

1 Ask students to write the sentences using the words in brackets. Let them check in pairs before feedback. Remind the students to think about whether the hypothesis is about the past or present, and, therefore, which form is needed.

Answers
1 I wish I spoke English fluently.
2 If you didn't speak very (so) fast, I would understand.
3 I wish I weren't an only child./I wish I had a brother or sister.
4 If only we had enough money for a holiday.

---

5 I wouldn't get up at six o'clock every morning if I didn't have to go to work.
6 If I had learned to ski when I was younger, I would be good (better) now. (note that this is a mixed conditional – it starts as a past hypothesis, and ends with a 'hypothetical result' now)
7 She wishes she were* (was) older. (*note that modern usage allows both *were* or *was* here – in fact, *was* is now more common in spoken English. It is only in the expression, *If I were you*, that *were* is generally preferred)
8 I'd rather he/she didn't borrow things without asking./I'd rather he/she asked before borrowing things.
9 If I knew something about computers, I could/I'd help you.
10 It's time we had a break. (*It's time to have a break* is also possible)

Broken dreams

2 Ask students to look at the picture of Sozos. Ask, *How does he feel? What do you think his regret is?*
Ask students to read the story, explain the title, and complete the regret.

Answers
The title is a play on words. The expression, *Crime doesn't pay*, usually means that crime is a bad idea because in the end you lose. So, here, politeness is a bad idea because in the end you lose.
How different my life would have been if only I'd **bought that ticket/hadn't offered the woman my place in the queue**!

3 Ask students to form sentences from the prompts. Let students check in pairs before feedback.

Answers
1 Sozos shouldn't have allowed the old lady to jump the queue.
2 If he hadn't followed his mother's advice, his life would have been very different.
3 If he'd contacted the old lady, she might have given him the (some) money.
4 What would have happened if he'd kept his place in the queue?
5 Supposing he hadn't given away his place in the queue?

Ask students in pairs to think of answers to question five. Elicit a few answers from each pair in the feedback.

Possible answers
If he hadn't given away his place, he would have become a millionaire./he might have travelled round the world./he could have bought a yacht/mansion/desert island.

4 **T11.3** [CD 3: Track 28] Play the recording. Ask students to listen to Marty's story, then work in pairs to complete the sentences. You may need to play the recording a second time if students have trouble completing the sentences. Ask some pairs to read out their sentences to the class.

5 Ask students in pairs to complete the question and think of answers to it.

Talking about you

6 Model the activity by telling students about a few of the things on your wish list, (*I wish I had a bigger house./If only I earned more money./I wish I had more holidays.*) Try to model a 'regretful' intonation pattern, and stress *wish* and *only*. For example:

I wish I had a bigger house.

If only I earned more money.

Ask students to look at the wish list, and make sentences using the prompts. Tell students to discuss their wishes in small groups, then ask a spokesperson from each group to summarize their group's wishes.

SPOKEN ENGLISH – Expressions with *if*

Ask students in pairs to match the expressions in **A** with the expressions in **B**.

T11.4 [CD 3: Track 29] Play the recording. Students listen and check their answers. What are the extra lines and contexts? Put students in pairs to practise the conversations.

Context: Two people talking about a team's chances in a match

7 **A We arrived on the Tuesday and ...**
   B It was a Thursday, not a Tuesday, if I remember rightly.
   A Oh Tuesday, Thursday – the day doesn't matter. I'll just never forget the blue of the water and the white of the sand.
   Context: Two people remembering a holiday

8 **A** Well, if the worst comes to the worst, we can always postpone it for a day or two.
   B I'd rather not. I've just got a bit of a headache. The sea air will do me good.
   A OK, if you're sure.
   Context: two people talking about a trip to the coast – one feels ill

9 **A** You haven't made much progress, if any at all.
   B What d'you mean? I've written five hundred words.
   A Yeah, but you have to write ten thousand.
   Context: person prompting someone to get on with a writing task

10 **A I don't think much of Nancy's new boyfriend. He's really cold and arrogant.**
   B Actually, I don't think he's cold or arrogant. If anything, he's a bit shy.
   A Shy?! You wouldn't say that if you'd seen him at Ned's party!
   Context: friends talking about Nancy's new boyfriend

ADDITIONAL MATERIAL

Workbook Unit 11

Exercise 1 Real time or unreal time?

Exercises 2–4 Wishes and regrets

Exercise 5 Third conditional

Exercise 6 All conditionals

Exercise 7 Ways of introducing conditionals

VOCABULARY AND PRONUNCIATION (SB p97)

Word pairs

The aim of this section is to introduce some common word pairs, fixed expressions involving two words, joined by a conjunction (usually *and* but not always).

You could lead in by writing two or three word pairs on the board, (*odds and ends*, *now and then*, *give and take*), then asking students if they can think of any other ones.

Read the introduction in the box as a class. Then ask students to read the example sentences (from Sozos' story on p96) aloud. They should stress the word pairs. Ask students to complete the well-known word pairs.

Answers
Life's full of **ups and downs**. (high points and low points)
There are always **pros and cons** in any argument. (arguments for and against)
We'll find out the truth **sooner or later**.

1 Ask students to match the word pairs to definitions. Let them check with a partner before feedback.

Answers

A	B
ifs or buts	excuses or arguments
wait and see	be patient and find out later
ins and outs	exact details
give and take	compromise/be flexible
by and large	generally speaking
grin and bear it	tolerate it as best you can
odds and ends	small items
take it or leave it	accept it or refuse, I don't care

2 Ask students to complete the sentences with a word pair from exercise 1.
   T11.5 [CD 3: Track 30] Play the recording. Students listen and check their answers.

Answers and tapescript
1 In any relationship you have to be prepared to **give and take**. You can't have your own way all the time.
2 I didn't buy much at the shops. Just a few **odds and ends** for the kids. Socks for Ben and hairbands for Jane.
3 I don't want to hear any **ifs and buts**. Just finish the job as soon as you can.
4 It's difficult to explain the **ins and outs** of the rules of cricket. It's so complicated.
5 'What have you got me for my birthday?' 'You'll have to **wait and see**.'
6 'Oh, no! The Burtons are coming for lunch! I hate their kids!' 'I'm sorry, but you'll just have to **grin and bear it**. It's only for an hour or so.'
7 OK, you can have it for £90. That's my final offer, **take it or leave it**.
8 Britain has lots of faults, of course, but **by and large**, it's a pleasant place to live.

3 Ask students in pairs to match words from the three columns to make word pairs. The clue is that word pairs are often synonyms or antonyms. Ask students to make their own sentences, using the word pairs.

Answers
now and then (occasionally – I go to the theatre now and then.)
sick and tired [of] (fed up with – I'm sick and tired of eating pasta. We eat it every day.)

more or less (approximately/almost – I earn £400, 000 a year, more or less./The team is more or less the same as last season.)
touch and go (uncertain and at risk – the operation was touch and go. We thought she might die.)
peace and quiet (quiet – I went to the library for some peace and quiet. My room was so noisy.)
safe and sound (safe and healthy – The children got lost in the forest, but were found safe and sound)
slowly but surely (gradually – Although writing this book is taking a long time, I'm getting there slowly but surely.)
there and then (immediately – We saw the house, and bought it there and then.)

4   **T11.6** [CD 3: Track 31] Play the recording. Ask, what the friends are talking about. Ask the students to note down all the word pairs they hear. You may need to play the recording twice.

Answers
They are talking about holiday plans, and the difficulty of taking holidays with small children.
Word pairs

wait and see	peace and quiet
touch and go	grin and bear it
by and large	ifs and buts
give and take	take it or leave it
sick and tired	pros and cons
now and then	

5   Ask students in pairs to practise reading the conversation, paying particular attention to the stress and intonation. It is on p157 of the Student's book.

EXTRA IDEA
Ask students in pairs to write their own conversations, including as many word pairs as they can.
Word pair Pelmanism
Word pairs lend themselves to the game of Pelmanism. Photocopy and cut out the words on p163 of the Teacher's Book. There are 24 words, making 12 possible word pairs. Make enough sets of cards for each group of four to six in your class. Hand out the cards to the students in groups of four to six. The students must spread the cards face down in front of them, in 6 rows of four. One person turns over any two cards. If they go together as a word pair the student may claim them, and have another go (but make sure the student explains the meaning of the word pair!) If they don't, they turn the cards back over, and then it is the next student's go. The key to the game is remembering where different words are. The aim of the game is to win the most word pairs.

READING AND SPEAKING (SB p97)

Have you ever wondered?

The aim here is to improve the students' ability to read for specific information, and to read intensively to complete gaps in the text.

1   Ask students to discuss the questions in pairs or small groups, and make notes of their ideas. You could ask a few creative students to share their ideas with the class before reading, just to make sure everybody has plenty of predictions.

2   Ask students to read the text and find the answers. Let students discuss the answers in their groups before feedback.

Answers
1   Physiological theory: we dream to exercise the brain cells. Psychological theory: dreams are a way of dealing with immediate concerns in our lives.
2   Meteors which hit the earth's atmosphere and then fall towards earth in a display of light.
3   Everything not fixed to the ground would fly off in a straight line.
4   Because of the jet stream – a high altitude wind that blows west to east.
5   There would be less rainfall and less beautiful sunsets.
6   Monks in the Middle Ages used it as a quick way of writing 'ad', which is Latin for 'at'.

3   Ask students to read the text again and insert the missing line. Let students check in pairs before feedback.

Answers
1 e   2 c   3 a   4 f   5 d   6 b

4   Ask students to answer the questions in pairs or groups.

Answers
1   Rapid Eye Movement
2   Immediate concerns in our lives, such as unfinished business from the day.
3   It is a meteor if it burns up in the Earth's atmosphere, and a meteorite if it lands on Earth.
4   Meteor showers
5   Many buildings would not find it easy to fly off, as they are rooted into the earth. People inside them would shoot upwards until they hit the ceiling.
6   It blows from west to east across the Atlantic, so planes going west go more slowly because they are flying against the wind.
7   There would be less rain because rain drops are formed around a dust particle. The more dust particles in the air, the more colourful a sunset – so less dust means less spectacular sunsets.

8 As a quick way of writing *ad*, the Latin word for *at*.
9 Elephant's trunk, hanging monkey, little duck, worm, pig's tail, and little dog.

Vocabulary work

Ask students in pairs to find the highlighted words and work out meanings from the context.

Answers
perpetual motion = moving continually
swarms = large, moving groups, (for example, swarms of bees or locusts)
display = show
rotating = going round
spin = turn round and round very quickly
shoot upwards = go up quickly
altitude = height above sea level
stemmed (from) = came from/resulted from
painstakingly = taking great care
tedious = very boring
strokes = individual marks made with an ink pen or paintbrush

What do you think?

The aim here is to use the reading text as a springboard for discussion.

Divide the class into small groups to discuss the questions. You can have fun with the last question. Model the example with a student, and use the persistent, demanding intonation that a child would use. Keep going on as long as you can! These dialogues often end with the adult answering, 'Oh … because it is!'

POSSIBLE WHY QUESTIONS

Why is the sky blue?   *Why are elephants big?*
Why can you see   *Why do dogs bark?*
through water?
Why is the night dark?

EXTRA IDEA
This is a useful extension if you have access to computers. Ask students in pairs to think of interesting *Have you ever wondered?* questions, e.g. *Have you ever wondered where flies go at night?* Draw up a class list, either on the board or on a handout, then ask students to choose one of the questions to research on the internet (they can try to do this on sites written in English first, and also find further information in their own language if necessary). When you follow this up in a later lesson, let the rest of the class offer their speculations on the question, and then ask the student(s) who have done the research to tell the class what they have found.

LISTENING AND SPEAKING (SB p100)

The interpretation of dreams

The aim is to improve the students' ability to listen for specific information. In the speaking activity, students are asked to discuss and interpret dreams.

1 Lead in by asking students to discuss the questions in groups. Have a brief class feedback.

Sample answers
2 You often forget the dream.
3 Common themes: falling, running, flying, being enclosed in a narrow space, being in an exam that you haven't revised for (and teaching a lesson that you haven't prepared!).

2 Ask students to read the descriptions, and discuss what they might mean in groups.

3 Ask students to read the interpretations of the dreams on p158 of the Student's Book, and match them to the dreams described on the page. Then discuss how the students' interpretations of the dreams compare to the ones given.

Answers
1 c 2 a 3 b

4 **T11.7** [CD 3: Track 32] Play the recording. Ask students to listen to Paul's dream, and answer the gist question, *What is really strange about the dream?* Then put students in pairs to correct the false statements. You may need to play the recording again.

Déjà vu is a French term, used in English, to describe an experience that feels like it's already happened before (*déjà vu* means 'already seen' in French).

Answers
What is strange is that he had exactly the same dream as his girlfriend.
1 True. (*down-to-earth*)
2 False. He was at his girlfriend's house.
3 False. They were in separate rooms.
4 False. It took place at his girlfriend's house in her home town.
5 False. They bumped into each other (met by accident).
6 False. She had *exactly* the same dream.
7 True.
8 False. He believes they were as a result of 'dream telepathy'.

T11.7 See SB Tapescripts p137

Language work

Ask students in pairs to look at the tapescript on p137 of the Student's Book, and answer the questions.

Answers
1 The fact that he had a 'supernatural' experience / the atmosphere in the dream / the fact that his girlfriend could describe a town that she'd never been to / the disturbing nature of the experience
2 weird/inexplicable/spooky (strange and slightly frightening)

What do you think?

The aim here is to use the text as a springboard for speaking.

Ask students in small groups to discuss and interpret Paul's dream. Ask a spokesperson from each group to summarize what was said. Have a class discussion, asking students to describe their dreams.

Sample interpretations
It really was dream telepathy.
Young lovers often dream about meeting unexpectedly and being watched while they kiss – it's because they are nervous and self-conscious about their relationship.
Because they are in love, they are thinking along similar lines.
Paul had perhaps told his girlfriend about his home town, so she had dreamt about it (though it's unlikely he would have told her about it in such detail).
It was a coincidence.

Writing Unit 11

Narrative writing 2 – Linking words and expressions SB p122

EVERYDAY ENGLISH (SB p101)

Moans and groans

The aim of this section is to practise ways of complaining.

1 Ask students in pairs to match the complaints and responses, and decide which items the complaints refer to.

Answers
1e	an exam	5b	boots
2a	email	6c	a dishwasher
3g	a bookcase	7f	a leather jacket
4h	a TV programme	8d	ordering by phone

2 **T11.8** [CD 3: Track 33] Play the recording. Students listen and check their answers. Then ask students to practise the conversations in pairs, adding extra lines to the dialogue.

T11.8 See SB Tapescripts p138

MUSIC OF ENGLISH

T11.9 [CD 3: Track 34] Read through the *Music of English* box as a class, then play the recording so that the students can listen and repeat the stress and exaggerated intonation.

3 Ask students to think of ways of moaning about typical events in their lives using the expressions in exercise 1. Ask them to share their 'moans' in small groups.

4 Have a brief class discussion, asking students what they feel like moaning about.

EXTRA IDEA
Write a series of subjects that people regularly moan about on small pieces of paper. Divide the class into groups of four or five. Hand out the pieces of paper in a pile face down. Students take it in turns to turn over a piece of paper, and moan about the subject. The other students can sympathise or not with the moans.
Some suggested subjects
Smoking in restaurants
Homework
The government
Waiting for the bus

ADDITIONAL MATERIAL

Workbook Unit 11
Exercise 8 Vocabulary
Exercise 9 Phrasal verbs
Exercise 10 Listening – What a pain!
Exercise 11 Pronunciation – Ways of pronouncing *ea*

12

Articles • Determiners
Hot words – *life, time*
Linking and commenting

It's never too late

Introduction to the unit

The theme of this unit is age and life
stages. The main grammatical focus of
the unit, determiners, is contextualized
in a quiz about the pace of life.

In the main reading text, seventy-
seven-year-old Mary Hobson describes
a typical day. The listening text features
four people talking about themselves,
and what is typical for people at their
stage of life.

Language aims

Determiners   The aim is to revise and practise determiners, including articles
(*a(n)*, *the*, no article), possessives (*my*, *your*, etc.), demonstratives (*this*, *that*,
these, *those*), and quantifiers (*each*, *every*, *some*, *any*, etc.).

Articles   Students whose first language does not have articles often miss them
out. Speakers of Latin languages often overuse *the*. Watch out for these errors.
*~~I come from small town.~~
*~~I am teacher.~~ (professions often don't take *a* in other languages)
*~~It's a nice weather.~~ (in English, there is no *a* with uncountables)
*~~The life is short.~~ (English doesn't take *the* before abstract words like *life* and
love when talking in general)

Demonstratives   Basically, we use *this* (singular) and *these* (plural) to talk
about here and now, and we use *that* (singular) and *those* (plural) to talk about
there and then.

Quantifiers   The unit looks at a lot of different uses. One area it focuses on,
however, is the difference between *both*, *each*, *every* and *all*. Compare:
Each/every student passed. (+ singular noun)
All the students passed. (+ plural noun)
Both students passed. (two people)
The difference between *each* and *every* is very subtle, and they are often
interchangeable. Basically, *each* is used with two or more people or things, when
we are thinking of them separately, e.g. *Each house in the street was designed
differently.* *Every* is used with three or more people or things, seen as a group,
e.g. *Every house is for sale.*

Vocabulary   This section looks at expressions using *life* and *time*.

Everyday English   This section introduces and practises linkers often used in
spoken discourse.

Notes on the unit

TEST YOUR GRAMMAR (SB p102)

The *Test your grammar* section aims to test the students' ability to use articles
correctly.

This exercise should be done quickly. Don't get involved in lengthy grammar
explanations at this stage.

1   Ask students in pairs to match lines from **A** and **C** with an article from **B**.
Do the first as an example. Ask the students to tell the story to their partner.

Answers
1 My grandfather used to be a judge.
2 He retired the year before last.
3 He decided to go on a sea cruise.
4 He enjoyed the cruise very much.
5 He sailed all round the world.
6 He met an attractive widow.
7 He invited her to have dinner with him.
8 They got on really well with one another.
9 My grandfather says you can find love at any age.
10 They were married by the captain of the ship.

2 **T12.1** [CD 3: Track 35] Play the recording. Ask students to listen and compare their answers. Ask, *What extra information do you hear?*

Answers and tapescript (extra information is in bold)
My grandfather, **who's a widower**, used to be a judge **and when** he retired the year before last, he decided to go on a sea cruise. He enjoyed the cruise very much **indeed**. He sailed all round the world **and it sounded like a great experience. Anyway, the most interesting thing about this cruise was that** he met an attractive widow – **I think she's pretty rich as well. She comes from California. Well, my grandfather** invited her to have dinner with him **and** they got on really well with one another. **And would you believe it, my grandfather fell in love? No kidding! He** says you can find love at any age, **and the next thing** we knew he'd asked her to marry him. Apparently, they were married by the captain of the ship. **It's so romantic. The whole family's amazed, but we're all very happy for him 'cos he's been rather lonely since my grandmother died. I just hope I find love one day, like Grandpa.**

THE PACE OF LIFE (SB p102)

Articles and determiners

This section contextualizes and practises determiners. The practice activities focus on meaning and use.

1 Ask students to do the quiz to find out about their pace of life. When they have finished, ask them to discuss their answers with a partner before turning to p158 in the Student's Book to find out what kind of person they are.

2 Ask students in pairs to find the highlighted words, and underline the nouns that follow. Ask students to deduce rules by asking questions: *Which words are followed by a singular noun? Which are followed by a plural, and which by an uncountable noun?*

Answers
(*determiners below can be followed by plural or uncountable nouns unless otherwise stated*)
enough <u>time</u>
the whole <u>time</u> (followed by singular [and occasionally uncountable] noun)
all the <u>rest</u>
each <u>item</u> (followed by singular noun)
plenty of <u>things</u>
a great deal of <u>enthusiasm</u> (followed by uncountable noun)
several <u>things</u> (followed by plural noun)
none
no <u>uncompleted projects</u>
each of <u>my projects</u> (*of* + plural noun)
no <u>patience</u>
a few <u>hobbies</u> (followed by plural noun)
few <u>hobbies</u> (followed by plural noun)
little <u>leisure time</u> (followed by uncountable noun)
the whole of <u>my life</u> (*of* + singular noun)
several <u>ways</u> (followed by plural noun)
most of the <u>time</u>
every <u>moment</u> (followed by singular noun)

3 Ask students in pairs to find the similar lines in the quiz, and compare the differences.

Answers
1 I leave **enough** time for relaxation.
2 Non-stop **the whole** time.
3 **Plenty of** things.
4 **A great deal** of enthusiasm.
5 **Hardly any**, just **one or two** minor things.
6 There **are no** uncomplicated projects.
7 I see **each** of my projects through.
8 **I have no** patience.
9 I have few hobbies **and little** leisure time.
10 In **several** ways.
11 In **any way I can**.
12 **Most** of the time by email.

4 Ask students to discuss the differences in pairs before discussing as a class.

Answers
A few and *few* are followed by a plural noun
I have a few hobbies (I'm happy – I enjoy having several hobbies) = the meaning is positive
I have few hobbies (I need more – my life is dull) = the meaning is negative, *not enough*
A little and *little* are followed by an uncountable noun
I have a little leisure time (I'm happy – I enjoy this time) = the meaning is positive
I have little leisure time (I need more – I work too much) = the meaning is negative, *not enough*

5 Ask students to discuss the difference and answer the questions in pairs, before discussing as a class.

> **Answers**
> *I completed each project* = each particular, individual one.
> *I completed every project* = all the projects in the group.
> We use *each* when there are *two* or more things, and *every* when there are *three* or more things. Both can be used to mean that you had lots of projects.

LANGUAGE FOCUS

See TB p8 for suggestions on how to teach this section.

Don't forget to look at the *Language aims* section on TB p121, which looks at problems students may have. You should also read the Grammar Reference on SB p152.

> **LANGUAGE INPUT**
>
> ### Determiners
>
> **1** Ask students in pairs to match the determiners with the nouns.
>
> > **Answers**
> > the other book/books/good book
> > another book/good book
> > many other books
> > his only book/good book
> > such a good book
> > what a book/good book
> >
> > both books
> > neither book
> > each/every book/time
> > little time
> > all books
> > the whole book/time
> > no book/books/time
>
> **2** Ask students in pairs to make expressions using *of*.
>
> > **Answers**
> > both of the/my/those books
> > neither of the/my/those books
> > each of the/my/those books
> > all of the/my/those books
> > all of the/my book/time
> > some of the/my/those books
> > some of the/my book/time
> > the whole of the/my book
> > the whole of the/my time
> > none of the/my/those books
> > none of the/my books/time
>
> Refer students to the Grammar Reference on SB p152.

Talking about you

1 Ask students to complete the sentences with determiners to make true sentences about themselves.

> **Possible answers**
> 1 I have no/some/enough time to relax.
> 2 All (of)/None of/Some of my friends think I work too hard.
> 3 All (of)/None of/Some of my teachers think I work too hard.
> 4 I spent all/the whole weekend relaxing.
> 5 I have some/no/many interests and hobbies.
> 6 All (of)/None of/Some of my hobbies are sports.
> 7 Both (of)/Neither of my parents look like me.
> 8 All (of)/Some of/None of my family have fair hair.
> 9 My aunt gives each of/all of us birthday presents.
> 10 My grandparents watch TV all of/some of/most of the time.

Discussing grammar

2 Ask students in pairs to discuss the difference in meaning between the sentences.

> **Answers**
> 1 *... all the students* (I spoke to the whole class as a group)
>   *... each student* (I spoke to individual students, one by one)
> 2 *None of them...* (not one individual in a group of three or more)
>   *Neither of them...* (not one of two individuals)
> 3 *The doctor's here.* (we know which doctor – the doctor we know or expect)
>   *A doctor's here.* (we don't know which doctor – could be any doctor)
> 4 *There's a man...* (a man – don't know which one)
>   *there's some man...* (used to refer to a person or thing without being specific – here, the implication is that you don't know who it is or why he's here)
> 5 *... a pair of socks missing* (two matching socks)
>   *... a couple of socks* (two socks that don't match)
> 6 *Whole families...* (everybody in each family – mum, dad, kids, granny)
>   *All the families ...* (the total number of families in the area)

3 Ask students in pairs to match the lines.

> **Answers**
> Would you like an egg?
> Do all birds lay eggs?
> Where did I put the egg?
>
> I have two cars. Borrow either one.
> It was great to see everyone.
> I have five nieces. I gave £10 to each one.
>
> Love is everything.
> A love of animals is vital for a vet.

The love I have for you is forever.
Both my parents are Scottish.
All my friends like dancing.
Every person in my class is friendly.

4 **T12.2** [CD 3: Track 36] Play the recording (it consists of **A**'s first lines from tapescript 12.3 below). Ask students to listen and respond to the lines with a sentence from exercise 3. Do the first as an example.

T12.3 [CD 3: Track 37] Play the recording so that students can listen and check. Ask students to look at the tapescript on p138 of the Student's Book and practise the conversations in pairs.

Answers and tapescript
1 **A** I don't like cereal for breakfast.
   B Well, would you like an egg? A boiled egg and some toast?
2 **A** Do any of your friends like dancing?
   B What d'you mean *any*? *All* my friends like dancing. We go every Saturday night.
3 **A** What are the people in your class like?
   B They're great. Every person in my class is really friendly. We all get on really well together.
4 **A** I've just sent my nephew £10 for his birthday.
   B Well, I have five nieces, I gave £10 to each one for Christmas – cost me a fortune!
   A I only have the one nephew at the moment. Thank goodness.
5 **A** Did you know Bob's training to be a vet and he doesn't even like animals?
   B I'd have thought that a love of animals was vital for a vet.
   A Me too. I think it's 'cos he wanted to be a doctor but he failed the exams.
6 **A** Isn't your mother Scottish?
   B In fact *both* my parents are Scottish. My father was born in Glasgow but he moved to London when he was eighteen.
7 **A** What do you think the most important thing in life is?
   B I think love is everything. If you can find true love you'll be happy forever.
8 **A** I bet you've told loads of girls that you love them.
   B This time it's different. The love I have for you is forever. I've never felt like this before.
9 **A** It's very kind of you to offer but I can't take your car. You might want to use it this afternoon.
   B Look, I have *two* cars. Borrow either one, I don't mind. I probably won't be using either anyway.
10 **A** There was quite a crowd at your birthday party, wasn't there?
   B Yeah, it was great to see everyone and I think they all had a good time.

SPOKEN ENGLISH – Demonstratives and determiners

Ask students to look at the demonstratives in the lines from the quiz. Use check questions to check the students understand their use.
Which ones are used with singular nouns or uncountables? (this and that)
Which ones are used with plural nouns? (these and those)
Which ones refer to here and now? (this and these)
Which ones refer to there and then? (that and those)

Ask students to find all the examples of *each*, *every*, and *all* in the quiz.

Answers
2 How do you tackle **all** the things you have to do **each** day?
2b I do the important things and put off **all** the rest.
2d ... that I tick off after **each** item is completed.
3d I see **each** of my projects through ...
8d Grasp **every** moment.

Demonstratives – *this / that / these /* those

5 Ask students to complete the sentences with the correct demonstrative.

T12.4 [CD 3: Track 38] Play the recording so that students can listen and check.

Answers and tapescript
1 What's that song you're singing?
2 Look at this ladybird on my hand!
3 Did you hear that storm in the middle of the night?
4 Mmm! These strawberries are delicious!
5 Take those dirty shoes off! I've just cleaned in here.
6 I can't stand this weather. It's really getting me down.
7 Who was that man you were talking to this morning?
8 Do you remember when we were young? Those were the days!
9 Children have no respect for authority these days, do they?

Determiners – *each / every / all*

6 **T12.5** [CD 3: Track 39] Play the recording. Ask students to listen and say what each is about. Then ask students in pairs to complete the replies, using *each*, *every* or *all*. You may need to play the recording a second time.

Ask students to practise the conversations in pairs.

Answers and tapescript
1 Talking about a meal, probably in a restaurant.
2 Somebody has done something wrong in front of a large group of people at a party, or wedding.
3 Talking about a group of students who have taken an exam.
4 Someone is collecting for a charity, etc.
5 Talking about travelling to a destination.
6 Friend or colleague invites someone for a pint of beer in a pub.

T12.5

1 **A** What was the meal like?
   B It was revolting, every bit as bad as you said it would be.
2 **A** Did you apologize to all the guests?
   B Each and every one of them. I felt I had to.
3 **A** They didn't all pass, did they?
   B All but three did. Seventeen out of twenty, that's not bad.
4 **A** Sorry, I only have 50p on me.
   B Don't worry. Every little helps you know.
5 **A** When do you think you'll get there?
   B All being well, we should be there about six.
6 **A** Do you fancy a quick pint?
   B If it's all the same to you, I'd rather not.

Writing Unit 12

Adding emphasis in writing – People of influence SB p123

ADDITIONAL MATERIAL

Workbook Unit 12

Exercise 1 Articles

Exercise 2 Determiners

Exercise 3 Demonstratives

Exercise 4 Revision of articles, determiners, and demonstratives

Exercise 5 Nouns in groups

LISTENING AND SPEAKING (SB p105)

Happy days

The aim here is to improve the students' ability to listen for specific information.

1 Lead in by dividing students into small groups to discuss the questions.

Sample answers
Students' own ideas. However, here are some suggestions for the stage of life and typical behaviour.
infancy 0 – 5 (playing, crying, learning to walk and talk)
childhood 5 – 12 (going to school, playing)
teenage years 13 – 19 (going out with friends, using mobiles, listening to music, doing exams)
adulthood 18 – 45 (getting a job, getting a partner, having children)
middle age 45/50 – late 60s (gardening, having dinner parties, retiring)
old age 70+ (going for walks, sleeping)

2 Ask students to discuss the statements in small groups, and decide which stage of life the four speakers are at. Do the first as an example. You will probably need to check the vocabulary explained below.

DIFFICULT VOCABULARY
settle down = get married, buy a house and have children
potter = do things in a slow and enjoyable way (typical of old people)
weed the flower bed = pull unwanted plants out of the part of the garden with flowers
get off on (dancing) = get your excitement from (dancing) (typical phrase of young people)
the world has gone to pot = it's become terrible

Answers
1 teenage years/adulthood
2 middle age
3 childhood
4 old age
5 teenage years
6 middle age/old age
7 childhood
8 could be adulthood, middle age or old age

3 **T12.6** [CD 3: Track 40] Play the recording. Pause after each speaker so that the students can discuss the questions in pairs.

Answers
Bernie Danziger
1 adulthood
2 2 and 8
3 Typically, he talks about his wife and children and working. Untypically, because he has had a life-saving operation, he talks about being happy to be alive and what a gift life is in a way that is more typical of older people.
4 Being alive makes him happy, and his children.
Hayley
1 teenage years
2 1 and 5
3 Typically, she talks about dancing, going clubbing, chatting to girlfriends, and says she wants to travel the world before settling down. Untypically, she says that she doesn't want to be tied down by having a boyfriend.
4 Dancing and chatting to friends makes her happy. Talking about football is boring.
Tony
1 old age
2 4 and 6
3 Typically, he goes for walks with his dog, potters about the garden, has aches and pains and gets tired, and criticizes politicians and thinks the world has gone to pot. Perhaps less typically, he and his wife often go out for lunch with friends, or have friends come and stay for the weekend.
4 happy: gardening, walking, watching sunset, entertaining friends.
   unhappy: politicians.

Tommy
1 childhood
2 3 and 7
3 Typically, he likes beaches and playing with his brother.
4 happy: Bigbury beach, the sea tractor, playing.
   unhappy: dead birds

T12.6 See SB Tapescripts p138

What do you think?

Divide students into groups of three or four to discuss the class. Ask them to make a list of advantages and disadvantages of each stage of life. Ask a spokesperson for each group to present their list to the class.

READING AND SPEAKING (SB p106)

You're never too old

The aim is to improve the students' ability to read for gist and specific information, but also to develop their ability to infer from and speculate about a text.

CULTURAL INFORMATION
This article comes from a regular feature of the *Sunday Times* magazine, *A Life in the Day*, in which a well-known person reveals aspects of their life and lifestyle by describing a typical day in their life.
Alexander Sergeievich Pushkin (1799-1837) was one of Russia's greatest poets. He wrote *Boris Godunov* and *Eugene Onegin*.
Earls Court is a district of London.
War and Peace is a novel by Leo Tolstoy.
Scrabble is a board game in which players have to make words from letters on plastic tiles.
Radio 4 is a BBC radio station which broadcasts a variety of programmes, but notably news and current affairs.

1 Lead in by asking the students to tell you about old people they know. Ask students in small groups to discuss which activities are typical for old people.

Answers
Students' own answers.
Most of the activities in the list are typical of old people, with the exception of going to university, studying foreign languages, living in the centre of the city, and using the Internet (though this is becoming increasingly common amongst older people, known as *silver surfers*).

2 Ask students to read the text quickly, and find out which of the activities in 1 are part of Mary Hobson's life.

Answers
finding it difficult to sleep
liking routine
going to university
studying foreign languages (Russian, ancient Greek)
talking about the past
living in the centre of a city

A life in the day suggests that a person's life can be shown by one of their typical days. It is a play on the common phrase, *A day in the life of ...*

3 Ask students to read the text again, then discuss the questions about the highlighted lines in pairs.

Answers
1 l.4   Learning ancient Greek – because it is a dead language that no-one speaks
2 l.10 'It' is breakfast. Marcus Aurelius' philosophy helped Mary get through the death of her son in a motorcycle accident.
3 l.22 Translating (Pushkin). It implies that she doesn't need to work for money, but that she likes to keep busy and loves her work.
4 l.24 'He' is Pushkin. She (Mary) is 'some old bat' ('an old bat' is used humorously or derogatively to describe an eccentric old lady).
5 l.30 The cerebral abscess and resulting disability was hell for Neil, her husband. Mary looked after Neil, and later wrote novels. After 28 years, she left him.
6 l.35 It was Neil's weekly 50-minute music therapy session. Mary wrote her novel during it.
7 l.47 It's a good time. For Mary it was when she studied Russian at the University of London.
8 l.55 Because she goes to Moscow at the coldest time of year.
9 l.65 TV. She doesn't like being passive, watching TV.
10 l.67 It is Radio 4. She dreams of anxiety and loss – probably as a result of the death of her son and the difficult times she had with her disabled husband.

Language work

Ask students in pairs to find and correct the mistakes. All the mistakes involve the use of articles and possessives.

Answers
1 ... back to **bed**. (we say, *go to bed, get into bed*, etc. We are interested in the activity not the specific bed)
2 ... was **a** talented musician. (we say *a* with professions)
3 You've got only **one** opportunity... (being specific about the number – one *not* two)
4 ... at **the** University of London. (we say *the University of London* but *Cambridge University*)
5 ... in **the** coldest weather. (we use *the* before a superlative)

6 ... a bit of **life**... (life in *general*)
7 ... over **the** country (*the country* as opposed to *the town*, not *a country* meaning 'a nation')
8 ... because **my** feet are awful (showing possession)

What do you think?

The aim here is to use the text as a springboard for speaking.

Divide students into small groups to make lists. Pair students from different groups to share their ideas, then have a class discussion.

Suggested lists
The disadvantages of being young
you don't get much respect
Lack of rights – can't drive before 17, vote before 18, etc.
No money
Difficult to find a job
Have to study
Peer pressure
You are immature and inexperienced
The advantages of being old
Can do what you want
Don't have to work
May have plenty of money if you've saved for retirement
Mature
Experienced
Wise
Don't need to worry about making an impression any more

VOCABULARY AND LISTENING (SB p108)

Hot words – *life* and *time*

This section looks at expressions using the hot words, *life* and *time*. It concludes with the song, *That's Life*.

1 Ask students in pairs to complete the expressions, using a dictionary if necessary.

Answers
not on your life (= no chance)
take your time (= no need to hurry)
get a life (= your life is dull and boring – you need to get some new interests and activities)
kill time (= waste time waiting for something)
third time lucky
no time to lose (= hurry, it's urgent)
that's life (= there's nothing we can do to change the situation)
not before time (= said angrily, to say that something is late)
any old time (= any time you want)
a cushy time (= an easy, undemanding time)
you can bet your life (= definitely)
better luck next time

get a new lease of life (= get the chance to live longer, with a better quality of life)
it's high time (= something needs to happen now)
for the time being (= temporarily)
stand the test of time (= last a long time without going out-of-date)
see life (= see/do exciting things)
in the nick of time (= just in time)
dead on time (= exactly on time)
anything for a quiet life (= I'll do anything to avoid trouble and confrontation)

2 Ask students to complete the lines with expressions from 1. Let students check in pairs before feedback.

Answers
1 No need to hurry. Take **your time**.
2 For goodness' sake, hurry up. There's no **time to lose**.
3 The operation was so successful that grandpa got a new **lease of life**.
4 Shakespeare's writing is still relevant today. It's really stood **the test of time**.
5 I got to the bank in the **nick of time**. It was just about to close.
6 You can give them back any **old time**. I'm not going skiing again until next year.
7 OK, OK, stop crying. You can have another ice-cream. Anything **for a quiet life**.

3 **T12.7** [CD 3: Track 41] Play the recording. Ask students to listen and answer the questions. Ask students in pairs to look at the tapescript on p139 of the Student's Book, and practise the conversation.

Answers and tapescript
1 Taking a driving test.
2 Parent or housemate telling son/daughter/housemate to do something more useful than watch TV all day.
3 Two friends have just missed a train home after going shopping.
4 Talking about having part of the house redecorated.
5 Talking about Dave – a lottery winner.

T12.7
Expressions from exercise 1 are in **bold**.
1 A I can't believe it. I failed again.
  B Never mind. You'll have **better luck next time**.
  A But that was the second time.
  B They say the best drivers pass on the third try.
2 A Come on! Get up! **Get a life!**
  B What d'you mean?
  A Well, **it's high time** you did something other than watch TV soaps all day.
  B Like what?
  A I dunno. Travel, see the world. **See life**.
  B Boring.
  A I give up. Be a couch potato if that's what you want.

3 **A** Oh no! We've missed it. It must have left **dead on time**.
  B I thought we might just get it.
  A What do we do now? There isn't another until 1 o'clock.
  B That's nearly **two hours to kill**!
  A More shopping?
  B **Not on your life**. I'm shopped-out! Let's just get a coffee. There's a café on platform 1.
4 **A** How's it going?
  B Well, they've finished at last but **not before time** – only four weeks late.
  A And how much is it all going to cost?
  B We haven't had the final bill yet.
  A Well, you can **bet your life** it'll be more than they estimated.
  B I know. We *were* going to have the kitchen decorated as well, but enough's enough **for the time being**.
5 **A** How come Dave has such **a cushy life**? He never seems to do any work.
  B Didn't you know? He won the lottery.
  A You're kidding! I had no idea. I do the lottery every week and never win a thing.
  B Me neither. **That's life**.

A song

4 Ask students to look at the title of the song. Ask, *What do you think the song will be about?*
  T12.8 [CD 3: Track 42] Ask students to listen to the song, then work in pairs to note all the differences between the words on the page and the words in the song. Play the song again and pause it until the students have caught all the differences.

5 Play the recording again. Ask students to listen again, and sing along (if they want to).

Answers and tapescript
(The differences are in bold.)
That's Life – Robbie Williams
That's life, that's what **people** say.
You're **riding' high** in April,
Shot down in May.
But **I know** I'm gonna **change** that tune,
When **I'm back on top** in June.
That's life, **funny** as it seems.
Some **folks** get their kicks,
Steppin' on dreams;
But I don't **let** it **get** me down,
'Cause this ol' world **keeps spinnin'** around.
I've been a puppet, a pauper, a **pirate**,
A **poet**, a pawn and a king.
I've been up and **down** and **over** and out
And I know **one thing**:
Each time I find myself **flat** on my face,
I **pick** myself up and get back in the race.

That's life, I can't deny it,
I thought of **quitting**,
But my **heart** just won't buy it.
If I didn't think it was worth a try,
I'd roll **myself** up in a **big ball** and **die**.

EVERYDAY ENGLISH (SB p109)

Linking and commenting

The aim of this section is to introduce and practise linkers often used in spoken discourse.

1 Read the introduction, and ask students to look at the examples. Ask students to find other examples in tapescript 12.6 on p138 of the Student's Book.

Answers
Bernie
Anyway, I had the transplant …
This time though, after …
Eventually I started working …
Hayley
Well, actually, most of us …
Honestly, my best times are …
Tony
I suppose …
And then …
Honestly!
Suddenly, I could …
The first thing we did … was …
Having said that, we often …

2 Ask students in pairs to choose the correct linking or commenting expression.
  T12.9 [CD 3: Track 43] Play the recording. Ask students to listen and check their answers, then practise some of the dialogues in pairs.

Answers and tapescript
1 **A** Did you see the match last night?
  B No, but **apparently** it was a good game. We won, didn't we?
  A **Actually**, it was a draw, but it was really exciting.
2 **A** What do you think of Claire's new boyfriend?
  B **Personally**, I can't stand him. I think he'll dump her like all the rest. **However**, that's her problem, not mine.
  A Poor old Claire! She always picks the wrong ones, doesn't she? **Anyway**, we'll see soon enough.
3 **A** I don't know how you can afford to buy all those fabulous clothes!
  B **Hopefully**, I'm going to get a bonus this month. My boss has promised. **After all**, I did earn the company over £100,000 last year. **Basically**, I deserve it.
4 **A** She said some terrible things to me. I hate her!

B **All the same**, I think you should apologize to her. **If you ask me**, you lose your temper too easily. You're being very childish. It's time you both grew up!

A What?! I never thought I'd hear you speak to me like that.

B **Honestly**, I'm not taking sides. I just think you should make up.

5 **A** So, Billy. You say that this is the last record you're ever going to make?

B **Definitely**.

A But **surely** you realize how upset your fans are going to be?

B **Obviously**, I don't want to hurt anyone, but **basically** I'm fed up with pop music. I'd like to do something else. **Ideally**, I'd like to get into films.

3 Ask students in pairs to complete the sentences with a suitable line.

Sample answers

1 They had a terrible holiday. Apparently, it rained every day.

2 It should have been a happy marriage. After all, they had so much in common.

3 I know you don't want to go to Harry's party. All the same, you should go for an hour or two.

4 I had the interview yesterday. Hopefully, I'll get the job.

5 I'd rather you didn't let this go any further. Obviously, it is a private affair.

6 I couldn't believe it, he just walked out and left her. Presumably, he was having an affair.

7 I don't like flying very much. As a matter of fact, I'm terrified of it.

8 So that's that. All's well that ends well. Anyway, how are things with you?

ADDITIONAL MATERIAL

Workbook Unit 12

Exercise 6 Vocabulary

Exercise 7 Prepositions revision

Exercise 8 Listening – The holiday of a lifetime

Exercises 9–10 Pronunciation – Nouns and verbs – Emphasis in speaking

Writing

UNIT 1 Applying for a job – A CV and a covering letter (SB p110)

1, 2 Lead in by asking the questions open class.

Answers
A CV or curriculum vitae is a summary of your personal details, work experience and educational qualifications. The aim is to give an employer an informative and positive view of you as a potential employee. It is usually sent when applying for a job.
A covering letter is a short, formal letter which says which job you are applying for, where you saw the job advertised, and gives key details of why you are suitable for the job.

3 Ask students in pairs to write the headings from **A** in the correct spaces in the CV in **B**.

Answers
Name
Personal details
Profile
Education
Work experience
Interests
Additional information
References

4 Ask students to discuss the questions in pairs.

Answers
1 Watford
2 Psychology and education
3 One of Kate's referees – she works in the Department of Education at Bristol University, and was probably one of Kate's teachers
4 No

5 Discuss this question as a class.

Answers
Students' own answers

6 Ask students to read the advertisement, and say whether Kate is well qualified for the job.

Answers
Yes. She is the right age, and has work experience in organising sports and working with kids.

7 Ask students to read Kate's covering letter, and decide which sections are too informal. Then ask students in pairs to replace the informal parts with the words on the right of the letter.

Answers 1
(informal parts underlined)
Dear Mark

I am applying for the post of camp leader, which I saw advertised somewhere recently. Here's my CV.
I reckon I have just about everything needed for this job. I have worked loads with kids, doing all kinds of stuff. They generally do what I tell them, and we manage to have a great time together. Having studied psychology and education at university, I know quite a bit about the behaviour of kids.
I am really into sport, and have lots of experience of organizing training events. I am a very practical person, easy-going, and it's no problem for me to make friends. I've been all over the place, and enjoy meeting new people.
I can't wait to hear from you.

Best wishes

Kate Henderson

Kate Henderson

Answers 2
17 March 2004

Dear **Mr Sullivan**

I am applying for the post of camp leader, which I saw advertised **in the March edition of the magazine** *Holiday Jobs for Graduates*. **Please find enclosed** my CV.
I **feel** I have **many of the relevant qualifications** needed for this job. I have worked **extensively** with **young adults**, **organizing a variety of activities**. They generally **respect my leadership abilities**, and we manage to **establish a good working relationship**. Having studied psychology and education at university, I **have a certain understanding of** the behaviour of **young adults**.

I am **very interested in** sport, and have **considerable** experience of organizing training events. I am a very practical person, easy-going, and **I find it easy** to make friends. **I have travelled widely**, and enjoy meeting new people. **I look forward to hearing** from you.

Yours sincerely

Kate Henderson

Discuss with the class the differences between the layout of this formal letter and that of formal letters in their country.

8   Ask students to write their own CV and covering letter for a job that they would like to do.

> **EXTRA IDEA**
> Bring in a page of job advertisements from an English-speaking newspaper or from the Internet. Ask students to choose one that they would like to apply for, and ask them to write their CV and covering letter with this job in mind.

UNIT 2 Informal Letters – Correcting mistakes
(SB p112)

1   Read through the correction symbols as a class, and ask students in pairs to correct the mistakes in the sentences. Do the first as an example.

> **Answers**
> 1   I **was** born in 1971 in **a** small town in Mexico.
> 2   My father is **a** diplomat, so **all my life** I've **lived** in **different** countries.
> 3   **After school**, I went **to a business** college **for four years**.
> 4   I've **been married for** five years. **I met** my wife while I was a student.
> 5   My town **isn't** as exciting **as** London. **It** is very **quiet in** the evening.
> 6   I've **been learning** English for five years. **I started** when I **was** eleven (years old).
> 7   My father wants **me to** work in a bank **because it** is a good **job/career/profession**.
> 8   I'm **doing an** evening course in English. I enjoy **learning** languages **very much**.

In feedback, ask students which of these mistakes are typical of speakers of their first language. Ask students to make a list of mistakes they typically make when writing, and to record them in their notebooks with corrections.

2   Ask students to read the letter and answer the questions.

> **Answers**
> 1   São Paolo, Brasil.
> 2   Fernando is the guest; James is the host.
> 3   São Paolo; It is the biggest and noisiest city in Brazil. It is not really for tourists. It is a commercial centre with a lot of pollution and traffic. There are a lot of things to do, and it has bars which stay open all night.
> 4   Summer (Christmas).

3   Ask students in pairs to find mistakes in the letter, and mark them with symbols, using a pencil. Monitor and help. When the students have finished, go through the answers as a class. If you have access to an OHP, you could make copies of the two sets of answers below, so that you can clearly show answers to students at the end of the activity.

Once the students have marked the text with the correct symbols, ask them to work in pairs to rewrite the text, correcting all the mistakes.

> **ALTERNATIVE IDEA**
> If you make photocopies of the letter, you can make this activity more interactive. Make enough copies so that the students have one between two. Ask students in pairs to mark up the mistakes with symbols. Then ask students to pass on their letter to another pair. This pair must check the marking up and make sure that it is correct. Monitor closely at this stage. Ask students to pass on the letter to another pair. They must now write in the corrections. Pin the corrected letters to the class notice board so that students can read and compare the corrected letters.

> **Answers 1**
>
> Avenida Campinas 361 ap. 45
> 01238 São Paulo
> Brasil
>
> 23 December
>
> Dear James
>
> ```
>                              T      Gr
> Thank you⋀your letter. I receive it the last week. Sorry I
>   T
> no reply⋀ you before, but I've been very busy. It's Christmas
>               Gr      Gr           T
> soon, and everyone are very exciting! In two weeks I am with
>          Gr   WW                          Gr
> you in England. I can no belief it! I⋀looking forward ⋀meet
>          Sp                             Gr
> you and your familly very much. I'm sure we will like us very
> WW                              Sp          Sp
> well. My city, São Paulo, is⋀biggest and noisyest city in Brasil.
>                    Gr          WO            WO  WW
> ⋀Is not really for tourist. ⋀Is a centre commercial. Also it have
>   Gr                        Gr
> very much pollution and traffic. But there is⋀lot of things to
> ```

do. I like <u>very much</u> listen ⋏music. There are bars <u>who</u> stay
WO   Gr   Gr

open all night! My friend went <u>in</u> London last year, and he
Prep

<u>has seen</u> a football match at Arsenal. He <u>said</u> me ⋏was
T   WW

<u>wonderfull</u>. I ⋏like to do that <u>also</u>.
Sp   WW

My plane <u>arrive</u> <u>to</u> Heathrow at 6.30 am <u>in</u> 3 <u>Janury</u>. ⋏Is very
T Prep   Prep   Sp

kind ⋏you ⋏meet me so early ⋏morning.

I hope very much ⋏improve my <u>english</u> <u>during</u> I am with you!
P   WW

See you soon and <u>happy</u> New Year!
P

Fernando

Answers 2

Avenida Campinas 361 ap. 45

01238 São Paulo

Brasil

23 December

Dear James

Thank you for your letter. I received it last week. Sorry I haven't replied to you before, but I've been very busy. It's Christmas soon, and everyone is very excited!
In two weeks I will be with you in England. I can't believe it! I am looking forward to meeting you and your family very much. I'm sure we will like each other very much (or get on very well).
My city, São Paulo, is the biggest and noisiest city in Brazil. It is not really for tourists. It is a commercial centre. There is also a lot of pollution and traffic. But there are a lot of things to do. I like listening to music very much. There are bars which stay open all night!
My friend went to London last year, and he saw a football match at Arsenal. He told me (that) it was wonderful. I would like to do that, too.
My plane arrives (or will arrive) at Heathrow at 6.30 am on 3 January. It is very kind of you to meet me so early in the morning.
I hope very much to improve my English while I am with you!

See you soon and Happy New Year!

Fernando

4 Ask students to write one of the letters for homework. It is a good idea to get them to make notes under the following headings first: your family, interests, school, your town.
Remind students to check their work carefully for mistakes before handing it in.

UNIT 3 Narrative Writing (1) – Using adverbs in narratives (SB p113)

1 Lead in by asking students to think about and prepare notes on a dangerous situation they have been in. When they are ready, ask students to share their stories in pairs or groups. You could model this task by telling a brief story of your own first – a real or imaginary story of a dangerous sport you have tried, or a hair-raising travel experience.

2 Ask students in pairs to put the adverbs and adverbial phrases in the correct place in the sentences. Ask pairs to read aloud their stories.

Answers
1 I used to go skiing in winter frequently.
  I frequently used to go skiing in winter.
  I used to go skiing frequently in winter.
2 I especially enjoyed going to Colorado with my family.
  I enjoyed going to Colorado, especially with my family.
3 Then, two years ago, I had a really bad accident.
  Then I had a really bad accident two years ago.
4 I skied headfirst into a tree.
5 Unfortunately, I broke my leg in three places.
  I broke my leg in three places, unfortunately.
6 I'd definitely like to go skiing again, one day.
  One day, I'd definitely like to go skiing again.
7 But I don't feel confident enough yet.
  But I don't yet feel confident enough.
8 However, my family still go skiing every February.
  My family, however, still go skiing every February.
  Every February, however, my family still go skiing.
  My family still go skiing every February, however.

3 Ask students to read the story and answer the questions. Let students discuss their answers in pairs before the class feedback.

Answers
Where were they? On Piz Badile – a mountain in the Swiss Alps
What went wrong? The weather changed – there was an electric storm and it started to snow, so they couldn't climb down safely.
How were they saved? Rachel sent a text to a friend in London, who called the emergency services in Switzerland.
What does the text message mean? It means that they need to be rescued by helicopter from the ridge (long, narrow top) of Piz Badile in the Swiss Alps.

4 Ask students in pairs to place the adverbs on the right in the correct place in the same line of the story (though an alternative placing may be in a different line). Monitor and help.

Answers
TEXTING TO THE RESCUE
On a mid-September day, **several years ago**, (or *Several years ago*, *on a mid-September day*,) British climbers Rachel Kelsey and Jeremy Colenso were climbing **high** in the Swiss Alps **with great confidence** (or *were climbing* **with great confidence**, **high** *in the Swiss Alps*). They were both **relatively** experienced climbers, and when they left their base, the weather was good. They **easily** reached the summit (or *reached the summit* **easily**), but as they started the climb down, **suddenly** an electric storm (or *an electric storm* **suddenly**) struck the mountain. Snow began to fall **heavily**, making it **extremely** difficult to see where they could **safely** put their hands and feet (or *put their hands and feet* **safely**) on the rock. After several frightening minutes, they found a narrow ledge and **gratefully** climbed (or *climbed* **gratefully**) on to it, **desperately** hoping (or *hoping* **desperately**) the snow would stop and they could continue their descent. **However**, the snow did not stop (or *The snow did not stop*, **however**,) and, **dangerously**, the temperature dropped (or *dropped* **dangerously**) to −10°C. 'We had to stay awake,' said Rachel **afterwards**, 'because it was so cold that, **undoubtedly**, we would have died (or *we would* **undoubtedly** *have died*, or *have died* **undoubtedly**). So we told stories and rubbed our fingers and toes **continuously** to keep them warm.'
Eventually, they decided (or *They decided*, **eventually**,) that they had to get help. But what could they **possibly** do? **Fortunately**, Rachel had brought her mobile phone with her, (or *with her*, **fortunately**) but, **unfortunately**, the only number contacts she had were in London (or *were*, **unfortunately**, *in London*, or *in London*, **unfortunately**). She sent a text message at 1.30 a.m. to get help. **In fact**, she sent the same text to five friends (or *the same text*, **in fact**, *to*) in the UK. It read: '**Urgently** need heli rescue (or *Need heli rescue* **urgently**) off north ridge of Piz Badile, Switz'. They were all asleep, so **for hours** nothing happened (or *nothing happened* **for hours**). **Then**, at 5.00 a.m., one friend, Avery Cunliffe, got the message. He jumped into action **immediately** (or **Immediately**, *he jumped into action*), called the rescue services in Switzerland, and **then** called Rachel to tell her that help was coming.
For the next 24 hours, the weather was too bad (or *The weather was too bad* **for the next 24 hours**) for the helicopters to operate, but Avery kept sending text messages to the climbers. **Finally**, at about 10.00pm they were **safely** lifted (or *lifted* **safely**) off the mountain (or **finally** *lifted off the mountain* **safely**). 'We owe our lives to Avery', they said **exhaustedly** when they were back at base.

5 Discuss the questions as a class.

Answers
What background information are you given in the article?
The date, the place, the weather, the people involved
When does the actual story of what happened start? It starts with the line, 'as they started the climb down, suddenly an electric storm struck the mountain'.

6 Ask students to use the notes they made in 1 to write the story of their dangerous experience. Get students to plan their story carefully, by writing notes on background information, and then notes on the events of the story in the order they happened. Monitor and help with vocabulary.

Ask students to write their stories for homework, using plenty of adverbs to describe people's feelings and actions.

In the next lesson, ask some students to read their stories.

UNIT 4 Linking Ideas – Conjunctions (SB p114)

1 Read through the examples, then ask the class to make sentences, and write them on the board.

Some possible answers
She's rich and famous, but she's unhappy.
Although she's rich and famous, she's unhappy.
She's rich and famous. However, she's unhappy.

2 Read through the explanation as a class, then ask students in pairs to complete the sentences with suitable conjunctions.

Answers
CONTRAST
1 **Although/Even though** I can't speak much Spanish, I can understand a lot.
2 I can't speak Spanish well. **However**, I can understand most things.
3 He can't speak Spanish well, **even though/although** he lives in Spain. (**even though** is the best answer here because the contrast is *very* surprising)
4 **Despite** living in Spain, he can't speak Spanish.
REASON AND RESULT
1 I didn't sleep well last night, **so** I'm tired.
2 I'm tired **as/since/because** I didn't sleep well last night.
3 I wanted to go, but **as/since/because** it was late, I decided not to.
4 **As/Since/Because** John can't be here today, I've been asked to chair the meeting.

5 He always looks **so** innocent **that** he gets away with murder.
6 He's **such** a terrible liar **that** no one believes him.

TIME

1 I called you **when/as soon as** I could.
2 He refused to talk to the police **until** his lawyer arrived. (**when**, **as soon as** and **after** are grammatically correct, but strange things to say in the context)
3 I feel sad **when(ever)** I hear that song.
4 They were burgled **while** they were away on holiday.
5 I've known her **since** I was a small child.
6 I'll help you with this exercise **when/after/as soon as** I've had dinner.

CONDITION

1 **If** I'm going to be late, I'll call you.
2 You won't pass **unless** you work harder.
3 Take an umbrella **in case** it rains.
4 You can borrow my car **as long as** you drive carefully.

3 Discuss the question as a class. Write up any information the students know on the board.

BACKGROUND INFORMATION

blonde; actress; 1950s film star; died young; lived 1926 to 1962; sex symbol; icon
Films: *Some Like it Hot*, *Gentlemen Prefer Blondes*, *The Seven Year Itch*, *The Misfits*
Husbands: Arthur Miller (playwright); Joe DiMaggio (baseball star)
Lovers: JFK (?); Frank Sinatra (?)
Real name: Norma Jean Baker

4 Ask students to read the text, and join the sentences with the correct conjunctions.

Answers
THE DEATH OF A STAR

(1) since	(10) However
(2) but	(11) even though
(3) Whenever	(12) after
(4) although	(13) unless
(5) such	(14) so
(6) However	(15) while
(7) even though	(16) in case
(8) When	(17) as soon as
(9) as	

5 Ask students to write about someone famous for homework. Tell them to research information on the Internet, and make notes under the headings suggested.

UNIT 5 Emailing Friends (SB p115)

1 Lead in by discussing the question as a class, and listing differences on the board.

Answers
Using a keyboard/using a pen.
Can correct, delete, change order of sentences or paragraphs on the screen/Can't correct or delete when writing letters without making a mess – so have to write out neat copy.
Emails are informal and don't have any real conventions/ Letters have conventions – even informal letters require *Dear ___, Best wishes,* etc., and formal letters have lots of conventions.
Emails are often written in abbreviated form/Letters require whole sentences and correct grammar and punctuation.
Emails are quick, so they are good for 'chatting', inviting people out, keeping in touch, doing business/Letters are personal and kept forever, so they are good when you want to say something special or important.

2 Read through the introduction as a class. Ask students in pairs to express the typical email phrases more formally, and decide which words are omitted.

Answers

(I'm) Glad you're OK.	I'm pleased (to hear) that you are well.
(It's) Great news – (I've) got the job!	It's excellent news – I've been offered the job!
(I'm) Sorry, (I) can't make next Sat(urday).	I'm sorry, but I'm afraid I can't see you next Saturday.
(Are) You still OK for Friday?	Can you still keep the arrangement we made for Friday?
Thanks loads.	Thank you very much.
(That) Sounds fantastic.	That is fantastic.
(I/We) Can't wait to see you.	I'm looking forward to seeing you.
(Let's/We'll) Speak soon.	I'll talk to you soon.

3 Ask students to read the email and note any features that are typical to emails. Ask students to discuss with a partner what changes they would make if it were a letter.

Answers
Typical features: *Hi* not *Dear*; missing out subjects and unimportant verbs, (e.g. (*It was*) *GREAT...*); using brackets to give asides; using capitals, dashes, and exclamation marks to show that the style is 'chatty'.
Changes to make if it were a letter: Address and more formal date (July 31st 2005) in place of email heading; *Dear* not *Hi*; complete sentences, (e.g. *It was really great to see you...,* not *GREAT to see you*); longer sentences, using relative clauses and conjunctions; no capitals or brackets.

4 Ask students to read the letter and answer the questions. Ask students in pairs to make it more like an email.

> **Answers**
> *What is the main reason for writing?* To arrange a get-together with old friends.
> *What parts of the letter give extra information?* At the start the writer mentions a previous meeting with Rob and Penny; at the start of the main paragraph, the writer talks about receiving a postcard from Graham.

> **Sample email version of the letter**
>
> Hi Rob,
> Got a postcard from Graham Pellowe. Really wants to meet up and discuss old times. Could go to the Green Olive, or the Red Pepper – both excellent. Can you come? – don't fancy a whole evening with old Graham on my own. Finish work at about six – he can't make the restaurant until 8.30 – so loads of time to catch up. Let me know if any of this possible. Please call or email when you can – I'll book the restaurant. Could be fun!
>
> Love
> Jane

5 Ask students to follow the instructions, and write an email in response to Jane's letter.

UNIT 6 Report Writing – A Consumer survey
(SB p116)

1 Lead in by discussing the questions as a class.

> **Answers**
> *Fast food*: food that is prepared and served quickly – typically, hamburgers, hot dogs, pizza, etc.
> It is generally considered to be unhealthy, as fast food is typically high in carbohydrates, salt and sugar.
> *Organic food*: food grown without pesticides and other chemicals.

2 Read through the report headings as a class, and check the vocabulary.

Ask students to match the expressions with the headings. Do the first as an example.

> **Answers**
> | | |
> |---|---|
> | For the attention of … | b |
> | Title | f |
> | Background and objectives | e/c/l |
> | Research and findings | j/h/d/m |
> | Summary and recommendations | a/g |
> | Action next | i/k |

3 Ask students to read the report, and put in the expressions from the box in exercise 2.

> **Answers**
> (1) The Managing Director
> (2) 'Survey into Potential Demand for Organic Burgers'
> (3) The history of this issue
> (4) The purpose of this report
> (5) We were asked to investigate
> (6) were asked to say what they thought
> (7) The results
> (8) two main findings
> (9) not enough evidence
> (10) In conclusion,
> (11) We recommend that
> (12) We propose that
> (13) within the next six months

Writing a survey and a report

4 Read through the introduction as a class, and focus students on the pictures. Ask students whether they buy *Fairtrade* products, and whether they support the idea.

Ask students in pairs to prepare and carry out a survey, following the instructions given. You could do this in class, if your class is large, and has a good range of ages. Alternatively, you could ask students to carry out the survey on friends or family at home, or on students and staff at your school.

> **Some suggested 'statements' for the report**
> 1 I want to know where the things I buy come from.
>   SA A DK D SD
> 2 I prefer to buy products direct from the producer.
>   SA A DK D SD
> 3 I always buy well-known brands.
>   SA A DK D SD
> 4 I believe in helping the economies of developing countries.
>   SA A DK D SD
> 5 I am prepared to pay more than I pay now.
>   ‹10% 10% 20% 30% 40% ›40%

5 Ask students to write the report, using the data they have collected. They should use expressions from the exercises above, and use the structure of the report as a model.

UNIT 7 Arguing your case – For and against (SB p118)

1 Lead in by asking students to discuss the questions in pairs, then as a class.

2 Write, *Is email a good or a bad thing?* on the board, and divide the board into *Pros* and *Cons* sections. Nominate two students to stand at the board, and write ideas up as the rest of the class suggest them.

In the feedback, ask students what they discovered – is it good or bad?

Some sample answers
PROS (+)

Keeping in touch with old friends, especially when they are abroad.

Quick way of making appointments and getting together with people.

Good way of sending things to people like photos, CVs, etc.

In business, it has revolutionized the speed of office work, replacing memos and letters.

Allows people to work at home, on holiday, etc., because they can regularly communicate with colleagues and can send work they have done to their office.

The text mentions: it's easy, cheap, fast, the emails are easily stored, it's environmentally-friendly, and 'universal' – everybody uses email.

CONS (–)

People no longer write letters and postcards to each other – which is a shame.

The informal style encourages poor grammar and punctuation.

People spend more time emailing and texting than actually talking to the people they are with.

The text mentions: it's impersonal, too easy, security is lax so people can get access to your emails, and emails can take over your life – you spend all your time reading and writing them.

3 Ask students to read through the article quickly, and answer the questions.

4 Ask students to study the article more carefully, and answer the questions. Let students discuss their answers and findings in pairs.

Answers

1 By saying, *In recent years email has become an increasingly important means of communication. However, in my opinion like most things, it has both advantages and disadvantages.*

2 There are two personal examples: *Nowadays, whenever I send regular mail (or snail mail as email users call it), I can't believe that it's actually going to take days to reach its destination.* And *Even my great aunt in Galashiels, Scotland is using it these days.*

3/4 See underlined words in the text extracts below.
Similar phrases from the two texts: *First of all/Firstly; A second point is that/Secondly; not only... also, Also* and *in addition to this/Another point is that; Last but not least/A final and very important point is that...*

5 The article is concluded with the writer's personal opinion: *Overall, however, to my mind...* is how the writer expresses his/her opinion.

EMAIL – A GOOD THING OR A BAD THING?

On the plus side:

- <u>First of all</u>, email is easy…
- <u>A second point is that</u> email is fast…

- Email is <u>not only</u> fast, it is <u>also</u> cheap…
- <u>Also</u>, email messages are easily stored…
- <u>In addition to this</u>, email is environmentally friendly because…
- <u>Last but not least</u>, email is practically universal.

On the minus side:

- <u>Firstly</u>, email is impersonal…
- <u>Secondly</u>, it can be argued that…
- <u>Another point is that</u> email security is lax…
- <u>A final and very important point is that</u> email can take over your life…

5 A good way of doing this is to ask students which of the three topics they would like to write about, then divide the students into groups of four depending on the topic they have chosen. So, for example, you might have two groups of four brainstorming *Mobile phones*, and one brainstorming *Adults living at home*.

Ask students to brainstorm the arguments for and against, then write their essay using the language in the model.

UNIT 8 Describing places – My favourite part of town (SB p119)

1 Lead in by asking students to discuss the questions in pairs, then as a class.

2 Ask students to look at the words in the box, and discuss the questions in pairs.

Answers

lively = positive/a person (full of fun and action)

dash around (v) = neutral/a person (run around in a hurry)

shabby = negative/a person or place (dirty/badly-dressed)

dull = negative/a person, place or food (boring)

brand-new = positive/place (very new)

snoring = negative/a person (making noise when sleeping)

a down-and-out = negative/a person (a homeless person)

cosmopolitan = positive/a person or place (having experience of people from different parts of the world)

pedestrianized = neutral/a place (area where no cars are allowed)

buzz (v) = positive/a place (have an atmosphere of fun and liveliness)

trendy = positive/a person or place (fashionable)

boutiques = neutral/a place (clothes shops)

packed = neutral/a place (full of people)

flock (v) = neutral/place (go to because everybody is going)

mouth-watering aromas = positive/food (delicious, nice smells)

a magnet = neutral/person or place (something or someone that attracts others)

3 Ask students to read the description of a part of London, and match the pictures with lines in the text.

Answers
The top picture shows Shaftesbury Avenue, with its many theatres. The bottom picture shows Piccadilly Circus and the statue of Eros.

4   Ask students in pairs to do these tasks.

Answers
See text below, which is divided into paragraphs.
The purpose of each paragraph: 1 Introduction; 2 Why he/she likes Soho; 3 The history of Soho; 4 Famous people and great food; 5 Conclusion
A suggested heading for each one: 1 My favourite part of town; 2 Why I like Soho; 3 The history of Soho; 4 Famous people and great food; 5 The centre of the world!

SOHO – MY FAVOURITE PART OF TOWN

I'm a Londoner, and proud of it. I'm not a Cockney – that's someone from the East End of London. I live in the West End, in Soho, <u>which is right in the centre</u>, and includes Piccadilly Circus, Shaftesbury Avenue, and Leicester Square. It's my favourite part of town.

So why do I like it so much? It is always lively and colourful, with people <u>dashing around</u>, <u>going about their business</u>, <u>which is mainly honest but not always</u>. Some of the streets may be a bit shabby but life in Soho is never dull. There's a surprise round every corner – maybe a brand-new night club <u>that wasn't there last week</u>, a snoring down-and-out <u>sleeping in a doorway</u>, or a celebrity <u>being pursued</u> by paparazzi and fans.

A sense of history pervades Soho. The name is derived from a hunting call, 'So-ho', <u>that huntsmen were heard to cry</u> as they chased deer in <u>what were the royal parklands</u>. It has been a cosmopolitan area since the first immigrants, <u>who were French Huguenots</u>, arrived in the 1680s. They were followed by Germans, Russians, Poles, Greeks, and Italians. More recently there have been a lot of Chinese from Hong Kong. Gerrard Street, <u>which is pedestrianized</u>, is the centre of London's Chinatown, and buzzes all year round, but especially at the New Year celebrations in February.

Many famous people have lived in Soho, <u>including</u> Mozart, Karl Marx, and the poet TS Eliot. It has a reputation for attracting artists, writers, poets, musicians, and people in the media. Shaftesbury Avenue is in the heart of London's theatre land, and there are endless clubs, pubs, trendy boutiques, and of course, restaurants. A large part of the Soho experience is to do with food. Soho is packed with continental food shops and restaurants. Mouth-watering aromas are everywhere, from first thing in the morning till late at night. Soho is a genuine 24/7 part of town.

Piccadilly Circus is like a magnet for young people. They flock from every corner of the world to sit on the steps under the statue of Eros, <u>celebrating the freedom</u>

<u>and friendship of youth</u>. My mother, <u>who was a Cockney</u>, used to say that if you wait long enough at Piccadilly Circus, you'll meet everyone you've ever known!

5   Ask students to find examples of fact and opinion in the text.

Answers
Facts: in the centre of London; named after a hunting cry; cosmopolitan; famous people have lived there; lots of restaurants
Opinions: lively; colourful; never dull; mouth-watering aromas

6   Ask students to find and underline examples of relative clauses and participles in the text.

Answers
See text in **4**, which has underlined examples of relative clauses and participles.

7   Ask students to write a description of their favourite part of town, using the paragraph plan to help them.

UNIT 9   Writing for Talking – What I want to talk about is … (SB p120)

1   Give students three or four minutes to think about what they want to talk about.

Ask students to write notes about their topic and talk to a partner briefly. You could give students a two-minute time limit.

2   **T9.13** [CD 3: Track 14] Ask students to read and listen to someone talking about a man called Christopher and answer the questions. Play the recording.

Note that the text is in American English, and involves American usage, (*cheap* = mean with money; *thrift store* = second-hand shop; the spelling of *humor*).

Answers
1   cousin
2   Because he doesn't like spending money – and prefers to buy cheap things. *Cheap* means *mean* in American English. *Stingy* also means *mean with money*.
3   He is a part-time journalist. He makes about $50,000 a year. He's married with two children, and his wife has a good job.
4   He never spends money on himself. He never buys new clothes. He gets them second-hand from thrift stores for about $5 an item. He never eats out in restaurants. When his work colleagues invite him out to lunch, he stays in his office and says he's expecting a phone call. He hardly ever uses his car. He says he can live on $10 a week. He never invites friends to dinner.

5 He went to a friend's wedding without a present. He just took some wrapping paper and a card saying 'Love from Christopher' and put it on the table with the other presents. Afterwards he got a thank-you letter from the bride because she thought she'd misplaced the present.

6 He'd give her a bouquet from her own garden.

7 He likes him because he's his cousin, and he's got a lot of other good qualities, like his sense of humor.

8 His wife doesn't seem to mind that he's so cheap. She says he's just 'careful with his money.'

3 Ask students to read the talk carefully and answer the questions in pairs. Ask students to mark stress and intonation in the first paragraph, then practise reading it aloud.

Answers

1 *The title of my talk is* = to introduce talk
Let's start with = to introduce first point
First, let me tell you = to make first point
Another thing, = to add another point
All these things are pretty bad, but in my opinion = to make a further point
The obvious question = to introduce a key question
Finally, I'd like to say that = to conclude

2 So why is Christopher so stingy?
Can you believe that?
Do you know what he says?
Why is he so stingy?
Why, you may ask?
A rhetorical question is a question that does not expect an answer. They are often used in speeches to keep the attention of the audience.

3 Examples of when the speaker gives his personal opinion: *in my opinion the stingiest thing he's ever done is... He went to a friend's wedding without a present. / I still like him. / he's got a lot of other good qualities...*

4 See text below for marked pauses, main stress and intonation in paragraph 1.

CHEAP CHRISTOPHER

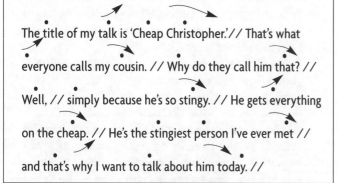

The title of my talk is 'Cheap Christopher.' // That's what everyone calls my cousin. // Why do they call him that? // Well, // simply because he's so stingy. // He gets everything on the cheap. // He's the stingiest person I've ever met // and that's why I want to talk about him today. //

Preparing your talk

4 Ask students to follow the guidelines to prepare their talks.

5 Ask students to read through their talk and mark pauses and words they want to stress. Ask them to practise before presenting their talks to the class.

UNIT 10 Formal and Informal Letters and Emails – Do's and don'ts (SB p121)

1 Ask students to do the 'quiz' on informal letters and emails, and check their answers with a partner before discussing as a class.

Answers

1 True, for emails. With informal letters, *Dear Rob* is still typical, although *Hi Rob* is OK.

2 True.

3 True.

4 Part true. *Bye for now* is not typical on informal letters, but might be used by some people. *Goodbye* and *Cheers!* are normally found in spoken English. *Best of wishes* is wrong – the phrase *Best wishes* is common in *formal* letters and emails, and *All the best* is also quite formal. *Take care, Yours,* or *Love* are typical of both informal letters and emails. *Love* is only used with family and close friends.

5 False.

6 True.

2 Ask students to do the 'quiz' on formal letters and emails, and check their answers with a partner before discussing as a class.

Answers

1 True: *Dear Mr Brown,*
False: *Dear Robert Brown, Dear Brown, Dear Mr Robert Brown,* or just *Brown!*

2 True. You could also write *Dear Mrs Black* (if married), or *Dear Miss Black,* (if not), but only if this is how these people usually refer to themselves. Nowadays, *Dear Ms Black* is the most commonly used method of address in a formal letter.

3 True.

4 True. Although very formal writing tends to avoid all contractions, much formal writing uses the contracted forms of *do*.

5 Part true. If you begin with *Dear Sir* or *Dear Madam*, you should end with *Yours faithfully*, but never with just *Yours*.
True: If you begin with the person's name, you should end with *Yours sincerely*.
(There is a useful way to remember which one to use: *Dear Sir* or *Dear Madam* are more **f**ormal, so remember that **f**ormal = **f**aithfully.)

6 True.

3 Ask students to read the letter, and decide which parts sound too formal. Ask them to replace them with words on the right, and check with a partner.

Answers

4-2 Nagayama 3-chome
Tama-shi, Tokyo 206

Hi Amber!
How are things with you? I **hope** you and your family are **all well**, and that you **had a great time** in France. I went to the mountains for a few days with **a few friends**. **I'm sending you** a photo of us at an ancient temple. Hope you like it.
It's great news that you are coming to Japan **soon**! You didn't **say when exactly. Please let me know. I'll do my best to make sure** I have some free time **so I can show** you around Tokyo. **Believe me**, there is a lot to see and do here. We'll have lots of fun! The shops here are **absolutely fantastic**, too, so **we're bound to** end up buying **loads of** clothes!
Anyway, I have to finish now. It's time for bed! Please **get in touch** soon. **I can't wait to hear** from you.
Love and best wishes
Keiko
PS Please **say hello** to your parents. Tell them I miss them!

4 Ask students to write an informal letter to another student in the class, following the guidelines suggested.

UNIT 11 Narrative Writing 2 – Linking words and expressions (SB p122)

1 Ask students to prepare notes in response to the questions, then tell their partner about the event. It is always a good idea to model this sort of activity for the students first, by telling a short story of a dream goal you have had fulfilled.

2 Ask students in pairs to reconstruct the story. Then ask two or three students to read their story to the class.

Possible answers
(*Students should come up with a wide variety of possible takes on the story – here is a very simple version, using the words given.*)
Larry's dream was to fly aeroplanes. One day, he bought twenty balloons and tied them to a garden chair. He packed a few sandwiches and an air pistol, then cut the rope that was holding the chair on the ground. He floated around because the winds were blowing until he was seen by a British Airways pilot at 3,500 metres. Soon a helicopter arrived with a TV reporter.

3 Ask students to read the full story, and compare it to their own. Ask students in pairs to decide what each heading refers to, and match it with the correct paragraph.

Answers
[4] *Serious problems* refers to the problems Larry had while flying – nightfall and strong winds.
[2] *Preparing for take-off* refers to what Larry actually did as he got ready to take off in the 'balloon'.
[5] *Down to earth with a bump* refers to the end of the story. Larry didn't actually, literally, land with a bump, (he was rescued by helicopter). However, idiomatically, if you 'come down to earth with a bump', it means that you suddenly have to face reality after living in a dream world.
[1] *Larry and his dream* refers to the start of the story – Larry's dream of flying.
[3] *Flying high* refers to the time when Larry was flying very high in his home-made machine. Idiomatically, *flying high* means doing well/being successful/having a great time.

4 Ask students to read the story again and complete it with a correct linking word or expression from the box.

Answers
(1) All day long
(2) Then, one day
(3) However
(4) first of all
(5) Next
(6) Finally
(7) in order to
(8) Unfortunately
(9) until
(10) so
(11) By this time
(12) Fortunately, just at that moment
(13) Immediately
(14) because
(15) Eventually
(16) As soon as

5 Ask students to use their notes from exercise 1 to write their own story of a dream that's been fulfilled.

6 Ask students to read each others' stories and ask and answer questions about them.

UNIT 12 Adding Emphasis in Writing – People of influence (SB p123)

1 Ask students to discuss the questions in pairs, then share their ideas with the class. Encourage a brief discussion.

Sample answers
Students' own ideas – however here are a few suggestions.
Today
The President of the USA
The Secretary General of the United Nations
Media moguls like Rupert Murdoch and Silvio Berlusconi
Leading film stars, pop stars and footballers who influence our taste in clothes and lifestyle
The past
Emperors, kings and popes
Artists and writers
People who led political or religious movements, (the prophet Mohammed, Martin Luther, Karl Marx)

2 Lead in briefly by asking students what they know about Michelangelo. Write any information they give you on the board, e.g. artist, sculptor, Florence, Sistine Chapel, David.

Ask students to read the two texts about Michelangelo. Then ask them to work in pairs to find examples of the differences in each section, and discuss the questions, *Which text sounds better? Why?*

Answers
The second section sounds better. The first is clear and simple, but flat. The second is more expressive and powerful. This is achieved by changing word order to emphasize particular words and ideas, using stronger words (e.g. *tremendous* not *great*), adding emphasis by using sentences beginning *It was...* and *What...*, and referring back using *this*.

Answers (by section)
1 Two sentences are joined into one by incorporating the list of jobs as a subordinate clause. The stronger word, *tremendous*, replaces *great*.
2 *Although* replaces *but*. *It was...* and *What... was...* are used to add emphasis. *Above all* is added to add emphasis.
3 *Initially* and *in 1501* are brought to the start of the sentence to add emphasis, (bringing these words, and *later*, in the next paragraph, to the start of the sentence helps the story-telling structure as they effectively introduce each sentence by saying when it happened). *This* is used to refer back.
4 *Later* is brought to the start of the sentence. Two sentences are incorporated into one, comprised of dramatic, short clauses.
5 Two sentences combined, using *it was...* Second sentence uses *What...* Use of *There is...* and *this* to change the order of the sentence for dramatic effect.
6 The order of the sentences is changed, so that the final sentence has dramatic emphasis, using *this* to refer back.

3 Ask students to rephrase the sentences in different ways to make them more emphatic.

Answers
1 What I love about my grandfather is his kind, wrinkly smile.
   The thing I love about my grandfather is his kind, wrinkly smile.
2 It's the President's policies (that) they don't understand.
   What they don't understand is the President's policies.
3 What makes Norah Jones' voice special is its softness.
   It's the softness of Norah Jones' voice that/which makes it special.
4 What I admired about Mother Teresa was her courage.
   It was Mother Teresa's courage that I admired.
5 What was amazing was the way Pele could head a football.
   What amazed me was the way Pele could head a football.

4 Ask students to write about the career of someone they consider influential. Ask students to research information about the person from books or the Internet, and make notes using the paragraph headings. Ask them to write a clear, simple account first, then to rewrite their profile, using some of the structures for adding emphasis from exercises 3 and 4.

Photocopiable material

The following material may be photocopied freely for classroom use. It may not be adapted, printed, or sold without the permission of Oxford University Press.

Extra material and ideas for Units 1–12 pp 142–163

Stop and checks pp 164–174

Progress tests pp 175–180

Answer keys (including teacher's notes for songs) pp 181–186

Word list pp 187–192

Unit 1

Getting to know your Student's Book!

The *flick* test

Before starting out on *New Headway Upper-Intermediate*, flick through the book and become familiar with it. The tasks below will help you.

1 Match the topics to the units. Guess from the unit title, then check by looking at the units.

Unit 1	*No place like home*	remembering people
Unit 2	*Been there, done that*	telling lies
Unit 3	*What a story!*	relationships with people
Unit 4	*Nothing but the truth*	success in business
Unit 5	*An eye to the future*	age
Unit 6	*Making it big*	travel
Unit 7	*Getting on together*	unusual experiences and places
Unit 8	*Going to extremes*	dangerous adventures
Unit 9	*Forever friends*	life in the future
Unit 10	*Risking life and limb*	telling stories
Unit 11	*In your dreams*	living and working away from home
Unit 12	*It's never too late*	interpreting dreams

2 Some of the unit titles in exercise 1 are idiomatic. Match them to the following.

  a An expression meaning 'being very successful'
  b Part of the oath taken in a court of law
  c An expression meaning 'thinking about the longer term'
  d An expression typical of bored, rich kids who have experienced everything
  e An expression meaning 'having a friendly relationship'
  f An expression meaning 'doing dangerous things'
  g An expression meaning 'doing something in a way that is far from normal'
  h A proverb meaning 'it's nice to travel, but it's even nicer to return'
  i An expression meaning 'there's no chance of this happening to you'

3 In which unit can you practise the following?

hypothesizing   narrating   using homonyms   speculating   exclaiming

4 On what page do the following sections start?

Contents   Grammar reference   Tapescripts   Writing

5 Find the following regular sections in Unit 1, and match them to their aims.

Test your Grammar	introduces spoken functional phrases
Language Focus	finds out how well you can use grammar at the start of the unit
Everyday English	shows you intonation and stress patterns
Music of English	explains grammatical rules

Unit 1

Song Don't leave home

1 Listen to a song called *Don't leave home*. Are these statements true or false?

The singer has a child.
The singer is in love.
The singer isn't serious about the relationship.
The singer is worried that her lover will leave home.

2 Read the song and choose the correct word for each space. Listen again, and check your answers.

3 Which of these words could describe the singer in the song? Why?

> loving   easy-going   selfish   possessive

4 Discuss the questions in pairs or groups.

1 How do you think the singer's lover feels about the situation in the song?
2 What advice would you give the singer in this song?
3 Do you think it is possible to love someone too much?
4 In a relationship, do you think it is important to give your partner space to do their own things?

"Don't Leave Home"

Like a _____, I don't need a key	ghost/guest
Your best friend I've come to be	
Please don't think of _____ up for me	getting/dressing
You don't even need to speak	
When I've been here for just one day	
You'll already _____ me if I go away	kiss/miss
So close the _____ and shut the door	windows/blinds
You won't need other friends anymore	
Oh don't leave home, oh don't leave home	
If you're _____, I'll keep you warm	cool/cold
If you're _____, just hold on	blue/low
'Cause I will be your safety	
Oh don't leave home	
And I arrived when you were weak	
I'll make you _____, like a child	sweeter/weaker
Now all your love you give to me	
When your _____ is all I need	art/heart
Oh don't leave home, oh don't leave home	
If you're _____, I'll keep you warm	cool/cold
If you're _____, just hold on	blue/low
'Cause I will be your safety	
Oh don't leave home	
Oh how quiet, quiet the world can be	
When it's just you and _____ me	brittle/little
Everything is _____ and everything is new	clear/dear
So you won't be leaving will you	
Oh don't leave home, oh don't leave home	
If you're _____, I'll keep you warm	cool/cold
If you're _____, just hold on	blue/low
'Cause I will be your safety	
Oh don't leave home	

Unit 3

Vocabulary and speaking (SB p29)

Genre	Fantasy
Setting	In an imaginary world called Middle earth.
Characters	The central character is Frodo Baggins, a hobbit. Other characters include Gandalf the wizard, Aragorn, Boromir, and a strange creature called Gollum
Plot	It is a long story, made up of three books, but basically, Frodo Baggins must travel to the evil kingdom of Mordor in order to destroy a ring that only he has the power to carry. He is accompanied by brave princes, elves and dwarves on his journey. The evil powers of Mordor desperately try to take the ring from Frodo, but eventually he is successful, and destroys the ring.

1

Genre	Classic
Setting	In rural Dorset, England, notably Blackmoor Vale, during the late nineteenth century.
Characters	Tess Durbeyfield, a poor village girl, Alec D'Urberville, and Angel Clare
Plot	Tess is seduced by Alec D'Urberville, but their baby dies at birth. She then works as a dairymaid on a large farm, and falls in love with a clergyman's son called Angel Clare. They get married, but when Tess admits that she had a relationship with Alec, Angel abandons her. She eventually ends up living a loveless relationship with Alec. When Angel returns from Brazil, and wants to be with her again, she murders Alec. Angel and Tess hide in the New Forest, but soon Tess is arrested and hanged.

5

Genre	Classic/Romance
Setting	It is set in various English country houses, notably Longbourn in Hertfordshire, in the early nineteenth century.
Characters	Mr and Mrs Bennet and their five daughters. The second sister is Elizabeth, who eventually marries Mr Darcy
Plot	The story is about the relationships between the girls in the Bennet family and various male suitors. One suitor, Mr Darcy, who is a very proud man, is at first rejected by Elizabeth, but later she realizes that he has a positive side and agrees to marry him.

2

Genre	Romance/history
Setting	The Greek island of Cephallonia in 1941
Characters	Pelagia, a Greek girl, Mandras, a Greek boy, and Antonio Corelli, a young Italian officer
Plot	It is the story of what happens on Cephallonia before and after the Second World War. It starts with a love story between Pelagia and Mandras, then, after the Italians invade the island, there is a love story between Pelagia and Corelli. When the Germans take over the island, life gets hard and Corelli must leave. The story ends with an earthquake on Cephallonia which changes the inhabitants' way of life.

6

Genre	Detective thriller
Setting	San Francisco's criminal underworld in the 1930s
Characters	Sam Spade, a private detective, his client Miss Wonderley, and a group of desperate criminals, including cowardly Joel Cairo, pompous Kasper Gutman, and a femme fatale, called Brigid O'Shaugnessey.
Plot	Miss Wonderley comes to Sam Spade's office, asking him to find her sister. The next night, Sam's partner, Miles Archer, is murdered. In trying to solve the murder, Sam has to deal with a gang of criminals who are desperate to get their hands on a statuette of a bird that contains jewels.

3

Genre	Romance
Setting	It is set among the houses of the very wealthy in 1920s California
Characters	Jay Gatsby is the central character
Plot	Gatsby is a very wealthy and mysterious gentleman, who lives a fabulous lifestyle. However, he is of poor and mysterious origins, and made his money from bootlegging, (making and smuggling alcohol illegally). Now that he is rich, he works to win back the girl he once loved, who is now married to a rich and harsh man.

7

Genre	Allegory
Setting	On a deserted island after a plane crash
Characters	A group of teenage boys; Ralph has leadership qualities; Piggy is fat and persecuted by the others
Plot	A group of teenage boys are marooned on a desert island following a plane crash. They go native, and divide into two tribes, and end up killing each other. The story is an allegory of the way society organizes itself along divisive religious and social lines, and how easily our 'mask' of civilization can be dropped.

4

Genre	Satire
Setting	The imaginary lands of Lilliput, Brobdingnag and others
Characters	Lemuel Gulliver, a sailor, and various fabulous characters
Plot	Gulliver is shipwrecked on an island called Lilliput, and finds himself a giant among the tiny Lilliputians. He has many adventures. In later stories, he lands in Brobdingnag, where he is tiny and the people huge, on Laputa, a flying island, and in the country of the Houyhnhnms, where the horses are endowed with reason, and the men, called Yahoos, are beasts. Basically, it is a satire on man and human institutions.

8

Unit 4

Song I Never Loved You Anyway

1 When relationships end, people often feel 'bad'. The words below describe how they feel. Put the words into pairs with similar meanings.

> angry   bitter   upset   furious   hurt   resentful

2 Listen to the song. How do you think the woman who is singing the song feels?

3 Choose the correct answer to complete the song. Listen and check your answers.

4 Tick the correct sentences according to what the singer says. Rewrite the incorrect sentences in the negative.

> 1 He was interesting. ☒
> *He wasn't interesting.*
> 2 Their relationship has ended. ☐
> 3 She is sorry it's over. ☐
> 4 She left him. ☐
> 5 He's got a new girlfriend. ☐
> 6 She always loved him. ☐
> 7 He spends lots of money. ☐

5 Do you think the singer is telling the truth in the song? How do you think she really feels? What do you think really happened?

6 Find words in the song which mean:

> 1 suffered something unpleasant for a long time
> 2 gentle
> 3 made to believe something that was not true

7 In the song, the singer is bitter and wants to say things that will hurt her ex-partner. Look at the words below. Why are they hurtful?

> 1 *I never really loved you anyway…*
> 2 *You bored me… I endured you…*
> 3 *Valentino, I don't think so*
> 4 *… that girl*

8 Put the words in the correct order to make questions. Discuss the questions in groups.

> 1 people / Why / love / do / in / fall?
> 2 end / relationships / do / Why?
> 3 should / end / you / you / when / say / What / relationship / a?
> 4 with / angry / was / time / When / felt / last / very / the / someone / you?

I never loved you anyway

You bored me with your stories
I _____ believe that I endured   *can/can't*
you for as long as I did
I'm _____ , it's over, I'm only   *sad/happy*
sorry
That I didn't make the move
before you
And when you go I will _____   *forget/remember*
To send a thankyou _____ to   *letter/note*
that girl
I see she's holding you so tender
Well I just wanna say …

I never really loved you anyway
No I didn't love you anyway
I never really loved you anyway
I'm so _____ you're moving   *sad/glad*
away

Valentino, I don't think so
You watching MTV while I lie
_____ in an MT bed   *dreaming/sleeping*
And come to think of it
I was _____   *misread/misled*
My flat, my food, my everything
And thoughts inside my
_____   *bed/head*

Before you go I must remember
To have a quiet _____ with   *chat/word*
that girl
Does she know you're not a
spender
Well I just have to say …

I never really loved you anyway
No I didn't love you anyway
I never really loved you anyway
I'm so happy you're moving away

And when you go I will remember
I must remember to say …
I never really loved you anyway …

Unit 5

Everyday English (SB p53)

Beginning and ending a phone conversation

Beginning a phone conversation

Answering the phone	Hello. 267890. Hello. Simpson's Travel Agents. Hello. The Regent Hotel. Kathy speaking. How can I help you?
Introducing yourself	Hello, James. This is Sarah Jackson. Hi, Sarah. It's Alan, Alan Cunningham. (Is that Mr Brown?) Speaking.
Asking who is speaking	Is that Sarah? Who's calling? (This is Keith Jones.)
Asking how someone is	How are things? How's the family? How's everything?
Saying how you are	Not too bad, thanks. We're surviving. Pretty good, thanks.
Asking about someone's work	What are you up to? Have you got a lot on at the moment? How are things at work?
Talking about work	I've got a lot on. Things are looking up. I mustn't complain.

Ending a phone conversation

Signalling that you want to end	So, Barry. It was good to talk to you. Anyway, Barry … Right, Barry. I must fly. I'm late for a meeting.
Confirming arrangements at the end of a phone call	So you'll give me a ring when you're back, right? And you'll send me a copy of the report? It'll be in the post tonight. I'll see you on the fourteenth in the bar of The County.

Unit 5

Everyday English (SB p53)

Role cards for telephones

Student A1

You are James from the listening activity about *The reunion* on p52 of the Student's Book.

You are married with two girls, and you work in a travel agent's.

You are going to phone Alan, who is an old university friend. Alan now runs a small engineering company in the Midlands. He isn't married. He likes football very much. He supports Sheffield United. You also like football. You support Sunderland.

Alan thinks you're going to meet at the Lotus Garden Restaurant on the fourteenth, so you need to tell him that it has closed. You also need to tell him that you're going to meet at the Kwai Lam at about 7.15. He'll probably need to know where this restaurant is.

Student B1

You are Alan from the listening activity about *The reunion* on p52 of the Student's Book.

You run a small engineering company in the Midlands. You aren't married. You are a big football fan. You support Sheffield United, who are doing well at the moment.

Your old university friend, James, is going to phone you. James works in a travel agent's in Sunderland, in the north of England. You haven't spoken to each other for a while.

Remember that you are meeting up with him and Sarah on the fourteenth. You're going to have a meal in the Lotus Garden Restaurant in Durham, where you all went to university about ten years ago.

Remember! You answer the phone. Begin by giving your phone number.

Student A2

You are a student of English. You are going to stay with a host family, Mr and Mrs Brown, who live in London, for a month while you study at International House. An agency has organized your stay with the Browns.

You are going to phone Mr and Mrs Brown to introduce yourself, and to give details of when you're arriving. Decide how you're travelling (By plane? By Eurostar?), what day you're travelling, and what time you expect to arrive.

End by saying something like 'I'm very excited about coming to London', or 'I'm really looking forward to meeting you'.

Student B2

You are Mr or Mrs Brown. You are English, and you live in London. Both Heathrow Airport and Waterloo Station, where the Eurostar train arrives, are pretty close to your house.

You are going to be a host family to a foreign student, who is coming to London for a month to study English. He/she is going to phone you to say hello, and to give details of his/her travel arrangements. You could offer to meet him/her.

Remember! You answer the phone. Begin by giving your phone number.

Student A3

You are going to phone a taxi firm to book a taxi to take you to the airport. Decide where you're going, on what date, and at what time. Which airport are you going from? Which terminal? What time does the plane leave? What time do you need to check in? How long does it take to get to the airport from your house? Will the traffic hold you up?

Student B3

You work for Tony's Taxis. Someone is going to ring to book a taxi. You need to get the following information.

What day? What time? What's the address? What's the name of the person? Where are they going?

You will need to decide a time to pick up, as you know what the traffic can be like at different times of day.

Remember! You answer the phone. Begin by saying 'Tony's Taxis. (Pat) speaking. How can I help you?'

Student A4

You are James from the listening activity about *The reunion* on p52 of the Student's Book.

You are married with two girls, and you work in a travel agent's.

You are going to phone your friend Martin, who lives in Durham, about fifteen miles away. He runs a bookshop. He isn't married. He's mad about dogs – he breeds German Shepherds, which he takes to dog shows. His favourite dog is called Wizzer.

You want to ask Martin if you can stay the night at his house on the night of Friday the fourteenth, because you are meeting up with two old university friends, Alan and Sarah, in Durham, and you want to be able to spend time with them.

Student B4

You are Martin. You are a friend of James from the listening activity about *The reunion* on p52 of the Student's Book. James works in a travel agent's in Sunderland, and he is married with two girls.

You live in Durham, about fifteen miles away from where James lives. You run a bookshop. You aren't married, but you adore dogs! You breed German Shepherds, and you take them to dog shows. Your favourite dog is called Wizzer.

James is going to ask you a favour. Maybe you can oblige, but maybe you're busy that night!

Remember! You answer the phone. Begin by giving your phone number.

Student A5

You want to book two seats to see a film, so you phone the cinema.

You want to see *Fear of the Dark* next Friday, either early in the evening or at about nine o'clock-ish.

You need to ask what time the film starts, how much the tickets are, and whether there's a booking fee.

Have your credit card details ready.

Student B5

You work for the Odeon Cinema. You take bookings, and give details of when films are showing.

Someone is going to phone you, asking for details about the film *Fear of the Dark*. Decide what time it starts in the evening. Presumably there are at least two showings per evening.

How much are the tickets? Is there one price, or several different ones? Is there a booking fee?

You need to get the person's credit card details.

Remember! You answer the phone. Begin by saying 'Odeon Cinemas. (Pat) speaking. How can I help you?'

Student A6

You are going to phone your local hairdresser to make an appointment to have your hair done.

You know the person who takes the bookings quite well, so you could have a little chat first. It's Monday today, so you could ask about the weekend. Or you could chat about the weather, which has changed very suddenly! Your mother has been ill recently, but she's getting better now.

Decide when you want an appointment for, what day and what time. What do you want to have done to your hair?

Student B6

You work for Jason's Hair Salon. You take bookings over the phone.

Someone is going to ring who you know quite well, so before you get details of the booking you could have a little chat first. It's Monday morning, so you could ask about the weekend that's just gone by. You could ask the person about his/her mother, who has been ill recently.

Finally, get details of the booking. What day? What time? Would the person like any particular hairdresser?

Remember! You answer the phone. Begin by saying 'Jason's Hair Salon. (Pat) speaking. How can I help you?'

Unit 6

Speaking (SB p60)

44

You are ready to open the fast food restaurant, but no one knows about it. You need to generate some awareness in the town, but you only have a limited budget. You must spend the money wisely.

> The budget could be spent on traditional advertising in the local press. It has an excellent readership so everyone will see the ads.
>
> **GO TO** 37
>
> Or you could do a public relations stunt! You could make some 'funny food' costumes and dress up as a carrot! Then you could go around town handing out leaflets to everyone. Wouldn't it be fun?
>
> **GO TO** 20

22

Your friend agrees to join you and contribute half the funds. Now you have to decide what type of restaurant you want.

He / she wants to open a fast food restaurant as there aren't any in town, and it would be easy to set up.

You don't want to be serving fast food. You'd rather open an upmarket bistro. As well as being more enjoyable work the profits will be far higher.

What are you going to do?

> Open a fast food restaurant.
>
> **GO TO** 44
>
> Open a bistro.
>
> **GO TO** 31
>
> Conduct some market research.
>
> **GO TO** 2

64

You give the police the information. Fortunately there is no trace of your 'ex-friend'.

Your good relations with the police mean that they use your fast food restaurant quite a bit. It makes a lot of money but the presence of the police does tend to keep other customers away.

> So what? The police give you easily enough business to keep going and you're not likely to get burgled with so many police around. You could tailor your restaurant to them.
>
> **GO TO** 55
>
> You politely and very tactfully persuade the police to use a different restaurant from yours.
>
> **GO TO** 6

2

You conduct some research and discover that a bistro will be opening in town before yours. However, there aren't any plans for more fast food restaurants.

> You are determined to carry on with the bistro and are not worried about competition.
>
> **GO TO** 31
>
> Maybe a fast food restaurant would be easier to run anyway.
>
> **GO TO** 44

69

Discounting prices doesn't seem to be working. People now think your food is of poor quality just because it's cheap, but they haven't even tried it yet!

You can't win! If you put prices up, people will stay away too! What can you do to make the restaurant busier and make more money?

> You put the prices back up but give the customers something extra for free. Your friend still has the soft drinks that he / she can sell you so that you can give them away.
>
> **GO TO** 39
>
> How about staying open 24 hours a day? There are factories nearby that do night shifts. There is sure to be lots of business.
>
> **GO TO** 29

8

The banks agree to lend you as much money as you need. That seems very generous, until you see the amount of interest they want to charge.

> The interest charges look huge. You decide to look for a partner to share the start-up costs.
>
> **GO TO** 22
>
> It's a high cost but you'll be successful enough.
>
> **GO TO** 33

20

Oh dear! It was a great stunt and everyone in town certainly knows about your restaurant. Unfortunately your partner has been arrested for obstruction of the pavement. The problem is the bail money would take the last of your cash and may stop you from opening on time.

> You decide to use the money to pay your partner's bail.
>
> **GO TO** 38
>
> You decide to open the restaurant.
>
> **GO TO** 59

59

You don't pay your partner's bail, but open up instead. Business is pretty slow, so you don't miss your partner.

When he / she is finally released, you need to start attracting more people into the restaurant. You have two ideas on how to do it.

> A friend of yours has offered you several cases of soft drink at an extremely good price. You could give free drinks with every meal.
>
> **GO TO** 39
>
> Or you could discount your food as a special offer.
>
> **GO TO** 69

38

You've got your partner out of jail and still managed to open on time. However, all this activity hasn't brought in many customers. You need a special opening offer. You have two ideas. You could buy some cheap soft drinks from a friend, and give them out free with every meal. Or you could discount your prices.

You want to give soft drinks out free with every meal.
GO TO 39

You discount your prices on food as an opening offer.
GO TO 69

39

Success! The free drinks idea has gone down very well. It's bringing the people in. However, it has also brought the police in! Apparently that consignment of drinks was stolen from a nearby factory and they want to know where you got them from.

You tell the police the truth, that you bought the drinks in good faith from a friend of yours and give the police his / her name and address.
GO TO 64

You lie to protect your friend and say that a travelling sales representative came to the restaurant and sold them to you.
GO TO 73

11

Word gets around town that you sacked him. Feeling is running very high, and people start to boycott the restaurant. Boy, was that guy popular! You try to track him down without success. Business gets worse and worse, you're ruined.

You have come to the end of this activity.

BAD LUCK!

6

The police understand your position and now are far less regular visitors. However, instead of the rest of the town now rushing to use your restaurant you only get the local kids coming in. You've got nothing against kids but they just use the place as a meeting place and buy one drink between ten of them that lasts for two hours.

You tell them to leave or you'll report them to the police for loitering.
GO TO 63

You leave them alone. After all, they haven't got anywhere else to go.
GO TO 54

63

Things are very quiet now! You got rid of the police and now the kids as well. Is there anyone left?

You've got one last chance to make it all work. The situation is that bad.

You could try and get the police to come back and use the restaurant.
GO TO 55

You could sell out to a large national chain of restaurants. They've guaranteed you a job and a good price for the restaurant.
GO TO 18

55

You are doing quite well since you specialized for the police. Unfortunately, a canteen opens at the police station itself, and overnight half of your business has gone. You need to find some more customers from somewhere.

As the market is competitive you look for a niche to exploit. You could open a fast food vegetarian restaurant.
GO TO 23

People are all so obsessed with their weight these days. A place that specializes in low-fat food could be successful.
GO TO 47

37

The ads appear and trade starts to pick up, but it's not great. One of your customers tells you that the restaurant in the next town is doing special offers, so most people are going there. You need some special offers of your own to bring them into the restaurant.

A friend of yours has offered you several cases of soft drinks at an extremely good price. You could give free drinks with every meal.
GO TO 39

You could discount your food to be more competitive with the other restaurant.
GO TO 69

73

You tried to protect your friend, but they really want to know where you got the drinks from. You have to tell them the truth to be able to get on with running your restaurant.

You tell the police where the drinks came from.
GO TO 64

18

Well, at least you've got a job and a nice uniform to go with it!

It is certainly not what you had in mind when you set out to run a restaurant. You have very little control over what goes on. You're never going to be happy there.

You have come to the end of this activity.

BAD LUCK!

23

It sounded like a good idea, but the number of vegetarians is still quite low in the area, and you are fed up with telling people that no, you don't sell hamburgers.

You decide to try the low-fat fast food restaurant idea.

GO TO 47

26

You took the food around and got the money. You nearly got away with it, until someone with an allergy to butter falls ill the next day. They find out the truth, demand the money back and the story makes the headlines in all the local press. Your restaurant is ruined.

You have come to the end of this activity.

BAD LUCK!

29

Now you're making more money. The night-time business is good. The problem is you're drinking most of your extra profits in the amount of coffee you need to stay awake! It's time you employed some staff. Unemployment is high so you won't need to pay them much, and you need to save some money. However, if you pay a reasonable wage you'll probably get a better standard of applicant.

You offer a low wage for the position.

GO TO 56

You offer a high wage for the position.

GO TO 32

57

You tell the customer you cannot make the food. They ask for whatever you can do. You prepare a range of completely oil-free foods that are a massive success with all the health freaks in the area. The restaurant becomes famous for its recipes and you become a wealthy and healthy restaurateur.

You have come to the end of this activity.

WELL DONE!

35

Your new 'celebrity' restaurant is proving to be very popular with families. To add atmosphere you put up some signed pictures of Hollywood actors. People start to ask you whether the actors have actually eaten in the restaurant. The fact is that they haven't, but will it upset the customers if you tell them the truth?

You tell them that a famous actor did pop in for a snack one day to keep them impressed.

GO TO 17

You admit that you simply put the photographs up to impress customers. No one famous has actually eaten in the place.

GO TO 67

47

It's a very original idea and the people eating fast food like the idea that yours is better for them. You do outside catering for special events and offices as well. You get a large order one day, but unfortunately you have run out of olive oil. You've only got butter. You don't want to lose the order. Will you make the food using the butter or turn down the order?

They won't notice the difference. You can make the food and take it around. You need the money after all.

GO TO 26

You have to turn the order and the money down. They won't be impressed, but if they found out what was in the food you could be in even more trouble.

GO TO 57

54

You let the young people stay. Word soon gets around and you end up having so many young people in that you start to make a profit.

You worry your restaurant isn't trendy enough. You could lose your business! Should you renovate the restaurant to appeal to all the young customers?

You decide to renovate the restaurant to appeal to your young customer base.

GO TO 25

Don't bother! Hopefully, the restaurant will be just as appealing to the new youngsters in the area.

GO TO 58

67

You told them the truth, but customers don't seem to mind. They keep coming in just in case someone really famous is there. When they never see anyone famous, you become well-known as the Restaurant of the Stars where no star has ever eaten.

You have come to the end of this activity.

WELL DONE!

32

You get a lot of good applicants and employ someone who works extremely hard. Your twenty-four hour fast food restaurant is doing really well. An opportunity arises to expand into next door. You're sure you could fill the seats.

Expand in to next door. It's quite a lot of money, but nothing ventured, nothing gained.

GO TO 34

Wait a while, you've only just become this busy and successful. It would be best to consolidate your position and build up some cash reserves.

GO TO 51

56

The people turning up for interviews are pretty appalling. You don't see anyone you would consider employing, and decide to increase the wages you are offering.

You increase the wage you are offering for the position.

GO TO 32

34

The risk has paid off! Business is excellent. You and your partner are very confident in your ability to run a restaurant. You believe the concept would work in lots of other locations. You could become extremely rich. If you do this, you will need to raise some investment capital.

You decide to take the idea further and bring in a number of investors to open up more restaurants.

GO TO 71

Stick with what you've got. You might not become extremely wealthy, but things will be all right.

GO TO 16

71

You now have a chain of restaurants in the area. The problem is, there are now a lot of people who influence the business, not just your partner and yourself. The other investors are demanding some changes be made to increase profitability. You don't believe they will work, but the others could fire you from the company if you don't agree.

Agree to their demands. They are all respected business people, so they should know what they are talking about, even if they don't run restaurants.

GO TO 65

Refuse their demands and stick to your plans, even though you're risking being made redundant.

GO TO 15

17

They're extremely impressed and soon tell their friends. Business picks up as people come in just in to see a celebrity dining. As the talk continues, the famous Hollywood actor finally gets to hear about it. He / she promptly files a lawsuit against you. You lose the case and your restaurant as part payment of the fees. The restaurant is now owned by a famous person but you've lost your livelihood.

You have come to the end of this activity.

BAD LUCK!

51

You haven't expanded. There are now queues at certain times of day. This is no bad thing, as some of the most fashionable eating places always have queues outside. You have a couple of ideas that could work in this situation.

Expand into next door. You think people might become fed up with queueing for fast food at some point.

GO TO 34

Take the restaurant upmarket like Planet Hollywood, which is run by celebrities. They make lots of money and always have a queue outside.

GO TO 35

66

That is a lot of money! You're not going to have to work for a year.

After all the hard work you've put in, you feel it's been worth it and will get stuck into another project next year.

You have come to the end of this activity.

WELL DONE!

31

Your bistro is being decorated and will soon be open. However, another one has opened before you and is quickly building up its business. There is going to be a lot of competition in town. Will you both be successful?

Maybe fast food wouldn't be so bad. There is still time to change your mind.

GO TO 44

Competition never hurt anyone and you're confident that your restaurant will be successful.

GO TO 5

65

The changes they forced you to make are a disaster. To increase profit you buy cheaper food from a bad supplier and lower the wages. This makes your staff unhappy. Customers soon notice the changes and stay away from your restaurant. You're ruined.

You have come to the end of this activity.

BAD LUCK!

70

You don't sell up, but as a result your working relationship suffers. You didn't realize how much your partner wanted to sell. It has damaged your working relationship and the restaurant as a result. You don't remain open for long.

You have come to the end of this activity.

BAD LUCK!

5

The bistro is ready to open. Your partner feels that you should spend the last of your money on a big opening night party for family and friends who have helped. You would prefer to start generating revenue and have paying customers in.

Have a big party for family and friends.

GO TO 21

Have an opening party for paying customers.

GO TO 43

16

You didn't take the opportunity to open a chain. However, the investors you were going to link with have offered a very high price for your restaurant. Are you going to sell or not?

Sell up for half a million pounds and give something else a go. This restaurant business is pretty hard work.

GO TO 66

Don't sell even though your partner wants to. You have come a long way since your first idea.

GO TO 70

68

Business is OK just being open in the evening. You're getting more calls from local companies asking whether they can bring in clients for lunch. You can't bear turning money away, so decide to open for lunch-times.

You decide to open for lunch-times as well.

GO TO 53

15

You refuse their demands and gain a lot of respect. You prove through your management that the running of the restaurants should be left to you and your partner. You make a lot of money for the investors and yourselves.

You have come to the end of this activity.

WELL DONE!

21

Great party! Everyone had a wonderful time. So good in fact that they drank a lot more of your opening supplies of drink than you expected. You don't have the money to replace all of the stocks immediately. How are you going to open without sufficient stocks of alcohol to offer the customers?

You could become a Bring Your Own restaurant where the customers bring alcoholic drinks in themselves.

GO TO 36

There is a lot of profit on drink and you don't want to lose this. You know where you can get some cheap drink to tide things over until you can afford more.

GO TO 50

4

This is extremely unpopular. Customers are furious when you ask them to give up the table at the end of the meal. It's giving you a very bad name. You think it might ruin you eventually and decide to do something different.

You'll lose all your customers if you persist with this plan. You decide to try charging a bottle opening fee.

GO TO 60

36

It proves to be extremely popular with your customers. The problem is they bring an awful lot of drink with them and stay for a long time. You're not making enough money from them to keep the business profitable.

You could restrict the amount of time people are allowed to stay. Lots of restaurants have a number of 'sittings' in a night – so can you.

GO TO 4

Charge a bottle opening fee for the drink that they bring in. At least then you'll be making some money from it.

GO TO 60

43

Your party for customers was very successful! They love the place. A number of people tell you to open at lunch-time as well as the evening. You'll make more money, but you'll also need more staff. Is it worth it?

You decide to open at lunch-time as well as the evening.

GO TO 53

You think you'll just stick to being open in the evening.

GO TO 68

10

Your business is now highly profitable and relations with the companies are excellent. The regulars ask for special table booking rights above all other people as they eat in your restaurant so frequently.

You think its a good idea. After all, they are the best customers.

GO TO 30

You decide not to agree with them as it will tie you in with these companies too closely.

GO TO 62

60

The bottle opening charge makes money but it still does not cover the loss from not selling drinks. You decide to offer live entertainment but you have to decide what type of entertainment.

You decide to put on regular live music – that's always a popular event.

GO TO 46

You've heard people talking about a restaurant that does live comedy while people eat. Sounds like a good idea.

GO TO 7

30

It goes very well for a while. Your special relationship with the local companies is very good for business. Unfortunately recession hits, and the first savings companies make are in entertainment. You are soon looking at an empty restaurant and need to attract some more customers.

You go looking for other companies. You're a specialized business restaurant now, and need to maintain a similar profit margin.

GO TO 49

You cut prices drastically in an attempt to get your old customers back through the door.

GO TO 3

53

Lunch-time trade is good, business people buy the expensive food and wine to impress clients. They also tip well. You could easily increase prices on everything and start making very expensive dishes. You know they'll sell very well.

You introduce your new and more expensive menu and drinks list.

GO TO 10

You worry about losing your normal customers. You stick with the original menu.

GO TO 27

3

Luckily for you everyone still appreciates a bargain! People return to your restaurant and the low prices in the recession prove to be very popular. Even through the bad times your restaurant remains successful. You've been through a lot but you've proven that you can run a restaurant in any circumstances.

You have come to the end of this activity.

WELL DONE!

62

Recession hits! What a good job you didn't tie up too closely with those businesses! You've still lost a large percentage of your turnover though. How are you going to keep the restaurant going in a recession?

There must be companies still making money in the area. You've specialized for businesses, so that's who you will attract.

GO TO 49

You cut prices drastically in an attempt to get your old customers back through the door.

GO TO 3

45

It's a good idea. The food is still very good but people can't eat as much. They even think it's better value than before because they're so full. You now have a permanently busy restaurant that you and your partner enjoy running. You're a great success!

You have come to the end of this activity.

WELL DONE!

49

So many companies have closed down that there is no business lunch market at all. Your highly specialized restaurant is doomed until the economy picks up markedly. The local people do not have much sympathy for you as you forgot them when better profits came along. You have to close down.

You have come to the end of this activity.

BAD LUCK!

19

You scrap the buffet, and lunch-time trade soon disappears. You are convinced people will change their minds, so you do nothing to reverse the trend. By the time you realize they aren't coming back, you've lost too much money and are forced to close.

You have come to the end of this activity.

BAD LUCK!

40

The all-you-can-eat buffet is very popular, and people in the area soon start putting on weight at your expense. This is the problem! It's so popular and people so greedy that the buffet is a large drain on your profit. Something needs to change.

Scrap the idea. It's done the job of making the place popular. You don't need it now.

GO TO 19

Change the food you offer and include a lot more filling recipes to make people eat less.

GO TO 45

27

You keep your normal menu without specializing. It does not bring in enough daytime revenue so you need to consider other options.

You can't resist specializing for businesses at lunch-time. The prospects look too good.

GO TO 10

You introduce an all-you-can-eat lunch-time buffet. These are always popular and bound to increase business.

GO TO 40

25

You adapt your restaurant into what you think will appeal to people of this age. However, in their eyes your place is now for 'kids' and there is no way that they will keep coming in. You have doomed your business by deciding to specialize in one section of the market.

You have come to the end of this activity.

BAD LUCK!

48

You say nothing, but the situation steadily deteriorates. He soon begins turning up late for work. It forces you to speak with your employee about the problem.

GO TO 14

50

Your choices of cheap drink do not go down well with the customers. You hardly sell any at all, and you need to think of a new strategy.

Go into debt and employ a beer and wine specialist. If you're going to serve drink why not do it properly?

GO TO 24

Change your views on letting them bring their own drink in when eating.

GO TO 36

14

He states that this is the way he has always worked, but he will try to improve his time-keeping.

Your partner does not believe he will improve and wants to sack him.

GO TO 42

You would like to give him a chance as he is popular with the customers.

GO TO 61

24

Your specialist certainly knows his trade. His choices of drinks and his character are a very popular addition to the restaurant. The only problem is that the specialist is very keen on his purchases as well. He's drinking a lot of any profits that might be made.

You decide not to say anything to him. He is doing the job well, after all.

GO TO 48

You decide to tackle him on the subject of the amount he is drinking.

GO TO 14

42

You have sacked him, but you underestimated just how popular with the customers he was. People are starting to wonder when he is coming back and they will be disappointed if he doesn't. Should you change your mind?

Your partner and yourself made the decision to fire him and are sticking to it. People will soon forget.

GO TO 11

You bring him back to keep your customers happy.

GO TO 28

61

You keep him on, but he is still not very dependable. He believes he would be much better if he had extra responsibility and a profit share of the wine takings. This would be a risky move.

You decide to take the risk with him and give him a more important role in the restaurant.

GO TO 12

There's no way you can give him more responsibility. Who knows what could happen?

GO TO 22

28

Being given the sack was a sobering experience for him. He is a changed person on return and makes an extremely valuable member of the team. You've made your restaurant a success!

You have come to the end of this activity.

WELL DONE!

72

With no extra responsibilities his drinking problem gets worse. You are just thinking about warning him again when there is an accident with a flaming brandy and the restaurant is burnt down. Everyone is safe but you have not got a business any more.

You have come to the end of this activity.

BAD LUCK!

58

You stuck with what you are good at, which is appealing to young people who don't have anywhere else to go. You've got a guaranteed business for many years if each new generation follows the one before. They're also a lot easier to please than older people. Your restaurant remains a success for many years.

You have come to the end of this activity.

WELL DONE!

12

It's a gamble, but it pays off. The added responsibility leads to a whole new attitude from your drinks expert. You now have a very good team and a profitable restaurant, a success.

You have come to the end of this activity.

WELL DONE!

46

The live music experiment is working, but you need to specialize with one type of music. People are confused about what sort of restaurant you are running.

You could specialize in jazz music. You're not keen on it, but the band you had in was liked by the customers.

GO TO 13

Or you could have some music you can really dance to! You're still young, as are a lot of the customers.

GO TO 9

9

You don't sell much food at the gigs but you don't need to. Everyone gets through such large amounts of soft drinks that you're making vast amounts of money and having a great time as well. You're the proud owners of a Rock Café and loving every second of it.

You have come to the end of this activity.

WELL DONE!

7

Your most popular acts use some very bad language. This offends some of your customers. You tell them that comedy is only at weekends but they seem very upset by it.

Change the comedians to some safer ones who will not upset anyone.

GO TO 41

Stick with the acts you have. They might be rude but they are very popular with most people.

GO TO 52

13

You and your partner have so little idea about jazz music that you hire some truly awful bands. This means that people actually stay away. This, together with the cost of the bands, damages your profitability so much you're forced to close.

You have come to the end of this activity.

BAD LUCK!

41

Your new comedians are certainly inoffensive, they are also not very funny. People are actually staying away from the bistro and you do not make enough money to keep the place in business. You tried your best but simply could not make it a success.

You have come to the end of this activity.

BAD LUCK!

33

You run into trouble very quickly. As well as paying the large interest payments there is only one of you to do the work. That means it will be twice as long before you open and are able to start repaying the bank.

The prospect of setting up with a partner who will pay off the bank with his share and help set up is too attractive. You change your mind and go in with him / her.

GO TO 22

52

Rude but funny, the comedians are very popular and ensure that you have regular packed nights in the bistro. You have now covered the revenue from not selling alcohol, and you have a very successful and busy restaurant.

You have come to the end of this activity.

WELL DONE!

Unit 7

Speaking roles

THE LEADER

You enjoy leading the discussion, and making sure that other people in your group get a chance to speak. So, take control, and make sure you involve everybody.

Useful language

I think we should talk about ... first.
Let's turn to ...
What do you think, Paula?
Just let Paula finish.
Does anybody else have anything to say about this?
OK, I think we've covered everything.

THE DREAMER

You enjoy being creative and imaginative. You often come up with a lot of new ideas, which are not always very practical.

Useful language

I think/reckon ...
One way of looking at this is to ...
Have you thought of ...
It might be a good idea to ...
It might seem strange, but what about ...
There's another way of looking at this.

THE NEUTRAL

You enjoy being objective. Rather than saying how you feel, you would rather remain neutral, seeing both sides of any argument. You like nothing better than presenting objective information and facts.

Useful language

There are two sides to the argument.
On one hand, ... On the other hand, ...
Let's look at the evidence/facts.
It's a fact that ...
It's clear from the evidence that ...
What exactly do you mean by ...?

THE PERSUADER

You don't like disagreeing with people, and prefer to persuade them gently to your point of view. You tend to see the positive aspects of what people say, and you are very supportive.

Useful language

That's a good/interesting point.
I see what you mean.
I see your point, but ...
I thought Joe made a good point, but ...
I'm with you 100% on that.

THE FIGHTER

You love an argument – but sometimes you get very emotional. You tend to say exactly how you feel, rather than reacting logically.

Useful language

I feel strongly that ...
Surely, ...
I am convinced that ...
There's no doubt that ...
I can't agree with you.
Don't talk rubbish.

THE PESSIMIST

You are very pessimistic and negative. You tend to see the bad side of everything, and you usually feel negative about other people's suggestions and solutions.

Useful language

I can't see how that works.
But surely ...
But what if ...
I don't see the point of ...
That's out of the question.
I think we're wasting our time here.

Unit 7

Song Fast Car

1 In the song Fast Car, a girl is talking to her boyfriend. Look at the phrases from the song, then discuss the questions.

I want a ticket to anywhere
Any place is better
We leave tonight or live and die this way
I could be someone

- How does she feel about her life now?
- Where does she want to go?
- What does she want her boyfriend to do?
- What do you think she wants from her life?

2 Listen to the song. Were your predictions correct? Does she get what she wants from life?

3 Listen to the song again and complete it with expressions using *get*.

4 Match the phrases from the song to their definitions.

1	*starting from zero*	a	drinks too much alcohol
2	*make a deal*	b	drive around for fun
3	*convenience store*	c	leave school
4	*lives with the bottle*	d	beginning again with no money or prospects
5	*quit school*	e	make an agreement
6	*go cruising*	f	place for the homeless
7	*the shelter*	g	small supermarket

5 Discuss these questions in groups.

1 What do you find out about the singer's background?
2 What does she do to try to change her life?
3 What do you think her boyfriend is like?
4 Do you think she still feels optimistic about life?
5 What about you? Have you ever tried to change your life in a dramatic way? Did it work out?

FAST CAR

You _____ a fast car
I want a ticket to anywhere
Maybe we (can) make a deal
Maybe together we can _____
Any place is better
Starting from zero we _____
Maybe we'll make something
But me myself I _____

You _____ a fast car
And I _____ to get us out of here
I've been working at the convenience store
Managed to save just a little bit of money
We won't have to drive too far
Just cross the border and into the city
You and I can both _____
And finally see what it means to be living

You see my old man _____
He lives with the bottle, that's the way it is
He says his body's too old for working
His body's too young to look like his
My mama went off and left him
She wanted more from life than he could give
I said somebody _____ take care of him
So I quit school and that's what I did

You _____ a fast car
But is it fast enough so we can fly away?
We _____
We leave tonight or live and die this way

I remember we were driving driving in your car
The speed so fast I felt like I was drunk
City lights lay out before us
And your arm felt nice wrapped round my shoulder
And I had a feeling that I belonged
And I had a feeling I could be someone, be someone, be someone

You _____ a fast car
And we go cruising to entertain ourselves
You still ain't _____
And I work in a market as a checkout girl
I know things will _____
You'll find work and I'll _____
We'll move out of the shelter
Buy a bigger house and live in the suburbs

I remember we were driving...

You _____ a fast car
And I've _____ that pays all our bills
You stay out drinking late at the bar
See more of your friends than you do of your kids
I'd always hoped for better
Thought maybe together you and me would find it
I _____ I ain't going nowhere
So take your fast car and keep on driving

So remember we were driving...

You _____ a fast car
But is it fast enough so you can fly away?
You _____
You leave tonight or live and die this way

Unit 8

Making descriptions longer (SB p72)

Describe the picture

Unit 10

Speaking (SB p89)

Plan of the room — Fireplace (A, B, C, D)	The men's names are Jones, Smith, Brown, and Robinson.
Four men are sitting in their club lounge. In the room, there is a sofa and two armchairs. Suddenly, one of the men, Jones, drops dead. His whisky has been poisoned!	Robinson is sitting next to the general on the sofa.
The school-teacher is sitting next to Smith on his left.	There are four people in the room.
Smith is sitting in one of the armchairs.	Smith is the admiral's brother-in-law.
Their jobs are general, school-teacher, admiral, and doctor.	No-one has left his chair.
Jones was drinking a whisky.	Brown is drinking a beer.
The school-teacher doesn't drink.	Neither Smith nor Brown has any sisters.

Unit 10

Song One of these things first

1 Read the regrets about the past below. Write two or three regrets about your own life, then tell the class.

I could have worked harder at school.
I should have been kinder to my parents.
I could have been an artist.

2 Listen to the song. What do you think the singer regrets?

3 Complete the gaps in the song. The missing word rhymes with the word at the end of the previous line. Listen again and check your answers.

4 What is the message of the song? Which of the opinions below do you agree with? Do you have your own theory?

> I think he's saying that he hasn't done much with his life – he wishes he had got a good job or done something interesting or useful.

> I reckon he's expressing regret about past relationships. He wasn't reliable or supportive so he has ended up single and alone.

> I think the song is a sort of apology to his wife or girlfriend. He's saying that he regrets that he wasn't loving and supportive in the past, but now he wants to be. He's saying, give me another chance.

5 The singer uses lots of metaphors. Choose five from the list below, and tell a partner why they might describe a good lover.

> a sailor   a cook   a signpost   a clock
> a kettle   a rock   a pillar   a door   a statue
> a whistle   a flute   a boot

I could have been *a book: It's interesting, relaxing, comforting. It's always there when you need it. You can take it to bed with you …*

ONE OF THESE
things first

I could have been a sailor, could have been a cook
A real live lover, could have been a _____ .
I could have been a signpost, could have been a clock
As simple as a kettle, steady as a _____.

I could be here and now
I would be, I should be, but _____ ?
I could have been
One of these things first
I could have been
One of these things first.

I could have been your pillar, could have been your door
I could have stayed beside you, could have stayed for _____ .
Could have been your statue, could have been your friend,
A whole long lifetime could have been the _____ .
I could be yours so true
I would be, I should be through and _____
I could have been
One of these things first
I could have been
One of these things first.

I could have been a whistle, could have been a flute
A real live giver, could have been a _____ .
I could have been a signpost, could have been a clock
As simple as a kettle, steady as a _____ .

I could be even here
I would be, I should be so _____
I could have been
One of these things first
I could have been
One of these things first.

Unit 11

Vocabulary and pronunciation (SB p97)

Pelmanism cards

ifs	sick	wait	touch
peace	safe	tired	quiet
sound	surely	buts	go
give	cons	by	see
odds	pros	downs	ends
take	slowly	large	ups

Stop and check 1

General revision

Complete the dialogue between two people who have just met with the correct form of the verb in brackets.

Sam So where (1) _____ (you come from), Chris? London itself?

Chris No, actually I (2) _____ (grow up) in Oxford, though I (3) _____ (be) here for ages now. Since I (4) _____ (leave) school, in fact. How about you?

Sam Well, as you probably (5) _____ (notice) from my accent, I'm Australian. From Rockhampton on the Queensland Coast. I (6) _____ (look for) work in the UK for quite some time, so when I (7) _____ (offer) a job in London a short while back, I (8) _____ (fly in) straightaway. And ever since then I (9) _____ (try) to find somewhere to live!

Chris Where (10) _____ (you stay) at the moment?

Sam With friends near Earl's Court. They're good people but it's a small place, and to make matters worse the flat (11) _____ (re-decorate) right now. We (12) _____ (just tell) today that the painters (13) _____ (finish) by the weekend, but that still (14) _____ (mean) several more days of utter chaos. The six of us (15) _____ (live) in one room since New Year!

Chris Six! I'm not surprised you (16) _____ (try) to find a place of your own these last few weeks. (17) _____ (you check out) the local small ads on the Internet yet?

Sam That's an idea. If there's anything new, it (18) _____ (list) there first, for sure.

Chris As it happens, the other day somebody (19) _____ (say) they (20) _____ (see) a small inexpensive flat to let quite near here. It (21) _____ (advertise) last week, I think, but it's possible they (22) _____ (still try) to rent it out.

Sam Do you know how much a month it is?

Chris Can't remember, I'm afraid. To be honest I (23) _____ (think about) something else when I (24) _____ (hear) it mentioned. I (25) _____ (find out) though, and give you a call if you like.

Sam Great. This is my mobile number.

Chris Here's mine.

Sam Thanks. I (26) _____ (call) you around 6 if that's all right.

Chris Ah – I (27) _____ (still work) then. Usually I (28) _____ (leave) the office at 5.30 but this evening I (29) _____ (not be able to) get away until quite a bit later.

Sam Does that mean you get extra money?

Chris Yes, we (30) _____ (always pay) at least double for overtime.

Sam So how (31) _____ (the job go)? Are you enjoying it?

Chris It's not bad. There's a lot to learn but right from the first day everyone in the office (32) _____ (be) very helpful. And I (33) _____ (take out) for dinner every evening this month!

33

Present Perfect: simple and continuous

Tick the correct sentence.

1 a ☐ My daughter's eyes are red because she's cried.
  b ☐ My daughter's eyes are red because she's been crying.

2 a ☐ The athletes have now run twenty kilometres.
  b ☐ The athletes have now been running twenty kilometres.

3 a ☐ My toe hurts so much I think I've broken it.
  b ☐ My toe hurts so much I think I've been breaking it.

4 a ☐ Have you waited here a long time?
  b ☐ Have you been waiting here a long time?

5 a ☐ I haven't understood a word he's said.
  b ☐ I haven't been understanding a word he's said.

6 a ☐ I've learned how to play the violin but I'm still not very good.
  b ☐ I've been learning how to play the violin but I'm still not very good.

6

Narrative tenses

Complete the sentences with the correct form of the verbs in brackets.

1 We _____ (sit) on the beach when it _____ (start) to rain.

2 Simon _____ (return) the money he _____ (borrow) a week earlier.

3 While I _____ (shop), my purse _____ (steal).

4 My letter _____ (not arrive) because I _____ (forgot) to put a stamp on it.

5 While he _____ (travel) in central Africa, Michael _____ (caught) malaria.

6 When I _____ (wake up), a man _____ (stand) next to me, asking me my name.

7 When Paula _____ (read) the book, she _____ (lend) it to me.

8 Sonia _____ (hit) by a car when she _____ (cycle) to school.

9 We _____ (carry on) driving when we _____ (fill up) with petrol.

10 I _____ (stand) there for hours when at last it _____ (be) my turn to speak to the official.

11 Frank _____ (know) he _____ (make) a terrible mistake as soon as he _____ (see) the message 'file deleted'.

12 When I _____ (open) the curtains this morning, I _____ (realise) it _____ (snow) all night.

	26

Vocabulary

1 Match a phrasal verb in **A** with a meaning in **B**.

A	B
1 do without sth	a would really like to have sth
2 make up for sth	b invent sth
3 could do with sth	c compensate for sth
4 make of sb	d manage without sth
5 do away with sth	e steal sth and take it away
6 do sth up	f end the existence of sth
7 make off with sth	g have an opinion of sb
8 make sth up	h decorate and repair sth

	8

2 Write *do* or *make* for each group of words.

1 _____ a profit
a start
an effort

2 _____ business
your best
overtime

3 _____ arrangements
connections
suggestions

4 _____ yourself understood
something clear
way for something

5 _____ a degree
some damage
somebody a favour

6 _____ a good impression
the big time
my day

	6

3 Form compound words by using each of these words once only.

| alarm | air | bag | escape | food | line |
| mail | office | pill | shelf | software | way |

1 Bring a sleeping _____ because we only have two beds.

2 I work in Singapore but the company's head _____ is in Shanghai.

3 We get more junk _____ through our letter box than letters.

4 Designing popular computer _____ can make you rich.

5 We heard the fire _____ and everyone ran out of the building.

6 You'll need a strong book _____ for all those dictionaries.

7 It's an open-_____ concert in England, so I hope it doesn't rain.

8 Progress was slow at first, but now we're making real head _____ .

9 There was no fire _____ , so we had to jump from a window.

10 I took a sleeping _____ , but still stayed awake all night.

11 A well-known air _____ charges only 1 euro to fly to Moscow.

12 Many people say that eating only junk _____ makes you fat.

| | 12 |

Spoken English

Cross out the words that people would often miss out in conversation.

1 ~~Have you~~ read any good books lately?
2 I'll see you tonight.
3 Do you want a chocolate? Take one!
4 I'm back. Have you been missing me?
5 Are you going to the match tonight?
6 'United might lose.' 'I hope so.'
7 Have you seen the new Harry Potter film yet?
8 Are you late again? Nine o'clock in future, please.
9 Nice material. I don't like the colour, though.
10 I'm sorry I upset you. Next time I'll be more careful.

| | 9 |

TOTAL | 100

Stop and check 2

General revision

Emily is staying in Singapore. Read the letter to her friend Olivia and choose the correct answers.

Dear Olivia,

Jenny and I finally got here yesterday, after a flight that took (1) *ages / our time*! Neither of us got (2) *much / many* sleep, but we quickly forgot about that when we landed at Changi. Even after such a long (3) *travel / journey*, we just had to spend (4) *a bit of / a couple of* time looking around the airport here. It's a fantastic place, with (5) *loads / a huge amount* of shops. We've decided that when we fly home, we (6) *'re getting / 're going to get* there really early so we have (7) *plenty of / several* time for shopping. Our flight (8) *will leave / leaves* at midnight on Monday, so we (9) *check in / 'll check in* much earlier than we need to.

Anyway, back to our arrival. To get into town we took the bus, which only cost (10) *a couple of / very little* Singapore dollars, and then walked to our hotel. It wasn't (11) *many / much* more than a kilometre, but even at night it was still hot and sticky, with (12) *no / none* cooling breeze from the sea. When we got to our room, we turned the air conditioning full on, then slept all night and (13) *almost all / the majority* of the morning too!

So here we are now, sitting in a lovely little bar, just (14) *putting / taking* it easy and planning what we (15) *'re doing / 're going to do* later. We're drinking Singapore Slings, of course, which cost much (16) *less / fewer* here than in the famous Raffles Hotel opposite, which seems to be (17) *full of / plenty of* big tourist groups all the time.

Later, Jenny (18) *goes / 's going* shopping in Orchard Road, where (19) *much of / most of* the smartest malls are, but with the Chinese New Year coming soon I think they (20) *are / 'll be* far too crowded this afternoon. Instead, I've put my name down for a tour of the Little India district, so I (21) *'m meeting / 'll meet* the guide at 3.30. After that, Jenny and I (22) *think to go / are thinking of going* on a river cruise. I'm not sure about that (last year's rough ferry crossing put me (23) *away / off* boats a bit), though the weather forecast says it (24) *isn't / won't be* windy tomorrow, so I should be OK. We (25) *'ll / are going to* see!

By the time the cruise (26) *is / is going to be* over, I imagine we (27) *'ll have / 'll have had* enough of sightseeing for one day, so perhaps we (28) *'re going to / 'll* go back to the hotel for a rest before we (29) *sample / are sampling* the nightlife. Anyway, I've just noticed it's after 3 o'clock, so I (30) *close / 'll close* now.

I hope all's well at home,

Love, Emily

| | 30 |

Question forms

Make questions.

1 with / out / she / who / now / going / is?

_____

2 want / you / about / talk / to / what / do?

_____

3 parents / think / how / do / visits / he / his / you / often ?

_____

4 to / any / you / come / never / work / how / seem / do?

_____

5 kind / what / that / you / flower / of / know / is / do?

_____

6 it / to / long / him / fix / how / it / take / will ?

_____

| | 6 |

Short questions

Match a statement in **A** with a short question in **B**.

A		B	
1	I played tennis yesterday.	a	Who by?
2	A plane has just landed.	b	What about?
3	I was told off for being late.	c	Where from?
4	I had a horrible dream.	d	What for?
5	I sold some of my CDs.	e	Who from?
6	We all plan to go abroad.	f	Who with?
7	I need some cash from you.	g	Who to?
8	I received a Valentine card.	h	Where to?

| | 8 |

Future forms

Write the correct future form of the verb, expressing the idea in *italics*.

1 They _____ (build) a new hospital there. (*intention*)

2 Brazil _____ (win) the next World Cup. (*prediction*)

3 Your flight _____ (leave) at 08.40. (*future fact based on timetable*)

4 I _____ (meet) her in the bar later. (*arrangement between people*)

5 I _____ (take) him to hospital right now. (*spontaneous decision*)

6 _____ (we go) for a drink somewhere? (*suggestion*)

| | 6 |

Expressions of quantity

Put the expressions in the correct columns.

a little   most   less   several   a great deal of   almost all no   hardly any   a few   a huge amount of   not one the majority of   fewer   not much   enough   a lot of a bit of   far too much   plenty of   not a single   loads of only a couple of

Used with count nouns, e.g. *book / books*	Used with uncount nouns, e.g. *music*	Used with count or uncount nouns

| | 22 |

Vocabulary

1 Match the opposite adjectives.

1 ☐ failure	a innocent
2 ☐ generous	b easy
3 ☐ guilty	c thick
4 ☐ dark (hair)	d wealth
5 ☐ safe	e mean
6 ☐ hard (= difficult)	f praise
7 ☐ boring	g love
8 ☐ genuine	h admit
9 ☐ poverty	i tiny
10 ☐ criticize	j success
11 ☐ deny	k live (adj.)
12 ☐ get worse	l fair
13 ☐ loathe	m fake
14 ☐ huge	n dangerous
15 ☐ recorded	o exciting
16 ☐ bright (= clever)	p improve

| | 16 |

2 Add a prefix from the box to form antonyms. There is one prefix you don't need to use.

ir-   dis-   in-   mis-   il-   im-   un-

1 _____kind   4 _____responsible

2 _____sincere   5 _____mature

3 _____honest   6 _____legal

| | 6 |

3 Use the words in the box with either *put* or *take* to form phrasal verbs which match definitions 1–6.

away   back   in   off   on   out

1 suddenly become successful   **take off**

2 admit you said something wrong   …… it ……

3 stop you wanting something   …… you ……

4 play something (a CD, cassette etc) …… it ……

5 understand what you hear   …… it ……

6 employ people   …… them ……

7 make something stop burning   …… it ……

| | 6 |

TOTAL | 100 |

Stop and check 3

General revision

Read the article about sharing a flat with other people and choose the correct answers.

Whether you're a student (1) *and / or / whether* you've just moved to the big city, the chances are you (2) *can / may / need* be thinking of sharing a flat with other young people. If so, there are some questions you (3) *are supposed to / should / are able to* ask yourself about anyone (4) *who / which / what* wants to be your flatmate. Particularly if you aren't used (5) *living / to live / to living* away from the family home.

Firstly, if you're already (6) *absolutely / very / highly* good friends there's a risk you (7) *might / are likely to / are bound to* spoil that friendship if you discover you don't get (8) *on / in / off* so well after several months under the same roof. Think about any time (9) *when / what / that* you've spent with them, on holiday for instance. Did they have any habits that got on your (10) *irritations / feelings / nerves*?

Obviously, many friends (11) *which / that / what* move in together find everything works out (12) *extremely / exactly / fully* well, and real problems are much more (13) *likely / probably / bound* to arise with complete strangers. In this case you need to know what each person is (14) *as / like / about*, so why (15) *you won't / don't / not* arrange a meeting to find out?

Begin by asking about basic things like (16) *which / that / what* they do, how much they (17) *'re able to / manage to / 'd better* pay in rent and how long they want to share with you. Also try to find out whether they're the kind of person (18) *whose / which / who* will do their fair share of the housework, or whether they'll (19) *reject / refuse / require* to wash the dishes or put the rubbish out. Will they (20) *be leaving always / always be leaving / leave always* dirty mugs and plates around the place? Are they the type of person who (21) *isn't / hasn't / won't* keep the bathroom clean?

Of course, it (22) *can / may / must* be that you're not all that clean and tidy yourself. In that case perhaps you (23) *'d better not / 're not supposed to / aren't able to* choose someone (24) *who's / whose / what's* too obsessed with cleanliness and tidiness!

Ask if they smoke, drink a lot or have any (other) habits (25) *what / who / which* you either don't share or don't approve of. Do they spend hours (26) *listen / to listen / listening* to loud music? Is it the kind of music (27) *that / what / whose* you like?

If, finally, you're (28) *exactly / quite / precisely* sure you could live with them, agree on some basic ground rules. These could cover, for example, paying for things (29) *when / where / which* are shared, like cleaning materials, or how long guests are (30) *allowed / required / bound* to stay without having to pay rent. It's essential that you (31) *mustn't / don't have to / shouldn't* decide things like these after weeks of sharing – (32) *what / that / when* it may be too late.

[32]

Modals and related verbs

Match the groups of modals and verbs with their meanings.

| ability   advice   obligation   no obligation |
| permission   probability   prohibition |
| request   willingness   unwillingness |

1 _____	can allowed to may
2 _____	won't refuse to
3 _____	can you could you would you
4 _____	don't have to needn't don't need to
5 _____	mustn't not allowed to can't
6 _____	be likely to will be bound to
7 _____	I'll I promise to
8 _____	should had better why don't you
9 _____	can able to manage to
10 _____	supposed to have got to required to

[10]

Expressing habit

Complete the sentences. Use each expression once only.

| get used to is used to use to used to usually would |

1 At this school we _____ play hockey in winter.
2 There _____ be a cinema where that supermarket is now.
3 By now, Sonia _____ travelling on her own.
4 Whenever I went by train, she _____ meet me at the station.
5 Did you really _____ dance like that, Dad?
6 It takes time to _____ living in a new town.

[ ] 6

Relative clauses

Combine the sentences using a relative pronoun. Add punctuation where necessary.

1 Those are the people. They shouted at us.
   Those _____
   _____ us.
2 Sandra loved the roses. Her favourite colour is red.
   Sandra _____
   _____ the roses.
3 Our flat has 3 bedrooms. It's in the town centre.
   Our flat _____
   _____ has 3 bedrooms.
4 That's the shop. I saw the suit there.
   That's the shop _____
   _____ the suit.
5 His elder sister is having a party. She's 17 today.
   His elder sister _____
   _____ a party.
6 In summer we go to the mountains. It's hot then.
   In summer _____
   _____ the mountains.
7 That's the dog. It bit the postman.
   That's the dog _____
   _____ the postman.
8 In the desert there's little vegetation. It seldom rains there.
   In the desert _____
   _____ little vegetation.

9 That's the man. His car is badly parked.
   That's the man _____
   _____ parked.
10 January's the month. We go skiing then.
   January's the month _____
   _____ skiing.

[ ] 10

-ed or -ing?

Write -ed or -ing.

1 Megan fell off her bike, hurt_____ her leg.
2 Embarrass_____ by his mistake, Neil said nothing.
3 The athlete was exhaust_____ after the race.
4 We spent the weekend relax_____ at home.
5 The comedian told an amus_____ story.
6 It was a depress_____ day: cold and grey.
7 It says 'Print_____ in Portugal' inside the book.
8 She was disappoint_____ to lose the game.
9 Jan looks relax_____ after her holidays.
10 The course was challeng_____ academically.
11 The gallery has a picture paint_____ by Goya.
12 You should get a job look_____ after children.
13 Many people are bor_____ by politics.
14 My aunt's depress_____ after her illness.
15 It's exhaust_____ to climb at high altitude.
16 One day, Harry made a shock_____ discovery.

[ ] 16

Vocabulary

1 Replace the verbs in *italics* with a form of *get* and a particle from the box.

> at   out   over   round   through   up

1 He hasn't *recovered from* the shock of losing the game yet.

_____

2 I always *spend* too much money when I go to a fairground.

_____

3 Sheila's boss never stops *criticizing* her.

_____

4 I'll have to *be out of bed* by 6.30 tomorrow morning.

_____

5 Once the truth *became known*, the Minister's reputation was ruined.

_____

6 Andy *passed* the Proficiency exam with a 'C' grade.

_____

7 What I'm *suggesting* is that the money may have been stolen.

_____

8 We can *successfully avoid* this problem by trying another approach.

_____

9 I've been trying to *talk on the phone* to someone in authority.

_____

10 My sister *avoided the job* of tidying up by saying she was ill.

_____

☐ 10

2 Complete the sentences with *very* or *absolutely* and a word from the box.

> interesting   hilarious   surprised
> awful   priceless   clever

1 Even a small diamond is valuable, but one that size is _____ .

2 It is not enough to be _____ to work here; you have to be absolutely brilliant.

3 Most episodes of *The Simpsons* are funny, but the best ones are _____ .

4 A single dinosaur bone is _____ , but the complete skeleton is absolutely fascinating.

5 Jack was _____ by his exam results and his parents were absolutely amazed.

6 His early CDs were bad but his latest one is even worse. It's _____ .

☐ 6

3 Correct the wrong word in these sentences. The answers are homophones.

    plane
1 The ~~plain~~ from Madrid to Buenos Aires takes 12 hours.

2 There's a big whole in your sock.

3 The burglar was court by the police.

4 Bart was so board he fell asleep.

5 Every day I rowed my bike to school.

6 The soldiers war their old uniforms.

7 Talking during the exam isn't aloud.

8 I'm not shore what time the tide comes in.

9 Slimming pills are a waist of money.

10 All we are saying is give piece a chance.

11 The Daily Sun says there are too many students in hire education.

☐ 10

TOTAL ☐ **100**

Stop and check 4

General revision

Read the newspaper article. Choose the correct answers or, if there is a gap, write one suitable word: an article, a preposition, an adverb, etc.

TWO MISSING IN SNOWDONIA

Two walkers are reported to (1) *being / have / been* gone missing close to the summit of Snowdon, (2) _____ highest mountain in Wales. Bryan McCall, aged 21, and Karen Wilson, 19, failed to return by nightfall, leading to fears that they (3) *may / may be / may have been* forced to spend last night on the mountain.

(4) _____ conditions when the pair set off yesterday morning were fairly good, by afternoon (5) _____ weather had got much worse. Thick cloud quickly covered the whole (6) _____ the area and there was such (7) _____ sharp drop in temperature (8) _____ the surface of local lakes began to freeze within (9) _____ few hours. Blizzards began in the evening, with a great deal (10) _____ snow falling above 500 metres.

Friends of (11) _____ two walkers, surprised (12) _____ to have heard from either (13) _____ them, think their mobile phones (14) *might / can / have* to have become unusable for (15) _____ reason. Karen's friend Janet Richards believes Karen (16) *called / would call / would have called* her to say they were alright if her phone (17) *is / has been / had been* working properly. Joe Hills, a friend of Bryan's, admits he is worried they (18) *could have / could have had / were able to have* had an accident last night, but insists they are experienced hill walkers who (19) *would have found / would be finding / would be found* shelter if they (20) *had forced / had been forced / forced* to stay on the mountain (21) _____ last night.

Mountain Rescue teams, who began looking for them early (22) _____ morning, say that one or both (23) _____ the walkers (24) *may / must / will* have slipped and fallen in the treacherous conditions, especially as (25) _____ of them (26) *used to / is used to / gets used to* walking in mountains in winter.

The hope is, though, that they will be found safe and (27) _____ before long, especially as the weather is forecast to clear up within (28) _____ next few hours.

| | 28 |

Modals in the past

Rewrite the sentences in the past.

1 She may forget.

_____

2 You shouldn't look.

_____

3 It must be him.

_____

4 Could they know?

_____

5 He might be lying.

_____

6 She can't tell him.

_____

7 You needn't wait.

_____

8 I don't need to stay.

_____

9 Won't he go?

_____

10 They'll be arrested.

_____

| | 10 |

wish and *if only*

Complete the second sentence so that it means the same as the first.

1 It's a pity you can't come with us.
  I wish you _____
  _____.

2 It's a shame there are some rocks on the beach.
  I wish there _____
  _____.

3 Sadly, they didn't see the warning sign.
  If only they _____
  _____.

4 Those people won't stop shouting.
  I wish those people _____
  _____.

5 I'm sorry I went to bed so late last night.
  I wish I _____
  _____.

6 It's annoying having to tidy up every day.
  I wish I _____
  _____.

7 My parents are always arguing.
  I wish _____
  _____.

8 I regret not wearing my seat belt at the time of the accident.
  If only _____
  _____.

9 Aren't you sorry you didn't stay longer?
  Don't you wish _____
  _____.

10 Unfortunately we weren't given all the information.
  If only _____
  _____.

☐ 10

Conditional sentences

Make past conditional sentences.

1 I _would've bought_ (buy) those shoes if I _I'd had_ (have) the money.

2 If the lifeboat _____ (not rescue) the sailors, they _____ (drown).

3 We _____ (set out) earlier if we _____ (know) how far it was.

4 If you _____ (ask) me to keep it secret, I _____ (not say) a word.

5 He _____ (not fail) his driving test if he _____ (not crash) the car.

6 We _____ (might win) the match if the referee _____ (allow) that goal.

7 If you _____ (not spot) the danger there _____ (can be) a disaster.

8 What _____ (you do) if you _____ (be attacked) by a crocodile?

9 If you _____ (not sleep) at the time, you _____ (hear) the phone ring.

☐ 8

Articles and determiners

Tick the correct sentences. Correct the wrong sentences by adding *a*, *an*, *the*, *one*, or *of* where necessary.

1 We live next to health centre on Victoria Street.
2 Some patients have to stay in hospital for months.
3 Neither of her brothers is very tall.
4 I want to work as chemical engineer.
5 It's starting to rain. Let's go on bus.
6 There's plenty food for everyone.
7 I usually have cereal with milk for breakfast.
8 Fortunately, there are few attractive places in this town.
9 We've checked every one of the cables.
10 Laura is very intelligent girl.
11 It was such lovely day we went to the seaside.
12 Every child loves chocolate and sweets.
13 They're divorced so they never speak to another.
14 When I was eating nuts, I broke tooth.
15 Hurry up. There's no time to lose.
16 Free elections are important feature of democracy.

☐ 16

Vocabulary

1 The idioms in these sentences use the wrong parts of the body. Write the correct part.

1 Our washing machine makes a terrible noise. It's on its last feet.

on its last _____

2 Suddenly becoming famous went to his leg and he started behaving badly.

went to his _____

3 I'm afraid you have to head the fact that you failed.

_____ the fact

4 He's a generous man and people say he has a head of gold.

a _____ of gold

5 She's still finding her legs in her new job.

finding her _____

6 To manage a multinational you need an excellent hand for business.

an excellent _____ for business

7 Are you really a member of the Royal Family or are you pulling my hand?

pulling my _____

8 There's lots of shopping in the car. Can you give me a face?

give me a _____

9 After his girlfriend left him, Tom put on a brave heart, but he was very upset.

put on a brave _____

10 In some countries, people shake face every time they meet.

shake _____

| | 10 |

2 Make word pairs from the words in the box to produce the meanings in brackets.

| ins   sooner   now   nothing   give   downs   surely   less then   odds   take   weird   all   outs   tired   by   ends more   sick   slowly   large   later   ups   wonderful |

1 _____ and _____ (generally)
2 _____ and _____ (details)
3 _____ and _____ (small items)
4 _____ and _____ (exchange of ideas, compromise)
5 _____ and _____ (fed up)
6 _____ and _____ (occasionally)
7 _____ and _____ (good and bad times)
8 _____ and _____ (exotic)
9 _____ but _____ (gradually)
10 _____ or _____ (eventually)
11 _____ or _____ (completely or not at all)
12 _____ or _____ (approximately)

| | 12 |

3 Match the synonyms in the box with the underlined words. There is one synonym that you don't need.

| beginning   guess   help   appalling   fat   describe   tasty |

1 Esther eats enormous meals but she isn't <u>overweight</u>. _____

2 It was such a <u>delicious</u> meal that I could eat it all again! _____

3 Customer Care will <u>assist</u> you if you have any problems. _____

4 After weeks lost in space, the astronauts began to <u>relate</u> their experiences. _____

5 The work will be done during the week <u>commencing</u> June 7. _____

6 Following the war, many people are living in <u>dreadful</u> conditions. _____

| | 6 |

TOTAL | 100 |

Progress test 1

Tenses

Put the verb in brackets in the correct tense. Sometimes more than one tense is correct.

A lift into trouble

It was the middle of the night and Paul (1) _____ (get) worried. The two unsmiling police officers obviously (2) _____ (not believe) his story and one of them (3) _____ (talk) quietly but urgently on the phone. From the look on their faces they _____ (4) (suspect) him of something, but Paul still had no idea what.

All he knew was that at 3.30 in the morning he (5) _____ (walk) home when a police car (6) _____ (come) to a sudden stop right next to him. The two officers jumped out and demanded to know who he (7) _____ (be) and where he (8) _____ (be).

'Paul Hughes,' he replied, 'and I (9) _____ (be) at the 2020 Club downtown. Now I (10) _____ (go) home.'

It (11) _____ (rain), Paul was tired and he wanted to get home quickly, but the police (12) _____ (be) suspicious.

'Where's home?', asked the younger policeman.

'The Stonechurch estate,' answered Paul, aware of the reputation for crime it (13) _____ (acquire) in recent years.

'So what (14) _____ (you do) round here?' said the older one, 'This isn't the way from the city centre.'

'I know,' said Paul, feeling a bit irritated, 'but I (15) _____ (give) a lift by a guy at the 2020. He (16) _____ (drop) me off at Bank St Station about 15 minutes ago. Since then I (17) _____ (walk).'

'What was his name?'

'No idea.'

'What (18) _____ (he look like)?'

'Tall, heavily-built, skinhead. Kind of tough-looking. He (19) _____ (wear) a blue denim jacket.'

'And the car?'

'A convertible BMW; a 5-Series. Green, I think.'

The policemen (20) _____ (look at) each other for second.

'That car (21) _____ (find) a few minutes ago. It (22) _____ (leave) behind the station.

'So what's that got to do with me?, said Paul, starting to feel uneasy.

'Quite a lot,' replied the older policeman. A report (23) _____ (receive) just after 3 a.m. that a green BMW (24) _____ (steal). From outside the 2020. Then, a few minutes later a young man (25) _____ (observe) walking away from the vehicle near Bank St Station. That person (26) _____ (describe) as average height, dark-haired and slim. Very much like you, in fact. And since then nobody else (27) _____ (see) anywhere near the car. You're in trouble, Paul, and we (28) _____ (take) you to the police station for further questioning. When we (29) _____ (get) there we (30) _____ (tell) you what we've found in that car.

| 30 |

Future forms

Choose the correct answer: a, b, or c.

1 This time tomorrow, we _____ in the Pacific.
   a swim   b 'll swim
   c 'll be swimming

2 The shop _____ you your money back if you explain.
   a are giving   b will give
   c will have given

3 What _____ for dinner tonight, Mum?
   a 're we having
   b do we have
   c 'll we have had

4 They _____ married by the end of the year.
   a 're getting   b 'll have got
   c 'll be getting

5 He'll still _____ in bed at two this afternoon.
   a be lying   b lie
   c have lain

6 I _____ you with the dishes if you like.
   a 'm helping
   b 'm going to help
   c 'll help

7 Here's your ticket. The train _____ platform 9 at 8.42.
   a leaving   b leaves
   c will have left

8 I finish work this week because _____ a baby in June.
   a have   b 'll have
   c 'm going to have

| 8 |

Negatives

Tick the right sentences and correct the wrong ones.

1 My aunt asked us to not make a noise.
2 He didn't speak to anybody all evening.
3 In the exam, you don't have to copy from other students.
4 I haven't already tidied my room.
5 I don't think what he did was very clever.
6 **A** Aren't they staying here?
   B I don't hope so.
7 We don't like Monday mornings, either.
8 I am not agree with what that man says.

[8]

Question forms

Complete the questions for the answers.

1 **A** What was the neighbour talking to you
         _____ ?
   B Oh, just the weather and things like that.
2 **A** How _____ have English lessons?
   B Three times a week.
3 **A** Could you tell me what date _____ today?
   B It's February 29th!
4 **A** What _____ you like?
   B Anything that's easy to read, like novels.
5 **A** How _____ you to have breakfast?
   B Only a minute. I just have tea and biscuits.
6 **A** What does your new coat _____ ?
   B Well, it's blue, quite long, with big pockets.

[6]

Countable or uncountable?

For each count noun, write an uncount noun related in meaning.

1 job   ___work___
2 table   _____
3 bus   _____
4 suitcase   _____
5 murder   _____
6 euro   _____
7 banana   _____

[6]

Numbers

Write the numbers as you would say them.

1 365   three hundred and sixty-five
2 4,941,208   _____
3 1990s   _____
4 14 Oct   _____
5 ³/₄   _____
6 72%   _____
7 34.57   _____
8 1789 (year) _____
9 730 4465 (phone number) _____

[8]

put and *take*

These sentences have the wrong expressions with *put* or *take*. Exchange the words in *italics* to correct them.

1 The whole village took *place* in the celebrations.

2 Sometimes you have to take *a stop* if you want to succeed.

3 You're old enough to take *offence* for your own actions.

4 Put yourself in my *responsibility*. How would you feel?

5 James took *part* when I asked if his Rolex watch was genuine.

6 The physics exam will take *notice* at 9 am on Monday.

7 You'll be in trouble if you don't take any *word* of what the boss says.

8 He'll waste all that money he won. Take my *risk* for it.

9 We must put a *foot* to violence by football fans.

10 Sarah put her *shoes* in it by asking about the wedding. It's been called off.

[10]

Expressing quantity

Put the expressions in order, from the most to the fewest.

| several people   most of the people   hardly anybody |
| nearly everybody   more than half the people   a few people |

Everybody (20 people)

1 _____ (18 or 19 people)

2 _____ (about 15 people)

3 _____ (over 10 people)

4 _____ (4 or 5 people)

5 _____ (about 3 people)

6 _____ (1 or 2 people)

Nobody (0 people)

[6]

Compound words and affixes

Complete each gap with the correct form of the word in capitals on the right.

When I arrived here in England I felt a bit

(1) _____ at first, and even, at times,   SICK

a little (2) _____ , but that soon   HAPPY

passed as I got used to the different

(3) _____ , and the meals. I know   LIFE

some people really (4) _____ English   LIKE

food, but it's not that bad and the criticism

seems (5) _____ to me. The family   FAIR

I'm staying with are nice, too. Nobody's

ever (6) _____ to me and they help   KIND

me with my English, even my

(7) _____ ! My teacher reckons   WORK

there's been a big (8) _____ in my   IMPROVE

speaking, and says I should be

(9) _____ in the end-of-course tests.   SUCCESS

Sometimes that kind of (10) _____   COURAGE

helps, doesn't it?

[10]

Everyday English

What would you say in these situations? Complete the sentences.

1 You phone a small company to speak to the manager and the secretary answers. What do you say?

Could _____ ?

2 Your friend Julia ends a phone conversation by saying 'Have a good evening!'. What do you reply?

Same _____ .

3 You're at a new school and you want to find the office. Ask another student where it is.

Do you happen _____ ?

4 At the railway station you see an old lady with a heavy suitcase. Politely offer to carry it for her.

Would _____ ?

5 You want to sell your old bicycle. Somebody offers you more money than you expected for it. Accept the offer enthusiastically!

Great! It's _____ !

6 You have phoned a shop for information about computers, but it's a bad line and you miss the last thing the assistant says. Apologise and ask her to repeat it.

Sorry, I didn't _____ .

7 A friend suggests spending a week in the casinos of Las Vegas, but neither of you have much money. What do you say?

We just _____ .

8 You go outside into the pouring rain and see a neighbour in the street. What exclamation would you use about the weather?

What _____ !

[8]

TOTAL [100]

Progress test 2

Grammar and vocabulary

Look at this formal letter from Patricia Ryan to a travel company. Write one word in each gap.

Dear Sir or Madam,

I am writing to complain about our recent Super City Break holiday, (1) _____ we booked through your company at (2) _____ beginning of February. My companion and I feel that (3) _____ advertising of this holiday was misleading, the organisation poor and the cost too high. If we (4) _____ known what it was really going to be like, we definitely (5) _____ not have chosen it.

Right from check-in at the airport, (6) _____ was supposed to be at 5.45 in the morning, things started to go wrong. Your staff there, (7) _____ appeared to be half asleep, said they had (8) _____ record at all of our booking and neither (9) _____ them seemed interested in finding out why. They said we must (10) _____ been given the wrong tickets and suggested we (11) _____ in touch with Head Office, (12) _____ of course was closed at that time of the morning. Our holiday (13) _____ have ended there and (14) _____ if the supervisor had (15) _____ appeared by chance and eventually sorted things out.

The flight itself, which (16) _____ have taken off at 7.45 but was delayed for almost the whole (17) _____ the morning, was uncomfortable and the food, (18) _____ at last it was served, was almost inedible. When we landed, we found the buses (19) _____ we had been promised had long since left. By the time we reached the hotel, we were already wishing we (20) _____ stayed at home, but even worse was to come.

The hotel, (21) _____ in the brochure as 'luxury accommodation', was appalling. The rooms were tiny and the food, (22) _____ my opinion, disgusting. I would (23) _____ have eaten fast food every day. There was, (24) _____ fact, so much wrong with the place that we collected evidence in the form of photos, (25) _____ I enclose.

Needless to say, the return flight was also late, (26) _____ off more than six hours behind schedule. I travel frequently, and am not used (27) _____ such poor service. My companion and I feel there (28) _____ be no excuse for this and we expect you to offer us a considerable (29) _____ of money in compensation. If this is not forthcoming, both (30) _____ us will take legal action to obtain it.

Yours faithfully,

Patricia Ryan

	30

Participles

Rewrite the sentences using present or past participles instead of relative clauses.

1 People who live near the airport are fed up with the noise.
   People living near the airport are fed up with the noise.

2 We were kept awake by a dog that barked all night.
   _____

3 The figures which were given by the government were wrong.
   _____

4 Cars that are parked on the pavement will be removed.
   _____

5 Employees who handle food have to wear gloves.
   _____

6 Products that are made in China now have a good reputation.
   _____

7 All the money that has been spent has been wasted.
   _____

8 Passengers who arrived late missed their flight.
   _____

	7

Unnecessary words

Some of the lines in this text are correct and some have a word which should not be there. Tick the correct lines and cross out the incorrect words.

SURVIVAL IN THE DESERT

0 The Atacama Desert is one of the most driest places on Earth.
00 Though flanked on one side by the Pacific Ocean and by the ✓
1 snow-capped Andes on the other, very little of water ever reaches
2 this parched area, which it extends for thousand of kilometres
3 through northern Chile and up into Peru. In some of places, there
4 must has been no rain for hundreds of years, certainly since the
5 Spanish conquest of the sixteenth century and possibly even longer.
6 Near the coast, however, some water does get to the few plants
7 that can survive there; but in the form of fog, not a rain. These
8 plants can have adapted to the conditions by taking moisture from
9 the air when the clouds roll in from the Pacific. Further of south,
10 in the slightly less arid region near Vallenar, the parched brown
11 earth now and also then undergoes a remarkable change when the
12 rains come and the phenomenon that known as the 'flowering
13 desert' occurs. Suddenly, purple, yellow and blue flowers spring
14 up from long-buried seeds, which forming a spectacular sight, but
15 one which occurs only once every of four years or so.

---

[15]

Linking

Choose the best answer: a, b, c or d.

1 I'm late for school. _____ , no-one will notice.
   a Hopefully   b Personally
   c Basically   d Generally speaking

2 I thought that was Sue over there. _____ , it's Ann.
   a After all   b Ideally
   c Certainly   d Actually

3 Vicki's not very popular. _____ , I quite like her.
   a Definitely   b Personally
   c Surely   d Apparently

4 Thomas lost his job. _____ , he'd been rude to the boss.
   a Still   b However
   c Apparently   d Absolutely

5 David and Anna went home separately. _____ , they've had a row.
   a Anyway   b All the same
   c Hopefully   d Presumably

6 I'm not surprised she's passed easily. _____ , she studied very hard.
   a In fact   b Hopefully
   c Still   d After all

7 Steve's 14 years old. _____ , he's too young to drive on the roads.
   a Obviously   b Honestly
   c Probably   d Presumably

8 I don't want to go into the water. _____ , I can't swim.
   a Definitely   b Personally
   c Presumably   d As a matter of fact

9 It's very late. _____ you're not going out now?
   a Surely   b Probably
   c Certainly   d In fact

10 That's a badly designed machine. _____ , it won't work.
    a Absolutely   b Still
    c All the same d Basically

11 He had said it was his last Championship. _____ , he's back again this year.
    a After all   b Hopefully
    c Certainly   d However

12 I didn't manage to persuade them. _____ , I'll keep trying.
    a Apparently   b Anyway
    c Presumably   d As a matter of fact

[12]

Hypothesizing

Complete the second sentence so that it has a similar meaning to the first, using the word in capitals. Don't change this word. Write between two and five words.

1 I think you should stay at home. RATHER
   I _____ at home.
2 You ought to give up smoking. TIME
   It _____ smoking.
3 It's tragic that Kim arrived too late. ONLY
   If _____ too late.
4 Unfortunately, he didn't pay attention. SHOULD
   He _____ attention.
5 I wasn't there, which I regret. WISH
   I _____ there.
6 Martin isn't pleased you told her. RATHER
   Martin would _____ told her.
7 They should do something about crime. TIME
   It _____ done about crime.
8 We could have lost. Imagine that. SUPPOSING
   We didn't lose, but _____ ?

| | 8 |

used to

Tick the correct sentence.

1 a ☐ Mark and Kate got married last year.
   b ☐ Mark and Kate used to get married last year.
2 a ☐ Sailors used to stormy weather.
   b ☐ Sailors are used to stormy weather.
3 a ☐ There used to be a railway in this valley.
   b ☐ There would be a railway in this valley.
4 a ☐ At last I get used to my new PC.
   b ☐ At last I'm getting used to my new PC.
5 a ☐ Nowadays people use to send emails.
   b ☐ Nowadays people usually send emails.
6 a ☐ I'm still used to working at night.
   b ☐ I'm still getting used to working at night.

| | 6 |

Homonyms

Write a word that has both meanings.

1 rather angry / go from one side of the road to the other
   _____

2 healthy / be the right size
   _____

3 not hot / trendy, fashionable
   _____

4 green area in a town / leave a car somewhere
   _____
5 large fierce animal / stand, tolerate
   _____
6 satisfactory / money you must pay
   _____
7 day of the month / appointment with a boy/girlfriend
   _____
8 place to keep money / side of a river
   _____

| | 8 |

Meanings of *get*

Rewrite the words in italics with a form of **get**. Add any other necessary words.

1 I *don't have* time to watch TV.
   _____
2 It's about time we *bought* a DVD recorder.
   _____
3 Chrissie is always *becoming* angry.
   _____
4 Please *contact* the office immediately.
   _____
5 It's clear to everyone else but he doesn't *understand*.
   _____
6 The kids are *growing* bigger all the time.
   _____
7 We don't *have a good relationship* these days.
   _____
8 The sound of car horns *irritates me*.
   _____

| | 8 |

Everyday English

Complete the exaggerated statements.

1 I can't _____ sight _____ !
2 He was totally _____ order!
3 They're obviously _____ love.
4 She's going to _____ roof!
5 I _____ you walk on.
6 I'm absolutely _____ drink!

| | 6 |

TOTAL | 100 |

Answer keys

Unit 1 Getting to know your Student's Book!

Before starting on the course, it is a good idea to familiarize your students with the layout and features of the book. Photocopy copies of the *Getting to know your Student's Book* worksheet on p141 of the Teacher's Book. Hand them out and ask students to work in pairs to complete the tasks. In the feedback, ask students what their 'first impressions' are.

Answers

1 Unit 1   *No place like home* = living and working away from home
   Unit 2   *Been there, done that* = travel
   Unit 3   *What a story!* = telling stories
   Unit 4   *Nothing but the truth* = telling lies
   Unit 5   *An eye to the future* = life in the future
   Unit 6   *Making it big* = success in business
   Unit 7   *Getting on together* = relationships with people
   Unit 8   *Going to extremes* = unusual experiences and places
   Unit 9   *Forever friends* = remembering people
   Unit 10 *Risking life and limb* = dangerous adventures
   Unit 11 *In your dreams* = interpreting dreams
   Unit 12 *It's never too late* = age

2 a = Unit 6; b = Unit 4; c = Unit 5; d = Unit 2; e = Unit 7; f = Unit 10; g = Unit 8; h = Unit 1; i = Unit 11

Note on the titles

Note that the titles are often abbreviations of proverbs or expressions. For example:
Be it ever so humble, there's no place like home. (from a song in a play by John Howard Payne, 1791–1852)
Been there, done that, (got the T-shirt!) is the cry of bored young people, and was used as an advert for Pepsi Cola, in which of course the only thing new and interesting was a can of Pepsi!
In a British court of law, witnesses swear, *I promise to tell the truth, the whole truth, and nothing but the truth.*
Risking life and limb is often used ironically, e.g. 'I risked life and limb to drive here in time to pick you up!'
In your dreams! is a jokey way to tell someone that they're being unrealistically optimistic and need to wake up to reality.

3 hypothesizing = Unit 11
   narrating = Unit 3
   using homonyms = Unit 9
   speculating = Unit 10
   exclaiming = Unit 2

4 Contents = page 2
   Grammar reference = page 140
   Tapescripts = page 124
   Writing = page 110

5 *Test your Grammar* = explains grammatical rules
   Language Focus = finds out how well you can use grammar at the start of the unit
   Everyday English = introduces spoken functional phrases
   Music of English = shows you intonation and stress patterns

Song Don't leave home

Notes

Dido (real name, Florian Cloud De Bounevialle Armstrong) was born in London on Christmas Day in 1971. She was a law student at Birkbeck University, and played in her brother's band Faithless, before recording her own solo albums *No angel* (1999) and *Life for rent* (2003), which featured *Don't leave home.*

Answers

1 *The singer has a child.* False
   The singer is in love. True
   The singer isn't serious about the relationship. False
   The singer is worried that her lover will leave home. True

2 See tapescript

3 Students' own ideas. However, one interpretation of the song is that she is loving (she clearly loves her partner), but she is very possessive, (she wants him to only love her, not see his friends, shut the door to the outside world). She is not easy-going. Arguably, she is selfish.

4 Students' own ideas.

Tapescript [CD1 Track 15]

Like a ghost, I don't need a key
Your best friend I've come to be
Please don't think of getting up for me
You don't even need to speak

When I've been here for just one day
You'll already miss me if I go away
So close the blinds and shut the door
You won't need other friends anymore

Oh don't leave home, oh don't leave home

Chorus

If you're cold, I'll keep you warm
If you're low, just hold on
'Cause I will be your safety
Oh don't leave home

And I arrived when you were weak
I'll make you weaker, like a child
Now all your love you give to me
When your heart is all I need

Oh don't leave home, oh don't leave home

Chorus

Oh how quiet, quiet the world can be
When it's just you and little me
Everything is clear and everything is new
So you won't be leaving will you

Oh don't leave home, oh don't leave home

Chorus

Unit 4

Song I never loved you anyway

I never loved you anyway was recorded by the Irish band, the Corrs, on their album *Talk on Corners*, in 1997. It was written by the Corrs and American singer-songwriter, Carole Bayer Sager.

Answers

1 angry/furious
   bitter/resentful
   upset/hurt

2 The woman who is singing the song probably feels all of the above, although she says that she feels happy, glad and delighted that he has left.

3 See tapescript

4 2 ✓
   3 ✗ She isn't sorry it's over.
   4 ✗ She didn't leave him.
   5 ✓
   6 ✗ She never loved him.
   7 ✗ He doesn't spend much money.

5 Ask students to discuss whether they think the singer is telling the truth in the song. If she really never loved him and is so happy it's over, why didn't she make the move before him? It is possible that things happened very differently, and that what she is saying in the song is an attempt at protective self-deception.

6 1 endured
   2 tender
   3 misled

7 1 Stressing *really* here stresses the fact that if she did love him, it wasn't a strong feeling.
      anyway = here, used to state that none of the arguments and details are important
   2 *bored/endured* = strong words suggesting he was a boring person.
   3 *Valentino, I don't think so* = Rudolf Valentino was a great screen lover in 1920s Hollywood movies – so, here, she is implying that he was not very romantic.*
   4 *...that girl* = she is referring to his new girlfriend – it is a quite rude, angry way of referring to someone.

*Explain the line, *You watching MTV while I lie dreaming in an MT bed*. She is saying that he is so unromantic that he prefers watching pop videos while she is in bed – *MT* is a word play on *empty*.

8 1 Why do people fall in love?
   2 Why do relationships end?
   3 What should you say when you end a relationship?
   4 When was the last time you felt angry with someone?

Tapescript [CD 1: Track 51]

You bored me with your stories
I can't believe that I endured you for as long as I did
I'm happy, it's over, I'm only sorry
That I didn't make the move before you

And when you go I will remember
To send a thankyou note to that girl
I see she's holding you so tender
Well I just wanna say...

I never really loved you anyway
No I didn't love you anyway
I never really loved you anyway
I'm so glad you're moving away

Valentino, I don't think so
You watching MTV while I lie dreaming in an MT bed
And come to think of it
I was misled
My flat, my food, my everything
And thoughts inside my head

Before you go I must remember
To have a quiet word with that girl
Does she know you're not a spender
Well I just have to say...

I never really loved you anyway
No I didn't love you anyway
I never really loved you anyway
I'm so happy you're moving away

And when you go I will remember
I must remember to say...

I never really loved you anyway
No I didn't love you anyway
I never really loved you anyway
I never really loved you anyway
Never really loved you anyway
No I didn't love you anyway
Never truly loved you anyway
I'm so happy you're moving away
Yeah I'm delighted you're moving away

Unit 7

Song Fast Car

Notes

Fast Car was written by American singer-songwriter Tracy Chapman in 1988.

Answers

1 and 2 Students' own ideas. She doesn't get what she wants from life.

3 See tapescript

4 1d, 2e, 3g, 4a, 5c, 6b, 7f

5 1 She left school to look after her alcoholic father who couldn't work. Her mother left to find a new life. She has no qualifications, and works in a convenience store.
   2 She gets jobs in convenience stores to try and save some money. She persuades her boyfriend/husband to move to the city.
   3 He is probably lazy – he never gets a job, and spends more time drinking with his friends than looking after his family.
   4 She wants him to drive away and leave. She says she's 'going nowhere', but she is still strong-minded, thinking she can do better without him if necessary.

Tapescript [CD 2: Track 37]

You've got a fast car
I want a ticket to anywhere
Maybe we (can) make a deal
Maybe together we can get somewhere
Any place is better
Starting from zero we've got nothing to lose
Maybe we'll make something
But me myself I've got nothing to prove.

You've got a fast car
And I've got a plan to get us out of here
I've been working at the convenience store
Managed to save just a little bit of money
We won't have to drive too far
Just cross the border and into the city
You and I can both get jobs
And finally see what it means to be living

You see my old man's got a problem
He lives with the bottle, that's the way it is
He says his body's too old for working
His body's too young to look like his
My mama went off and left him
She wanted more from life than he could give

I said somebody's got to take care of him
So I quit school and that's what I did

You've got a fast car
But is it fast enough so we can fly away?
We've got to make a decision
We leave tonight or live and die this way

I remember we were driving driving in
your car
The speed so fast I felt like I was drunk
City lights lay out before us
And your arm felt nice wrapped round my
shoulder
And I had a feeling that I belonged
And I had a feeling I could be someone, be
someone, be someone

You've got a fast car
And we go cruising to entertain ourselves
You still ain't got a job
And I work in a market as a checkout girl
I know things will get better
You'll find work and I'll get promoted
We'll move out of the shelter
Buy a bigger house and live in the
suburbs

I remember we were driving driving in
your car
The speed so fast I felt like I was drunk
City lights lay out before us
And your arm felt nice wrapped 'round my
shoulder
And I had a feeling that I belonged
And I had a feeling I could be someone, be
someone, be someone

You've got a fast car
And I've got a job that pays all our bills
You stay out drinking late at the bar
See more of your friends than you do of
your kids
I'd always hoped for better
Thought maybe together you and me
would find it
I've got no plans I ain't going nowhere
So take your fast car and keep on driving

So remember we were driving driving in
your car
The speed so fast I felt like I was drunk
City lights lay out before us
And your arm felt nice wrapped 'round my
shoulder
And I had a feeling that I belonged
And I had a feeling I could be someone, be
someone, be someone

You've got a fast car
But is it fast enough so you can fly away?
You've got to make a decision
You leave tonight or live and die this way

Unit 10

Song One of these things first

Notes
One of these things first was written by
British singer-songwriter Nick Drake. It is
on the album, Bryter Layter, released in
1970. Nick Drake was prominent on the
British folk-rock scene in the late sixties
and early seventies, but did not gain a lot
of recognition, partly because he rarely
performed live. He suffered from
depression, and died, in his mid-twenties,
in 1974, of an overdose of anti-depressant
medication. In recent years, there has
been a revival of interest in his music.

Answers
1 Students' own ideas.

2 Students' own ideas. The song is
probably regretting not being a more
reliable, supportive lover/partner in a
relationship.

3 See tapescript.

4 Students' own ideas. However, the
third opinion is probably most
accurate.

5 Suggested answers:
a sailor = knows how to navigate the
seas of life, always comes home/
interesting stories
a cook = provider of good
nourishment
a signpost = reassuringly points the
way
a clock = tells the time /reliable
a kettle = reliable/makes comforting
hot drinks
a rock = always there/strong/
unmoveable
a pillar = strong/holds things up/
supportive/can lean on it
a door = strong/opens things up for
you
a statue = strong/can lean on it/always
there
a whistle = useful when you're in
trouble
a flute = soothing and nice to listen to
a boot = strong/comfortable/protects
your feet from contact with the hard
world

Tapescript [CD 3: Track 25]
I could have been a sailor, could have
been a cook
A real live lover, could have been a book.
I could have been a signpost, could have
been a clock
As simple as a kettle, steady as a rock.

I could be
Here and now
I would be, I should be
But how?
I could have been
One of these things first
I could have been
One of these things first.

I could have been your pillar, could have
been your door
I could have stayed beside you, could
have stayed for more.
Could have been your statue, could have
been your friend,
A whole long lifetime could have been the
end.
I could be yours so true
I would be, I should be through and
through
I could have been
One of these things first
I could have been
One of these things first.

I could have been a whistle, could have
been a flute
A real live giver, could have been a boot.
I could have been a signpost, could have
been a clock
As simple as a kettle, steady as a rock.

I could be even here
I would be, I should be so near
I could have been
One of these things first
I could have been
One of these things first.

Stop and Check 1

General revision

1 do you come from
2 grew up
3 've been
4 left
5 noticed / have noticed
6 'd been looking for
7 was offered
8 flew in
9 've been trying
10 are you staying
11 is being re-decorated
12 've just been told
13 will finish / will have finished
14 means
15 have been living
16 've been trying
17 Have you checked out
18 'll be listed
19 said
20 'd seen
21 was advertised
22 're still trying
23 was thinking
24 heard
25 'll find out
26 'll call
27 'll still be working
28 leave
29 won't be able to
30 're always paid
31 's the job going
32 has been
33 've been taken out/'m being taken out

Present Perfect: simple and continuous

1 b   2 a   3 a   4 b (*a* is possible, but *b* is better for stressing the length of time)   5 a   6 b

Narrative tenses

1 were sitting, started
2 returned, had borrowed
3 was shopping, was stolen
4 didn't arrive/hasn't arrived, 'd forgotten
5 was travelling, caught
6 woke up, was standing
7 had read, lent
8 was hit, was cycling
9 carried on, 'd filled up
10 'd been standing, was
11 knew, 'd made, saw
12 opened, realised, had been snowing

Vocabulary

1 1 d   2 c   3 a   4 g
  5 f   6 h   7 e   8 b
2 1 make   4 make
  2 do   5 do
  3 make   6 make
3 1 bag   7 air
  2 office   8 way
  3 mail   9 escape
  4 software 10 pill
  5 alarm   11 line
  6 shelf   12 food

Spoken English

2 I'll   7 Have you
3 Do you   8 Are you
4 Have you   9 I
5 Are you   10 I'm
6 I

Stop and Check 2

General revision

1 ages   16 less
2 much   17 full of
3 journey   18 's going
4 a bit of   19 most of
5 loads   20 'll be
6 're going to get 21 'm meeting
7 plenty of   22 are thinking of
8 leaves   going
9 'll check in   23 off
10 a couple of   24 won't be
11 much   25 'll
12 no   26 is
13 almost all   27 'll have had
14 taking   28 'll
15 're going to do 29 sample
                   30 'll close

Question forms

1 Who is she going out with now?
2 What do you want to talk about?
3 How often do you think he visits his parents?
4 How come you never seem to do any work?
5 Do you know what kind of flower that is?
6 How long will it take him to fix it?

Short questions

1 f   2 c   3 a   4 b
5 g   6 h   7 d   8 e

Future forms

1 are going to build   4 'm meeting
2 will win   5 'll take
3 leaves   6 Shall we go

Expressions of quantity

With count nouns: several, a few, not one, the majority of, fewer, not a single, only a couple of
With uncount nouns: a little, less, a great deal of, a huge amount of, not much, a bit of, far too much
With count or uncount nouns: most, almost all, no, hardly any, enough, a lot of, plenty of, loads of

Vocabulary

1 1 j   2 e   3 a   4 l   5 n   6 b
  7 o   8 m   9 d   10 f 11 h
  12 p 13 g 14 i 15 k 16 c
2 1 unkind   4 irresponsible
  2 insincere   5 immature
  3 dishonest   6 illegal
3 2 take it back 5 take it in
  3 put you off   6 take them on
  4 put it on   7 put it out

Stop and check 3

General revision

1 or   17 're able to
2 may   18 who
3 should   19 refuse
4 who   20 always be leaving
5 to living   21 won't
6 very   22 may
7 might   23 'd better not
8 on   24 who's
9 that   25 which
10 nerves   26 listening
11 that   27 that
12 extremely   28 quite
13 likely   29 which
14 like   30 allowed
15 not   31 don't have to
16 what   32 when

Modals and related verbs

1 permission   6 probability
2 unwillingness   7 willingness
3 request   8 advice
4 no obligation   9 ability
5 prohibition   10 obligation

Expressing habit

1 usually   4 would
2 used to be   5 use to
3 is used to   6 get used to

Relative clauses

1 are the people who shouted at
2 , whose favourite colour is red, loved
3 , which is in the town centre,
4 where I saw
5 , who's 17 today, is having
6 , when it's hot, we go to
7 that / which bit
8 , where it seldom rains, there's
9 whose car is badly
10 when we go

-ed or –ing?

1	hurting	9	relaxed
2	embarrassed	10	challenging
3	exhausted	11	painted
4	relaxing	12	looking
5	amusing	13	bored
6	depressing	14	depressed
7	Printed	15	exhausting
8	disappointed	16	shocking

Vocabulary

1
1	got over	6	got through
2	get through	7	getting at
3	getting at	8	get round
4	get up	9	get through
5	got out	10	got out

2
1 absolutely priceless
2 very clever
3 absolutely hilarious
4 very interesting
5 very surprised
6 absolutely awful

3
2	hole	7	allowed
3	caught	8	sure
4	bored	9	waste
5	rode	10	peace
6	wore	11	higher

Stop and check 4

General revision

1	have	15	some
2	the	16	would have called
3	may have been	17	had been
4	Although	18	could have had
5	the	19	would have found
6	of	20	had been forced
7	a	21	all
8	that	22	this
9	a	23	of
10	of	24	may
11	the	25	neither
12	not	26	is used to
13	of	27	sound
14	might	28	the

Modals in the past

1 She may have forgotten.
2 You shouldn't have looked.
3 It must have been him.
4 Could they have known?
5 He might have been lying.
6 She can't have told him.
7 You needn't have waited.
8 I didn't need to stay.
9 Won't/Wouldn't he have gone?
10 They'll have been arrested.

wish and if only

1 could come with us
2 weren't any rocks on the beach
3 'd seen the warning sign
4 would stop shouting
5 hadn't gone to bed so late last night
6 didn't have to tidy up every day
7 my parents weren't always arguing
8 I'd been wearing my seat belt at the time of the accident
9 you'd stayed longer?
10 we'd been given all the information

Conditional sentences

2 hadn't rescued, would've drowned
3 would've set out, 'd known
4 'd asked, wouldn't have said
5 wouldn't have failed, hadn't crashed
6 might've won, had allowed
7 hadn't spotted, could have been
8 would you have done, 'd been attacked
9 hadn't been sleeping, would've heard

Articles and determiners

1 the health centre
2 ✓
3 ✓
4 a chemical engineer
5 the bus
6 plenty of
7 ✓
8 a few
9 ✓
10 a very intelligent girl
11 such a lovely day
12 ✓
13 speak to one another
14 a tooth
15 ✓
16 an important feature

Vocabulary

1
1 on its last legs
2 went to his head
3 face the fact
4 a heart of gold
5 finding her feet
6 an excellent head for business
7 pulling my leg
8 give me a hand
9 put on a brave face
10 shake hands

2 (correct order within pairs essential)
1 by and large
2 ins and outs
3 odds and ends
4 give and take
5 sick and tired
6 now and then
7 ups and downs
8 weird and wonderful
9 slowly but surely
10 sooner or later
11 all or nothing
12 more or less

3
1	fat	4	describe
2	tasty	5	beginning
3	help	6	appalling

Progress test 1

1 Tenses

1 was getting
2 didn't believe
3 was talking
4 suspected
5 had been walking / was walking
6 had come / came
7 was
8 had been
9 've been / was
10 'm going
11 was raining
12 were
13 had acquired
14 are you doing
15 was given
16 dropped
17 've been walking
18 did he look like
19 was wearing
20 looked at
21 was found
22 had been left
23 was received
24 had been stolen
25 was observed
26 was described / has been described
27 has been seen
28 're taking / 're going to take
29 get
30 'll tell

2 Future forms

1 c 2 b 3 a 4 b
5 a 6 c 7 b 8 c

3 Negatives

1 not to make
2 ✓
3 mustn't copy
4 haven't tidied my room yet
5 ✓
6 I hope not
7 ✓
8 I don't agree

4 Question forms

1 about
2 often do you
3 it is
4 kind of books do
5 long does it take
6 look like

5 Countable or uncountable?

2 furniture
3 traffic
4 luggage
5 crime
6 money
7 fruit / food

6 Numbers

2 four million, nine hundred and forty-one thousand, two hundred and eight
3 the nineteen nineties
4 the fourteenth of October / October the fourteenth
5 three-quarters
6 seventy-two per cent
7 thirty-four point five seven
8 seventeen eighty-nine
9 seven three oh, double four six five

7 *put* and *take*

1 took part
2 take a risk
3 take responsibility
4 put yourself in my shoes
5 took offence
6 take place
7 take any notice
8 Take my word
9 put a stop to
10 put her foot in it

8 Expressing quantity

1 nearly everybody
2 most of the people
3 more than half the people
4 several people
5 a few people
6 hardly anybody

9 Compound words and affixes

1 homesick
2 unhappy
3 lifestyle
4 dislike
5 unfair
6 unkind
7 homework
8 improvement
9 successful
10 encouragement

10 Everyday English

1 (Good morning, etc.) Could I speak to the manager, please?
2 Same to you, too! Bye, Jane.
3 Do you happen to know where the office is?
4 Would you like me to carry your suitcase?
5 Great! It's a deal. It's yours!
6 Sorry, I didn't quite get that last bit. What was it again?
7 can't afford it
8 What dreadful / awful / horrible weather!

Progress test 2

1 Grammar and vocabulary

1 which
2 the
3 the
4 had
5 would
6 which
7 who
8 no
9 of
10 have
11 get
12 which
13 would/might/could
14 then
15 not
16 should
17 of
18 when
19 which / that
20 had
21 described
22 in
23 rather
24 in
25 which
26 taking
27 to
28 can
29 amount
30 of

2 Participles

2 a dog barking
3 The figures given
4 Cars parked
5 Employees handling
6 Products made
7 the money spent
8 Passengers arriving

3 Unnecessary words

1 of
2 it
3 of
4 must
5 ✓
6 ✓
7 a
8 can
9 of
10 ✓
11 also
12 that
13 ✓
14 which
15 of

4 Linking

1 a 2 d 3 b 4 c 5 d 6 d
7 a 8 d 9 a 10 d 11 d
12 b

5 Hypothesizing

1 'd rather you stayed
2 's time you gave up
3 only Kim hadn't arrived
4 should have paid (some) attention
5 wish I'd been
6 rather you hadn't told
7 is time something was / were
8 supposing we had (lost)

6 *used to*

1 a 2 b 3 a 4 b 5 b 6 b

7 Homonyms

1 cross
2 fit
3 cool
4 park
5 bear
6 fine
7 date
8 bank

8 Meanings of *get*

1 I haven't got
2 got
3 getting
4 get in touch with
5 get it
6 getting
7 get on (well)
8 gets on my nerves.

9 Everyday English

1 stand the sight of him
2 totally out of order
3 madly in love
4 hit the roof
5 worship the ground you walk on
6 dying for a drink

Word list

Unit 1

aerial n /'eəriəl/
albatross n /'ælbətrɒs/
apartment n /ə'pɑ:tmənt/
archery n /'ɑ:tʃəri/
astronomical adj /æstrə'nɒmɪkl/
(be) attached to v /(bɪ:) ə'tætʃt tu:/
awesome adj /'ɔ:səm/
barrier n /'bæriə(r)/
bear v /'beə(r)/
bend n /bend/
beyond recognition id /bi:'jɒnd ˌrekɒg'nɪʃn/
big deal n /bɪg 'di:l/
big shot (inf) n /'bɪg ʃɒt/
bother v /'bɒðə/
boundaries pl n /'baʊndri:z/
briefcase n /'bri:fkeɪs/
cell phone n /'sel ˌfəʊn/
classy adj /'klɑ:si/
converse v /kɒn'vɜ:s/
cool (temperature) adj /ku:l/
desktop support n /'desktɒp ˌsə'pɔ:t/
diplomat n /'dɪpləmæt/
dolphin n /'dɒlfɪn/
drag n /dræg/
ear plugs pl n /'ɪə(r) ˌplʌgz/
excessive adj /ˌek'sesɪv/
extended adj /ˌek'stendɪd/
extensive adj /ˌek'stensɪv/
firm n /fɜ:m/
fussy adj /'fʌsi/
glove box n /'glʌv ˌbɒks/
hang in there (stick with) id /ˌhæŋ 'ɪn ðeə/
harrowing adj /'hærəʊɪŋ/
homecoming party n /'həʊmkʌmɪŋ ˌpɑ:ti/
homesick adj /'həʊmsɪk/
host v /həʊst/
housebound adj /'haʊsbaʊnd/
house-proud adj n /'haʊspraʊd/
housewarming party n /'haʊswɔ:mɪŋ ˌpɑ:ti/
invaluable adj /ɪn'væljuəbl/
itchy feet id /'ɪtʃi ˌfi:t/
jet-lagged adj /'dʒet lægd/
kangaroo n /ˌkæŋgə'ru:/
keep an eye on id /ˌki:p ən 'aɪ ɒn/
kid (inf) v /kɪd/
knack n /næk/
knowledge n /'nɒlɪdʒ/
litter n /'lɪtə/
locate v /ləʊ'keɪt/
managing director n /mænɪdʒɪŋ daɪ'rektə/
masses pl (inf) /'mæsɪz/
master v /'mɑ:stə(r)/
mechanical adj /mə'kænɪkl/
mountain biking n /'maʊntɪn ˌbaɪkɪŋ/
mousse n /mu:s/
municipal adj /mu'nɪsɪpl/
observatory n /ˌəb'zɜ:vətri/
overtake v /əʊvə'taɪk/
pace n /peɪs/
particular adj /ˌpə'tɪkulə/
platypus n /'plætɪpəs/
possessions pl n /pə'zeʃn/
probe v /prəʊb/
provide v /prə'vaɪd/
pyjamas n /pə'dʒɑ:məz/
(get) puffed v /(get) 'pʌft/
reassuring adj /riə'ʃɔ:rɪŋ/
satellite n /'sætəlaɪt/
second-hand adj /sekənd hænd/
served pp /sɜ:vd/
solid adj /'sɒlɪd/
spectacular adj /spek'tækulə/
split up v /ˌsplɪt 'ʌp/
stink v /stɪŋk/
stuff (inf) n /stʌf/
subway n /'sʌbweɪ/
take a toll on v id /ˌteɪk ə 'tɒl ɒn/
take trouble to v id /ˌteɪk 'trʌbl tu:/
telescope n /'telɪskəʊp/
thorough adj /'θʌrə/
tons (inf) adj /tʌnz/
trade v /treɪd/
transfer v /ˌtræns'fɜ:(r)/
tune into v /'tju:n ˌɪntu/
twiddle v /'twɪdl/
universe n /'u:nɪvɜ:s/
unruly adj /ʌn'ru:li/
walkway n /'wɔ:kˌweɪ/
wander v /'wɒndə/
whale n /'weɪl/
wildlife n /'waɪldlaɪf/

Unit 2

adjust to v /ə'dʒʌst ˌtu:/
advocate v /'ædvəkeɪt/
affordable adj /ə'fɔ:dəbl/
ancient adj /'eɪntʃnt/
annual adj /'ænjuəl/
apply for v /ə'plaɪ ˌfɔ:(r)/
assets pl n /'æsetz/
assistant n /ə'sɪstənt/
(be) associated with id /(bi) ə'səʊsi:eɪtɪd ˌwɪð/
attitude n /'ætɪtjud/
awe n /ɔ:/
backpacking trip n /'bækpækɪŋ ˌtrɪp/
benefit n /'benəfɪt/
biography n /baɪ'ɒgrəfi/
boom (inf) n /bu:m/
broaden v /'brɔ:dən/
bug (inf) n /bʌg/
buzzing adj /'bʌzɪŋ/
cash in on id /ˌkæʃ 'ɪn ɒn/
chore n /tʃɔ:/
civilisation n /ˌsɪvɪlaɪ'zeɪʃn/
coach (person) n /kəʊtʃ/
compound n /'kɒmpaʊnd/
considerable adj /kən'sɪdərəbl/
constantly adv /'kɒnstəntli/
consume v /kən'sju:m/
convinced pp /kən'vɪnst/
cooped up (inf) pp /'ku:pt ˌʌp/
covering letter n /'kʌvərɪŋ ˌletə(r)/
decade n /'dekaɪd/
demolished pp /dɪ'mɒlɪʃt/
diarrhoea n /daɪə'riə/
(be) due v /(bi) dʒu:/
economy n /ɪ'kɒnəmi/
edition n /ɪ'dɪʃn/
eerie adj /'ɪəri/
emperor n /'empərə(r)/
energetic adj /ˌenɜ:'dʒetɪk/
engineering n /ˌendʒɪn'ɪərɪŋ/
entire adj /ɪn'taɪə/
establish v /ɪs'tæblɪʃ/
evicted pp /ɪ'vɪktɪd/
exhausting adj /ɪk'zɔ:stɪŋ/
exotic adj /ɪk'zɒtɪk/
exploit v /eks'plɔɪt/
explorer n /eks'plɔ:rə/
extensively adv /ek'stensɪvli/
favour n /'feɪvə/
formed pp /fɔ:md/
fortune n /fɔ:tʃu:n/
graduate n /'grædjuət/
handle v /'hændl/
hang out (inf) v /ˌhæŋ 'aʊt/
headquarters n /hed'kɔ:təz/
hectic adj /'hektɪk/
hot air balloon n /hɒt 'eə ˌbəlu:n/
idyllic adj /ɪ'dɪlɪk/
impact n /'ɪmpækt/
jewellery n /'dʒu:lri/
leader n /'li:də(r)/
mining n /'maɪnɪŋ/
monarchy n /'mɒnəki/
motivated adj /'məʊtɪveɪtɪd/
mugged pp /'mʌgd/
(be) opposed to id /(bi) ə'pəʊzd ˌtu:/
outstanding adj /aʊt'stændɪŋ/
overtime n /'əʊvətaɪm/
package tour n /'pækɪdʒ ˌtɔ:(r)/
paradise n /'pærədaɪs/
pickpocketed pp /'pɪkˌpɒkɪtɪd/
piped pp /'paɪpt/
practical adj /'præktɪkl/
privileged adj /'prɪvɪlɪdʒd/
profile n /'prəʊfaɪl/
publishing n /'pʌblɪʃɪŋ/
qualified adj /'kwɒlɪfaɪd/
qualifications pl n /kwɒlɪfɪ'keɪʃnz/
range n /'reɪndʒ/
rationed pp /'ræʃnd/
references pl n /'refrənsɪz/
relentless adj /rə'lentləs/
relevant adj /'reləvənt/
rely on v /rɪ'laɪ ˌɒn/
remote adj /rɪ'məʊt/
respect n /rɪ'spekt/
revenue n /'revənju:/
ridge n /'rɪdʒ/
route n /ru:t/
safari n /sə'fɑ:ri/
scuba diving n /'sku:bə ˌdaɪvɪŋ/
shares pl n /ʃeəz/
shimmering adj /'ʃɪmərɪŋ/
summit n /'sʌmɪt/
supervisor n /'supəvaɪzə(r)/
territory n /'terətri/
tourist spot (inf) n /'tɔ:rɪst ˌspɒt/
training session n /'treɪnɪŋ ˌseʃn/
trampoline n /ˌtræmpə'li:n/
trek v /trek/
triplets pl n /'trɪplətz/
unique adj /ju:'ni:k/
valley n /'væli/
value v /'vælu:/
variety n /və'raɪəti/
venture n /'ventʃə/
vital adj /'vaɪtl/
white water rafting n /waɪt wɔ:tə 'ra:ftɪŋ/
worsen v /'wɜ:sən/

Unit 3

alerted pp /ə'lɜːtɪd/
alligator n /'ælɪgeɪtə/
apparent adj /ə'pærənt/
assassin n /ə'sæsɪn/
attempt n /ə'tempt/
avalanche n /'ævəlɑːntʃ/

bargain n /'bɑːgɪn/
barred pp /bɑːd/
beggar n /'begə(r)/
bet v /bet/
broke (inf) adj /brəʊk/
(go) bust id /(gəʊ) 'bʌst/

capture v /'kæptʃə/
chatter (shake) v /'tʃætə(r)/
claustrophobic adj
    /ˌklɒstrə'fəʊbɪk/
clinically adv /'klɪnɪkəli/
collapsed pp /kə'læpst/
compelling adj /kəm'pelɪŋ/
concern n /kən'sɜːn/
corruption n /kə'rʌpʃn/
creek n /kriːk/

dare n /deə/
dependable adj /dɪ'pendəbl/
descent n /dɪ'sent/
download v /'daʊnləʊd/
dress code n /'dres ˌkəʊd/

element n /'elɪmənt/

faith n /feɪθ/
fashionable adj /'fæʃənəbl/
fashion-conscious adj /'fæʃn
    ˌkɒnʃs/
fatally adv /'feɪtəli/
figure v /'fɪgə/

gadget n /'gædʒɪt/
glint v /glɪnt/
grief n /griːf/

hack (into) v /hæk ('ɪntu)/
helicopter n /'helɪkɒptə(r)/
howl v /haʊl/

inquest n /'ɪnkwest/
intense adj /ɪn'tens/
issue v /'ɪʃuː/

jammed (inf) adj /'dʒæmd/

ledge n /ledʒ/

military adj /'mɪlətri/
mountain climber n /'maʊntɪn
    ˌklaɪmə(r)/

nerd n /nɜːd/
nostalgic adj /nɒs'tældʒɪk/
numb adj /nʌm/

operate v /'ɒpəreɪt/
oval adj /'əʊvl/
owe v /əʊ/

passionate adj /'pæʃənət/
penitential adj /penɪ'tentʃl/
plea n /pliː/
plummet n /'plʌmɪt/
plunge v /plʌndʒ/
protection n /prə'tekʃn/
psychologically adj

/ˌsaɪkə'lɒdʒɪkli/
ravine n /rə'viːn/
rescued pp /'reskjud/
rigid adj /'rɪdʒɪd/
rub v /rʌb/
ruthless adj /'ruːθləs/

scale down v /'skeɪl ˌdaʊn/
scoop up v /ˌskuːp 'ʌp/
serial number n /'sɪəriəl
    ˌnʌmbə(r)/
several adj /'sevrəl/
shed n /ʃed/
shelter n /'ʃeltə(r)/
solemn adj /'sɒləm/
stack n /stæk/
strands pl n /strændz/
streetcar n /'striːtˌkɑː/
struck pp /strʌk/
suspended pp /sə'spendɪd/
suspense n /sə'spens/
suspiciously adv /sə'spɪʃəsli/
swirling adj /'swɜːlɪŋ/

tense adj /tens/
text message n /'tekst ˌmesɪdʒ/
tiger n /'taɪgə/
torn adj /tɔːn/
tow v /təʊ/
trace (find) v /treɪs/
track down v /træk daʊn/
tragic adj /'trædʒɪk/
tranquillizer dart n
    /'trænkwɪlaɪzə ˌdɑːt/
trapped pp /træpt/

veil n /veɪl/

(be) worth id /(bi) wɜːθ/
wreckage n /'rekɪdʒ/

Unit 4

affair (relationship) n /ə'feə/
allege v /ə'ledʒ/
analysis n /ə'næləsɪs/
arbitrary adj /'ɑːbətri/
assassinated pp /ə'sæsɪneɪtɪd/
assert v /ə'sɜːt/
atheist n /'eɪθiɪst/
authentic adj /ɔː'θentɪk/

bearable adj /'beərəbl/
bizarrely adv /bɪ'zɑːli/
breathtaking adj /'breθteɪkɪŋ/
buy into id /ˌbaɪ 'ɪntu/

campaigner n /kæm'peɪnə(r)/
career path n /kə'rɪə ˌpɑːθ/
chair v /tʃeə/
coincidentally adv
    /kəʊˌɪnsɪ'dentli/
conceal v /kən'siːl/
conference n /'kɒnfərəns/
confess v /kɒn'fes/
consequences pl n
    /'kɒnsɪkwensɪz/
conspiracy theory n /kən'spɪrəsi
    ˌθɪəri/
counter-theory n /'kaʊntə ˌθɪəri/
curse n /kɜːs/

depression n /dɪ'preʃn/
developed pp /dɪ'veləpt/
devise v /dɪ'vaɪz/
dyslexic adj /dɪs'leksik/

elaborate adj /ɪ'læbərət/
existence n /ek'zɪstəns/

farce n /fɑːs/
fascinate v /'fæsɪneɪt/
fiendish adj /'fiːndɪʃ/
flutter v /'flʌtə(r)/
follow on from v /ˌfɒləʊ 'ɒn
    frɒm/
formed pp /fɔːmd/
frumpy adj /'frʌmpi/

geological adj /ˌdʒiːə'lɒdʒɪkl/
grate n /greɪt/

hatched pp /hætʃd/
hint n /hɪnt/
hoax n /həʊks/
housekeeper n /'haʊskiːpə(r)/
hypotheses pl n /haɪ'pɒθəsiːz/

innocent adj /'ɪnəsənt/
insomniac n /ɪn'sɒmniæk/
interfere v /ˌɪntə'fɪə/
ironically adv /aɪ'rɒnikli/

lawyer n /lɔɪjə/
leak (information) v /liːk/
legendary adj /'ledʒɪndri/
linked pp /lɪŋkt/

meanness n /'miːnnəs/
memoirs pl n /'memɑːz/
mundane adj /mʌn'deɪn/

naturist n /'neɪtʃərɪst/

official adj /ə'fɪʃl/

pacifist n /'pæsɪfɪst/
paranoia n /ˌpærə'nɔɪə/

parsnips pl n /'pɑːsnɪps/
pastime n /'pɑːstaɪm/
patently adv /'peɪtəntli/
pierced pp /'pɪəst/
plausible adj /'plɔːzɪbl/
protester n /'prəʊtestə(r)/
psychiatrist n /saɪ'kaɪətrɪst/
published pp /'pʌblɪʃt/

recall v /rɪkɔːl/
reputation n /ˌrepju'teɪʃn/
reputed pp /rɪ'pjuːtɪd/
reveal v /rɪ'viːl/

sin n /sɪn/
spank v /spæŋk/
stub out (inf) v /'stʌb ˌaʊt/
stuffy adj /'stʌfi/
(be) subjected to id /(bi)
    səb'dʒektɪd tuː/
suicidal adj /ˌsuːɪ'saɪdl/
suspicious adj /sə'spɪʃəs/

tampered pp /'tæmpəd/
teetotal adj /'tiːˌtəʊtəl/
tragedy n /'trædʒədi/
turbulence n /'tɜːbuləns/

unanimously adv /ju'nænɪməsli/
untimely adj /ʌn'taɪmli/

vegan n /'viːgən/
verdict n /'vɜːdɪkt/

weird adj /wɪəd/
witness n /'wɪtnəs/

Unit 5

address v /ə'dres/
adequate adj /'ædəkwət/
advice n /əd'vaɪs/
afford v /ə'fɔ:d/
agency n /'eɪdʒənsi/
aid n /eɪd/
alienated pp /'eɪliːənˌeɪtɪd/
arms trade n /'ɑ:mz ˌtreɪd/
article n /'ɑ:tɪkl/
aspiration n /ˌæspɪ'reɪʃn/
assistance n /ə'sɪstəns/
assume v /ə'sju:m/
bleat (inf) v /bli:t/
boost v /bu:st/
brochure n /'brəʊʃə/
cabin crew pl n /'kæbɪn ˌkru:/
canvassed pp /'kænvəst/
catch up on (inf) v /ˌkætʃ 'ʌp ɒn/
client n /'klaɪənt/
climate n /'klaɪmət/
conscientious adj /ˌkɒnʃi'enʃəs/
cruising-speed n /'kru:zɪŋ ˌspi:d/
customer services n /ˌkʌstəmə 'sɜ:vɪsɪz/
dealt (with) pp /delt (wɪð)/
debt n /det/
department n /dɪ'pɑ:tmənt/
desperately adv /'desprətli/
disillusionment n /ˌdɪsɪl'u:ʒnmənt/
disturb v /dɪs'tɜ:b/
dramatically adv /drə'mætɪkli/
due v /dʒu:/
efficiently adv /ɪ'fɪʃəntli/
election n /ɪ'lekʃn/
ensure v /en'ʃʊə/
enterprise n /'entəpraɪz/
equal rights pl n /ˌi:kwəl ˌraɪtz/
factory farming n /'fæktri ˌfɑ:mɪŋ/
fancy (inf) v /'fænsi/
finance company n /'faɪnæns ˌkʌmpəni/
flight attendant n /'flaɪt ə'tendənt/
gender n /'dʒendə/
generation n /ˌdʒenə'reɪʃn/
gig (inf) n /gɪg/
globalization n /ˌgləʊbəlaɪz'eɪʃn/
goal n /gəʊl/
high-flier n /'haɪ ˌflaɪə(r)/
idealistic adj /ˌaɪdɪə'lɪstɪk/
income n /'ɪnkʌm/
interrupted pp /ˌɪntə'rʌptɪd/
jacuzzi n /dʒə'ku:zi/
lecture n /'lektʃə/
literature n /'lɪtrɪtʃə/
loan n /ləʊn/
lousy adj /laʊzi/
loyalty n /'lɔɪəlti/
make redundant v /ˌmeɪk rɪ'dʌndənt/

(on the) mend id /(ɒn ðə) mend/
mortgage n /'mɔ:gɪdʒ/
motto n /'mɒtəʊ/
operator n /'ɒpəreɪtə(r)/
optimistic adj /ˌɒptɪ'mɪstɪk/
plumber n /'plʌmə(r)/
politics n /'pɒlətɪks/
presume v /prɪ'zju:m/
processed pp /'prəʊsest/
promotion n /prə'məʊʃn/
property ladder n /'prɒpəti ˌlædə(r)/
prospects pl n /'prɒspektz/
psychology n /saɪ'kɒlədʒi/
query v /'kwɪəri/
raise v /reɪz/
rat race id /'ræt reɪs/
redistribute v /ˌri:dɪs'trɪbu:t/
refreshments pl n /rɪ'freʃmənts/
regardless adv /rɪ'gɑ:dləs/
remain v /rɪ'meɪn/
requested pp /rɪ'kwestɪd/
resign v /rɪ'zaɪn/
responsibility n /rɪˌspɒnsə'bɪləti/
reunion n /ri:'ju:nɪən/
(be) scared stiff id /(bi) skeəd stɪf/
secure adj /sɪ'kʊə/
select v /sɪ'lekt/
sexual orientation n /ˌsekʃu:l ɔ:riən'teɪʃn/
social adj /'səʊʃl/
staff n /stɑ:f/
standards pl n /'stændədz/
take for granted id /ˌteɪk fə 'grɑ:ntɪd/
take notice of v /ˌteɪk 'nəʊtɪs əv/
take offence v /ˌteɪk ə'fens/
take place (happen) v /ˌteɪk 'pleɪs/
upright prep /'ʌpraɪt/
vote v /vəʊt/
wealth n /welθ/
wonder v /'wʌndə(r)/

Unit 6

acclaimed adj /ə'kleɪmd/
ail v /eɪl/
appeal n /ə'pɪəl/
attachment n /ə'tætʃmənt/
attitude n /'ætɪtju:d/
bitterly adv /'bɪtəli/
blend n /blend/
bloke (inf) n /bləʊk/
branch (of bank) n /brɑ:ntʃ/
brand n /brænd/
campaign n /kæm'peɪn/
capital (money) n /'kæpɪtl/
catering college n /'keɪtərɪŋ ˌkɒlɪdʒ/
chef n /ʃef/
commercialism n /kə'mɜ:ʃlɪzm/
competitive adj /kəm'petətɪv/
consumer n /kən'sju:mə(r)/
count (matter) v /kaʊnt/
count yourself lucky id /ˌkaʊnt jɔ:self 'lʌki/
currently adv /'kʌrəntli/
data n /'deɪtə/
deadline n /'dedlaɪn/
dealer n /'di:lə(r)/
deposit n /dɪ'pɒzɪt/
devotion n /dɪ'vəʊʃn/
dirt n /dɜ:t/
export n /'ekspɔ:t/
evidence n /'evɪdəns/
fair-trade adj /ˌfeər 'treɪd/
feature v /'fi:tʃə/
findings pl n /'faɪndɪŋz/
fluffy adj /'flʌfi/
formula n /'fɔ:mjələ/
founder member n /'faʊndə ˌmembə(r)/
gathered pp /'gæðəd/
gradually adv /'græduəli/
import n /'ɪmpɔ:t/
ingredients pl n /ɪn'gri:dɪəntz/
inherit v /ɪn'herɪt/
initially adv /ɪn'ɪʃəli/
insult n /'ɪnsʌlt/
insurance n /ɪn'ʃɔ:rəns/
interior n /ɪn'tɪərɪə(r)/
irresistible adj /ɪrɪ'zɪstəbl/
issue n /'ɪʃu:/
keen adj /ki:n/
league n /li:g/
model on v /'mɒdl ɒn/
objective n /əb'dʒektɪv/
offence n /ə'fens/
offhand id /ɒf'hænd/
opposition n /ˌɒpə'zɪʃn/
organic adj /ɔ:'gænɪk/
originally adv /ə'rɪdʒənəli/
outlet n /'aʊtlət/
passionately adv /'pæʃənətli/
potential adj /pə'tenʃl/
powder n /'paʊdə(r)/
preliminary adj /prɪ'lɪmɪnəri/
presence n /'prezəns/

previously adv /'pri:vɪəsli/
product n /'prɒdʌkt/
profitability n /ˌprɒfɪtə'bɪlɪti/
propose (suggest) v /prə'pəʊz/
purpose n /'pɜ:pəs/
quote n /kwəʊt/
rapidly adv /'ræpɪdli/
recipe n /'resɪpi/
recommendation n /ˌrekəmen'deɪʃn/
reduction n /rɪ'dʌkʃn/
reluctantly adv /rɪ'lʌktəntli/
research n /'ri:sɜ:tʃ/
retailer n /'ri:teɪlə(r)/
rival n /'raɪvl/
rule out v /ˌru:l 'aʊt/
scale n /skeɪl/
significantly adv /sɪg'nɪfɪkəntli/
sleek adj /sli:k/
speciality n /speʃi'ælɪti/
specialize in v /'speʃəlaɪz ˌɪn/
statistics pl n /stə'tɪstɪks/
status n /'steɪtəs/
stunning adj /'stʌnɪŋ/
stylish adj /'staɪlɪʃ/
summarize v /'sʌməraɪz/
summary n /'sʌməri/
survey n /'sɜ:veɪ/
swiftly adv /'swɪftli/
technique n /tek'ni:k/
whack (inf) v /wæk/
zip (rush about) (inf) v /zɪp/

Unit 7

accumulate v /əˈkjuːmuleɪt/
acronym n /ˈækrənɪm/
adore v /əˈdɔː/
affair (occasion) n /əˈfeə/
alongside prep /əlɒŋˈsaɪd/
appropriate adj /əˈprəʊpriˌət/
arranged marriage n /əˈreɪndʒd ˌmærɪdʒ/

background n /ˈbækgraʊnd/
beneficial adj /ˌbenəˈfɪʃl/
breeze (inf) n /briːz/

call up v /kɔːl ˈʌp/
carton n /ˈkɑːtən/
chaperone n /ˈʃæpərəʊn/
charge v /tʃɑːdʒ/
chilly adj /ˈtʃɪli/
clue n /kluː/
communication n /kəˌmjuːnɪˈkeɪʃn/
contribute v /kənˈtrɪbjuːt/
controlled adj /kənˈtrəʊld/
correspondence n /kɒrɪsˈpɒndəns/

designated adj /ˈdezɪgneɪtɪd/
destination n /ˌdestɪˈneɪʃn/
divorce n /dɪˈvɔːs/
domestic adj /dəˈmestɪk/

electronic adj /eləkˈtrɒnɪk/
engagement n /enˈgeɪdʒmənt/
environmentally friendly adj /enˌvaɪrəˈmentəli ˈfrendli/
erode v /ɪˈrəʊd/
exaggerated adj /ikˈzædʒəreɪtɪd/

flood n /flʌd/
forfeit v /ˈfɔːfɪt/

haunt v /hɔːnt/

ignore v /igˈnɔː/
impersonal adj /imˈpɜːsənəl/
intercept v /ˌɪntəˈsept/
irritation n /ɪrɪˈteɪʃn/

knackered (inf) adj /ˈnækəd/
know-how (inf) n /ˈnəʊ ˌhaʊ/

lax adj /læks/
loaded (inf) adj /ˈləʊdɪd/

manners n /ˈmænəz/
matter n /ˈmætə(r)/
means n /miːnz/
minus adj /ˈmaɪnəs/

obtain v /əbˈteɪn/
operation n /ˌɒpəˈreɪʃn/
outweigh v /aʊtˈweɪ/
overlook v /əʊvəˈlʊk/

perks pl n /pɜːks/
permitted pp /pəˈmɪtɪd/
plus adj /plʌs/
postpone v /pəʊsˈpəʊn/
pride n /praɪd/
primitive adj /ˈprɪmɪtɪv/
prose n /prəʊz/

rent v /rent/
required pp /rɪˈkwaɪəd/
reserved adj /rɪˈzɜːvd/

resources pl n /rɪˈzɔːsɪs/
respond to v /rɪˈspɒnd ˌtu/
retirement n /rɪˈtaɪəmənt/
(for the) sake (of) id /(fɔː ðə) seɪk (əv)/
salary n /ˈsæləri/
snail n /sneɪl/
software n /ˈsɒftweə/
soul n /səʊl/
sponge (inf) v /spʌndʒ/
spontaneous adj /spɒnˈteɪniːəs/
stamp n /stæmp/
store v /stɔː/
strapped (inf) v /stræpt/
stated pp /ˈsteɪtɪd/
subtle adj /ˈsʌtl/
suit v /suːt/
suitable adj /ˈsuːtəbl/
system n /ˈsɪstəm/

technical adj /ˈteknɪkəl/
temperamental adj /ˌtemprəˈmentl/
titbit n /ˈtɪtbɪt/
transformed pp /trænsˈfɔːmd/
tuition n /tjuˈɪʃn/

understated adj /ʌndəˈsteɪtɪd/
universal adj /juniˈvɜːsəl/
unwilling adj /ʌnˈwɪlɪŋ/

visa n /ˈviːzə/

wealthy adj /ˈwelθi/
wits pl n /wɪtz/
worship v /ˈwɜːʃɪp/

Unit 8

access n /ˈækses/
adorn v /əˈdɔːn/
anonymous adj /əˈnɒnɪməs/
aroma n /əˈrəʊmə/
appointment n /əˈpɔɪntmənt/
apt adj /æpt/
aviation n /ˌeɪviˈeɪʃn/

bald adj /bɔːld/
bliss n /blɪs/
boast v /bəʊst/
border v /ˈbɔːdə(r)/
boutique n /buːˈtiːk/
buzz v /bʌz/

capture (interest) v /ˈkæptʃə/
carved pp /ˈkɑːvd/
caution n /ˈkɔːʃn/
cockpit n /ˈkɒkpɪt/
collide (with) v /kəˈlaɪd (wɪð)/
commercial licence n /kəˈmɜːʃl ˌlaɪsəns/
commute v /kəˈmjuːt/
continental adj /ˌkɒntɪˈnentl/
cope v /kəʊp/
cosmopolitan adj /ˌkɒsməˈpɒlɪtən/
crumpled adj /ˈkrʌmpld/

deer pl n /dɪə(r)/
dehydrate v /ˌdiːhaɪˈdreɪt/
demands pl n /dɪˈmɑːndz/
derived pp /dɪˈraɪvd/
distinction n /dɪˈstɪnkʃn/
down and out n /ˈdaʊn ənd aʊt/
downpour n /ˈdaʊnpɔː(r)/
dull adj /dʌl/

electrical appliances pl n /iˈlektrɪkl əˌplaɪənsɪz/
estate n /ɪˈsteɪt/

fall behind with v /ˌfɔːl bɪˈhaɪnd wɪð/
fantasy n /ˈfæntəsi/
flock v /flɒk/
fluid n /ˈfluːɪd/

get rid of v /ˌget ˈrɪd əv/

hammer n /ˈhæmə(r)/
hilarious adj /hɪˈleəriːəs/
honest adj /ˈɒnɪst/
hunt v /hʌnt/

inhabitant n /ɪnˈhæbɪtənt/
interest (money) n /ˈɪntrest/
intimate adj /ˈɪntɪmət/

jet n /dʒet/

magnet n /ˈmægnət/
mansion n /ˈmænʃn/
media n /ˈmiːdiə/
mere adj /mɪə/
minimum n /ˈmɪnɪməm/
motive n /ˈməʊtɪv/
mouth-watering (inf) adj /ˈmaʊθ ˌwɔːtərɪŋ/

nauseous adj /ˈnɔːziəs/
nostrils pl n /ˈnɒstrəlz/
notice (time period) n /ˈnəʊtɪs/

outskirts n /ˈaʊtskɜːtz/
overdraft facility n /ˈəʊvədrɑːft fəˌsɪlɪti/

paparazzi n /pæpəˈrætsi/
pedestrianized adj /pəˈdestriənaɪzd/
pervade v /pəˈveɪd/
predict v /prɪˈdɪkt/
profusely adv /prəˈfjuːsli/
province n /ˈprɒvɪns/
pursue v /pɜːˈsjuː/

quotation n /kwəʊˈteɪʃn/

refunded pp /rɪˈfʌndɪd/
rehydration salts pl n /riːhaɪˈdreɪʃn ˌsɒltz/
rent n /rent/
resentful adj /rɪˈzentfəl/
resources pl n /rɪˈzɔːsɪs/
risk v /rɪsk/

savings account n /ˈseɪvɪŋs əˌkaʊnt/
screwdriver n /ˈskruːdraɪvə/
shabby adj /ˈʃæbi/
shattered (inf) adj /ˈʃætəd/
(be) situated v /(bi) ˈsɪtueɪtɪd/
snoring adj /ˈsnɔːrɪŋ/
sought pp /sɔːt/
straddle v /ˈstrædl/
sumptuous adj /ˈsʌmptjuəs/
surrounded pp /səˈraʊndɪd/
sweat v /swet/

terminal building n /ˈtɜːmɪnəl ˌbɪldɪŋ/
thrilled adj /θrɪld/
trendy adj /ˈtrendi/

ultimate adj /ˈʌltɪmət/
utter adj /ˈʌtə(r)/

walrus tusks pl n /ˈwɔːlrəs ˌtʌsks/
withdrawal n /wɪðˈdrɔːəl/

Unit 9

absent-minded adj /ˈæbsənt ˌmaɪndɪd/
argumentative adj /ɑ:gumentətɪv/
aura n /ˈɔːrə/
blank out (inf) v /ˈblæŋk ˌaʊt/
blew (up) pp /ˈbluː (ʌp)/
bouquet n /buˈkeɪ/
cheek v /tʃiːk/
cleanliness n /ˈklenlinəs/
clumsy adj /ˈklʌmsi/
comics pl n /ˈkɒmɪks/
convenience food n /kənˈviːniəns ˌfɔː/
credit with v /ˈkredɪt wɪð/
crisis n /ˈkraɪsɪs/
cute adj /kjuːt/
defence mechanism n /dɪˈfens ˌmekənɪzm/
define v /dɪˈfaɪn/
dense adj /dens/
discipline n /ˈdɪsɪplɪn/
disdain n /dɪsˈdeɪn/
documentary n /dɒkjuˈmentri/
dumb adj /dʌm/
easy-going adj /iːzi ˈɡəʊɪŋ/
eccentric adj /ɪkˈsentrɪk/
encounter v /ɪnˈkaʊntə/
enviable adj /ˈenviːəbl/
envy n /ˈenvi/
episode n /ˈepɪsəʊd/
estimated adj /ˈestɪmeɪtɪd/
fault n /fɒlt/
fluid adj /ˈfluːɪd/
fond (of) adj /ˈfɒnd (əv)/
fortunate adj /ˈfɔːtʃunət/
furious adj /ˈfjʊəriəs/
fussy adj /ˈfʌsi/
giggle v /ɡɪɡl/
habit n /ˈhæbɪt/
harm n /hɑːm/
humour n /ˈhjuːmə(r)/
imperious adj /ɪmˈpɪəriəs/
incorporate v /ɪnˈkɔːpəreɪt/
influence n /ˈɪnfluəns/
infringement n /ɪnˈfrɪndʒmənt/
insanely adv /ɪnˈseɪnli/
insecure adj /ˈɪnsɪˌkʊə/
intensify v /ɪnˈtensɪfaɪ/
interrogator n /ɪnˈterəɡeɪtə(r)/
joint (inf) n /dʒɔɪnt/
journalist n /ˈdʒɜːnəlɪst/
laid back (inf) adj /ˈleɪd ˌbæk/
laziness n /ˈleɪzinəs/
lifestyle n /ˈlaɪfstaɪl/
masseuse n /mæˈsɜːz/
mean adj /miːn/
memorable adj /ˈmemərəbl/
mess with (inf) v /ˈmes wɪð/
microcosm n /ˈmaɪkrəkɒzm/
misplaced pp /mɪsˈpleɪst/
nickname n /ˈnɪkneɪm/
nosy adj /ˈnəʊzi/

pace v /peɪs/
prior /ˈpraɪə/
recite v /rɪˈsaɪt/
relate to v /rɪˈleɪt ˌtu/
represented pp /ˌreprɪˈzentɪd/
sarcasm n /ˈsɑːkæzm/
scald v /skɔːld/
scatty adj /ˈskæti/
screech v /skriːtʃ/
self-obsessed adj /self əbˈsest/
sensible adj /ˈsensɪbl/
sensitive adj /ˈsensɪtɪv/
series n /ˈsɪəriːz/
sitcom n /ˈsɪtkɒm/
slicked back (inf) adj /ˈslɪkt ˌbæk/
soap opera n /ˈsəʊp ɒprə/
spine n /spaɪn/
spiritual adj /ˈspɪrɪtjuəl/
spoil v /spɔɪl/
stingy adj /ˈstɪndʒi/
stubborn adj /ˈstʌbən/
supportive adj /səˈpɔːtɪv/
surge n /sɜːdʒ/
tax v/n /t&ks/
teeter (inf) v /ˈtiːtə(r)/
thrift store n /ˈθrɪft ˌstɔː/
treat n /triːt/
trials pl n /traɪlz/
unsophisticated adj /ˌʌnsəˈfɪstɪkeɪtɪd/
uptight adj /ʌpˈtaɪt/
whine v /waɪn/
witty adj /ˈwɪti/
wonder n /ˈwʌndə/

Unit 10

acquaintances pl n /əˈkweɪntənsɪz/
ambushed pp /ˈæmˌbʊʃd/
ammunition n /ˌæmjuˈnɪʃn/
ancestors pl n /ˈænsestəz/
arrow n /ˈærəʊ/
assailant n /əˈseɪlənt/
assumptions pl n /əˈsʌmpʃənz/
assure v /əˈʃɔː/
atrocities pl n /əˈtrɒsətiːz/
axe n /æks/
befall v /bɪˈfɔːl/
benefit from v /ˈbenəfɪt frɒm/
blizzards pl n /ˈblɪzədz/
(be) bound to id /(bi) baʊnd tu/
buffalo pl n /ˈbʌfələʊ/
carnivore n /ˈkɑːnɪvɔː/
cape n /keɪp/
cave n /keɪv/
charcoal n /ˈtʃɑːkəʊl/
companion n /kəmˈpæniən/
conflict n /ˈkɒnflɪkt/
courageous adj /kəˈreɪdʒəs/
crops pl n /krɒps/
dagger n /ˈdæɡə(r)/
elements pl n /ˈeləməntz/
emigrate v /ˈemɪɡreɪt/
encountered pp /enˈkaʊntəd/
established adj /ɪsˈtæblɪʃd/
fatal adj /ˈfeɪtəl/
ferocious adj /fɪˈrəʊʃəs/
filthy adj /ˈfɪlθi/
flare v /fleə/
flint n /flɪnt/
foible n /ˈfɔɪbl/
furs pl n /fɜːz/
goat n /ɡəʊt/
harsh adj /hɑːʃ/
hazardous adj /ˈhæzədəs/
herbs pl n /ˈhɜːbz/
herdsman n /ˈhɜːdzmən/
hostilities pl n /hɒsˈtɪlətiːz/
hunter n /ˈhʌntə(r)/
imitate v /ˈɪmɪteɪt/
impassable adj /ɪmˈpɑːsəbəl/
inauspicious adj /ɪnɔːˈspɪʃəs/
indivisible adj /ɪndɪˈvɪzɪbl/
inevitably adv /ɪnˈevɪtəbli/
inflicted pp /ɪnˈflɪktɪd/
integrated pp /ˈɪntɪɡreɪtɪd/
lung n /lʌŋ/
migrants pl n /ˈmaɪɡrəntz/
migration n /maɪˈɡreɪʃn/
morale n /məˈrɑːl/
morsel n /ˈmɔːsəl/
obliged pp /əˈblaɪdʒd/
penetrate v /ˈpenətreɪt/
pester v /ˈpestə/
pharmaceutical adj /ˌfɑːməˈsuːtɪkəl/
pioneers pl n /ˌpaɪəˈnɪəz/
plagues pl n /ˈpleɪɡz/

plains pl n /pleɪnz/
precision n /prɪˈsɪʒn/
prehistoric adj /ˌpriːhɪˈstɒrɪk/
properties pl n /ˈprɒpəti:z/
quantities pl n /ˈkwɒntɪti:z/
reconstruct v /riːkɒnˈstrʌkt/
regarded pp /rɪˈɡɑːdɪd/
regards pl n /rɪˈɡɑːdz/
retail business n /ˈriːteɪl ˌbɪznɪs/
retrieve v /rɪˈtriːv/
savages pl n /ˈsævɪdʒɪz/
scarce adj /skeəs/
shepherd n /ˈʃepəd/
sincere adj /sɪnˈsɪə/
slaughtered pp /ˈslɔːtəd/
specify v /ˈspesɪfaɪ/
standard n /ˈstændəd/
starvation n /stɑːˈveɪʃn/
supply v /səˈplaɪ/
tamed pp /teɪmd/
tensions pl n /ˈtenʃnz/
tinder n /ˈtɪndə/
tool n /tuːl/
utmost n /ˈʌtməʊst/
valuable adj /ˈvælubəl/
virtually adv /ˈvɜːtʃuəli/
wagon n /ˈwæɡən/
warrior n /ˈwɒriə(r)/
weapon n /ˈwepən/
wound n/v /wuːnd/
wilderness n /ˈwɪldənəs/

Unit 11

altitude n /'æltɪtjud/
ambition n /æm'bɪʃn/
architect n /'ɑːkɪtekt/
arrogant adj /'ærəgənt/
atmosphere n /'ætməsfɪə/

cannon n /'kænən/
cellar n /'selə/
conscious adj /'kɒnʃəs/
cover for (inf) v /'kʌvə ˌfɔː/
cramped adj /'kræmpt/
crumbling adj /'krʌmblɪŋ/

dart v /dɑːt/
dash (inf) v /dæʃ/
decaying adj /dɪ'keɪɪŋ/
descend v /dɪ'send/
droplets pl n /'drɒpləts/
dust n /dʌst/

earthquake n /'ɜːθkweɪk/
eliminated pp /ɪ'lɪmɪneɪtɪd/
emotion n /ɪm'əʊʃn/
equator n /ɪ'kweɪtə/
expand v /ɪk'spænd/

failure n /'feɪlʊə/
finances pl n /'faɪnænsɪz/
flatpack (inf) adj /'flætpæk/
frustration n /frʌs'treɪʃn/
function n /'fʌŋkʃn/

gravity n /'grævəti/

hard up (inf) adj /ˌhɑːd 'ʌp/
hardware shop n /'hɑːdweə ˌʃɒp/
helium n /'hiːliəm/
huge adj /hjudʒ/

indicate v /'ɪndɪkeɪt/
inexplicable adj /ˌɪnɪk'splɪkəbl/
inflate v /ɪn'fleɪt/
insecurity n /ˌɪnsɪ'kjʊərəti/
interpretation n /ɪnˌtɜːprɪ'teɪʃn/

lack n /læk/
ladder n /'lædə/
literal adj /'lɪtərəl/
literally adv /'lɪtərəli/
load v /ləʊd/
looped pp /luːpt/

meteor n /'miːtiə/
meteorologist n /ˌmiːtɪə'rɒlədʒɪst/
mind n /maɪnd/
molecule n /'mɒlɪkjul/
momentous adj /mə'mentəs/
motion n /'məʊʃn/

neglected pp /nɪ'glektɪd/

obsessed v /əb'sest/

painstakingly adv /'peɪnsteɪkɪŋli/
particle n /'pɑːtɪkl/
permissive adj /pə'mɪsɪv/
perpetual adj /pə'petʃuəl/
phase n /feɪz/
phenomenon n /fə'nɒmɪnən/
physiological adj /ˌfɪsɪə'lɒdʒɪkəl/
pop v /pɒp/
preparations pl n /ˌprepə'reɪʃnz/
printing press n /'prɪntɪŋ ˌpres/
psychological adj /ˌsaɪkə'lɒdʒɪkəl/

rational adj /'ræʃənəl/

reflect (light) v /rɪ'flekt/
reporter n /rɪ'pɔːtə(r)/
represent v /reprɪ'zent/
repressed pp /rɪ'prest/
rotate v /rəʊ'teɪt/
rotor blade n /'rəʊtə bleɪd/

sceptical adj /'skeptɪkəl/
self n /self/
self-confidence n /ˌself 'kɒnfɪdəns/
self-image n /ˌself 'ɪmɪdʒ/
signed up pp /ˌsaɪnd 'ʌp/
spin v /spɪn/
spot v /spɒt/
stationers n /'steɪʃənəz/
stemmed pp /'stemd/
strokes pl n /'strəʊks/
suffer v /'sʌfə(r)/
supernatural adj /ˌsuːpə'nætʃrəl/
swarm n /swɔːm/
symbol n /'sɪmbəl/
symbolize v /'sɪmbəlaɪz/

tank n /tæŋk/
tedious adj /'tiːdiəs/
telepathy n /tə'lepəθi/
theme n /θiːm/
theorist pl n /'θɪərɪst/
tolerate v /'tɒləreɪt/
transcribed pp /træn'skraɪbd/
transmit v /træns'mɪt/

vapour n /'veɪpə(r)/

wobbly adj /'wɒbli/

Unit 12

achiever n /ə'tʃiːvə(r)/
afterlife n /'ɑːftəlaɪf/
appreciate v /ə'priːʃieɪt/
architecture n /'ɑːkɪtektʃə/
assistance n /ə'sɪstəns/
authority n /ɔː'θɒrəti/

balance n /'bæləns/
bonus n /'bəʊnəs/

centenary n /sen'tɪːnəri/
chaos n /'keɪɒs/
common sense n /ˌkɒmən 'sens/
convened pp /kɒn'viːnd/
corny adj /kɔːni/
couch potato n id /'kaʊtʃ ˌpəteɪtəʊ/
courage n /'kʌrɪdʒ/
creative adj /kri'eɪtɪv/
crises pl n /'kraɪsiːz/
cruise n /kruːz/
cushy adj /kʊʃi/

daydreamer n /'deɪdriːmə(r)/
denial n /dɪ'naɪəl/
design n /dɪ'zaɪn/
diagnosed pp /ˌdaɪəg'nəʊzd/
donor n /'dəʊnə/

elation n /ɪ'leɪʃn/
enthusiasm n /en'θjuːziːæzm/
estuaries pl n /'estjuəriːz/
exhilarating adj /ek'zɪləreɪtɪŋ/

frantic adj /'fræntɪk/

gained pp /'geɪnd/

horrendous adj /hə'rendəs/
humanity n /hju'mænəti/

infancy n /'ɪnfənsi/
influential adj /ˌɪnflu'enʃl/
initially adv /ɪn'ɪʃəli/
(get) irritated by v /(get) 'ɪrɪteɪtɪd baɪ/

judge n /dʒʌdʒ/

lease n /liːs/
life expectancy n /'laɪf ɪkspektənsi/
lunacy n /'luːnəsi/

nephew n /'nefuː/
niece n /'niːs/

obsessive adj /əb'sesɪv/
optimism n /'ɒptɪmɪzm/
orchard n /'ɔːtʃəd/
overpowering adj /ˌəʊvə'paʊərɪŋ/

pace n /peɪs/
pauper n /'pɔːpə/
pawn n /pɔːn/
philosophy n /fɪ'lɒsəfi/
physical adj /'fɪzɪkəl/
plunged pp /'plʌndʒd/
politician n /ˌpɒlə'tɪʃn/
potter (inf) v /'pɒtə(r)/
pour over (look at in detail) id /'pɔː ˌəʊvə/
pressure n /'preʃə/
prioritize v /ˌpraɪ'ɒrɪtaɪz/
punctuality n /ˌpʌŋktʃu'æləti/
quarrel n /'kwɒrəl/

rare adj /reə/
retired pp /rɪ'taɪəd/
revolutionary adj /ˌrevə'luːʃənəri/
ritual n /'rɪtʃuəl/
rottenly adv /'rɒtənli/
routine n /ruː'tiːn/
run down (unwell) v /'rʌn ˌdaʊn/

scaffolding n /'skæfəldɪŋ/
scandalous adj /'skændələs/
sculptor n /'skʌlptə/
smash v /smæʃ/
snatched pp /snætʃd/
stand (bear) v /stænd/
sufficient adj /sə'fɪʃənt/

tackle v /'tækl/
terrace n /'terɪs/
therapy n /'θerəpi/
torture adj /'tɔːtʃə/
transplant n /'trænsplɑːnt/

unfulfilled adj /ˌʌnfəl'fɪld/
urge v /ɜːdʒ/

vegetable patch n /'vedʒtəbl ˌpætʃ/

weed v /wiːd/
widow n /'wɪdəʊ/
widower n /'wɪdəʊə/
wrinkly adj /'rɪŋkli/